THE STARVING EMPIRE

THE STARVING EMPIRE

A HISTORY OF FAMINE IN FRANCE'S COLONIES

YAN SLOBODKIN

CORNELL UNIVERSITY PRESS

Ithaca and London

First published 2023 by Cornell University Press

Library of Congress Cataloging-in-Publication Data

Names: Slobodkin, Yan, 1985– author.
Title: The starving empire : a history of famine in
    France's colonies / Yan Slobodkin.
Description: Ithaca [New York] : Cornell University Press,
    2023. | Includes bibliographical references and index.
Identifiers: LCCN 2023004246 (print) | LCCN 2023004247
    (ebook) | ISBN 9781501772351 (hardcover) |
    ISBN 9781501772368 (epub) | ISBN 9781501772375 (pdf)
Subjects: LCSH: Famines—France—Colonies—History. |
    France—Colonies—Social conditions. | France—
    Colonies—Economic conditions.
Classification: LCC HC279 .S55 2023 (print) |
    LCC HC279 (ebook) | DDC 306.0944—dc23 / eng/
    20230605
LC record available at https://lccn.loc.gov/2023004246
LC ebook record available at https://lccn.loc.gov/
    2023004247

Mat
1987–2008

People who shut their eyes to reality simply invite their own destruction, and anyone who insists on remaining in a state of innocence long after that innocence is dead turns himself into a monster.

—James Baldwin, "Stranger in the Village"

Contents

ACKNOWLEDGMENTS

It is a unique pleasure to acknowledge the debts I have incurred over the long course of researching and writing this book. My first words of thanks are to those who taught me to be a historian. J. P. Daughton has been a tremendous mentor and friend. His perceptive advice and constant confidence have helped me find my way as a scholar. Richard Roberts inspired and cultivated my interest in the history of Africa with wisdom and kindness. Priya Satia, Kären Wigen, and Keith Baker opened my mind to many things. Leora Auslander welcomed me to the remarkable community of historians at the University of Chicago. Leonard V. Smith was my first teacher of French history and continues to be generous in his support.

I have had the incredible fortune to benefit from the expertise, perspectives, and sensibilities of colleagues and friends. I am profoundly touched by the sheer amount of thought and labor they invested in this book. My heartfelt thanks go to Mélanie Lamotte, Owen White, Haun Saussy, Alice Gregory, Josh Bauchner, Sam Dolbee, Alex Statman, Jenny Harris, Thomas Pringle, Alex Campolo, Steven Press, Simran Bhalla, Anne Wootton, Andy Schupanitz, Sam Riley, David Fedman, Sam Bloch, Sabrina Ramos, Chris Taylor, Caroline Bankoff, Rani Molla, Zachary Epcar, Leon Neyfakh, Vikrant Dadawala, and Colin Winnette. Special thanks to Haydon Cherry, whose erudition in Vietnamese history and just about everything else is awe-inspiring. Merlin Chowkwanyun helped me think about public health, and Kara Harvill about medicine. Daniel Pearce, brilliant stylist, made my prose better. Alex de Waal's thoughtful reading of the entire manuscript helped improve it dramatically. My coworkers and students at Sarah Lawrence College, the Institute on the Formation of Knowledge at UChicago, and the History and Literature program at Harvard provided collegial, vibrant, and challenging intellectual communities. It is impossible to reconstruct the social determinants of this book in all their complexity—many more people than can be named here made their mark, and I thank them all.

The writing of history cannot happen without the archivists whose work preserves the traces of the past. For welcoming and guiding me, emphatic thanks go to the staffs of the Centres des archives d'outre-mer in Aix-en-Provence, the Bibliothèque national de France, Missions évangéliques de Paris, Sociétés des missions étrangères, and Bibliothèque de l'académie des sciences d'outre-mer in Paris, the Archives nationales du Sénégal in Dakar, the National Archives Center 1 in Hanoi, and the United Nations Archives in New York City. Generous financial support was provided by the Georges Lurcy Fund, the Mellon Foundation, the Stanford University history department, the Institute on the Formation of Knowledge at the University of Chicago, and the Committee on History and Literature at Harvard.

I am grateful to Emily Andrew and Bethany Wasik for their guidance in the publication process. I would also like to express my deep gratitude to the anonymous reviewers, whose thoughtful readings strengthened the writing and arguments in many ways. The beautiful maps that appear in this book were designed by Meredith Sadler.

My family has inspired and sustained this book more than they know. Special thanks go to aunts, uncles, and cousins throughout the world for sharing conversations and experiences. I cannot name them all here (there are so many!), but I would like to acknowledge Shlomo and Danielle Malka, Victor and Alexa Malka, Muriel and Richard Dahan, Danielle and Jean-Claude Sicsic, and Séverine Allouche for opening their Paris homes to a wandering researcher. My father, David, my sister, Liaht, and my grandmother, Tami, are pillars of support. My mother, Orly, born into the French Empire and now a citizen, to her persistent bemusement, of the United States, is a truly special person. My deepest thanks are to them, for everything.

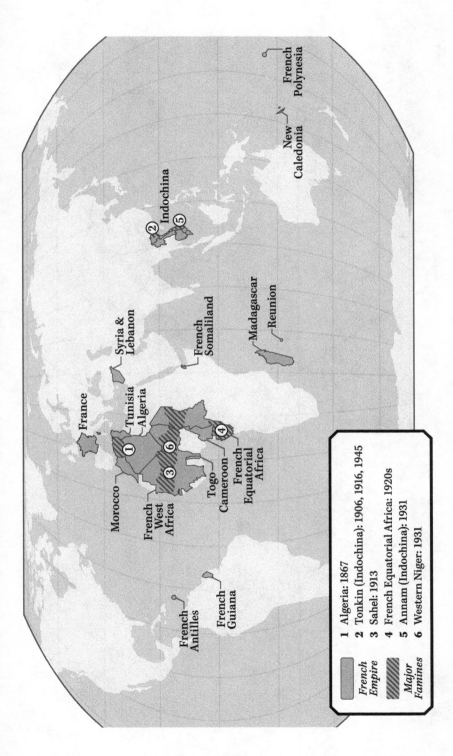

MAP 1. Major famines in the French Empire

French
Empire

Major
Famines

1 Algeria: 1867
2 Tonkin (Indochina): 1906, 1916, 1945
3 Sahel: 1913
4 French Equatorial Africa: 1920s
5 Annam (Indochina): 1931
6 Western Niger: 1931

France
Tunisia
Algeria
Morocco
French
West
Africa
Togo
Cameroon
French
Equatorial
Africa
Syria &
Lebanon
French
Somaliland
Madagascar
Reunion
Indochina
New
Caledonia
French
Polynesia
French
Antilles
French
Guiana

MAP 2. Algeria

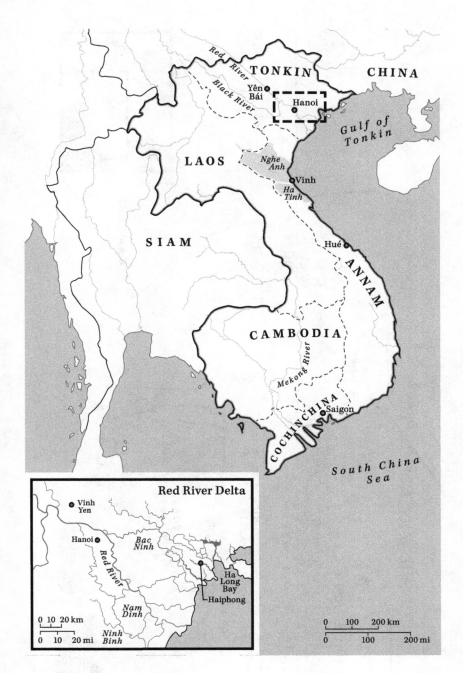

MAP 3. Indochina

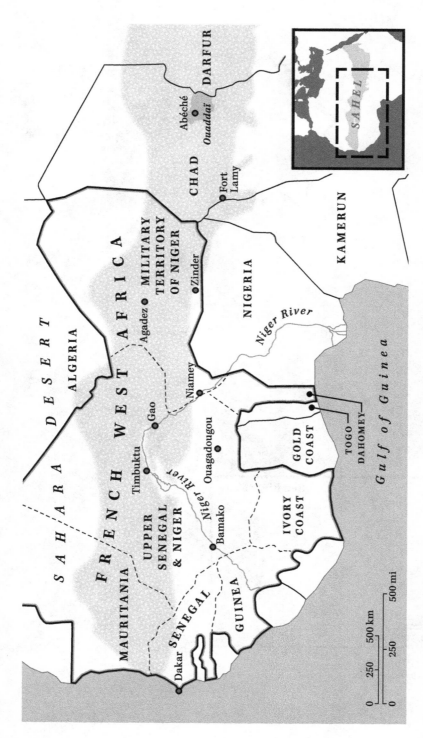

Map 4. French West Africa (AOF) circa 1913

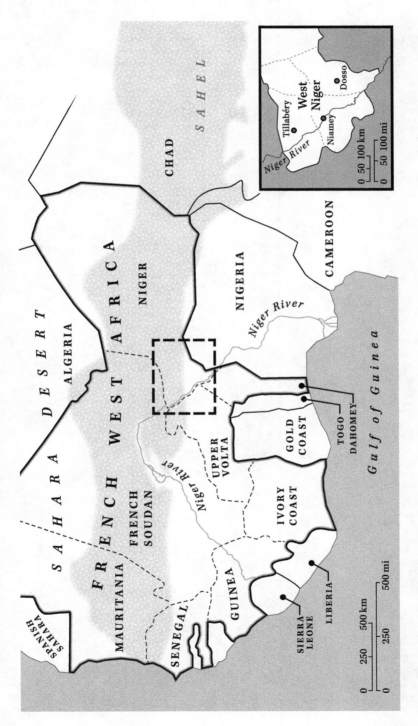

Map 5. French West Africa (AOF) circa 1931

THE STARVING EMPIRE

Introduction
Who Is Responsible for Famine?

> Under a colonial regime, man's relationship with the
> physical world and history is connected to food. In a
> context of oppression like that of Algeria, for the
> colonized, living does not mean embodying a set of
> values, does not mean integrating oneself into the
> coherent, constructive development of a world. To live
> simply means not to die.
>
> —Frantz Fanon (1961)

In 1867, hundreds of thousands of Algerians
starved to death. A French priest described the sight: "On the roads, in the
ditches, we encountered lifeless unfortunates already cadavers. Others still
breathed, heads hidden under the hoods of their cloaks, occasionally allowing a sigh to escape, a groan, they shook with convulsive jolts in the cruel trance
of the affliction."[1] In 1945, a priest in French Indochina witnessed a famine
that killed between one million and three million Vietnamese: "Distressing
spectacle, hundreds of families destined for extinction, thousands of famished
at the end of their strength and innumerable lifeless cadavers along the roads
and sidewalks."[2]

From the close-up vantage of the two clergymen, the "lifeless cadavers" on
public roads roughly eighty years and ten thousand miles apart looked much
the same; the priests were overwhelmed by the all-consuming horror in front
of their eyes. Their perspective conveys the brute physical reality of hunger.
But the tight framing can make famine appear timeless, severing starvation
from causes distant in time and space, obscuring the historical coordinates of
personal suffering.[3] Each one of the millions of famine victims lay at the heart
of a shifting nexus of regional, imperial, and transnational processes that
shaped, often invisibly, their lives and deaths. In the years between the tragedies of 1867 and 1945, understandings of famine in the French Empire and

the responsibilities it engendered changed dramatically. These changes, and the persistence of starvation across them, are the focus of this book.

Hunger was at once intensely local and sweepingly global, urgently immediate and evolving over time. This history of famine in France's colonies traces changing conceptions of and responses to starvation through Algeria, Indochina, West and Equatorial Africa, and Europe, all the while accounting for the connections that united these disparate places into a single narrative.[4] It brings together the stories of subsistence farmers struggling to make the harvest, disoriented colonial administrators trying to stay out of trouble with their superiors, physicians and scientists in clinics and universities, men and women of letters, elite politicians, and anticolonial revolutionaries. By integrating their stories into the broader development of imperial and transnational care, this book shows how the French imperial state and an emerging international community took increasing responsibility for managing famines, and ultimately failed to fulfill this responsibility.

Famine was a powerful force in the French Empire. Through physical ordeal, political symbolism, and emotional weight, it could do many things. Famine impoverished people, making them more susceptible to dispossession and exploitation by colonial states and settlers. It provoked uprisings and brutal repression, increasing the risk of future famines. It contributed to a recalibration of agricultural economies toward wage labor and world markets, and it drew hungry converts to Catholic missions that could feed them. Eventually, famine mobilized doctors, biochemists, engineers, statesmen, journalists, Nobel laureates in the arts and the sciences, and professional humanitarians in an international struggle to eliminate it. The suffering of hungry people drew the attention, pity, and anger of humanist reformers, marshaling the pens of some of the towering intellectuals and activists of the day. Once a purely local tragedy to be regretted and brushed off, starvation became a global problem demanding the intervention of the world community. But even as its hoped-for solution anchored fantasies of a rational and humane colonial modernity, famine's persistence was a conspicuous sign of modernity's failure. The chasm between confident promises and enormous suffering was in itself a historical force. In many ways, famine fueled French colonialism, but it also helped to end it. Famine was taken up as a rallying call by anticolonial nationalists and became a structuring concern of the international system poised to inherit the world of empires.

And famine, of course, killed. Some people died of acute malnutrition. Others died of infectious diseases such as cholera, smallpox, typhus, and measles, which thrived among mobile populations and malnourished immune systems. Some people died of dysentery from drinking filthy water, and others survived deprivation only to die during refeeding, a dangerous moment for the severely malnourished. Some were murdered amid the social breakdown that accompanied dearth. Some were poisoned by toxic, inedible foods. Famine's ever-present threat and periodic eruption had a profound impact on the experiences, ideas, decisions, life trajectories, and deaths of the people who constituted the French imperial world.

To capture the web of relationships surrounding each famine, this book interweaves several registers of historical inquiry. At the local level, it reconstructs specific food crises, considering how social and economic change, European conceptions of race and environment, and non-European famine strategies affected the causes and experiences of starvation. At the imperial level, it situates local histories in the context of the French Empire as a whole, asking how debates about colonial governance and responsibility interacted with conditions on the ground. At the transnational level, it explores how developments in nutrition and race science merged with deepening notions of humanitarian care to form new technical and ethical understandings of famine management within and across borders. As the story travels from Algerian wheat and barley fields to Indochinese rice paddies, from remote military outposts to cutting-edge medical laboratories, from desert refugee camps to conference rooms in Paris and Geneva, it is grounded by two simple questions: What kind of problem was famine? Who was responsible for it?

Following these questions wherever they lead reveals a story of changing forms of care that a focus on individual famines can overshadow.[5] Since the 1980s, the study of famine has been dominated by economist Amartya Sen's elegant insight that "starvation is the characteristic of some people not *having* enough food to eat. It is not the characteristic of there *being* not enough food to eat."[6] While it is intuitive to think of famines as situations in which there is simply not enough food to go around, Sen taught that it is in fact people's ability to obtain food that is at issue. What matters to hungry people is not how much food exists but how much food they can eat. A deficit of available calories is one reason people may fail to eat enough not to die, but it is not the only possible reason. Famines can and often have happened despite there being enough food for all.

The relentless imperial expansion of the nineteenth and twentieth centuries that brought the majority of the globe under European rule profoundly restructured peoples' capabilities to procure food—in Sen's vocabulary, their "entitlements."[7] Like all colonialists, French soldiers, administrators, and businessmen encountered a breathtaking range of peoples, places, and subsistence arrangements. Some volatile ecologies, such as the African Sahel or the Red River Delta in Indochina, had long been prone to chronic insecurity and periodic famine. But colonialism often heightened vulnerability to starvation and disrupted existing antifamine practices without providing replacements, likely increasing the frequency and intensity of famines. At the very least, no counterfactuals are needed to see that colonialism, presented as the precondition of progress for what was not yet called the Global South, obviously did not prevent millions from starving. This book follows the path paved by Sen by considering how people's ability to obtain enough food was eroded through global economics, local exploitation, racial stereotypes, and social transformation as well as by natural disasters and food shortages. However, it moves beyond the history of individual food crises to address famine as a broader social force, situating mass starvation events within the long development of French colonialism and international humanitarianism.

In academic history and popular imagination alike, one famine looms larger than others: the Irish one. The potato famine of the 1840s was a calamity that killed a million people, unmasked British colonial cruelty, and accelerated Irish immigration across the Atlantic.[8] For scholars of the British Empire who have dominated questions of colonial subsistence, it was also the prototype for modern famine management.[9] The Irish famine, the argument goes, inaugurated a form of relief that was also a form of social control. Prison-like famine camps and a food aid policy that required recipients to travel long distances and perform difficult labor formed an organized system that kept starving populations under discipline. Born in Ireland, the system was perfected in India, where it was formalized in the famous famine codes of the 1880s. British colonial administrators-turned-humanitarians internationalized this "British way of famine" in the twentieth century, forming the basis of modern global famine relief.[10]

This account of the British way of famine captures the critical connection between colonialism and humanitarianism. It has also encouraged a too-easy tendency to universalize the British case and draw a straight line from British imperialism to contemporary famine relief. The "French way of famine" was another vital strand in this history. It was, in a sense, the inverse of the British way. The British elaborated techniques of famine control without articulating a political obligation to guarantee subsistence. The French, between the terrible famines in Algeria in 1867 and Indochina in 1945, progressively accepted political responsibility for the subsistence of colonial subjects. However, they failed to build an imperial state capable of achieving it. Integrating French colonial famine into the history of modern humanitarianism helps complete the story by emphasizing the importance of political values as well as technical knowledge. It also suggests that famine relief was characterized by improvisation more than by systematic, technocratic governance.

French colonial administrators never came up with a definition of famine, a set of characteristics whose presence indicated a prescribed crisis response.[11] They never had anything like the Indian famine codes. Even as famines became unacceptable and embarrassing, relief on the ground remained reactive, voluntary, and conditional, born of the institutional vacuum and procedural chaos of severely underdeveloped colonial administrations. Under these conditions, grain distributions, public labor camps, and commercial controls were not coherent apparatuses of modern population management so much as the flailing reflexes of frightened administrators unsure what to do in the face of unthinkable trauma.[12] In the French case, famine relief did not look like sophisticated disciplinary governance; it did not look like governance at all.

Elements of the history of famine relief were distinctly French, even as they were influenced by and contributed to British and international ideas and practices. An enduring national myth chronicled the defeat of famines in France in the eighteenth and early nineteenth centuries under the guidance of technocratic economists and rational *intendants,* royal administrators in the mold of the storied liberal modernizer Turgot.[13] Traditionally, the kings of France had guaranteed subjects their daily bread in an implicit accord with the people; monarchs were the food suppliers of last resort.[14] Under reformist administrators, the burden of subsistence was transferred to markets, smoothed by the construction of roads and the liberalization of the grain trade in the years surrounding the French Revolution.[15] The story of a progression from old regime noblesse oblige to modern laissez-faire was belied by the persistence of price caps, public grain reserves, subsidies, and trade restrictions across eighteenth- and nineteenth-century regimes.[16] Nonetheless, the often-mythologized classical liberal approach to food policy would determine responses to colonial famines through the twentieth century. Even the British shared in this French history, as when the Indian Famine Commission of 1880 cited the "great administrator of famine relief in modern times" Turgot in support of labor tests for government aid.[17] The fact that Turgot's 1774 edict easing traditional controls on the buying and selling of grain was followed by the "flour war" food riots of 1775 and then by his dismissal from King Louis XVI's government in 1776 was conveniently overlooked.[18] But his insistence that unrestricted liberty of commerce was always the correct policy regardless of observable outcomes became orthodoxy.[19] Subsistence in France—at least in theory— would fall to the free market, supplemented in the last resort by private charity motivated by religion, civic virtue, or patriotic nationalism.[20]

The belief that enlightened administrators had vanquished famine in France through market liberalization was dominant among officials in the French Empire of the nineteenth and twentieth centuries. Most also believed that characteristics particular to African and Asian people and environments made analogous developments impossible. The backward races that inhabited the colonies, the thinking went, were simply incapable of the reasoned decision making that liberty of commerce presupposed.[21] Overseas, race was often a blunter force than the careful racial hierarchies worked out in nineteenth-century Europe, emerging from expedience rather than scientific method.[22] With regard to subsistence in the colonies, race had a specific function: it explained and excused the continued occurrence of famines in a modern world. Indeed, starvation itself sometimes appeared to be a racial attribute. French colonialists characterized famine victims across the empire, whether African, Asian, Arab, or any other grouping, as largely the same—weak, lazy, stupid. Even races sometimes praised as industrious or intelligent, such as North African Kabyles or the Annamites of Indochina, were criticized as deficient if they were unfortunate enough to experience famine. Above all, colonized races lacked the indispensable virtue required for participation in modern liberal society: foresight.[23]

Coupled with the natural shortcomings of colonized people was the perceived severity of colonial natural environments.[24] From the parched deserts and savannas of North and West Africa to the dense forests of Equatorial Africa to the flood-prone and overcrowded Red River Delta of Indochina, the challenges posed by these difficult natural settings could not be overcome by their inhabitants. The syllogism of improvident races coupled with harsh environments leading inexorably to famine was repeated with relentless regularity by French observers in all corners of the globe.

Primed to see famine as a natural feature of the colonial landscape, French administrators did not necessarily prioritize the alleviation of suffering. Rather, they understood their job to be the formation of self-sufficient, industrious, and provident colonial subjects capable, someday, of avoiding hunger through rational decision making.[25] This civilizing mission was an ideology of reason, not of sentiment. Administrators, repelled by the risk of reinforcing laziness and dependence, withheld or imposed conditions on aid rather than succumbing to emotion to relieve immediate distress at the cost of future progress. Between a race thinking that blamed famine on its victims and a civilizing mission that equated compassion with irrationality and weakness, those in power were often paralyzed.

Before World War I, French people across the empire were united in considering famine the natural consequence of backward races living in difficult environments. These blanket preconceptions had different effects in different contexts. In Algeria in 1867, starvation and cholera killed as many as eight hundred thousand people.[26] In this settler colony characterized by the geographic and social segregation of indigenous people, Muslims were excluded from the communitarian forms of care that provided charity for European Christians. Instead of dealing directly with the problem in front of them, French interest groups that spanned the Mediterranean integrated the famine into preexisting power struggles, using it as rhetorical ammunition to promote their preferred vision of an Algerian colonial state. The military regime of Emperor Napoleon III and Governor-General of Algeria Patrice de MacMahon argued that only the army had the intimate knowledge of Muslim culture required to manage famine. The Catholic Church, led by the charismatic Archbishop of Algiers Charles Lavigerie, believed the famine was a divine punishment. The only remedy was a Christian colonialism that had the conversion of Muslims as its ultimate goal. The European settler establishment used the famine to advocate against Napoleon III's Second Empire and in favor of liberal republicanism and a free press, while also taking the opportunity to dispossess indigenous people of their lands. In the debates between these French interests, the famine victims themselves receded from view.

In Indochina, as in Algeria, French witnesses ascribed famines to natural disaster and racial attributes. But the two colonies were very different places. When the French arrived in the Vietnamese-speaking areas of Indochina in the second half of the nineteenth century, they recognized a centralized imperial state with a strong tradition of famine prevention and relief based on neo-Confucian ideals of benevolent governance and technical control of watercourses. In the protectorates of Annam and Tonkin, the French maintained the Vietnamese imperial bureaucracy under the emperors of the Nguyen dynasty. This allowed France to place responsibility for famine on the aristocratic mandarin class and Vietnamese hydraulic engineers. During recurring food crises between 1884 and 1930, famine was primarily the problem of the protected Vietnamese state rather than the French administration.

In 1913, famine swept across the African Sahel, the desert-side region south of the Sahara that runs from the Atlantic Ocean to the Red Sea. French observers attributed the tragedy to severe drought and naturally indolent and improvident populations. Since famine was understood to be unavoidable in one of the world's driest and most fickle environments, French administrators considered their role to be reactive and voluntary, easing the effects of misfortune to whatever extent possible. Absent defined religious, social, or political ties between those in charge and those in need, administrators improvised a range of relationships defined at the poles by a bureaucratic rationality that erased the humanity of subjects and a pure sentimentality that had little capacity to help. These ways of seeing excused inaction as hundreds of thousands died.

The cataclysm of World War I and the crush of the Great Depression were turning points for European states, colonialism, and international humanitarianism alike.[27] The task of managing war economies and feeding some of the largest armies the world had ever seen endowed European technocrats with a strong sense of control over nature and society.[28] The tens of thousands of overseas subjects conscripted for the war effort saddled empires with a "blood debt" that veterans demanded be settled with more political participation and better living conditions.[29] Debates about welfare in France heated up, especially during the Depression when dire need was widespread and highly visible. Welfare advocates foregrounded the idea that state and society had formal and specific obligations toward individuals, challenging a long-dominant liberal orthodoxy.[30] The institutionalization of global interconnection in the new League of Nations gave rise to an enhanced sense of community with faraway people, deepening feelings of responsibility for distant as well as proximate suffering.[31] Humanitarians more readily intervened across political borders to help those deemed in need. During the Russian famine of 1921, a mission led by European and US charities distributed millions of meals.[32] Just a few years after its lackluster efforts in the Sahel, France launched a humanitarian mission that helped consolidate new colonial territories in Lebanon and Syria after half a million people starved during the Great War.[33] In these new "mandates"—former German and Ottoman territories whose civilizational development was entrusted to victorious countries—the League of Nations exercised a measure of formal oversight. This system often fell short. It failed, for example, to stop tens of thousands from starving in Belgian mandate Rwanda in 1929.[34] Powerful empires jealously guarded their territories against international intervention. Norms and pressure, though, could be as compelling as laws and institutions.[35] Heightened humanitarian standards in a climate of international scrutiny made subsistence a constitutive component of colonial rule.

The high modernist confidence in the ability to mitigate hunger coupled with the acknowledgment of a political responsibility to do so marked a turning point in the French Empire's relationship to its subjects and to nature itself. As France worked to bring its patchwork empire under centralized control, experts in medicine, ecology, economics, and other fields debated how best to raise living standards. Nowhere was the fusion of new responsibilities and new capabilities more fully encapsulated than in nutrition science.[36] The discovery of vitamins in 1912 opened vast new terrains for scientific knowledge and state management.[37] More than revolutionizing the medical care of individuals, a new awareness of vitamins, minerals, and amino acids transformed the problem of collective hunger. Famine had generally been thought of as the consequence of calorie deficits caused by exogenous shocks such as droughts, locusts, or wars. Nutritionists now argued that famines were socially embedded and biochemically complex. Through the League of Nations and other international organizations, experts such as the pioneering French nutritionist Étienne Burnet put forth a holistic vision of global public health centered around the fulfillment of newly discovered biological needs. Nutritionists offered a model of society and biochemistry as a single system linked by the production, distribution, consumption, and metabolism of food. In a twentieth century characterized by modernist projects that dreamed of bringing nature and populations under the will of human beings, the hope of mastering the links between biology and society made nutritionists among the most grandiose of the era's social engineers.[38]

French colonial experts first applied nutritional insights to physiology and medicine. Biochemists and doctors in Indochina and elsewhere participated in a transnational conversation on the disease beriberi which would lead to the 1912 discovery of vitamin B (later recognized as multiple distinct B vitamins).[39] In the 1920s, scientific experts shifted the focus of nutritional thinking from individuals to collectivities through the concept of race. Fearful that the workforce of French Equatorial Africa was dwindling due to starvation and malnutrition, administrators and physicians proposed that newly discovered chemical factors could be used to "regenerate" Black races to increase labor productivity. From its application to races, nutrition expanded to encompass populations in general. The idea of population as an internally differentiated and holistic social formation that could be the object of statistics and policy had existed in France since the eighteenth century.[40] In the interwar empire, this usage of population joined—and sometimes overlapped with but did not entirely supplant—race as a basic unit for understanding and managing groups of people. If the solution to hunger among homogenous races was biological regeneration, populations were susceptible to policies that addressed the social determinants of starvation, such as education programs and minimum wage. By the 1930s, the aim of nutrition was not only to maximize labor power, but also to provide for the well-being of colonial populations. Nutrition as articulated in international organizations was a totalizing framework optimized for the fulfillment of each individual's quantitative and qualitative food requirements. It was a grand plan for the management of national, imperial, and global populations, encompassing social, cultural, and biological dimensions of life.

The ubiquitous opinion that famine was inevitable where backward races encountered difficult environments was challenged on scientific and ethical grounds. A civilizing mission that sacrificed the present for the sake of the future came into conflict with a humanitarianism that prioritized the relief of immediate suffering across parochial divisions.[41] The ideal of a welfare state in which provision was universal, automatic, and determined by rules that pre-existed any particular need presented an alternative to conditional, voluntary, reactive charity. In an age of increasingly rigid scientific racism, nutrition unexpectedly encouraged a malleable and controllable idea of race. Old and new forms of care competed and converged through colonial famine.

The tension between time-honored understandings of starvation as natural and cutting-edge norms and knowledge was laid bare during a famine in western Niger in 1931. Just eighteen years after the devastating famine of 1913 passed with minimal impact on French consciousness, a far smaller famine—one that affected a fraction of the same geographic area and killed around thirty thousand people—was deemed unacceptable. The Antillean-born governor of Niger, Louis-Placide Blacher, one of the few high-ranking men of color in the French colonial service, followed precedent in considering the famine a natural disaster outside the purview of his responsibility. Buying into a simplistic environmental and racial determinism that naturalized famine in the Sahel as a routine tragedy, his administration's response was late and ineffective. This failure had a gendered element, as Blacher and his administrators interpreted starving women and children not as symptoms of an emergency, but as the normal functioning of African families supposedly designed to jettison unproductive members in times of stress. The view of famine as inevitable, however, was rejected by Blacher's superiors in France. No longer excusable as a side effect of natural disaster or the growing pains of primitive races, starvation became scandalous. For the first time, the colonial bureaucracy held administrators personally responsible. Famine was no longer a mere tragedy; it was now a problem.

The Niger crisis of 1931 forced French people across the empire to rethink their approach to famine just as nutrition science, the League of Nations, and the Great Depression were elevating the problem of hunger as a priority of states. The same year, a famine in central Indochina associated with the anticolonial Nghe Tinh uprising made subsistence an issue of security as well as of humanity and administration. The twin food crises prompted senior officials including Ministers of Colonies Albert Sarraut and Marius Moutet to demand the eradication of not only famine but also chronic undernutrition and malnutrition, now seen as related facets of a single problem. Humanist reformers such as the novelist André Gide and the innovative journalist Andrée Viollis, who published a best-selling eyewitness account of the Nghe Tinh uprising, brought colonial hunger home to a metropolitan audience, in the process opening a domestic front in the fight against famine. The sharpened focus on the alimentary well-being of the colonized reached its peak with France's left-wing Popular Front government and its 1937 Commission of Inquiry in the Overseas Territories. Spearheaded by socialist politician Henri Guernut, the empire-wide investigation sought to establish the "quality of life" and "legitimate aspirations" of subjects. French officials who had tended to think of colonial life as merely biological—it existed or it did not—were now concerned with the full range of physical, intellectual, and social flourishing of their overseas protégés.

Promises to improve the social, political, and cultural lives of non-Europeans were empty when the precondition of biological life was not assured. Asking *how* colonial subjects were living forcefully raised the question of *whether* they were living. Against lofty new standards of quality of life, persistent famine and malnutrition were conspicuous. The French theoretically accepted the obligation to ensure full nutritional health, but they could not achieve mere subsistence. The fall of the Popular Front in 1938 and then the outbreak of World War II interrupted the nascent project of forming an empire attuned to the needs of the colonized. In France, the location of responsibility for the future had moved from Divine Providence, to rational, provident individuals, to the social collectivity. But as the French welfare state—the *État-providence*, the provident state—began to be constructed in fits and starts, social provision in the colonies remained the burden of improvident subjects. French responsibility for colonial famine continued to blur the distinction between politics and humanitarianism, between law and pity.

The French Empire could not translate new physiological and sociological understandings of famine into a better quality of colonial life. Nonetheless, the history of colonial hunger profoundly altered ideas of what states owed the people under their protection. By World War II, famine management was a constitutive element of sovereignty. Reformist and anticolonial movements were fueled by the huge gap between what living standards had become in France at the infancy of social democracy and what they remained in the colonies. Having accepted famine prevention as one of colonialism's raisons d'être, France was now forced to defend its empire on this new terrain.

Both the French and British Empires experienced huge famines during World War II. Britain was in a position to intervene but chose not to; France wanted to intervene but was in no position to do so. Infamously, the British did not activate the Indian famine codes as three million people died in Bengal in 1943.[42] During the Great Famine of 1945 in northern Indochina, which killed between one million and three million people, the French administration was helpless under Japanese occupation. France was divided against itself as General Charles de Gaulle's republican Free French government-in-exile and Marshal Philippe Pétain's collaborationist Vichy regime both claimed to be the legitimate French government. Though it had no real presence on the ground, the French Republic competed from afar on the international stage for the right to care for Indochinese people. As actors including Vichy France, Japan, the Allied powers, and the United Nations jockeyed for influence in Indochina, republican France staked its claim through a performance of sovereignty, ostentatiously making famine relief plans that could not be executed. The fight over famine relief marked the culmination of a historical process in which providing subsistence became a privilege of sovereignty that the French tried and failed to assert.

France's inability to fulfill its sovereign duties toward the hungry left a void that nationalists could claim to fill. When in 1945 Ho Chi Minh became the first colonial leader to declare independence from France, he did so during the deadliest famine in the history of the French Empire. More than setting up the material conditions for a revolution that would expel the French in 1954, the famine itself became a battleground on which belligerents contested the right to govern. In the end it was the Vietnamese nation that emerged victorious, not only on the battlefield but in the battle for subsistence. The Great Famine marked the culmination of a reconceptualization of famine in the French Empire from a natural tragedy to a technical and political problem. It was at once one of the last colonial famines and one of the first international ones, marking a shift from an imperial responsibility for the subsistence of non-Western people to one rooted in nation-states and global humanitarianism. States, overseen by an international community, were now supposed to protect their people from starvation. When empires failed to do so, nations claimed that responsibility for themselves.

This book ends with independence, but the story does not.[43] The example of Vietnam is suggestive, pointing to how successor states and the international community inherited a colonial responsibility for famine. Empires and civilizing ideology, today largely discredited, and international humanitarianism, today considered ethical orthodoxy, emerged together and only later went their separate ways. Modern humanitarianism was left over when the formal political ties holding empire together fell away.[44] In the postcolonial era, rich nations intervene in the Global South on the grounds of humanitarianism rather than sovereignty, while ultimate responsibility for fulfilling needs falls on sovereign nations.[45] The welfare state was the logical endpoint of the ethical and technical developments of the interwar French Empire. In its attempts to provide a minimum quality of life in the absence of welfare states, modern humanitarianism remains reactive, conditional, and voluntary. To the extent that colonial governance reworked for a postcolonial era, it is a form of imperialism without sovereignty. And for those who continue to starve along roads and sidewalks, vast world-historical developments are of small consequence; to them, famine still appears timeless.

PART ONE

Studies in Neglect

CHAPTER 1

Bodies and Souls in Algeria, 1867

Marshal of France Patrice de MacMahon, duke of Magenta, a committed monarchist and devout Catholic, was reluctantly and deeply embroiled in the founding of the third French republic. He is remembered for losing the Franco-Prussian War that toppled Emperor Napoleon III in 1870 and then winning the "bloody week" campaign against the revolutionary Paris Commune in 1871. As president of the republic between 1873 and 1879, MacMahon overrode his legitimist devotion to the Bourbon dynasty to protect the fragile new political system, which would fall only after another German invasion in 1940. Less remembered is that shortly before starring in the initial scenes of the new republic, MacMahon, as governor-general of Algeria, presided over a famine that would shape how republican rule was lived across the French colonial empire.

In 1867, Governor-General MacMahon wrote to Napoleon III, "there is reason to hope that when the sun will have acted efficiently on the corpses of poorly-buried people" Algeria would return to its normal state.[1] Yet between half a million and eight hundred thousand people died, between a quarter and a third of indigenous Algerians.[2] The demographic shock and extreme immiseration had deep and durable consequences for indigenous society. But Europeans in Algeria and France approached the famine from a different perspective, that of a colonial narcissism in which everything that happened happened to them. For the men trying to make a new kind of colony—one that

15

was part of France but kept at arm's length, that was liberal but structured on difference—the famine cut to the heart of what this experiment in state building should look like. Would colonialism promote the development of indigenous society parallel to European modernity, or would its aim be assimilation under a universal French civilization? Would it be military or civilian, Catholic or laic, protectionist or laissez-faire? What did the French owe non-European subjects? The core principles of a republican colonialism that would impact millions of lives over the next century were debated even before the republic existed, in the context of famine. In these debates, the starving were all but forgotten.

What exactly France was supposed to be doing in Algeria had been disputed since the initial conquest of 1830. In 1827, during tense negotiations over unpaid grain advances from Jewish Algerian merchants to revolutionary France in the 1790s, the Ottoman ruler of Algiers had hit the French consul with a fly whisk. France invaded the Ottoman regency three years later, ostensibly to avenge the insult but more likely as a gambit by the Bourbon Restoration to rally waning popular support. Notwithstanding, barricades went up in Paris, the ultraconservative king of France Charles X was overthrown, and the "July Monarchy" came to power. Invited by the revolutionaries to take the throne as king of the French, Louis-Philippe inherited a confused situation in Algeria. He initially limited the French presence to the coast to control trade and piracy. But by the end of the decade, Louis-Philippe, like his predecessor, came to see imperial expansion as bound up with the legitimacy of his reign.[3]

The policy of "restricted occupation" gave way to deliberate conquest and settlement. In the 1840s, the French would defeat the two most powerful obstacles to military hegemony. They had taken the eastern city of Constantine in 1837, though its Ottoman ruler, Ahmed Bey, fled to wage guerilla war until finally surrendering in 1848. In 1832, the state-builder Abdelkader had established an emirate that within a few years comprised two-thirds of Algeria. Taking advantage of the aimlessness of the French presence, he alternated between seeking accommodation and waging jihad. But in the early 1840s, a French army eventually numbering over one hundred thousand soldiers undertook a scorched-earth campaign against the nascent state. The army intentionally starved the population by burning crops, destroying grain stores, and killing livestock. Abdelkader surrendered in 1847.

In 1848, as the French army was consolidating power in Algeria, barricades again went up in Paris, King Louis-Phillipe was overthrown, and the Second Republic came to power. Among its first reforms was to abolish slavery and extend citizenship and universal male suffrage to French overseas possessions. Both acts excluded indigenous Algerians. The Second Republic reorganized

Algeria as three French departments, in theory equivalent to those of territorial France. In 1851, Louis-Napoleon Bonaparte, president of the republic and nephew of Napoleon I, executed a coup-d'état. A referendum the next year made him Emperor Napoleon III. It was under his watch that the 1867 famine occurred.

Napoleon III's policy in Algeria was heavily influenced by followers of the revolutionary-era utopian philosopher Henri de Saint-Simon. Saint-Simonians posited a stadial theory of history in which all civilizations progressed toward a future ideal, but at different rates. Under the influence of Saint-Simonian advisors such as Muslim convert Thomas-Ismaïl Urbain, the mixed-race descendant of enslaved people from Guiana, Napoleon III envisaged the natural development of indigenous people under their own customs and laws. Civilian government was limited to heavily European areas in and around coastal cities and was subordinate to the military, which had ruled by decree since 1834. Muslims retained their traditional social organization under the protection of the army's "Arab Bureaus" and the emperor himself. Despite its authoritarianism and often astonishing violence, and in contrast to the republican civilizing mission, the French army adhered to a vague conception of "rights" that afforded indigenous societies a measure of autonomy.[4] The culturally and legally distinct "Arab Kingdom" was consistent with the Bonapartist stress on a sacred and direct bond between sovereign and people.[5] The indigenous people of Algeria were to live, die, and evolve separately from Europeans in a multinational polity. In his own words, Napoleon III was emperor of the Arabs as well as of the French.

This Arab Kingdom was intended to protect indigenous society, including Kabyles and Jews, from potentially harmful contact with European civilization. In fact, the existence of the kingdom did little to stop the unraveling of precolonial social forms. The violence of conquest, heavy taxation, and changing economic patterns weakened subsistence arrangements based in charitable institutions and communal granaries.[6] In the fight against Abdelkader and other resisters, the French intentionally broke rural economies in a lasting way. Property controlled by charitable religious institutions (habous or waqf), an important part of the social safety net, lost its legal protections or was simply confiscated. It was not until 1851 that summary seizure of indigenous land was prohibited, over the protests of settlers.[7] In 1863, the French promulgated a sénatus-consulte, an act of senate, that initiated a process giving Arabs definitive title to land in productive use.[8] Though the act was on its face meant to shelter collectively held indigenous land ('arsh) from being sold under French property law, the subjective meaning of the qualifier "productive" allowed it to serve as legal cover to wrest vast territories from Arabs and Kabyles.[9] This process, known as sequestration (*cantonnement*), relegated communities often reliant on wide-ranging nomadic lifestyles to ever-smaller areas, unsettling carefully calibrated subsistence strategies.[10] People who found it impossible to continue their normal economic activities adapted by taking advantage of new outlets in coastal cities and Europe to sell rather than store surpluses. The repression of a serious revolt in response to the *sénatus-consulte* between 1864 and 1866 further diminished the capacity to resist starvation.[11]

The connection between these material processes and weakened social resilience may seem self-evident, but European observers rarely made it.[12] Rather, they discussed the 1867 famine in terms of sweeping generalizations about Muslim culture and its proper place in a modern colony, tending "to sidestep the local context in order to find solace in broad civilizational paradigms."[13] The causes and solutions of the famine were sought in the abstract concepts of religion, civilization, and social theory. Europeans saw the famine as a battleground for their own political struggles, sometimes expressing sympathy for victims but otherwise treating them as incidental.

European opinion divided roughly into three camps: the Bonapartist military government, the economically liberal settler establishment, and the Catholic Church. The famine of 1867 was assimilated into longstanding debates between Arabophiles and Arabophobes that had been escalating over the previous few years.[14] The army's Arab Kingdom was despised by settlers who, in opposition to the Arab Bureaus—facetiously labeled the *bourreaux d'arabes*, the "executioners of the Arabs"—desired the abolition of military government.[15] The settler vision of colonialism was instead rooted in European immigration, agriculture, and markets, an "empire of virtue" distinct from an earlier colonialism based on mercantilist protectionism and slavery.[16] Settlers called for the extension of civilian rule and European property rights throughout the territory, as well as fuller integration into the French political system. This project for the civil rights of Europeans in a liberal Algeria intersected with that of reformers in France who were pushing for the liberalization of the Second Empire, forming a unified interest group that spanned the Mediterranean. Critics of Napoleon III used the famine to denounce his autocratic tendencies, with a special focus on press censorship. For them, the place of indigenous Algerians was a second-order problem to be dealt with once military rule was abolished. Some advocated simply forcing indigenous people from the territory (*refoulement*). Most speculated that the market, if allowed to operate freely, would find them roles suitable to their level of civilization.

Joining settlers in uneasy alliance was the Catholic Church. The Third Republic would be famously anticlerical, but in 1867 Catholics and republicans fleetingly united in common cause against the French army. Each held its particular universalism—one religious and the other laic—in opposition to the Arab Kingdom's communitarian protection of Muslim civilization. Led by the forceful archbishop of Algiers, Charles Lavigerie, the Algerian church believed that the army's protection of Islam was repugnant to Christianity. Catholics envisioned a Christian Algeria into which Muslims would be assimilated through conversion. During the famine, Lavigerie demonstrated the superiority of religious colonialism by distributing charity and setting up facilities for orphans. This experience would move him to establish the influential "White Fathers" missionary society in 1868. For soldiers, liberals, and Catholics maneuvering for influence in Algeria, the famine was of interest as much for its rhetorical utility as for the suffering it caused.

Under the victorious Third Republic, the liberal vision of colonialism would dominate. The military government was abolished in 1870. As the republic rose from the turmoil of the Franco-Prussian War, the Algerian leader Sheikh Mohammad al-Hajj al-Muqrani rose up against the colony's new civilian government. Having borrowed almost a million francs to distribute famine aid, he now found his autonomy curtailed by the end of military rule.[17] Al-Muqrani died in battle just a few weeks before MacMahon crushed the Paris Commune in the streets of Montmartre and Belleville. His rebellion was defeated soon after. Twenty thousand people were killed. The French imposed punitive land redistributions and fines of thirty-six million francs.[18] In contrast, the total amount allocated for famine relief in 1867 was two million francs. In 1873, all forms of Muslim property law were eliminated, ending restrictions on the sale and purchase of Muslim land as private property.[19] The famine and its aftermath helped prepare the ground for a massive redistribution of land to the burgeoning community of immigrants from France and southern Europe, numbering one hundred thousand in 1848, a quarter million in 1872, and nearly a million by the 1930s.[20] The famine was, in its way, among the foundational events of a universalist French republic predicated on colonial subordination.

A Plague of Locusts

The famine of 1867 appeared to the French to be two separate problems. The first was a locust infestation affecting, in their eyes, primarily European commercial farms. The second problem, severed almost entirely from the first, was starvation and cholera among indigenous people. The Arab Kingdom's separation of settlers and natives led to parallel rather than integrated responses, revealing stark differences in basic social responsibilities. The observation that empires treated the colonized differently is unsurprising. But the debate about if and how the French were responsible for subjects' subsistence is a starting point for the history of famine in the republican empire. The victory of liberal settlers against Arabophile Bonapartists placed final responsibility for subsistence on free markets and individual foresight.

In the spring of 1866, panic overcame Algeria as successive waves of locusts descended across the territory. The press, the Catholic Church, and the military administration dramatized the invasion in a concerted effort to elicit pity and money from the Algerian and French publics. Observers counted, impressively if unscientifically, billions of locusts in some swarms.[21] Settlers watched the insects eclipse the sun for minutes at a time, concealing even the closest objects from view as in a whiteout snowstorm.[22] Locusts insinuated themselves into homes and wells, their decomposing bodies emitting nauseating odors and unhealthy miasmas.[23] When they landed, they formed thick carpets on the ground and collapsed tree branches under their weight.[24] These "true wonders of insatiable greed and gluttony" consumed prairies, orchards, forests, and crops down to the roots.[25]

Settlers, sometimes supported by soldiers, waged a courageous but ineffective war.[26] Newspapers explained in great detail the life cycle, anatomy, habits, and mores (*mœurs*) of the locusts, instructing desperate farmers on how to kill them, their juveniles, and their eggs. Tactics ranged from incinerating them in fires (leading to more than one mortal accident) to crushing them with harrows to scaring them off with drums and guns. Some resorted to chemical weapons, engulfing locusts in vaporous clouds of sulfuric acid or dousing them with lime.[27] The Algerian military administration offered bounties of five francs per kilogram of dead locusts and eggs.[28] But the tenacious insects "always seemed to return from the ground they were buried in or were reborn from the ashes of the fires they were pushed into."[29] Ultimately, "the task was beyond the power of humans."[30] Instead of the sense of mastery over the environment that would characterize twentieth-century colonialism, there was an awed recognition of the helplessness of human agency in the face of nature and God.

In their powerlessness, settlers fell back on solidarity and good will. Public disaster was considered a religious and patriotic responsibility more than an administrative one. Charity drives were organized by church officials, newspapers, and even consulates as distant as Indochina, Puerto Rico, and San Francisco.[31] In the summer of 1866, Governor-General MacMahon convened a commission of seven European notables and a single Arab to coordinate charity efforts.[32] In all other respects, the Algerian administration preferred to "erase itself as much as possible."[33] Charity delivered far less money than was hoped, about a million francs compared to twenty million in estimated damages.[34]

The Catholic Church took a leading role in organizing donations. The Church had thrown its weight behind Algerian colonization since 1830, legitimizing the French presence through ecclesiastical letters and pastoral instructions (*mandements*).[35] Such tools remained available to the French and Algerian clergy "who never cede the front line in works of charity."[36] Just before his death, Bishop of Algiers Louis Antoine Augustin Pavy circulated an appeal that epitomized this blend of religion and nationalism. After recognizing the tests and punishments of Divine Providence, "equally mistress of the laws of nature and the laws of grace," it was incumbent on the faithful to help the victims. Pavy set the example by personally donating three hundred francs.[37]

Calls for alms emphasized the helplessness of humanity in the face of divinely inspired natural disaster: "What can human efforts do against these winged multitudes . . . ?" Only Providence could remove the natural causes of suffering, but it was the duty of French Christians to care for victims, as "Algeria is sister to France."[38] This religious submission to "Providence" coexisted with a newer, secular use of the term as a human characteristic.[39] For economic liberals, the future was in the hands not of God, but in those of provident, rational individuals who had inherited His faculty of foresight.

To instill responsibility for suffering settlers, journalists and clergy incorporated the locusts into nationalist and religious histories. Though locusts had ravaged French Algeria before—a journalist recounted a rumor that in 1848 swarms were so thick that one Arab army thought itself under attack and, embarrassingly, made a cavalry charge against them—observers preferred to assimilate the event into a long history of African locust plagues reaching back to antiquity and the Bible.[40] Scientists emphasized that the specific locust involved, known at the time as *acridium peregrinum*, was native to Africa. Indeed, even when locusts had afflicted Europe, they had always come from foreign lands. These "pernicious insects of the desert," which had plagued African and Asian peoples for thousands of years, "came through the centuries etched on the pages of the sacred and profane history of the most distant times."[41] The ancient Roman writers Pliny and Livy told tales of locusts. Saint Joan of Arc thought them a punishment from hell. One writer, reminded of the armies led by Darius, Xerxes, and Tamerlane, wrote, "Terror formed their advance-guard, famine and pestilence their rearguard, like they formed those of these barbarian hordes."[42] Using the word "native" to describe African locusts as well as African people suggested they were all part of a foreign and hostile natural environment.

The history of the "insect hurricane" or "living hail" could be traced, famously, to the Bible. Priests soliciting alms quoted Deuteronomy, "You will entrust to the earth a rich seed . . . and you will harvest little; for the locusts devour all," and Chronicles, "They are in my hand, says the Lord, and, if I open it, they will ravage the Earth."[43] At a public conference in Algiers, a professor of natural history invoked the plagues of Egypt, lecturing, "Brought by the Oriental wind, it is said in chapter ten of Exodus, the locusts did not leave the country until Pharaoh consented to the departure of the Hebrews. A violent wind rose from the West to rid the country."[44] The analogy between western winds and Western civilization ridding the world of "Oriental" plagues is hard to miss.

Some scientists tried to oppose this type of supernatural exoticism with rationality. A French-Algerian medical professor proved himself a passable literary critic, writing, "The biblical denomination *plagues of Egypt*, given to this pest in our holy books, suggests that its cause is inherent in and special to the land of Africa; that this pest is a supernatural phenomenon and extremely rare." In fact the affliction was "natural and universal." However, his sober natural history failed to capture the popular imagination and promote "civic and national solidarity" the way religious and patriotic myth did.[45]

Journalists and clergy drew on classical antiquity as well as on sacred texts, weaving the locusts into a narrative of France as the inheritor of Roman North Africa.[46] This story implied a religious, civilizational, and (metaphorical and sometimes incestuous) familial responsibility for Europeans while excising Muslims from history and society. Saint Augustine, who as the bishop of Hippo observed a locust-induced famine that killed eight hundred thousand people, provided much rhetorical ammunition for this Latin and Christian form of care. The cardinal archbishop of Bordeaux informed the faithful that, as in the time of Augustine, "so competent to describe the distress of Africa," insects had once more appeared to "reveal to man his powerlessness before certain evils." His Eminence implored his flock to donate to Algeria, "a daughter and a sister" to France.[47] Bishop Pavy, referring to "our African history," praised the example of the third-century archbishop of Carthage Saint Cyprian, who received an unending stream of alms from across Numidia during a terrible plague.[48] In antiquity, Roman legions had taken on the job of killing locusts, just as French soldiers did in modern times.[49] There was an environmental aspect to Latin continuity as well. North Africa had been so fertile that it had served as the granary of Rome. Then a "brutal and barbaric" conquest destroyed this farming culture and the ecology that allowed for it.[50] The conquest referred to was, of course, the Arab one rather than the French. An important task of colonialism would be the regeneration of the once-fertile North African environment.[51]

Fitting the locust infestation into the history of Christianity, Roman Africa, and France was necessary since Christian patriots served as settlers' "guarantee of security."[52] This followed a tradition of public almsgiving for disaster victims, most recently after a hurricane in Guadeloupe earlier in 1866.[53] Algeria, settlers reminded their compatriots, had donated to French flood victims in 1856 and to unemployed workers during the cotton crisis of 1863.[54] Now it was France's turn to prove it cared for Algeria "as a mother does her child."[55] A Parisian journalist framed the struggle in explicitly nationalist terms, praising the settlers fighting to "repulse the enemy, who, for lacking needle-guns and not speaking German, are no less redoubtable than the soldiers of Monsieur von Bismarck Schönhausen."[56] A professor of medicine appealed to coreligionists beyond France, labeling locusts "a humanitarian catastrophe" and calling on all Christians to join in "fraternal solidarity between civilized nations." It was taken for granted that this solidarity did not include indigenous people. The professor listed "Muslim fanaticism" alongside locusts as Algeria's greatest threats.[57]

Relief was a public performance of civic and religious virtue. Newspapers in France and Algeria listed the names of donors and the size of their gifts. Notables arranged public benefits such as regattas, raffles, and balls.[58] Napoleon III was very visible, not in his capacity as head of the government but as symbol and example of private generosity. The imperial family ostentatiously donated twenty thousand francs on behalf of the emperor, ten thousand from the empress, and five thousand from the imperial prince.[59] Napoleon III's donation as a private citizen reflected a responsibility rooted in national and religious culture rather than law. Administrators and clergy in France and Algeria leaned on his example, making appeals for this "truly national project" of salvation in the name of "our gracious sovereign."[60] Since indigenous Algerians were neither French nor Christian, they were excluded from this national and religious economy of care.

Some observers pointed out shortcomings in a social support system based on voluntary charity rather than political obligation. One French Algerian complained that in France the state as well as public charity assisted disaster victims, asking, "Do we not have the same rights as the French who live on the other shore of the Mediterranean?"[61] However, calls for public emergency funds, insurance policies, and funding for technical innovation were largely ignored.[62]

The most striking thing about this patriotic and religious language of care was the near-complete elision of indigenous Algerians. Descriptions of suffering and appeals for aid referred to settlers by default. When Europeans did talk about indigenous people, it was in ways that excluded them from Western Christian civilization and the charitable responsibility it implied. French people believed that the poverty of natives meant they had less to lose from the locusts. Moreover, naturally fatalistic Muslims felt losses less acutely.[63] Newspapers entertained their readers with the presumed simplicity of Arabs, who allegedly thought the locusts were an army led by a "sultan," a large blue insect with colored stripes and pearl eyes aided by a chief of staff. The Arabs, with the "practical instinct that replaces good sense in Oriental regions," would simply eat the locusts that had eaten their wheat, "recovering their harvest in slightly altered form."[64] In a sensationalist book interweaving personal observation with rumor and fiction, L'Abbé Burzet, a parish priest near Algiers, coupled mawkish sentimentality with harsh bigotry. Arabs, he wrote, lay around smoking and drinking coffee, watching indifferently as locusts ruined their livelihoods. According to Burzet, natives would interpret charity as "a legitimate reward for their laziness."[65] A French bishop agreed, arguing that locusts, long a favorite weapon in God's arsenal, were a punishment for those who did not follow His law. Until the French succeeded in delivering Muslims from "brutal fanaticism to the admirable light of Jesus Christ," Islam would continue to invite the retribution of Divine Providence.[66] Portraying Muslims as less susceptible to harm than Europeans, hopelessly stupid, and cosmically evil justified their exclusion from charitable forms of social responsibility.

Officially, the Algerian administration's distribution of charity was supposed to be neutral. Its central charity commission decided that as "one of the duties of the superior administration is to arrive at a complete unity between Europeans and natives, and to treat both on an equal footing," no distinction would be made on the grounds of "nationality." In the context of a multinational polity, equality meant something specific. The Algerian administration facilitated charity within Muslim society just as it did within French Christian society, in a parallel rather than an integrated way. All donations were deposited in the same Bank of Algeria account, but the "nationality" of donors was carefully recorded so as to "attribute to the natives a proportional and equitable portion."[67] The central charity commission and local aid committees took great care not to let natives benefit from charity given by and for Europeans.[68] Furthermore, indemnities for farmers were calculated according to exchange value rather than use value. The committees indemnified at a higher rate per hectare for farmers using the "European plow" rather than the "Arab plow," corresponding to the higher yields given by modern equipment. This suggests that the rescue was about commerce, not subsistence.[69] In these ways, Muslims were excluded from French and Christian communitarian care.

Starving under Military Rule

A Christian, patriotic spirit inspired generosity toward settlers but omitted the colonized. Europeans saw the locusts as a threat to investment and settlement rather than to subsistence. Charity reimbursed settler landowners for lost profits. The stakes were higher for indigenous Algerians whose institutions had been weakened by decades of war and dispossession. Locusts on top of drought led to poor harvests in the fall of 1866.[70] Starvation commenced in the spring of 1867, and by summer the enormous scale of the crisis came into view.[71] The problem was too serious and too visible to ignore. But what should be done about it? And who should do it?

Having been more concerned with commercial cultivators than with subsistence farmers and herders, administrators in indigenous areas were caught off guard. Once starvation and epidemic cholera were in progress, officers of the Arab Bureaus responded in three ways: by intervening directly with grain distributions, refugee camps, and public works; by facilitating loans; and by managing charity. Even while taking these actions, administrators insisted that final responsibility fell to patriotic Muslim solidarity. This approach paralleled patriotic Christian responsibility for locust victims. Algeria was not a single integrated community, but an association of distinct socioreligious spheres responsible for their own well-being. By stressing the incommensurability of European and native societies, insisting on the arbitrary and unforeseeable nature of natural disaster, and rehashing stereotypes about indigenous people's inherent unfitness for dealing with chance accidents, the French state minimized its own role in relief.

French people readily acknowledged the misery of famine, but they turned to civilizational thinking to explain and justify it. There was a widespread belief that Muslims did not experience suffering the way Europeans did, meeting the calamity with "the spirit of sublime resignation that constitutes the essence of their character."[72] Rather than following the dictates of modern medicine by, for example, avoiding the miasmas that caused cholera, Muslims put their faith in useless amulets written by insane religious leaders (marabouts).[73] In their "stupid simplicity," they refused even to accept the care of Europeans, as "these degraded natures are closed to all charitable thought, to all good sentiments of the human heart." Muslims felt no emotion watching loved ones die, trusting fanatically that all was preordained by God.[74] A French visitor argued that moral and physical degradation had left Arabs "without humanity," and wondered about letting the race go extinct: "Humanity is at first repulsed by this thought, but humanity must reason."[75] The supposed quiescence of indigenous people was repeatedly contradicted in the administration's own reports, but the claim was culturally embedded and politically expedient.[76]

The perceived barbarity of Arabs was expressed in the French fixation on cannibalism. Although cannibalism during famines is not unknown, a tone of excited fascination gave voice to titillation and exoticism rather than concern.[77] At the request of Governor-General MacMahon, administrators in Muslim districts submitted tables of "crimes attributed to misery" that included a category for "anthropophagy." These tables recorded perpetrators' nationality, whether the victims were native or European, and whether the cannibals had killed their victims or found them already dead.[78] While the tables indicated many cases of theft and some of murder, the officers admitted that the handful of cannibalism reports were unconfirmed rumors.[79]

This did not stop the media from making cannibalism a central feature of famine coverage. Lurid reports of Arabs eating French soldiers made good copy.[80] Burzet's 1869 book on disaster in Algeria was extreme but not entirely unrepresentative of how the French public learned about the famine. He illustrated with cartoonish gore how Arabs willingly chose theft, murder, cannibalism, and even death instead of working for their subsistence. Unlike the appeals for charity during the locust crisis, Burzet's depictions of suffering were meant to satisfy readers' taste for the shocking and the macabre rather than to inspire pity and action. Arabs, he wrote, "needed the sight of blood, the spectacle of agony, the drunkenness of murder." In obscene detail, Burzet recounted acts that put perpetrators "outside humanity."[81] Cannibalism provided his most gruesome material. It was not necessity but "the absence of any moral sentiment" that made this "degraded race" prefer human flesh over other food and murder over earning an honest wage.[82] Whether readers believed these stories or read them for fun, the tales functioned to exclude Arabs from the circle of European concern.[83]

The word "Arab" sometimes referred specifically to Arabic-speaking Muslims and sometimes to indigenous people in general. When convenient, Europeans contrasted Arabs with complimentary stereotypes of Kabyles, the scions of pre-Islamic Roman North Africa. Catholics and liberals each saw what they wanted to in Kabyle culture. Optimistic Catholics argued that Kabyles were of European origin, had been Christian, had retained the remnants of civilization beneath a forced and superficial conversion, and were on the verge of converting (even reconverting) to Christianity en masse. Liberals, following Alexis de Tocqueville, recognized in Kabyle culture a primitive form of democracy based on egalitarian ideals and electoral politics.[84] With very little evidence, observers reported that Kabyles escaped starvation through their "love of hard work and foresight," arguing that their "ancient Berber laws" protected them from Muslim barbarity and "the crushing protection of French militarism" alike.[85] But these stereotypes were deployed inconsistently. When it suited them, French people did not hesitate to include Kabyles among the depraved Arabs.

Images of savage, lazy, and improvident natives influenced relief efforts. In the summer of 1867, Governor-General MacMahon ordered his subordinates to stop the famine. Having relayed Napoleon III's direct instructions to "save native families from starving to death at any cost," MacMahon promised the emperor that officers would be personally responsible for any "accidents."[86] Despite this flattery of Napoleon's self-conception as emperor of the Arabs, no administrators in Algeria were held responsible. As the magnitude of the famine came into focus, the goalposts moved. Admitting itself powerless to prevent the public calamity, the military administration "at least greatly attenuated the sad consequences by all the measures of providence inspired by its solicitude for the indigenous populations."[87] What were these providential measures?

Relief was in the first instance a question of finding money. Indigenous Algerians had been involved in charity drives following the locust invasions but only tangentially, as donations were apportioned by "nationality." The sums collected were in any case negligible compared to the need.[88] More substantial were the subsidies authorized by the French government, eventually reaching two million francs. The French legislature approved the aid only begrudgingly, simultaneously warning against a reduction in tax receipts.[89] MacMahon dutifully resumed aggressive tax collection as quickly as possible. In 1868, as starvation was ongoing, revenues totaled 1.54 million francs compared to 760,000 francs the previous year.[90] He cut costs further by choosing not to spend the entirety of the funds approved by the legislature.[91]

Negative representations of indigenous people had material consequences. Reluctant to reward irresponsible behavior, the officers of the Arab Bureaus preferred to set up public works projects for men and reserve direct aid primarily for women, children, and the elderly. To inculcate good habits in subjects who were "allergic to work," the bureaus distributed food, clothing, and seed only in limited quantities.[92] In July 1867, MacMahon outlined a plan to get through the crisis cheaply and "without too much suffering" by leaning heavily on temporary jobs in road construction and maintenance.[93] A year later, after hundreds of thousands had died, he advised against renewed subsidies or loans. Relief works stayed open to provide jobs for men, but allocations for women, children, the infirm, and the elderly were severely cut in an effort to "awaken the spirit of solidarity" among Muslims.[94] Europeans openly admitted that the meager wages offered on public works projects could neither stimulate economic recovery nor ensure survival.[95] But regardless of the material efficacy of the relief works, they had the political advantage of placing the burden of responsibility on Muslim men.

The Algerian administration had a clear preference for relief as remuneration for work over free aid, but some of the two million francs went to distributions of cash or grain when judged absolutely essential. It was infinitely better to "stimulate private initiatives rather than put the state on the hook."

Nonetheless, government intervention was sometimes required by "duties of humanity" and fears of an "outburst of passions aroused by misery."[96] Uncomfortable with the very idea of state aid, administrators maintained as much control over resources as possible. When seed was distributed, it was on condition that planting be supervised by a senior Arab leader or a French officer. Under such supervision, the French claimed, indigents were rewarded for "their efforts and our sacrifice."[97]

Extending aid as repayable loans helped address concerns about overdependence on the state. The Arab Bureaus distributed advances on their own account, facilitated loans from European banks, and encouraged impoverished communities to borrow grain from well-off ones.[98] Though these solutions were favored by promarket critics of the regime, who believed that "alms are sterile, loans fecund," the eagerness to hold victims accountable precipitated a debt crisis. MacMahon foresaw this and instructed administrators to approve loans only when absolutely necessary.[99] Moreover, he asked officers to carefully calculate the value of communal property available as collateral. Tribal assets fell far short of his hopes, so the administration lent instead to wealthy individuals, recording personal liabilities in detailed ledgers.[100] On top of requiring communal and private collateral from tribes, banks demanded that the Arab Bureaus guarantee loans. The bureaus declined, urging banks to manage risk by simply extending less credit.[101]

For borrowers who met the requirements, loans were high-interest and short-term. Emergency loans granted in 1867 by institutions such as the French Landed Credit (Crédit Foncier de France) had to be repaid, including interest, half in 1868 and half in 1869.[102] Recipients faced debt service immediately after the fall harvest of 1868 while remaining responsible for taxes.[103] This proved impossible for many. One officer reported that the harvest in his district had once again failed. Inhabitants were butchering famished livestock and would be unable to settle the debts incurred the previous year. He begged for new relief works.[104] A group of European and Jewish businessmen, artisans, landlords, and professionals from the city of Constantine accused the government of disingenuousness, pointing out that the most needy lacked collateral to access aid funds. At the same time, neither the Algerian administration nor indigenous leaders, those "lords of the tent," had any interest in taking financial responsibility. Even if the money could get to the needy, they calculated that a subsidy of 2.4 million francs (a somewhat higher figure than other sources cite) amounted to a pathetic 2.4 francs for each of a million famine victims. This sum fell "like a drop of water into the abyss of misfortune dug under the feet of the Arabs by the Turks."[105] With no time to recover from an event that killed, in some places, half the population, famine debt hindered recovery and accelerated land transfers to Europeans.

In addition to public works, distributions in kind, and cash loans, the Algerian administration confined and repatriated people fleeing starvation. Famine management was largely about keeping subjects in their place. Refugees who swarmed European areas of Algeria were both social and sanitary threats, exuding nauseating odors and compromising security and public health. The administration did not tolerate vagabondage, forcing all able-bodied beggars home or to work sites under military guard. Women and children were sent to camps outside major towns, which remained open until the summer of 1868. Municipal police depots detained refugees until the army could send them away. Burzet observed thousands of people dehumanized by physical suffering gathered together for repatriation: "One saw in their lifeless gaze that all these stomachs were empty, that all these heads were hollow, that all these ears rang with the strange noises that result from the grip of hunger."[106] Over twenty-five thousand people were expelled from the province of Algiers alone.[107] Administrators were especially aggressive about repatriating Tunisians and Moroccans, who, they complained, came to Algeria only to die.[108] As mobility threatened order and hygiene, the French intensified their habitual spatial control of indigenous populations.

The strict management of movement was partly motivated by public health concerns. Typhus and, especially, cholera among hunger-weakened and mobile people caused a large proportion, perhaps the majority, of famine deaths. Refugee asylums were hotbeds of disease that Europeans were terrified would spread to cities.[109] Though mobile clinics were located away from towns, health professionals, soldiers, and others in close contact with refugees often got sick. Sanitary workers carefully disposed of human and animal remains to reduce the risk of spread, and doctors prioritized physical separation to keep Europeans safe from epidemics.[110]

A final antifamine strategy sidestepped issues of cost by encouraging charity within Muslim communities. The commander of Algiers, General Emmanuel Félix de Wimpffen, would soon be infamous for surrendering to Prussia at the Battle of Sedan after relieving a wounded MacMahon. In 1868, General de Wimpffen cited the French response to locusts and customary Muslim charity as models for famine relief. Traditionally, he explained, there had existed religious charitable organizations funded by pious bequests. Fearing hostile marabouts, the French state had "taken charge" of these funds. Now, the general thought, "It behooves us to reconstitute on a French basis the charitable institutions that politics forced us to suppress, and the absence of which had regrettable consequences this year." De Wimpffen also tried to incorporate Muslims into French philanthropy, recalling that the indigenous communities of Algiers had donated seventy-five thousand francs for French flood victims in 1856.[111]

Charitable institutions were not revived, and the French public did not donate but indigenous notables did. Just as the administration had done after the locusts, it promoted charity as a cheap form of famine relief.[112] The former soldier Amor ben Mohamed was nearly ruined spending twenty thousand francs on rescue grain. The caïd of Guelma, also a veteran, sheltered orphans in his home, adopting five of them. Both were awarded the Legion of Honor, the most prestigious of French awards.[113] The caïd Si Smaïl of the Hodna region bankrupted himself to the "honor of his society." Sufi institutions (*zaouias*) were commended for taking in starving people.[114] Public praise and awards for indigenous donors helped the French claim antifamine efforts they had little to do with. By intervening directly with aid and camps, facilitating loans, and encouraging charity, the French state fulfilled what it saw as its humanitarian charge.

Property and the Press

As Arab Bureau officers struggled with limited means and limiting prejudices, most French people observed starvation from a distance. The Algerian government's most desperate fight for survival was not physical but political. In a speech to the French senate delivered in January 1870, MacMahon mounted a failed last-ditch defense of the French Algerian military regime that would be abolished in March, just months before his failed last-ditch defense of the Second Empire against Prussia.[115] By personal conviction, MacMahon was relatively sympathetic to settlers, even at times indifferent to the Arab Kingdom.[116] Nonetheless, in his role as governor-general, he fought for military rule. He justified the "progress" of Algeria against critics such as Senator Michel Chevalier, sometime Saint-Simonian, professor of political economy, free-market champion, and advisor to Napoleon III.[117] Chevalier had visited the United States in the 1830s and admired Americans' handling of their own "native problem." Following the US model, Chevalier and other liberals advocated assimilating native land while ignoring natives, driving them away (*refoulement*), or, for some extremists, eradicating them.[118] MacMahon conceded that in the United States, the "insignificant" aboriginal populations were simply forced farther into the endless forests with minimal disruption to their hunting lifestyle. In Algeria, what he believed to be a larger indigenous population, 2.5 million strong, precluded such an easy solution. Stripping land from

Arabs would violate what he called their "rights" and furthermore could only be accomplished through violence. Instead, MacMahon defended the 1863 *sénatus-consulte* that opened hundreds of thousands of acres to settlement as a compromise between liberal capitalism and native rights. Against accusations that military rule had left natives "dead or ruined," MacMahon cited import and export data, for "despite their benevolence, our merchants would certainly not furnish [products] gratis."[119] Ostensibly about living conditions, the argument was tailored for senators concerned with the classic liberal function of colonies as providers of raw materials and buyers of metropolitan goods.[120] The standard of "dead or ruined," which MacMahon repeated several times, suggested that life for indigenous people existed or did not; there was little room for gradations in what kinds of lives they were living.

This debate occurred at a level so far removed that MacMahon and the senators referred to the famine only euphemistically as "the crisis." It entered French politics as rhetorical material for preexisting power struggles between settlers and soldiers, church and state, Bonapartists and republicans, and administrators and journalists. The crisis's material specificity was lost through its integration into competing abstract political projects. Liberals rarely explained how a civilian administration would prevent future famines; military officers did not propose policy changes for their Arab Kingdom; Catholics were concerned as much with souls as with bodies. Indigenous Algerians were minimally involved as participants or even objects. French discussions of famine were usually about something else entirely.

The single overriding aim of settler, republican, and Christian critics was the replacement of military rule with civil government and individual land tenure. This had been accomplished briefly in 1858 before Napoleon III reversed course and earned the permanent animosity of settlers.[121] In reestablishing military rule, the emperor believed he was protecting indigenous people from integration into a liberal economy in inevitably subordinate roles. Indeed, officers claimed that by protecting native rights, it was the army, not settlers, that championed "the cause of true liberalism."[122]

The famine became fodder for this decades-long quarrel. In a remarkable coincidence of interests, the army's opponents argued that the sole remedy for famine was to allow Arabs to sell them land.[123] Troubled by the distress of people and business, the Constantine Chamber of Commerce judged that state aid and private alms were ineffective and harmful to Arab civilization. Famines would occur "as long as the natives form in the colony a separate society, subject to particular laws and without direct contact with the European element." The chamber lobbied for an emergency exception to property laws that prohibited the selling of collectively held tribal land. This would provide immediate relief and increase the long-term productivity of indigenous farmland and people by subjecting both to European influence.[124] Across the colony, a spokesman for the city of Tlemcen argued, "The only thing left to them is land; but they cannot alienate or mortgage it as long as individual property is not established."[125] A free market in land was the only substantive famine remedy proposed by liberal settlers.

The debates about competing visions of colonialism played out in and around the press. Readers in France and Algeria had access to more information about the Algerian crisis than they would about any other French colonial famine. This was due to the presence of a large settler community and an established Algerian press corps and because emotionally evocative language was politically useful.[126] The sympathy elicited by descriptions of indigenous suffering was channeled toward the interests of free-market liberals, republican activists, and Catholic clergy. Advocates of these disparate interests formed an unorthodox front against the military government.

The famine struck at a significant moment in the history of journalism under the authoritarian Second Empire.[127] At the beginning of 1867, France abolished the system of press warnings (*avertissements*) that gave officials the power to censor and correct newspaper items by executive decree. MacMahon voluntarily followed the French example, leaving the enforcement of press laws and the suppression of "discrepancies" in Algerian newspapers to the courts. By 1868, however, newspapers were becoming more "violent" by the day. Editors, MacMahon complained, were nonetheless smart enough to stay within the law. They wrote in a "detestable spirit," but they did so in a way that avoided judicial condemnation. Protected from administrative and legal reprisals, journalists had crossed all decent boundaries to compromise public safety. The last straw was when the Algiers newspaper *L'Akhbar* ran an article, entirely devoid of evidence, blaming "the natives" for murdering a child whose body had been found in Algiers. MacMahon accused *L'Akhbar* of inciting violence, and in contravention of the new French law and its voluntary application in Algeria, he issued an *avertissement*.[128] The state's interest in protecting Arabs from defamation and violence, and Europeans from any counterviolence, justified the reestablishment of executive censorship. The governor-general thus invited his officers to exercise an "active surveillance" of the press.[129]

MacMahon cited a single incident to reinstate censorship by decree, but officials used their restored power freely. Officers believed they were protecting military order from a meddlesome liberal press, which some believed was backed by Jewish money.[130] Unsurprisingly, journalists were furious at this obstruction of their duty to "open their fists when they are full of truths."[131] The most dramatic truths in the fists of journalists had to do with famine, and it was around this issue that the conflict between the military administration and the press played out most intensely. Journalists claimed censorship was motivated not by security but by fear of public humiliation. Even before the reinstitution of executive censorship, the administration had aggressively sued newspapers for reporting on the famine. Now that censorship was once again practiced by fiat, the effect was even more repressive.

Journalists portrayed themselves as guardians of liberal society against military authoritarianism. A piece in the republican Parisian newspaper *Le Siècle* imagined a speech delivered by a masked man in Algiers. The famine, the orator disclosed, could not be attributed solely to drought and locusts. "I see that men united with the elements to perpetrate the ruin of an entire people, and this, *messieurs*, with the finest sentiments to be found, with the firm desire to do good." The shadowy figure accused the administration of obstinately refusing to instate liberal property laws "as the Arab Kingdom collapsed, burying in its ruins thousands of corpses." Who was this mysterious man who spoke truth to power so courageously? "I am the independent press," he disclosed as he withdrew amidst cheers and jeers.[132]

The press denounced the government for doing more to suppress news of the famine than to help its victims, in the process making the crisis common knowledge among all walks of the French reading public. Columnists for the gossipy Paris daily *Le Figaro* discussed famine in a playful but stinging style alongside analyses of the latest fashions and eyewitness testimony of upscale parties. *Le Figaro* argued that its own often silly coverage was more honest than administrative and ecclesiastical reports.[133] Édouard Lockroy, a militant anti-Bonapartist, former assistant to famed orientalist Ernest Renan in Syria, future leftist deputy and husband of Victor Hugo's widowed daughter-in-law Alice, complained that while France failed to send money or food to Algeria, it did serve the famished colony an appetizing menu of censorship, featuring a main course of *avertissements* with onions.[134] Another writer, noting that a quarter of the indigenous population had died, contrasted the situation with the petty preoccupations of Parisians: "There, they suffer, despair, and die; here, we look for diversion, and the calamity of the day is the cold drizzle that spoils the races and forces ladies to rethink their outfits." The rest of the column was devoted not to famine but to the vogue of shorter dresses.[135]

Famine entered the public sphere in a rhetorical mode that emphasized graphic scenes of horror, the backwardness of Arabs, and the incompetence of the military. Critics of army rule used emotional or titillating prose to draw readers in before making their case. One analyst simultaneously described and made use of this rhetorical tactic, observing that stories of cannibalism "fill the heart with pity and indignation." With an expenditure of thirty-eight years, four billion francs, and the blood of its most vigorous children, France had bought nothing but people eating each other. As soon as the reader's interest was piqued, the author dismissed "prejudicial and fanatical" Arabs from his vision of a civilian settler colony free of military oversight. Investors, he complained, had no confidence in the arbitrary military regime that provided only "force without security, and license [*bon plaisir*] without liberty." His ideal colony demoted the army from its governing role and reassigned it to form a barrier between Arabs and a civilian, European Algeria.[136]

Genteel readers of *Le Figaro* read jarringly lighthearted accounts of Arabs fighting in the streets over filth abandoned by animals, stealing and eating whatever they could get their hands on while fending off blows from settlers' clubs. In Oran, starving people fought with dogs over garbage thrown out by a hotel kitchen, devouring discarded chicken entrails with the voracity of hyenas or jackals.[137] A painter returning from Algeria claimed to have seen a woman roast and eat her daughter.[138] Another witness wrote that, denied bread, the Arabs "crunched on the kids."[139] Yet another recounted how he was swarmed by villagers, the men begging for alms, the girls "buying pity with the most distressing debasement, that of modesty. They lifted their veils and without shame . . . contorted in the sun" in a vulgar display of seduction. Some Europeans amused themselves by throwing coins into thickets of cactus, laughing as the girls emerged with their bronze shoulders dripping blood, "paying with their bodies the tax demanded by famine."[140] As with Burzet's graphic writing, these accounts are less interesting for their literal truth than for their ubiquity, provocation, and channeling of readers' gut reactions.

Le Figaro, like nearly all outlets, blamed the famine on the military. As it seemed improbable that it had rained on Europeans but not Arabs, the fault for the famine could not lie in nature. Rather, it was credited to a system of governance "more Turkish than French." Lockroy predicted that France would be forced to abandon Algeria and the army would put up a placard, as in a storefront, reading, "Closed by reason of death." The two-million-franc subsidy, he reproached, was like giving a naked man a pair of socks.[141] One writer demanded the resignation of the cabinet politician Adolphe Niel, who now, the journalist accused, held the ministerial portfolios for famine and cholera as well as war.[142] The Church was not immune to the sarcasm of *Le Figaro* columnists, who found it odd that though priests took vows of poverty, Muslims fulfilled them.[143] Church and press were allies against military rule, but the antagonisms that would characterize the Third Republic were only thinly papered over.

Journalists drew attention to discrepancies between official and eyewitness accounts of the famine. They accused the army of both negligence and lying, more interested in saving face than saving lives.[144] Using the Algerian army's own statistics, one reporter painstakingly calculated a death toll of 217 thousand, a figure that, while likely an underestimate, was "too eloquent to require commentary."[145] Witness accounts publicized the suffering the administration was anxious to hide. In refugee camps meant to provide care, meals consisted of "drink, river water; food, a ten-cent biscuit divided between four people; dessert, truncheon blows at will. We see that this diet is hardly fortifying, especially the last item on the menu."[146] The famine unfolded in full view of Europeans, as "the starving cross the boundaries imposed on them, invading our properties, our farms, our centers, our cities, and die on our roads, without the strength to beg for bread."[147] The presence of European witnesses and a robust print culture gave the French leaders of Algeria nowhere to hide: "the spectacle of last year, everyone saw it; the dangers of next year, everyone understands them; the cause and the remedy, everyone asserts them." And yet, "our pilots are deaf to all voices, blind or resistant to all information."[148]

Such arguments mapped French political fractures onto Algerian society. Trans-Mediterranean struggles over press censorship, liberal economics, and religion were the true referents of debate. If news outlets were expert at capturing attention with heartbreaking or exciting yellow journalism, action on behalf of the starving did not necessarily follow from awareness. The remedy for both famine and press censorship was, invariably, the suppression of the "barbaric and antisocial utopia" of the Arab Kingdom.[149] Some pundits denounced Arab chiefs who symbolically "ate" their people through theft and corruption.[150] Others blamed famine on the "communism" of land they saw as the root of Arab social organization, and they hoped it would discourage French leftists from pursuing similar utopias.[151] Regardless of the specific criticism, the solution was always the same: if the French failed to impose civilian government and private property, they would "make the Arabs disappear from Algeria like the Redskins from America."[152] One French observer asked ominously, "Is this then the fate to which all populations subjected to humanitarian France are doomed?"[153] The Catholic Church, for one, did not think it had to be, as long as the French adhered to a colonialism with Christianity at its core.

Christian Colonialism

In the spring of 1868, a conflict between two of the most powerful men in Algeria erupted into public view. In a heated exchange of letters, Governor-General MacMahon accused Archbishop Lavigerie of proselytizing among starving Muslims. In turn, Lavigerie accused MacMahon of not supporting the

Church's charity work. The dispute incarnated a tension between incompatible visions of colonialism, one based in protection of indigenous civilization,
the other in Christianity. In practical terms, it was about whether Algeria and
its Catholic Church would remain subject to military fiat or share in the privi-
leges of French governance. In this battle, the Church found itself on the side
of activists across the political spectrum who were interested in civil freedoms
and economic liberalization.

The material import of Lavigerie's charity was more than nothing but not
by much. Rather than the brotherly care of Christian toward Christian, it was
the paternal beneficence of the missionary.[154] Lavigerie's biggest contribution
was setting up orphanages that cumulatively housed about eighteen hundred
children, many of whom converted and half of whom died.[155] The Church,
in its quest for alms, pioneered techniques that would later be taken up by
twentieth-century humanitarians. French sponsors could "adopt" individuals,
buying the right to choose a child's Christian name and receiving yearly up-
dates and photographs. Some orphans toured France to warm the hearts of
potential donors.[156] Shared tactics notwithstanding, the Church was motivated
as much by evangelism and the political needs of the particular moment as
by the "do unto others" imperative inherited and secularized by later philanthropists. Humanitarianism's genealogy owes as much or more to the free-
market liberals and nascent republicans in uneasy alliance with the Church.

The dispute between Lavigerie and MacMahon originated in a personal letter that the archbishop wrote to a French donor and later published as an appeal for charity. In it, he described how alms were used to fund orphanages
and the "sweet and pious victims of charity and faith" who staffed them. There,
young famine survivors were molded into a class of "Christian Arabs," accom-
plishing the true assimilation and regeneration that "we seek without finding
because we look with the Koran, and with the Koran in one thousand years,
like today, we will be Christian dogs, and it will be meritorious and holy to slit
our throats and throw us in the sea."[157] For Lavigerie, secular colonialism, like
Muslim civilization, was a contradiction in terms.

Lavigerie's Christian colonialism was irreconcilable with the Arab Kingdom's
protection of indigenous civilization. MacMahon considered Church charity a
bad-faith effort to circumvent official restrictions on proselytizing under the
guise of caring for famine victims, giving Muslims bread only at the price of
their souls. He took particular issue with a line in Lavigerie's letter that presented a stark choice: "It is necessary to stop confining the Arab people to its
Koran, to give it, or at least allow it to be given, the Gospel; or to chase it into the
desert, far from the civilized world." For MacMahon, this passage threatened
Muslims' rights of conscience and of property. As significantly, he complained

FIGURE 1. "Famine in Algeria: Msgr. The Archbishop of Algiers Welcoming Orphans at the Episcopal Palace." Etching by Janet-Lange (Ange-Louis Janet), *Illustration: Journal Universel,* January 18, 1868.

that the archbishop had intentionally exaggerated the scope of the famine to embarrass the government.[158] Lavigerie strenuously denied the charge of involuntary conversion, except for those under the age of reason and at the moment of death. He stood his ground on his estimate of famine mortality, maintaining (correctly) that the published figure of one hundred thousand was actually conservative. He wrote, provocatively, that MacMahon's government-general had shirked its economic, political, and moral responsibilities, so it was the Church's duty to step up. Charity, he explained, was not undertaken to benefit the charitable.[159]

Cannibalism again had symbolic significance disproportionate to its real impact. In his original letter, Lavigerie told a grisly story he claimed to have heard from an orphan named Zohra, who said her parents had killed and eaten her siblings. The little girl was under the knife herself but managed to escape, ending up in a Church orphanage.[160] MacMahon accused Lavigerie of impugning Islam for the actions of a few individuals, pointing out that eminently Catholic Ireland had also seen cases of cannibalism during its famine. Cannibalism, he said, was a medical rather than religious issue, the result of brain seizures (*transports aux cerveaux*) caused by severe privation that eliminated the capacity for free will.[161] This enraged Lavigerie, who maintained that Christians, Irish or otherwise, did not engage in cannibalism under any circumstances.[162] He was supported by Jules Duval, a settler activist and disciple of Michel Chevalier, who in a tone of thrilled revulsion found MacMahon's medical explanation an absurd excuse for Arab barbarism: "A thousand times death—right, ladies?— before turning one's thoughts to such atrocities!"[163]

The confrontation between Church and state became public through the media, overlapping with debates about press freedom. *L'Akhbar* republished Lavigerie's original letter alongside a letter to the editor in which he emphatically denied that the Church baptized anyone by force. MacMahon, Lavigerie objected, had taken his obviously rhetorical line about driving Arabs into the desert out of context. Far from supporting violence, he wanted only to bestow upon Arabs the Christian virtue that alone could prevent future famines.[164] In response, the military authorities issued an *avertissement* against the newspaper, claiming that Lavigerie had disavowed the controversial passage. Lavigerie publicly insisted he had not disavowed anything.[165] The government also published an open letter addressed to "the Muslims of Algeria," assuring them that accepting charity would not compromise freedom of religion. Distinguishing between care and Christianity where Lavigerie would not, the army did not want Arabs to think that "the sentiment of humanity alone did not guide us in these sad circumstances, and that we could have given in to a desire for religious propaganda."[166] The tense situation was resolved in June 1868, at least publicly, when it was reported that the government would allow Lavigerie's orphanages to stay open as long as they respected freedom of conscience.[167] At this point, though, the conflict had already become a unifying cause for those opposed to military rule.

The archbishop became the face of the famine for Europeans. Lavigerie himself professed to put into words a widespread public spirit against an unpopular government.[168] Opinion was divided on the question of proselytizing. Some journalists trusted Lavigerie to restrain religious expression to its bare minimum—charity. Others saw no role whatsoever for Christianity in Algeria. Others split the difference. *Le Figaro* appreciated that Lavigerie saved children from being cooked in a little butter and served for lunch, but it also condemned his orphanages as steam factories "to manufacture five hundred little apostates an hour."[169] Regardless of journalists' feelings about clericalism, they praised Lavigerie's "humanitarian zeal" and condemned MacMahon's attempts to silence him.[170] A leftist deputy even invited Lavigerie to lead a demonstration against the military. He refused, but the request confirmed, as MacMahon noted, that Lavigerie was a symbol for those hostile to the gov-

ernment, regardless of their politics.[171] Overcoming their customary antipa-
thy to the Church, liberals and republicans rallied behind the Catholic leader.

The polemic crystallized a narrative that blamed famine on the army, ap-
plauded Lavigerie and the press for publicizing it, and prescribed private property as the remedy.[172] Hunger would be defeated only by replacing the "collective
right which kills" with the "personal right which vitalizes."[173] The dominance
of this view was evident in a French government inquiry commissioned in 1867
and published in 1870. Despite the timing, it was not motivated by famine but
formed part of a country-wide survey of French departments. The project organizers took oral depositions and created a form with 151 questions about
property, credit, wages, exchange, ecology, and law; the questionnaire was distributed to notables, mostly European, in government, agriculture, business,
and the professions. The respondents were virtually unanimous in pushing for
civil government and private property, often discussing the famine in support
of these aims. A few cited utopian Saint-Simonians such as Prosper Enfantin,
proposing to overcome Arab deficiencies through racial fusion within a single community.[174] Most argued that civilian government would prevent famines, but they did not explain how.[175] Whether or not settlers were sincere in
their concern for hungry people, civilian government would not bring about
a liberal utopia. As Napoleon III and Patrice de MacMahon foresaw, liberal
property law would accelerate the subordination of indigenous Algerians.

Famine in a Liberal Empire

Settler, republican, and Catholic opposition to military rule in Algeria coalesced
through famine. The anti-Bonapartist movement achieved its aim when the
army was replaced by a civilian government in 1870. Without animosity toward
the Second Empire to unify it, the opportunistic alliance unraveled. The Third
Republic would be characterized by friction between Church, state, and settlers. In 1873, Catholic legitimist Patrice de MacMahon, who had run Algeria
as a Bonapartist, found himself president of a third French republic of which
he was deeply suspicious. His "government of moral order" was ideologically
monarchist but respected the new republic's formal institutions. After elections
returned a moderate republican government in 1877, MacMahon dissolved the
chamber of deputies and flirted with a coup. In the end, he backed away, begrudgingly preserving the republic.[176]

Having been interpreted through the lens of a unique historical con-
juncture, the 1867 famine offered no lessons for dealing with famines in other
times and places. What it did do was help inaugurate a colonialism rooted

in economic liberalism that placed responsibility for subsistence on free markets, provident individuals, and charitable goodwill. France's first major experience with modern colonial famine was seen as a chance to think about French society and the form of its imperial power. The needs and the suffering of indigenous Algerians were incidental.

CHAPTER 2

The Mandate of Heaven in Indochina, 1884–1930

Everywhere the French saw famine, they explained it as the outcome of improvident races and inhospitable environments. It was a tragedy of nature more than a problem of government. Responsibility for subsistence fell on some combination of individual foresight, free markets, and charitable goodwill. French colonial administrators understood their role to be philanthropist of last resort. In Indochina under the Third Republic as in Algeria under the Second Empire, this vague collection of ideas and practices—they never cohered at the level of theory or policy—left administrators wide latitude to act, or not, unconstrained by specific instructions or desired outcomes. Absent a defined obligation, caring for the hungry could always fall to someone else first.

This flexible stance toward subsistence left plenty of room for contextual variation. Similar ideas and actions had unpredictable trajectories in the unique complex of forces surrounding each famine. In Indochina, three characteristics of the colonial situation were crucial: the existence of a Vietnamese state with a historically strong obligation to ensure subsistence; the existence of means to do so in the form of dikes and granaries; and sustained oversight from European journalists and missionaries. In Algeria in 1867, only the last of these conditions had obtained. The French had suppressed the Ottoman state. Decentralized subsistence strategies, regardless of their efficacy, were relegated to the realm of ethnological curiosity rather than serious administration.

Journalists had drawn attention to the famine, but they had not done so in a way that demanded a response on behalf of the hungry. Indeed, liberal critics had faulted Algeria's military administration for doing too much, not too little.

When the French conquered the Vietnamese-speaking regions of Indochina in the second half of the nineteenth century, they encountered a centralized imperial state that had long dealt with famine both technically and ideologically. Confucian ideals of benevolent governance, including that of "nourishing the people," helped regulate relations between rulers and ruled.[1] In the fourth century BCE the Chinese philosopher Mencius had written, influentially, "When people die, you simply say, 'It is none of my doing. It is the fault of the harvest.' In what way is that different from killing a man by running him through, while saying all the time, 'It is none of my doing. It is the fault of the weapon?'"[2] Such teachings remained vital sources of legitimacy and guidance in the nineteenth and twentieth centuries. They helped Vietnamese rulers, and indirectly, the French, claim the authority of ancient tradition through famine relief. According to neo-Confucian thinking, it was the obligation of rulers, communities, and landowners to ensure a minimum living for subjects and tenants.[3] Vietnamese lords were responsible for subsistence in a cosmological as well as sociopolitical sense. Famines were signs they had displeased supernatural forces and risked losing the "mandate of heaven."[4]

Compelled by Confucian norms of benevolent governance, nineteenth-century emperors, the "sons of heaven," implemented a variety of subsistence policies. Article 85 of the Nguyen dynasty founder Gia Long's 1815 legal code, which was closely modeled on that of the Chinese Qing dynasty, provided a framework for the care of the needy. These arrangements were expanded by his successors over the following decades. The Vietnamese imperial court in the central city of Hue required regular reports on weather conditions, crop yields, and rice prices. If these reports were unfavorable, the court had several tools available to stave off starvation, including tax relief, debt cancellation, and grain distribution.[5] Gia Long instituted a system of emergency price stabilization and aid based on decentralized provincial and community granaries. Centralized imperial stocks were made available in cases of dire need.[6] According to one estimate, the imperial state distributed fifteen million kilograms of rice between 1817 and 1842.[7] In the event of famine, mandarins—imperial administrators selected through a Confucian examination system—were held personally accountable. Article 85 of the Gia Long code stipulated that officials caught collecting taxes from famine-stricken villages would be fired and suffer one hundred strokes of the bamboo. Fraudulent claims on state aid were likewise punished with beating and fines.[8]

Alongside emergency relief, the court undertook long-term social and technical programs aimed at subsistence. The most important of these was water management. In the early nineteenth century, Gia Long, drawing on a centuries-long tradition, founded a department of dikes to build and maintain hydraulic infrastructure.[9] Dikes not only increased crop yields, but also protected against the killer floods that were a main trigger of famines in the region. In addition, emperors, who in theory owned all Vietnamese land, could reclassify property as communal. Controlled collectively by villages and legally inalienable, communal fields were meant to allow destitute people to grow enough rice for food and taxes. The state was complemented by civil society institutions such as mutual aid organizations and Buddhist charities.[10] These measures did not always prove satisfactory. In the late 1840s, famine and cholera killed ten percent of the population, almost a million people.[11]

In 1859, Napoleon III's navy began the French conquest of Indochina under the pretext of protecting persecuted European missionaries and Vietnamese Catholics. In 1862 and 1867, as Algeria starved, France signed treaties establishing the southern colony of Cochinchina. The Kingdom of Cambodia was made a protectorate in 1863. In the 1880s, France conquered the remainder of Vietnamese territory, forming protectorates over the central and northern regions of Annam and Tonkin in 1884. Laos was brought under French control in 1893.[12]

The French Indochinese Union created in 1887 was a patchwork of languages, cultures, and administrative jurisdictions. Cochinchina was a formal colony under direct French rule. In the protectorates of Annam and Tonkin, the French preserved the Vietnamese imperial state centered on the Forbidden City at Hue, grafting their administration onto existing institutions. Mandarins continued to take orders, subject to French approval, directly from the imperial court.[13] French administrators saw their job as "discreetly managing" Vietnamese officials.[14] Indirect rule gave France access to an established state apparatus with administrative capacity and political legitimacy. It also ensured that precolonial famine thinking remained in play.

French colonialism had an ambivalent relationship with the Vietnamese tradition of famine management. By maintaining continuity with the precolonial Vietnamese state, the French indirectly inherited its political and technical responsibilities. However, they also let many elements of the precolonial subsistence arrangement lapse. Communal lands lost their protected status and accumulated to the wealthy, both Vietnamese and foreign. Privatization of collectively held land, coupled with the cessation of periodic debt cancellation, swelled the ranks of sharecroppers and wage laborers. This, in turn, decreased access to direct food entitlements and increased exposure to creditors. At the same time, the French raised tax rates, introduced new taxes (the one on rice wine was particularly detested), and eliminated tax exemptions for categories of people such as the disabled and elderly. Personal taxes were raised by a factor of five in Tonkin in 1897 and in Annam in 1908.[15] The French tried to fight the poverty they themselves generated by providing cheap credit for peasants, but tenant farmers and sharecroppers had no collateral to access it. The low-interest money instead found its way to the wealthy, who loaned it at usurious rates to the poor, unintentionally exacerbating the problem it was meant to solve.[16] Inequality widened and living conditions worsened, largely at the expense of the very poorest. More and more farmers found themselves in a state of permanent landlessness and indebtedness. By 1930, twelve thousand people in Tonkin, 1.25 percent of landowners, controlled 16.6 percent of rice fields. In 1937, French social scientist Yves Henry estimated that the average Vietnamese ate 182 kilograms of rice per year, down from 262 kilograms in 1900.[17]

As elsewhere in the empire, the French in Indochina rarely made the connection between policy and poverty. They believed that the people they called "Annamites," a label derived from a Chinese exonym, suffered from famine because they were naturally improvident, suspicious, hypocritical liars, lazy and fatalistic even when faced with death.[18] Unable to see the big picture from the vantage point of their little corner of land, the Annamites were incapable of planning for the future.[19] These characteristics made them naturally unsuited to survival in environments like the Red River Delta of Tonkin. Though much of the delta's farmland had the enviable quality of yielding two rice harvests each year, it was also densely overcrowded and prone to catastrophic flooding.

French racial and environmental determinism was tempered ethically and politically by Confucianism, and technically by Vietnamese traditions of civil engineering and grain distribution. The same mandarins who had been responsible for managing famines in the precolonial period continued to bear that obligation under the protectorates, in both a practical and moral sense. The continued existence of the imperial court maintained the precolonial expectation of state intervention in famines while keeping the ultimate burden on the Vietnamese rather than the French. In addition, French-language newspapers were active in exposing famine and criticizing the colonial state. The presence of an old and strong Vietnamese Catholic community ensured that parochial Christian care had greater material benefits than it did in other colonies, as more people fell within the Christian circle of concern. Administrators, mandarins, engineers, missionaries, and journalists all took part in the debates provoked by recurring famines.

This chapter considers the period from the invasion of Tonkin and Annam in the 1880s to 1930, when anticolonial resistance and reformist colonial humanism ushered in a new phase in French thinking about famine. Of particular interest is the Red River Delta of Tonkin, which suffered from chronic precarity and frequent famines. The chapter does not proceed strictly chronologically but treats, in turn, certain particulars of the colonial situation in Indochina that affected how famines were understood and lived: the dynamic relationship between the French protectorate and the protected Vietnamese imperial state; the Vietnamese tradition of hydraulic engineering and grain storage; and the role of French journalists and Catholic missionaries in famine relief. These political and technical pressures tended to encourage attention, but this attention was rarely translated into substantive and enduring reform.

Food was a constant concern in the violent first decades of French rule in Tonkin and Annam. Fierce resistance to the French invasion between 1885 and 1889 threatened French power before it was even established and was accompanied by widespread hunger. A famine in Annam in 1897 killed thousands. In 1907, the Than Thai emperor rebelled and was forced to abdicate, and his son Duy Tan did the same in 1916, both years of dearth. Through this turbulent time, the questions of who was responsible for hunger and how best to address it were at the forefront of people's minds.

Administrators and Mandarins

Famine thinking in Tonkin and Annam was shaped by the relationship between the French protectorates and the protected Vietnamese state. This dynamic generated assemblages of ideas and practices drawing from sources including Confucian hierarchy, Vietnamese civil engineering, the colonial civilizing mission, market liberalism, and charitable philanthropy. The indeterminacy of responsibility allowed for flexibility. Policy was improvised according to the mix of political, financial, and humanitarian motivations in each particular case. The Vietnamese imperial court functioned both as competitor pushing the French to care for subjects and as scapegoat bearing final responsibility for famine.

The questions of how to intervene in famines and who should do so were already salient as France fought to consolidate power and establish legitimacy in the early, hungry years of its rule. Some colonial administrators believed the political benefits of Vietnamese antifamine measures would automatically redound to the French. During a dearth in Annam in 1889, one French official argued that "humanity supplements political interest for us to attempt even a partial remedy . . . at the least as an example of our active good will." His proposal to boost French humanitarian credentials was an irrigation scheme paid for and carried out by the imperial court.[20] The inverse of Vietnamese famine relief as a path to French legitimacy was anxiety about Vietnamese corruption that could "render the protectorate odious to the populations." The French feared that Vietnamese elites would take advantage of the cover of French rule, "which the people hold morally responsible," to engage in graft.[21] Relying on the Vietnamese state came with advantages as well as dangers.

It was often Vietnamese rather than French administrators who favored humanitarian considerations.[22] In 1890, the imperial commissioner (*kham sai*) of Tonkin, fearing that a series of bad harvests and floods would lead to famine, requested a ban on rice exports.[23] The French customs service opposed meddling with trade in the name of freedom of commerce.[24] A customs official laid out the conflict as he saw it: protectionism ran counter to the principles of political economy, but Annamites were "not ready for liberty of commerce, not even knowing its name." Vietnamese might blame famine on French improvidence, but it was antithetical to civilizational progress to assume the role of "paterfamilias of the Annamite people;" even the most primitive races, out of instinct if not reason, should be capable of avoiding starvation without coercion. Export bans were intended to preserve rice for local consumption, but farmers had no choice but to sell their crop for tax money.[25] Torn between market orthodoxy and fear of famine, the French administration continually imposed and withdrew market controls without choosing a definitive course of action. In this case, the French never resolved their competing interests in free trade, public relations, and humanitarian concern.

When French funds were committed for famine relief, it was usually under rigid conditions for repayment. During a shortage in Tonkin in 1896, the imperial viceroy (*kinh luoc*) asked the protectorate to intervene. The French approved loans of cash and rice imported from Cochinchina on condition of "strict supervision" and repayment within two years.[26] The administration's careful accounting was on display when exactly two years later, the resident-general of Tonkin complained that only 4,677.92 piastres of the 4,718.02 owed by one district had been collected. He demanded the balance immediately.[27]

French competition with the Vietnamese imperial state, belief in the free market and liberty of commerce, and charitable sentiment did not together form a consistent approach to famine. Rather, the weight of these various motivations shifted according to circumstance. In 1897 and 1898, several districts in Annam were hit successively by drought, locusts, and floods. In the environs of Hue, administrators encountered gaunt beggars barely covered with miserable rags, legs and feet swollen, sitting alongside the roads hoping for the pity of passersby. Every morning, several people were found dead in the streets of cold and hunger. Others fled to the mountains to pillage the granaries of ethnic minorities. A French functionary confirmed that rumors of "the darkest colors" had not been exaggerated: "The misery is extreme, one encounters at every step on the roads individuals who have nothing left but their breath, veritable skeletons covered in an envelope of skin!" There were so many dead that they were simply buried where they lay without any thought of proper ritual. Mortality was impossible to calculate, but according to one estimate over six thousand people died.[28]

The 1897 famine raised concerns about "political" consequences, a euphemism that usually referred to law, order, and the stability of French rule. The Annam countryside suffered from arson, pillage, and murder as starving men armed themselves with sticks and formed roving bands of thieves between ten and thirty strong. The population, some officials feared, had been pushed by hunger, taxes, and forced labor to the verge of a general revolt. The people lacked only a leader to organize them.[29] The French suspected this potential leader might well be the powerful court official Hoang Cao Khai, their "most mortal enemy." Administrators thought that Hoang Cao Khai and other mandarins, more interested in petty rivalries than in public well-being, saw famine as an opportunity for financial speculation and political advantage. Hoang Cao Khai was liable to start a rebellion simply to consolidate his personal power in Annam.[30] It was the French, though, who had elevated Hoang Cao Khai to the powerful role of imperial viceroy of Tonkin, as a reward for his support during the conquest of the 1880s. The fact that he was often praised as one of France's staunchest allies and reviled by many Vietnamese as a collaborator only highlights the protean character of Franco-Vietnamese relations.[31]

In response to the issues of security, legitimacy, and humanity raised by the 1897 famine, the Hue court reinforced military units, shipped rice, and issued an imperial edict appealing to rich people's spirit of solidarity. Hoang Cao Khai personally opened a charity drive. Nonetheless, the French did not trust the Vietnamese state to handle the famine. Proposals such as subsidies for officials charged with rice distribution, a pawning scheme that would allow the rich to amass valuables at low cost, and promotions for generous mandarins were seen, not unreasonably, as self-interested. The French accused mandarins of using their control of granaries to sell subsidized grain on their own behalf at a markup.[32] Much of the emergency rice was hoarded by officials or left to rot on roads and in junks, never arriving where it was needed. When the imperial granaries of Hue were opened, the spoiled rice within dated to the reign of the Minh Mang emperor fifty years earlier.[33] The French interpreted the Vietnamese court's response as unforgivably careless and even, in the case of mandarin corruption, criminal.

Upset by what they interpreted as the callousness of mandarins, the French pushed the imperial court to transport and distribute rice without regard to cost. Overriding Vietnamese ministers, French administrators arranged for reserve grain to be released for free rather than demanding money or labor from people enervated by hunger. They ordered that grain requisitions be sent directly to famine areas rather than to Hue, postponed labor conscription, and opened public works.[34] The administrators hoped these measures would earn the trust and recognition of the people, that "the sacrifices made will not have been useless."[35] The Annam famine of 1897 illustrates how the French simultaneously relied on and competed with the Vietnamese imperial state.

As France progressively secured power over the court and the population in the early twentieth century, relations with mandarins continued to affect famine relief. Vietnamese officials could be self-interested, but they could also serve as the conscience the French sometimes seemed to be lacking. In 1906, a low-level official named Doan Chien wrote a lengthy letter to his superior the French resident, head of the province of Ninh Binh in Tonkin. After successive typhoons and lost harvests, farmers in Doan Chien's district were trapped in a vicious cycle of debt. They had managed to survive for a time by borrowing, working for wages, and pawning ancestral heirlooms. But now the worst famine in memory was upon them. Even the well-off, having depleted their resources in the spirit of mutual aid, were now bereft. The poorest were eating wild plants and banana roots. The men Doan Chien tasked with distributing rice reported that nine out of ten of the destitute could be mistaken for skeletons. Some had gone a full week without food. Hundreds died. Charity and government advances had provided forty thousand piastres for relief, but Doan Chien estimated an additional one hundred thousand piastres were required. This was a substantial sum, but failing to make the request would be a neglect of duty and would shame him in front of his people.[36] His words moved the resident of Ninh Binh, who forwarded the request up the chain of command.[37]

In addition to motivating French action, Doan Chien and other mandarins provided French administrators with a degree of information often unavailable in other colonies. From the mandarins' reports, the French learned, in some cases, the exact number of people suffering from starvation in each village, the names of the women, children, and elderly at risk, the number of people who had left to seek work, and the amount of rice on offer from individual merchants.[38] The detailed data provided by mandarins allowed and pressured the French authority to "show the native population that it is not indifferent to its misfortune."[39]

As mandarins held them accountable, French administrators in turn pushed mandarins to fulfill their Confucian responsibilities. "From time immemorial," the French believed, emperors had urged mandarins to purchase promotion with charitable donations as a supplement to official grain distributions.[40] Continuity with such precolonial practices encouraged relief while easing moral and financial pressure on the French administration. During the Red River Delta famines of 1906 and 1916, Vietnamese officials could earn formal promotion through personal donations.[41] French decorations such as the Legion of Honor supplemented mandarin grades as incentives for charity.[42] Administrators seized on promotion and praise as cost-effective solutions, even as they worried that it risked cheapening both.[43]

Famine relief blurred the distinction between governance and philanthropy, fueling an economy of generosity, gratitude, and spectacle. Even in their official capacities, Vietnamese and French authorities often requested and granted aid using the language of charity and personal virtue. In 1906, a savvy mandarin in the Red River Delta province of Nam Dinh wrote flatteringly to his French supervisors. The inhabitants of his district, he claimed improbably, were all talking about how ably the French fed them. He had even posted his relief instructions on his office door as a public testament to French generosity.[44] True or not, the mandarin knew his French superiors would appreciate learning of their good reputation among the people. After flooding in Annam in 1910, the Council of Regents that ruled in the name of the child emperor Duy Tan profusely thanked the governor-general for his "generosity" in committing budget funds for aid, promising to make this act of "charity" known to the emperor and the population.[45] Likewise, the highest-ranking French official in Annam, the resident-superior, voiced extravagant gratitude on behalf of the Vietnamese government, the population, and himself.[46] Though budget funds were disbursed through official channels, they retained a flavor of Napoleon III's philanthropy for Algeria. State relief as an expression of personal character made it inconsistent, as some administrators proved more beneficent than others.

Vietnamese charity played a major role in famine relief through World War I. In the Red River Delta in 1916, a newspaper reported that death struck down Vietnamese civilians just as surely as it did French troops assaulting enemy trenches. "Hunger replaces 75 mm batteries and various illnesses represent machine guns."[47] The colonial administration again turned to the generosity of notables such as Trang Ngoc Quang of Nam Dinh, who conserved "the habit of doing good toward the poor" by distributing rice nine times a month. As many as five thousand people attended each distribution.[48] A mandarin in Ninh Binh province, Hoang Van Canh, convened a meeting of notables to organize charity. He used the example of the French resident-general of Tonkin to shame his countrymen into action. This Frenchman, Hoang Van Canh gushed, distributed aid with his own hand, unable to eat or sleep, sharing the hunger of the people, worrying day and night. How could compatriots of the Annamite race who honored the same ancestors "remain emotionless when we see our fellows dying of hunger next to us while we live in affluence?" The generous, according to Hoang Van Canh, would be recognized not only by Providence, but by the resident-general himself, who would inscribe their names on a list to be preserved in memory for long centuries.[49]

Cooperation and competition between French and Vietnamese officials could bolster relief or could just as easily give cover for state negligence and personal corruption. French complaints of mandarin graft were often instrumental, but rarely baseless. The famines of 1906 and 1916 saw numerous cases of Vietnamese using their positions to enrich themselves at the expense of the hungry. Some of this amounted to simple theft.[50] In Nam Dinh, the people of Van Bang village protested that emergency rice had been stolen by a local official.[51] But it was not necessary to break the law to profit from suffering. The wealthy were often motivated by cheap land prices offered by desperate smallholders more than by titles or honors, contributing to the inequality that increased vulnerability to future famines.[52] Villagers complained that merchants hoarded rice to sell at extravagant famine prices.[53] The synthetic Franco-Vietnamese responsibility for famine was fluid enough to fit a variety of needs, some honorable and some less so.

Water and Rice

In 1903, 1904, and especially 1905, violent typhoons flooded large areas of Tonkin and Annam. In June 1903, winds uprooted Hanoi's trees and tore the roofs off buildings. Pedestrians hacked their way through the debris with hatchets. Junks and sampans seeking to escape the storm near Nam Dinh were carried off and sank, killing two thousand people in less than an hour.[54] The same thing happened in 1904 when boats sheltering in Ha Long Bay were surprised by a typhoon.[55] In Hue, a French correspondent joined hundreds of Vietnamese taking refuge under a pagoda. After the roof blew away, they spent all night exposed to the elements, watching animal carcasses float by in the flooded streets. The wind leveled the city's Vietnamese neighborhood, which was more vulnerable than the European and Chinese quarters. The hospital collapsed on top of patients.[56] Newspapers reported as many as two thousand residents dead.[57] The next year, people needed boats to navigate the inundated countryside of Ninh Binh.[58] These repeated, relentless floods contributed to the serious famine of 1906.

The fact that flooding frequently triggered famines in Indochina accounted for some particularities of French thinking in the region. Floods could be controlled more easily than droughts. If famine resulted from backward races and hostile environments, the impact of the second of these factors could be softened through technical means. Following a long history of associating the spirit of the laws in the Orient with water management, French administrators saw hydraulic engineering as a key to state building in Asia. Constructing and maintaining the precolonial network of dikes that allowed cultivation and protected from floods was difficult. It necessitated a level of investment and surveillance that only a centralized state was capable of. Construction involved the work of elephants, in most cases too expensive to be privately owned. Once built, the system required constant repairs and an extensive bureaucracy to collect and archive information. Water levels needed to be continuously monitored and compared with historical records filed in Hue to ascertain the risk of disaster.[59] At the beginning of the nineteenth century, Gia Long united these functions under his department of dikes.

French administration had continuity not only with the abstract Confucian responsibility for famine, but also with precolonial physical infrastructure. Many observers admired the roughly 1,200-kilometer network of dikes in the Red River Delta, most of which predated the Nguyen dynasty. Even so, they acknowledged its shortcomings.[60] The dikes were periodically overwhelmed by the severe floods that, according to Vietnamese belief, struck roughly once a decade. As early as the 1890s, French engineers put forth comprehensive hydraulic programs to bring the network up to date.[61] These plans proved too expensive for the budget-conscious administration. Instead, it resorted to cheaper stop-gap measures such as renovating precolonial dikes and drainage canals that had fallen into disrepair.[62]

French fears were borne out when successive years of flooding triggered famines in the Red River Delta in 1906 and 1916. A Franco-Vietnamese commission that met twice after the 1906 famine urged against the "illusion" that palliative relief could make up for the inadequacy of the water regime.[63] When ten years later flooding again led to famine in the delta, a council of mandarins in Nam Dinh duly praised the achievements of precolonial engineers while pointing out persistent problems. It attributed the famine of 1916 to the inadequacy of drainage canals for evacuating floodwater from farmland. The council approved the renovation of a precolonial protective dike around the city of Nam Dinh, which the Tonkin protectorate had allowed to deteriorate. But like the commission of ten years earlier, the council, too, emphasized that a wholesale rethinking of the delta's infrastructure was in order.[64]

The now-retired high mandarin Hoang Cao Khai took the radical position that the entire system of dikes should be phased out. In a lengthy technical treatise responding to the floods of 1915, he situated his proposal within a long history of civil engineering that had begun with a dike built by the Ly dynasty (1009–1225 CE) to protect Hanoi. Efforts to build a comprehensive system to tame the length of the Red River, he believed, dated to the later Tran dynasty (1225–1400 CE). Dikes had broken throughout this history. But the previous hundred years, Hoang Cao Khai wrote, had seen a gradual rise of riverbeds increase the risk of ruptures. Flooding had intensified due to deforestation in China's Yunnan province, where the sources of the Red, Black, and Clear Rivers were located. As flooding grew more deadly, riverside populations built unofficial protective dikes, preventing drainage and exacerbating the rise of riverbeds. These uncoordinated local structures rendered the system incoherent. Floods during the reign of the Tu Duc emperor (r. 1847–1883) prompted a debate about whether the maintenance of the network was worth the enormous cost. The question remained unresolved when the French invaded and was now more urgent than ever.[65]

Hoang Cao Khai surmised that to protect against the worsening floods caused by rising riverbeds, dikes would need to be heightened and strengthened at huge expense. Higher dikes, in turn, would raise riverbeds by allowing sediment to accumulate, initiating a vicious circle. The whole system, Hoang Cao Khai suggested, should simply be dismantled. He conceded that eliminating the dikes would lead to temporary hardship for flooded populations. In the long term, though, sedimentation would slowly raise the level of riverside land, eventually allowing farmers to cultivate once more. The whole project would be overseen by an updated version of Gia Long's department of dikes.[66]

Hoang Cao Khai weighed in on a controversial question in Red River hydrology: that of the dike at Vinh Yen. This area functioned as a natural floodplain when the river overflowed its banks. The local administration often intentionally breached the dike to protect Hanoi downriver. This always destroyed crops and sometimes killed peasants who had not been forewarned, as in 1904 when an intentional rupture drowned at least four people.[67] The controversy continued beyond Hoang Cao Khai's contribution. In 1917, a French landowner reported that the administration forced people to cut the dike and flood their own fields and villages to divert floodwaters from Hanoi.[68] In 1926, the head of the public works service complained about the population's opposition to flooding Vinh Yen.[69] As late as 1945, the Viet Minh chastised the French for sacrificing Vietnamese to protect the European population of Hanoi, republishing a 1909 tract that explained, "When the waters rise excessively, and the dike protecting Hanoi threatens to break, the simple remedy consists of rupturing the dike above Hanoi and on the opposite bank, thus flooding the entire province of Vinh Yen, drowning livestock and, if needed, natives; in any case the harvest is destroyed." Once the threat to Hanoi dissipated, the ruined peasants were asked to rebuild the dike they had been compelled to demolish.[70] In his 1915 essay, Hoang Cao Khai observed that as the system stood, floodwaters had to drain at either Vinh Yen or Hanoi. The administration always chose to protect Hanoi by opening the dike at Vinh Yen, where "the population, receiving no prior warning, and thinking itself safe behind the dike that protects it, continues fieldwork." To avoid such "complications," it would be better, he thought, to dismantle the dike and create a permanent reservoir.[71]

A French engineer took issue with Hoang Cao Khai's assessment, offering an alternative history of Vietnamese water control. The system, the engineer wrote, originated in ancient times not with centralized construction but with local community dikes only later taken over by the state. Because each community was concerned with its own needs without a view of the big picture, the Red River system became tortuous and incoherent. This situation persisted into the present day. Furthermore, Annamite engineers had lacked the expertise to determine the dimensions needed to contain the most severe floods. His Excellency Hoang Cao Khai, like Vietnamese experts before him, paid more attention to appearances than to calculations. What he interpreted as stronger flooding due to deforestation and sedimentation was actually the consequence of stronger dikes built by the French without corresponding outlets. These dikes broke less often, making the riverbed appear higher. Vietnamese dikes, the engineer argued, had always been too low to contain the most serious floods. He condescendingly speculated that if Vietnamese engineers had been capable of correctly calculating the necessary dimensions, "It is probable that they would have been frightened and would perhaps not have undertaken the construction of dikes."[72]

Given the unfeasibility of building dikes capable of completely containing the Red River, the engineer argued for the creation of outlets to evacuate floodwater. He defended the repeated decision to break the dike at Vinh Yen, arguing that this saved not only Hanoi, but also thousands of hectares of rice paddies lower in the delta. The flooding also fertilized fields with deposits of alluvial sediment. The engineer believed that had the Vinh Yen dike been opened in 1915, deadly flooding would have been prevented. He did not mention the failure of this strategy in 1906. Along with improved drainage, it would be necessary to raise and reinforce the dikes, not to the impossible height of the strongest floods, but to practical and safe dimensions. As for the creation of a department of dikes, he agreed in principle, but the teams of dozens of trained hydraulic specialists that managed rivers in Europe were simply not available in Indochina. In short, the engineer summed up, Hoang Cao Khai's proposal to get rid of the dikes was preposterous.[73]

The administration never seriously considered dismantling the dikes, but the debate raised enduring questions of costs and benefits. In 1926, the Red River flood was measured at a record level of nearly twelve meters. Contradicting Hoang Cao Khai's hypothesis that flooding was getting more extreme, the public works service attributed the measurement to the strengthening of dikes earlier in the decade. Unlike precolonial dikes, the reinforced ones did not break. They were breached only when the water exceeded their height. This achievement contrasted with the "sad bitterness" of Tu Duc's failure to control floods of a mere nine meters in the 1870s. French success, however, made the system more rigid and potentially explosive. Expanding the riverbed to relieve pressure was one possible solution, but this would counter a thousand-year effort to contain the river as narrowly as possible to maximize paddy land in the crowded delta. On the other hand, increasing the capacity of the riverbed without widening its banks risked decreasing the frequency but strengthening the intensity of floods in the event of a breach.[74] These issues were not resolved. Projects to improve the system continued through the 1940s in a piecemeal way, but so did uncontrolled floods. Between technical challenges and budget constraints, the wholesale rationalization proposed by some engineers was never achieved under the French. Yet the very possibility of technical solutions made flooding, and thus famine prevention, a pervasive state concern.

Just as the French relied on and were constrained by Vietnamese river engineering, they had to contend with the legacy of Vietnamese granaries. In the nineteenth century, subsistence granaries were administered primarily at the village and provincial levels. In addition, the imperial court in Hue stocked granaries for the use of officials and soldiers, sometimes opening them to the public in emergencies. Information on granaries under the French is thin and contradictory. It appears that provincial state granaries were suppressed shortly after the conquest of Tonkin and Annam, leaving emergency grain storage to community initiative.[75] Subsequent debates about whether to reestablish official granaries pitted the modernizing colonial project against the necessity of leaning on precolonial ideologies and institutions. The recent memory of state granaries forced a discussion about relief during the famines of 1906 and 1916. Most officials concluded that granaries were inefficient, expensive, conducive to corruption, and anachronistic in a modern market economy.

During the 1906 Red River Delta famine, the absence of granaries loomed large as administrators sought to balance interests in relief, liberty of commerce, and, perhaps decisively, cost. Governor-General Paul Beau second-guessed his predecessors' suppression of precolonial granaries, wondering if responsible French leadership might have salvaged a conceptually sound system ruined by corrupt Annamite execution.[76] To resolve the question, European and Vietnamese functionaries were asked to compare the impact of the 1906 famine with a counterfactual scenario in which a granary system had been in effect.[77] Several respondents recommended the reinstitution of state granaries, usually at the village or district level rather than the provincial level as under the Nguyen.[78] However, most French and Vietnamese administrators thought looking to the past would interfere with modern progress. For reasons of efficacy and of optics, the administration concluded that "besides admitting it was a mistake to let [the granaries] disappear, there would today be no benefit to restoring them."[79] The French considered and rejected farming cooperatives and mutual aid societies as inappropriate to improvident and suspicious Annamites. Instead, the administration settled on emergency cash funds under French control.[80] Each province in Tonkin was ordered to stock capital so as "to no longer be at the mercy of natural phenomena or atmospheric accidents."[81] There is no evidence these orders were followed. In any event, the funds were not available during subsequent crises.[82]

The granary debate was rehashed in the following years as though it had never occurred. Whenever the issue arose, many functionaries, both French and Vietnamese, argued that precolonial granaries had been plagued by fraud, corruption, and deterioration of stocks. Even when granaries functioned properly, they had been designed for a premodern world that only utopians were nostalgic for. Though it was "very nice to remember the granaries of the old regime," they made sense only in a situation of economic protectionism and poor transportation. They were "a sign of infancy or weakness in a people."[83] Under the French, preventing famine was easy: simply allow markets to function freely, and fluke accidents like the 1906 famine would be avoided.[84]

Others were less sanguine about liberty of commerce as the definitive solution to famine. One mandarin felt that just as "bees know how to procure flowers in spring to feed themselves in winter," true compassion demanded foresight. He, too, looked to the precolonial period for inspiration, recalling that the imperial court had constituted an emergency cash fund as well as granaries. Though the money had been squandered by ignorant Annamites, such a fund could be restored under the competent supervision of the French, thereby avoiding the waste associated with granaries as well as the indifference of markets.[85] Just such funds were supposed to have been capitalized in 1907, but clearly did not exist when the mandarin wrote these words in 1910. This lack of follow-through was a hallmark of French rule. The same debates, influenced by the persistence of precolonial dikes and the memory of precolonial granaries, were repeated over and over. They led to few concrete results.

Missions and Newspapers

The Vietnamese imperial state and its legacy of dikes, granaries, and Confucian noblesse oblige drew the French colonial authority's attention to famine while relieving it of final responsibility. Missionaries and the French-language press added Christian and liberal traditions of care to the mix of pressures on the colonial state. At the time of the conquest, French missionaries under the auspices of the Paris Foreign Missions Society (Société des missions étrangères de Paris, MEP) had been operating in the region for two centuries. They ministered to a sizable but persecuted Vietnamese Christian community that numbered 270 thousand in Tonkin and Annam, and another 90 thousand in Cochinchina.[86] In contrast to Algeria, where evangelizing had little purchase and the Catholic Church served Europeans almost exclusively, communitarian Catholic care encompassed many Vietnamese. This was especially true in provinces such as Ninh Binh and Nam Dinh, which were both flood prone and home to many Christians. The French-language press based in large cities likewise bore witness to hunger and encouraged relief. These institutions brought nonadministrative European perspectives to bear on colonial famine. While attention need not logically entail sympathy or relief—in Algeria it did not—the specific confluence of interests and means in Indochina was somewhat more conducive to a caring disposition.

Not unlike conservative Confucians, Catholic missionaries subscribed to supernatural explanations of famine. Seeking natural causes and solutions in delta hydrology, they argued, ignored that famine was at root a punishment of Divine Providence.[87] One priest captured the providential understanding of famine when he preached, with possibly unintentional irony, "On earth as in heaven, one reaps what he sows."[88] The religious understanding of famine as a literal act of God limited care primarily to Christians. Vietnamese Catholics were a community apart. They were tolerated in the earlier years of the nineteenth century thanks to France's support of Nguyen dynasty founder Gia Long in his war for power. Gia Long's successor, Minh Mang, reversed his father's policy of tolerance in the 1830s, clearing the way for the murder of hundreds of thousands of Christians. The 1880s were a period of revived animosity against Catholics, who were commonly seen as collaborators with the French invaders. Developments such as the Save the King Movement, which called for the death of all Christians as well as the expulsion of the French, and the massacre of forty thousand Catholics in Annam in 1885, help explain the insular communitarianism on the part of missionaries.[89] Along a different axis, acrimony between anticlerical republicanism and the Catholic Church in France sometimes spilled into the colonies, further isolating missions.[90]

The French conquest of Tonkin and Annam in the 1880s contributed to widespread hunger. The MEP missionaries distilled what they saw into evocative images of desolation and suffering to extract pity and alms from French Catholics. Monseigneur Puginier, the head of the MEP mission in Hanoi, described a landscape of war, banditry, floods, and empty granaries. People caught up in the chaos subsisted on grass, roots, and other foods that "do not sustain the stomach."[91] Christians were especially vulnerable to violence.[92] By 1887, fifteen hundred of Puginier's flock had died of "physical or moral suffering."[93]

Moved by real but carefully curated scenes of anguish, the faithful in France donated for their coreligionists overseas.[94] Access to this funding source helped make missions a formidable regional force in Indochina. In 1887, the MEP contracted with a French merchant to import rice from Hong Kong, duty-free thanks to the Indochinese administration's cooperation. The missionaries helped Christians obtain cheap loans from the Bank of Indochina so they could purchase the grain.[95] Even with bank loans and French alms, the MEP's resources fell far short of what was needed for the 180 thousand Christians thought to be in need. But it was enough to make "pagans," according to one missionary, note the care of the ministers of the Lord with admiration and jealousy.[96]

When famine hit again in 1906 and again in 1916, missionaries spoke of an abject misery that was unimaginable without witnessing it firsthand.[97] In the delta province of Ninh Binh, where in 1907 missionaries estimated a mortality of at least three thousand, "one saw on the roads only beggars of cadaverous pallor, all appearing more dead than alive."[98] People tried to survive on rice bran and banana roots. Those who left looking for work found illness instead, returning home only to die. Many took to banditry as an alternative to "wast[ing] away in the tortures of hunger."[99] The starving wandered randomly in search of food, an "appalling army of misery, sowing the way with its dead."[100] Ten years later, this army marched once more, its soldiers cheating hunger with "unnamable scraps" until they expired on the sides of the roads.[101]

The MEP reports were intended not merely to bear witness but to raise money. To this end, stories and storytelling styles were chosen to grab readers' attention with thrilling exoticism, instill pity for suffering Christians, and arouse religious fervor. The practice of parents selling children they could not feed was useful in this regard. It was shocking, provoked sympathy for the children, and demanded heroic intervention. According to the MEP, one hundred Christian children were sold during the 1906 famine by parents trying to save their lives.[102] The numbers were endowed with emotional power through vivid stories. A missionary related how a "pagan" family, believing their newborn to be possessed by a devil, abandoned her under a bush. She was rescued by a Christian orphanage. Another couple sold their children, bought an extravagant meal, and drowned themselves in a river.[103] Helping the missions repurchase and care for such children was a cause worthy of a generous donation.

As a rule, missionaries prioritized the care of Christians.[104] Even with recourse to French alms, there was hardly enough money to feed the faithful. Some were driven by hunger, "poor counselor," to abandon the Church and try their luck with Buddhist relations. A little rice and some clothes usually returned them to the fold, for "such is the power of alms-giving."[105] Only once Christians were provided for did the MEP expand its charity to others, as when in a packed Nam Dinh churchyard in 1905 it served rice to seven thousand people with no regard to confession.[106] If some Vietnamese stubbornly resisted mission aid despite their desperation, others experienced hunger as revelation. As in the time of Jesus, the poor gravitated toward Christian charity. Limited supplies forced the MEP to reject converts and turn people away from its hospitals. Priests worried that conversions under famine conditions were less than sincere, motivated by material rather than spiritual needs. They fined apostates three centimes for each day they had been Catholic.[107] In the years following famines, though, missionaries complained that "this means of calling souls to us no longer exists" as people reverted to sensuality without a thought for the hereafter.[108]

Even in famine, church and state found it difficult to find common cause. Missionaries sometimes cooperated with the protectorates, but they were often stinging in their criticism of official policy. They accused administrators of actively perpetuating famine through violence, taxes, food exports, and forced labor.[109] The press, many Catholics thought, embodied the virtues of French civilization more fully than the administration did.[110] In reports of people scouring forests for edible roots or throwing themselves on rotting, weevil-infested grain, journalists were unafraid of calling out the administration's "inertia." Contrasting feeble French relief with the famine codes in British India, reporters condemned "ridiculous" rescue efforts that amounted to a mere "mouthful," a "drop in the ocean."[111] They accused the administration of failing to protect subjects from unscrupulous merchants who profited from famine, "first taking everything, and then taking what is left."[112] The MEP-owned newspaper *L'Avenir du Tonkin* scorned administrators as "improvident" and mocked the dearth of useful ideas to "hatch from their administrative brain."[113] Editor Henri Laumonier, incredulous that families continued to perish of hunger in the age of steam and electricity, was reminded of the great French famines of the Middle Ages. Administrators piled humiliation on top of sorrow, crowding naked men and women together indiscriminately in hospitals. Pointing out that taxes could not be collected from corpses, Laumonier wrote that such negligence made as little sense from an economic standpoint as from a humanitarian one.[114] While the press criticized government policy, it praised private charity from wealthy Asians and the Catholic Church.[115] Inverting the usual hierarchy of civilizations, Annamite philanthropy served as an example for the French.[116]

Journalists, like mandarins, made it harder for French administrators to plead ignorance. Functionaries sometimes learned of famine from the press rather than through official channels. For instance, in early 1906, the resident-superior of Tonkin read reports of starvation in L'Avenir du Tonkin and asked subordinates to investigate.[117] The resident of Ha Nam, despite his suspicion of the motives of Catholic journalists, confirmed the presence of extreme misery.[118] Likewise, the resident of Nam Dinh warned against giving too much credence to a hostile press, but, admitting that people were dying, he authorized rice distributions and emergency public works.[119] These officials either did not know or did not care about famine until they read about it in newspapers.

The press, like the missions, raised funds for famine victims. In 1906, Le Courrier d'Haiphong, which was owned by Auguste Raphaël Fontaine, a businessman who had made a fortune by securing the official Indochinese alcohol monopoly, opened a charity drive.[120] His newspaper listed the names of donors and published letters of thanks from the administration. Governor-General Paul Beau donated one hundred piastres. In total, around two thousand piastres were collected.[121] L'Avenir du Tonkin raised a similar amount.[122] Journalists admitted that these small sums were merely symbolic. They functioned as a public demonstration of care.

Newspapers were outlets for those who despised the starving as well as for the compassionate. Some writers argued that far from being negligent, the administration was overly generous to lazy Annamites taking advantage of public feeling.[123] For others, pity was tempered by disdain and disgust. An article in Le Courrier d'Haiphong read, "Without mentioning the strong odors released by the flea-ridden and ill, of sticky but necessary closeness, of the ardor of the sun which seems to ferment all these rags and bad smells," it was not easy to remain in control of one's faculties to distinguish the deserving poor from the frauds. Torn between sympathy and anger for unruly crowds, the author pitied the functionaries who undertook the distasteful task of dealing with the stink of the starving.[124]

Civil society organizations joined the press in pressuring the government. The members of the Haiphong chapter of the Human Rights League, a left-leaning French organization with origins in the Dreyfus affair, were unanimously moved by the plight of the hungry.[125] Following the principle that "the right to life is a primordial right of Humanity," the league asked Governor-General Beau to consider the reestablishment of precolonial granaries and the regulation of rice exports.[126] The governor-general took the request seriously, forwarding the league's suggestions to his subordinates.[127]

The presence or absence of French civil institutions, both religious and laic, was a key variable in how much attention colonial administrations devoted to famine. The mere existence of attention, however, did not by itself ensure better outcomes. In Algeria in 1867, high public awareness of famine was not accompanied by concern for its victims. In Indochina, European attention interacted with Vietnamese imperial bureaucracy and infrastructure in a way that encouraged administrative intervention. But though the French were more concerned about famine victims in Indochina than they had been in Algeria, the incapacity of the colonial state to fund and sustain antifamine policies meant this concern did not necessarily improve the lives of Vietnamese people.

Responsibility and Neglect

As the French authority in Tonkin and Annam matured from a fighting force in the 1880s to discreet manager of the Vietnamese state before the First World War to "rational" modern administration afterward, the burden of care for the hungry shifted in the direction of France. The 1919 suppression of the Confucian examination system that provided the Vietnamese state with classically trained functionaries exemplified the adjustment away from traditional rule.[128] At the same time, the "total war" effort in Europe expanded expectations of what an interventionist state could achieve in the management of societies, broadening administrative imaginations. As French administrators and Vietnamese reformers embraced the promises of modernization, the traditionalist court's usefulness as a source of authority and a ready scapegoat was eroded.

Before World War I, debate about famine was dominated by the themes of dikes, granaries, charity, and liberty of commerce. After the war, there was a marked change in tone as administrators embraced, at least rhetorically, a technocratic, interventionist management style. As the effects of famine lingered in 1917, the governor-general of Indochina, Albert Sarraut, convened a "commission to study the measures to increase the nutritive value of the in-dochinese diet." The group was composed of prominent French businessmen and agriculturalists as well as physicians and biologists from Hanoi's Pasteur Institute and the University of Toulouse's medical faculty.[129] The experts con-cluded that the development of the "Annamite race" required a "normal" diet including the proper amounts of fats, minerals, and "nitrogenous" foods (foods high in protein). Their linking of acute famine to "living conditions" and the quality as well as the quantity of food was an early formulation of an approach Sarraut would champion for the entire French Empire over the next two decades.

Governor-General Sarraut was not alone in favoring long-term develop-ment over emergency response. In 1921, the resident-superior of Annam, Pierre Pasquier, decided to eliminate famine in his protectorate. This goal stemmed from twin convictions that protection from famine was a universal raison d'être of all human societies and that Annamites were incapable of the task. Following the standard French liberal narrative, Pasquier identified three principal reasons for the "quasi-disappearance" of dearth in the civilized west: liberty of commerce, improved transportation, and industrialization. He saw no reason why Annam could not follow this template to prosperity. In a circu-lar as notable for its focus on sustained execution as for its unusual detail, he sketched the outlines of a system meant to ensure subsistence for all.[130] It was the most exhaustive famine plan devised in Indochina, and probably the em-pire, to date.

The standard story of France's defeat of famine in the eighteenth century furnished Pasquier with a model, but it had to be adapted to Annamite cir-cumstances. In medieval Europe and contemporary India, Pasquier observed, the problem of famine presented as periodic cataclysm. In contrast, famine in Annam was endemic. Chronic hunger did not strike the imagination like full-blown famine did, but it was more harmful in its physical and intellectual stunt-ing of the Annamite race. From this angle, the problem of famine was bound up with the problem of pauperism. The Annamite poor were not, Pasquier cautioned, like the European poor, individuals unfortunate in birth, ability, or circumstance. Annamite poverty was a collective problem, the lot of entire communities or regions rather than of isolated individuals or a single social class. An antifamine program was thus necessarily an antipoverty program.

Pasquier dismissed the prevailing expediency of emergency loans as overly reliant on the fallible discretion of administrators. Furthermore, the money for such loans simply did not exist. Instead, he envisioned a rational system that once instituted would function "automatically." This social machinery would be built methodically from the ground up by mapping "famine areas," using poverty as a proxy for vulnerability to starvation.[131] The map would be complemented by a detailed history of famines over the previous two decades, indicating whether their causes were "natural," including poor soil, droughts, floods, and epidemics; "exceptional," including typhoons, tidal waves, crop failures, and market failures; or "social," including landlessness, labor shortages, speculation, and lack of credit. The famine areas accounted for variations in ecology and society better than administrative divisions did, allowing for customized diagnoses and solutions. The coastal farmers and fishermen of Tuy Phuoc were vulnerable to floods, while Phan Rang suffered primarily from droughts. In Quang Nam, food shortages were usually due to fluctuations in the cinnamon market, while among the Moi—a Vietnamese term for ethnic minorities meaning "savage" or "barbarian"—they were a seasonal occurrence resulting from the laziness of these "semicivilized" people. A uniform policy was inappropriate for these different microcontexts.[132]

Identifying famine areas would lay the groundwork for a comprehensive antifamine system mobilizing public budgets and mutual aid societies, French and indigenous functionaries, settlers and missionaries, active and retired mandarins, teachers, and notables of all kinds, harmoniously coordinated by Annam's administration. By dividing Annam into sectors corresponding to the famine areas, engineers could tailor hydraulic systems to local needs. This involved restoring precolonial Vietnamese and Cham (an ethnic group from central and southern Indochina) infrastructure that had been left to deteriorate. Other teams of experts would rationalize food distribution by constructing roads and railways. To address economic as well as natural causes, the administration would enlist experts in agronomy and commerce. In fact, every public service would be mobilized in this "crusade against hunger," not only across domains of knowledge but also over time to "definitively engage the future." In other words, it would take a sustained effort of the kind that French colonial administrations were particularly bad at.[133]

As a palliative until Annam was freed from famine, administrators, with the map in front of them, would devise bespoke rescue plans for each famine area, thereby averting starvation before it took hold. Pasquier was not a proponent of emergency work camps. He cited "hecatombs" in Indian famine camps and typhus epidemics in Algerian ones as examples not to imitate. Preferring prevention to alleviation, he advocated public works before famine took hold instead of at its apex. To provide a model, Pasquier came up with a hypothetical rescue plan for an imaginary famine area comprising one entire district (*huyen*) plus two cantons of a neighboring district, favoring social and ecological coherence over administrative demarcations. There would be a supply center in the largest town, as well as two secondary supply centers in logistically appropriate villages. The plan included a timeline specifying when in the agricultural cycle administrators should determine if a food shortage was likely, when to request emergency rice, and when to begin distributions.[134] Through economic development and rationalized emergency protocols, famine prevention would no longer depend on fallible human judgment and fickle generosity; it would be entrusted to a machine-like automatic system.

In the following decades, French thinkers would question the conception of famine as something that happened to places rather than to people. In reality, Annam was not conveniently composed of discrete famine areas inhabited by undifferentiated masses uniformly prone to starvation. Yet, without the sociological or biochemical knowledge of later reformers, Pasquier was among the first administrators to insist on comprehensive development attuned to local needs rather than reactive improvisation. His emphasis on continuity and follow-through proved prescient. The plan was never implemented. The map of poverty and famine in Annam attests to its unfulfilled ambition (figures 2–5).

As the resident-general of Annam, Pierre Pasquier modeled creative, if flawed, thinking about famine. As governor-general of Indochina from 1928 to 1934, he succumbed to the inertia that wed the administration to staid practices. By this time, the mandarinate had been largely discredited in the eyes of many Vietnamese. The year 1925 was a symbolically salient one. The death of reformer Phan Chu Trinh and the house arrest of the more aggressively anticolonial Phan Boi Chau, two towering Vietnamese leaders, ushered in a period of heightened antagonism toward both French and traditional authority. It was also the year that Nguyen Ai Quoc, the future Ho Chi Minh, formed the Revolutionary Youth League in China, a precursor to the Indochinese Communist Party. After the mid-1920s, anti-French feeling increasingly went hand in hand with disdain for traditional Vietnamese leaders and values.[135] Still, France continued to rely on a traditional authority that had been deteriorating for some time. New fault lines solidified as the French propped up the power of mandarins against modernizing and sometimes anticolonial reformers.

In 1929, typhoons and floods led to widespread dearth. Governor-General Pasquier responded with an antifamine proposal that looked quite different from the one he crafted for Annam earlier in the decade. This was not because he was ignorant of alternatives, but because he was constrained by the exigencies of his new position. He framed the new project not as modernization but as an extension of timeless Annamite "foresight and charitable aid."[136] His aim was no longer to eradicate famine through rational management but to fill the gaps in traditional Vietnamese social assistance.[137] Tellingly, Pasquier first sought to determine who was already cared for, "in right and in fact," by Vietnamese social arrangements and could therefore be left out of his administration's

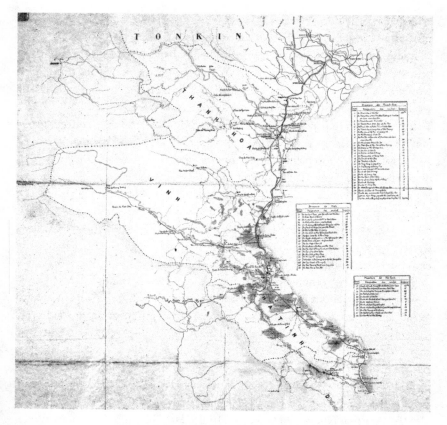

FIGURE 2.   Map of poverty and famine in Annam, 1921. ANOM, GGI 46395.

field of action. Whenever possible, the French preferred to "remind" the Vietnamese of their ancestral duties toward the marginalized.[138]

To determine just what these ancestral duties were, Pasquier canvassed mandarins. Most, perhaps sensitive about their fading authority, favored a policy based on precolonial Nguyen laws and promotions in exchange for charity. Article 85 of the Gia Long code provided for the care of disaster victims, including the requirement that villages pay for the repatriation of residents. An edict from the eighth year of Minh Mang's reign (1828) required each province to fund a refuge for widows and widowers, orphans, the infirm, and others with no means of support. Each was to receive a small stipend and a half bowl of rice daily. An ordinance from the eighteenth year of Tu Duc's reign (1865) specified who was eligible for grain distributions. Victims of fire, for example, were not.[139] The French looked to community custom as well as

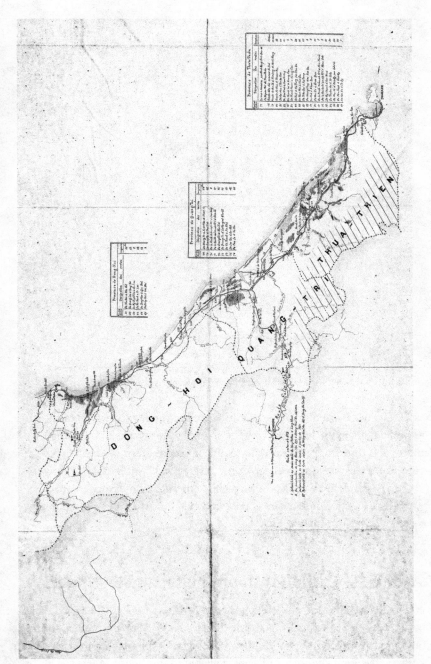

FIGURE 3. Map of poverty and famine in Annam, 1921. ANOM, GGI 46395.

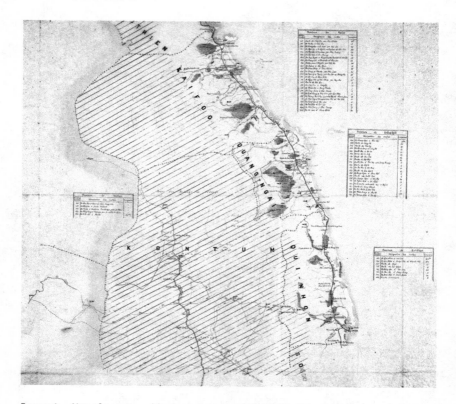

FIGURE 4.   Map of poverty and famine in Annam, 1921. ANOM, GGI 46395.

to codified law to disentangle which duties fell to the family, which to the village, and which, in the last resort, to the state.[140] After weeks of debating Vietnamese and French proposals, Pasquier ignored them and ordered the creation of a cash fund to be used at the discretion of individual administrators.[141] In the end, he resorted to the ad hoc emergency measures he had previously dismissed as ineffective. There is no evidence the fund existed during the shortages of the 1930s.

Confucians, Catholics, Journalists, and Engineers

In Indochina as in Africa, the French saw colonial famines as the unavoidable consequences of improvident races and difficult natural environments. Administrators intervened only with the utmost reluctance, in a reactive rather than systematic fashion. The forms of care available to fill the space left vacant by the French varied by colony. In Tonkin and Annam, the maintenance of the

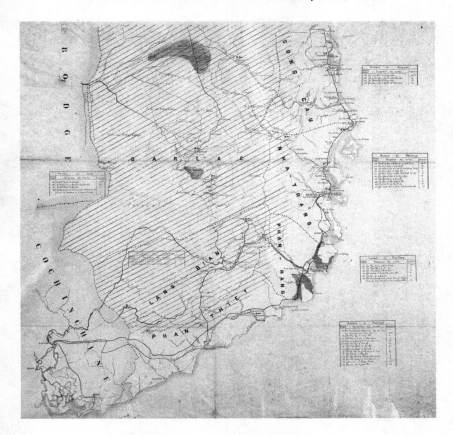

FIGURE 5.   Map of poverty and famine in Annam, 1921. ANOM, GGI 46395.

centralized Vietnamese state with its Confucian responsibility for social provision meant that the French had to deal with a preexisting expectation of government involvement. The fact that flooding was a major natural trigger of famines in the lowlands of Tonkin and Annam, as opposed to drought and vermin in Africa, gave French and Vietnamese civil engineers an obvious technical means to combat hunger. Finally, a strong Vietnamese Catholic community meant that Christian care encompassed many Vietnamese within its circle of concern. These specificities of the Indochinese colonial situation conditioned the standard debates about individual foresight, free markets, liberal charity, and republican responsibility that were present wherever the French went.

French and Vietnamese administrators in Indochina paid attention to famine in a more sympathetic way than in other parts of the empire. Yet they still failed to prevent tens of thousands of starvation deaths. Commissions were formed and solutions debated, but they were soon forgotten as the starving faded from sight. Comprehensive social and infrastructural reform was repeatedly called for but not undertaken. Plans for rescue protocols, granaries, and cash funds were repeatedly proposed, but they were never available when the next disaster struck. Each time a famine occurred, the same debates were reprised as though for the first time. The French tendency to withdraw from responsibility was not unique to Southeast Asia; it was an ideological and structural feature of colonial rule. Even as Confucians, Catholics, journalists, and engineers debated and competed over hunger in Indochina, underprepared and overwhelmed administrators in the African Sahel were stupefied by a catastrophic famine in 1913.

Chapter 3

The Nature of Famine in the Sahel, 1913

The crisis that killed between a quarter million and a million people in the Sahel in 1913 and 1914 is commemorated in the Songhai languages as "great famine."[1] In French colonial sources, it barely registers. Administrators in West and Central Africa echoed the attitude adopted in Algeria and Indochina that famine was natural where uncivilized races faced environmental challenges.[2] But the Sahelian colonies had few settlers, journalists, or missionaries to bear witness and communicate information as they had in Algeria. Unlike Indochina, the Sahel lacked functioning indigenous states or officially sanctioned technical means to check the causes of famine. Numerically slight and socially superficial French administrations were better suited to military operations than the routine management of people and environments.[3] Vast distances connected by lines of communication as thin and delicate as telegraph cables allowed and obligated isolated administrators to act autonomously.[4] In the presence of starvation and the absence of instructions, oversight, or public pressure, French reactions to famine were improvised. Subjects were linked to administrators not by politics or law, but by a set of relationships ranging from a bureaucratic formalism conveying the illusion of control to an interpersonal humanitarianism rooted in sentimental pity. The first insisted that all was well when it was not; the second recognized suffering but could do little to help.

The famine of 1913 was unusually extensive. It was experienced across the Sahel, the semiarid transcontinental transition zone between the Sahara and the savanna. This huge swathe included parts of the contiguous French colonies of Upper Senegal and Niger (split into Upper Volta and Soudan in 1919, contemporary Burkina Faso and Mali), the Military Territory of Niger, and Chad. United by climate and crisis but separated by distance, administrative jurisdictions, and myriad languages and cultures, these territories were at different stages in the French Empire's state-building project. What became the colony of Upper Senegal and Niger in 1904 was conquered in the 1880s and 1890s, capped by the taking of Timbuktu in 1894.[5] In 1913, the colony had been under civilian administration for a little over a decade. The southwestern corner of the huge Military Territory of Niger was brought under French administration around the turn of the century. Most of the territory was under nominal but tenuous French control by 1908. It was administered by the army until 1922, when it became the civilian Colony of Niger. Both Upper Senegal and Niger and the Military Territory of Niger were part of French West Africa (Afrique Occidentale Française, AOF), an administrative grouping governed from Dakar, Senegal.

In Chad, the famine struck at a time of ongoing war. For much of the nineteenth century, the region was in turmoil due to fighting and slave raiding between the Islamic sultanates of Wadai, Baguirmi, and Bornu. French explorers and soldiers arrived at the end of the nineteenth century during a period of intense violence. The powerful warlord Rabih Fadlallah, a slave from Khartoum who became a slave trader, had moved his army into the territory of the three sultanates. The French killed him in 1900, discarded his body in the Chari River, and displayed his head as a warning to his followers.[6] Wadai remained standing as the most powerful state in the central Sahel. The French defeated Wadai's Sultan Dudmurrah in 1909, installed his more pliant cousin as puppet ruler, and then abolished the sultanate in 1912.[7] When famine hit the following year, this fragile French foothold was being used as a base to conquer the desert regions of Borkou and Ennedi to the north.[8] In 1920, Chad was integrated into French Equatorial Africa (Afrique Équatoriale Française, AEF), administered from Brazzaville in the French Congo.

The inhabitants of the Sahel were far from uniform in culture and language, but all developed strategies for life at the desert's edge. Social arrangements were calibrated to deal with geographically variable rainfall and recurrent drought. These were often based in various forms of patronage and dependence including slavery, a term that encompassed a range of experiences unified by the characteristics of being property and kinless.[9] The practice of selling dependents or oneself into slavery during dearths was common enough that in some places "slaves of hunger" was an established category.[10] Those at the bottom of the social hierarchy were subservient, but they had some measure of protection against starvation. Additionally, Sahelians hedged against the risk of localized drought through geographically extensive economic arrangements such as seasonal migration of people and animals, exchange between pastoralists and farmers, and crop fields spread across large areas. For example, militarily dominant Tuaregs diversified their pastoralist economy by imposing tributary relationships on sedentary farmers and by establishing farming villages comprised of slaves whose bodies and produce they owned. During periods of stress, people could trade status for survival. In 1913, starving low-caste Tuaregs gave up their nomadic lifestyle and its associated prestige to assimilate into sedentary farming communities.[11] Other people sold themselves into slavery.

In 1903, the French prohibited courts from recognizing the legal status of slavery, denying enslavers the backing of the colonial state in controlling their property. This was followed by a 1905 decree prohibiting new enslavement. Along with the French administration's preoccupation with settling mobile populations, these legal changes complicated, though did not eliminate, traditional survival strategies. Difficult periods such as the 1913 famine saw substantial rises in pawning, an arrangement in which heads of households offered a dependent, usually a girl, as collateral for a loan. The pawn's body and labor were attached to the creditor until the loan was repaid. Unlike the enslaved, pawns kept their name, remained part of their lineage, and could not be sold. While slavery was not legally recognized and pawning occupied a gray area, French administrators were unwilling and unable to stop the practices. Some even conceded that these customs saved people who might otherwise die. Nineteenth- and twentieth-century antislavery activists, the archbishop of Algiers Charles Lavigerie foremost among them, protested France's toleration of unfree labor in Africa and Indochina. French administrations countered activist meddling by invoking respect for indigenous culture.[12]

The French in the Sahel rarely considered how social and economic changes brought about by colonialism increased vulnerability to starvation. In addition to the straightforward privations of wars of conquest, colonial taxation disrupted regional economies. Sahelian farmers did not practice subsistence in a narrow sense but planted with the expectation of having surpluses that could be stored against periodic droughts and poor harvests. Reserves could be consumed or sold as needed. French taxation unbalanced this decision-making calculus. To pay their taxes, farmers were forced to boost grain sales, shift production to export crops, and undertake labor migration. These changes made the agrarian economies of the Sahel less resilient against periodic droughts like that of 1913.

The disruption of economic patterns increased the exposure of farmers to volatile markets. One French answer to heightened market risk was to collectivize it through institutions called native provident societies (sociétés indigènes de prévoyance, SIPs). As their name implies, SIPs were supposed to practice, and to inculcate in natives, the paradigmatic liberal value of foresight. They could serve a variety of functions: storing and distributing seed, offering cash loans, lending equipment, purchasing and collectively marketing crops, managing granaries, and sometimes distributing food. The French introduced SIPs to Algeria and Indochina in the nineteenth century, then to West Africa in 1907. However, until the 1930s they were more or less limited to the peanut exporting regions of Senegal. This area, which had been subject to French administration for several decades, appears to have been less affected by the 1913 famine than regions further east. But even where they were established, the operation of SIPs was irregular. They were supposed to be the first line of defense against harvest shortfalls, but their role in 1913 was negligible.[13]

In much of the Sahel, the 1913 famine unfolded in something of an institutional vacuum. The precolonial order had been or was being violently suppressed while French power was not yet entrenched. Compared to Algeria and Indochina, there were relatively few administrators, missionaries, or journalists. In the military territories of Niger and Chad, there were almost no Europeans who were not affiliated with the army. The small number of French people over huge areas of land led to a dearth of knowledge and capacity. This was exacerbated at the beginning of the Great War by the siphoning of French soldiers and functionaries to fight in the trenches of Europe. Even when they were inclined to help, administrators had little power to do so.

Anemic administration and weak civil society oversight made official French documentation of the famine sparse and unreliable. Few non-administrative sources exist to provide an alternative point of view. For these reasons, the sources from the period do not allow for a reconstruction of what happened with any degree of confidence. Instead, this chapter relies heavily on close readings of official reports and unofficial memoirs to examine administrators' stance toward colonized subjects, asking if and how the French felt responsible for relieving starvation. It also examines how administrative practices of recording, reporting, and communicating affected famine relief.

French responses to famine depended on the extent to which suffering made demands on the witness as a rational administrator or as a sentimental human being; whether it triggered bureaucratic procedure or interpersonal pity. Some administrators, especially senior ones, tended to emphasize normality, efficiency, and control. Others, especially soldiers in newly conquered areas whose professional responsibility was primarily fighting, centered chaos and personal experience. Civilian administrators were supposed to prioritize rational governance, but like military officers, they ruled by decree and were often equally quick to resort to force.[14] In practice, administrators tended to blend the formal bureaucratic and unmediated interpersonal ways of relating to colonized people. All officials, civilian or military, saw their role in the famine as reactive, mitigating its effects to whatever extent was possible or convenient.

If routine reports are to be believed, the French had complete control over the famine. Food shortages were limited to small areas. Administrators easily reacted in time to provision the starving. These depictions of calm orderliness and efficiency stand in stark contrast to scattered sources that stressed helplessness in the face of breakdown. This difference in how the famine was preserved in the archives likely has more to do with ways of seeing and reporting than with any vast difference in the efficacy of relief. Rationality in style did not necessarily imply rationality in substance, just as candid descriptions of suffering did not necessarily imply care. Missing from both kinds of reports are the documents that do material work—the statistics, instructions, and financial instruments that move food from one place to another.

The famine of 1913 unfolded with little commentary from French people but took on greater significance in retrospect. In the changed imperial and international context of the 1930s, France was at pains to show that its colonialism had always had the well-being of subjects at heart. In response to German and Italian propaganda accusing the French of having allowed hundreds of thousands of people to die—propaganda that was surely correct—French officials of the 1930s countered with their own narratives of care that would have made little sense to the administrators present in 1913. Two decades after the fact, the memory of the famine was adapted to the political needs of the particular moment. The story of the 1913 famine cannot be separated from the story of how it was recorded and remembered.

The Role of Reports

The year 1913, one report read, "will remain in the memory of the natives."[15] The same could not be said for French colonial bureaucrats. Until the publication of memoirs in the 1930s, the only information about the famine to reach Europe, other than through word of mouth, was contained in periodic official reports. The reports sent to Paris tell a simple story of natural disaster and relief, communicated in dry, dull, at times self-congratulatory prose. Drought in the Sahel had caused poor harvests in parts of Senegal, Mauritania, and Upper

Senegal and Niger. Food shortages were especially severe in Timbuktu and environs. Motivated by an "urgent duty" owed in exchange for obedience and taxes, French administrators came to the rescue.[16]

The French, according to the routine reports, took a number of steps to stabilize prices in the volatile food market. Administrators in Timbuktu first noticed a rise in the price of millet in July of 1913.[17] They immediately granted tax relief and distributed, they claimed, five hundred tons of millet and three hundred tons of rice, an amount so large relative to other French reports it cannot be taken at face value. On top of the distributions, the administration invited private merchants to bring food supplies to the famine areas. The flood of grain onto markets quickly brought prices under control.[18] To provide their families with the means of subsistence, African men traveled south to public relief works and remitted wages to "those whose sex or age retained them in their home regions."[19] The June 1914 rains brought with them a flourishing of wild vegetation that provided yet another food source.[20] The crisis was declared over by the end of 1914. Good harvests let people "peacefully enjoy in their homes a material satisfaction of which they had long been deprived." The recovery was so complete that African donations for French victims of the Great War—probably not, in fact, voluntary—surpassed sixty thousand francs by the end of the year.[21]

Administrators in Upper Senegal and Niger were confident that as transportation improved, the economy grew, and export supplanted subsistence agriculture, famines would exercise "only a very minor secondary influence on the life of the country."[22] More immediately, compulsory reserve granaries, administrative supervision of farming, and a tax on food exports would protect against the vagaries of climate.[23] The French were convinced that "the colony . . . imposed on itself great sacrifices to confront the disaster and succeeded in large measure to check its effects."[24] Having been dealt with, famine gave way to the forcible recruitment of African soldiers for the European war—and the rebellions it provoked—as the focus of administrative attention.[25] Unlike famine, recruitment was seen as a potential threat to French authority.

As this sanguine account suggests, administrative reporting was concerned less with capturing reality than with constructing it. The bureaucratic formalism of official communication rendered the messiness of real conditions as simple, stable, unproblematic, and under control. Routine periodic reports were instruments to convey specific types of information in a succinct, easily digestible, almost ritualized manner. They were written by specialists of the various administrative services and focused on one category of administration, such as the "political," "economic," "agricultural," or "medical."[26] These categories encouraged the communication of certain types of information while

filtering out other types. Specialized reports were then summarized and compiled into general reports (*rapports d'ensemble*) according to standardized tem-
plates. They were meant to be digests of what happened in a colony in a given
period of time.[27] The famine entered these reports insofar as it affected topics
of interest including commerce, agriculture, taxes, or security. The reports
compiled during the famine often concluded that the situation was "entirely
satisfactory" or "excellent" because according to criteria such as import and
export figures or tax receipts, it was.

Such texts had as much to do with representation as with the practical work
of administration. In France, they were published as booklets and distributed
to politicians and other people who had an interest in the colonies. For this
reason, administrators were instructed to focus on "economic" issues that allowed readers to follow the "evolution" of the empire while sparing them the
tedium of routine governance. Authors were asked to write in an impersonal
style and include only news deemed appropriate for public consumption,
keeping the reports as brief as possible to maximize readability and mini-
mize printing costs.[28]

News of famine was not meant to be shared with the public. French readers
interested in the African colonies would have had little hint that tens of thousands of people were dying. When the famine did make it into official paperwork, the information was filtered and molded by the conventions regulating
its production. A *rapport d'ensemble* for the Military Territory of Niger from
1914, its author unnamed to augment the impression of impersonal objectivity,
was one of the few to acknowledge famine. It began by noting subjects' excellent "state of mind." This appears incongruous, but it made sense from the
perspective of the privileged criterion of security; it meant famine had not provoked rebellion. Tax receipts had increased, meeting only mild resistance. Confrontation between pastoral nomads over reduced pasturage did not threaten
general stability. People even contributed to a charity drive for French war victims. "Misery" was noted, but it was tangential to economics and security.[29]

Reports like this one referenced famine obliquely, to the extent that it affected other things. A section on "population" estimated that Niger had lost
eighty thousand people due to mortality and migration. A section on international commerce recorded increased food imports and a precipitous drop in
exports. The "justice" section conveyed that there had been a slight increase
in crimes because "hunger, poor advisor, had pushed unfortunates to more
theft and pillage than usual." In the report's conclusion, the author was freed
from bureaucratic categories and could consider the famine more directly. Natives, "improvident by their nature," had grown complacent under French
rule. They had forgotten the frequent famines of the precolonial period and

neglected to stock grain, leaving them defenseless against drought and jeopardizing their very existence. Having thus devoted more attention to famine than many of his colleagues, the unnamed author, following the instructions for compiling *rapports d'ensemble*, was careful to end on a positive note. Colonial subjects' loyalty through the hard times—the Great War, not the famine—was a harbinger of future colonial greatness.[30]

This report from the Military Territory of Niger was notable for its relatively open discussion of famine and frank assessment of the staggering mortality. Others, if they mentioned famine at all, hinted at it as a side effect of other concerns. A French physician in Upper Senegal and Niger reflected on how bureaucratic categorization and the administrative division of labor worked to marginalize famine. "If it were possible to include famine among facts of pathology, the numerous cases of cachexia followed by death would tend to permit such a classification, but the means suitable to check such a calamity are of an administrative and not of a medical order."[31] Doctors knew how to diagnose and treat patients, but this was close to useless in a crisis that demanded the full mobilization of the colonial administration. What was the point of translating starvation into medical terminology when the solution, access to food, was both obvious and not primarily a medical issue?

A narrowly professional point of view, whether medical, agricultural, economic, or otherwise, could capture only thin slices of the multivalent problem. A report on education in the military territory for 1914 noted that many students had migrated with their parents in search of food. An agricultural report mentioned excessive mortality but only among "the miserable herds reduced to famine."[32] Another agricultural report admitted that harvest shortfalls had reduced the population to a state "close to famine." In the conclusion, the report revealed, almost in passing, that these near-famine conditions had cost over twenty thousand lives.[33] The division of administrative labor into fields of specialist expertise created a situation in which it was nobody's job responsibility to deal with, or even discuss, the famine.

The story that reached Paris through official reports was simple: drought had caused harvest shortfalls and administrators had reacted quickly and effectively to restore normalcy. However, the famine took on a different aspect in correspondence between administrators within Africa. Unsatisfied with routine reports that hinted at famine but provided no details, the governor-general of French West Africa, William Ponty, requested additional information. In response to this prodding, the governor of Upper Senegal and Niger, François-Joseph Clozel, disclosed that the famine was more serious and widespread than he had originally suggested. By April 1914, the administration in Timbuktu alone had counted 3,428 famine deaths.[34]

Under these circumstances, it was essential to demonstrate the benefits of French rule. Clozel thought of aid as transactional. Beyond "the most elementary considerations of humaneness," it was important to show indigenous subjects "solidarity" in exchange for taxes. He tried to buy 180 tons of millet, but "goodwill confronted material obstacles." The Niger River was impassably low, and mortality itself complicated logistics. Though Clozel spent over four hundred thousand francs, the dearth of European personnel and the absence of the thousand tons of food needed to "save the country from death" prevented him from mounting the response he would have liked to.[35] This admission casts heavy doubt on the figure of eight hundred tons of rescue grain quoted in the reports sent to Paris.

Like French administrators throughout the empire, Clozel blamed indigenous racial characteristics and the climate for the famine. The apathetic Songhai in and around Timbuktu, he complained, "let themselves die of hunger in front of a river as teeming with fish as the Niger." They preferred to flee rather than plant the wheat and barley given out by the administration. Farmers who worked their crops diligently in the presence of Europeans abandoned the fields when unsupervised.[36] This helped explain poor results despite what Clozel described as the maximum effort on the part of his administration.

Governor-General Ponty was still unsatisfied with the quality of information. In June 1914, he urgently requested statistics about rainfall and harvests from the AOF governors.[37] He sent yet another letter to Clozel, asking him what he had done besides distributing grain. In particular, Ponty was interested in agricultural cooperatives and granaries.[38] The responses, if there were any, are not in the archives. But the repeated requests for information are revealing of the thinness of lines of communication, the autonomy of administrators, and the French state's incapacity to control, or even know much about, its enormous territory.

The untrustworthiness of official documentation is confirmed by vast discrepancies in reports. A medical report written by a doctor in Upper Senegal and Niger contradicted Clozel's account, even the revised one. The author wrote that of the 45,000 people living in the district of Gao, 8,304 were confirmed dead and 3,206 had "disappeared." The town of Mopti recorded a daily death toll of 25. The population of Timbuktu had dropped from 12,000 to 9,000, which accorded with Clozel's estimate. But if the surroundings were included, mortality jumped to 20,000. The figures, the doctor thought, spoke for themselves. But unlike Clozel, he included glimpses of the realities behind the numbers. "It was by the tens that in July, August we collected cadavers in Timbuktu, in the streets, in the squares, and under the bushes of the surroundings." Children had suffered disproportionately: "Those that survive this severe selection will long bear the marks of their physiological misery."[39] These sad sentences contrasted with Clozel's optimism and evasion.

Documents from the Military Territory of Niger, which was even more isolated than Upper Senegal and Niger, exhibited similar inconsistencies. From disconnected fragments, only an impressionistic account of the famine in Niger can be pieced together. Drought in 1913 forced farmers to replant repeatedly. Millet prices skyrocketed. Garden crops such as manioc, potatoes, and onions made little headway against the shortfalls. Livestock was decimated. Children suffered from a shortage of milk. Families fled. Some men migrated to Nigeria for work, others toward Lake Chad where exceptionally low water levels made fishing easy.[40] Those who remained foraged in the wilderness. Some refugees briefly came home in the spring of 1914 to plant before moving on again, leaving the bare minimum of people behind to tend fields.[41] When it finally rained, Africans gathered wild plants of little nutritional value. Refeeding after prolonged starvation is one of the most dangerous moments for the acutely malnourished, and the filling of unaccustomed stomachs killed many. The only signs of a response from the military administration are passing references to the prohibition of grain exports, punishments to exhort farmers to work harder, and one half-sentence proposing grain reserves.[42] In early 1915, the military governor of the Niger territory estimated that one hundred thousand people had died of famine. The population nonetheless remained in a "good state of mind." Despite the "horrifying misery," tax receipts exceeded expectations to reach 1.1 million francs. A further 35,000 francs were collected for soldiers wounded in the European war.[43]

A physician working in Niger, his observations filtered through his professional expertise, drew attention to infectious disease. Long-awaited autumn rains ended the drought but caused mortality to surge among all age groups as mosquitos spread malaria and hunger-weakened people drank dirty water, leading to a "veritable epidemic" of dysentery and other water-borne illnesses. Returning refugees brought a severe outbreak of smallpox to the city of Niamey. Between starvation and disease, made worse by a "Muslim fatalism" toward health and life, the doctor estimated that the population of the Military Territory of Niger had fallen by a quarter.[44]

These scraps of information offer glimpses into a world, but they are more directly a reflection of an administrative point of view. Repeated requests for information, large discrepancies in mortality estimates, oblique hints of disaster, and overly neat stories of mastery say as much about French mentalities and communication practices as about famine. Starting from the assumption that famine was an inevitable natural disaster, Clozel and other French administrators saw their role as reactive, bringing the situation back to a baseline normal as efficiently as possible. The dry accounts of grain prices and food distributions were meant to convey control. To do so, they occluded much. One result was that administrators addressed the problems they had created on paper, not the ones that existed in reality. If the famine was quickly and easily overcome in these documents, a different mode of witnessing, one that was emotional and personal rather than rational and objective, laid bare what bureaucratic procedure hid.

Disorder in Chad

The governor of Upper Senegal and Niger, François-Joseph Clozel, sought to downplay the crisis lest he incriminate himself. Only a handful of documents from the Military Territory of Niger discussed the famine at all. The case of Chad, where colonial conquest was ongoing, gives a different perspective. Fighting soldiers whose job was less the rational administration of Africans than the forcible control of them did not face the same pressures to cast famine in a rosy light. Although or perhaps because colonial administration was barely established, officials recorded more information about famine in Chad than in other Sahelian colonies. Whereas routine bureaucratic reports from Upper Senegal and Niger worked to conceal the famine, documents from Chad magnified and dramatized it. Acknowledgment of the severity of famine did not imply better intervention; rather, it suggested different professional standards. The most direct descriptions of famine often occurred when and where French responsibilities and capabilities were weakest. Attention could denote the absence rather than the presence of care.

In April of 1913, several months before the famine began, starvation made a curious appearance in military reports. In this case the French were not trying to relieve it, but to induce it. A contingent of French troops had laid siege to a village occupied by a band of rebels in Chad's mountainous Guéra region. The adversaries were armed only with spears and slings but had the advantage of the terrain. The French commander tried to break the stalemate by destroying crops and food stores. In this way, he "hoped to defeat the rebels by means of famine." The strategy failed with the coming of the rains. The French resorted to brute force. One French auxiliary was killed. The resistors suffered major losses. Some preferred suicide to surrender. "The tragic scene, in which we see entire families throw themselves into a chasm, shows just how far the fanaticism of these tribes of primitive mores (*mœurs*) can go."[45]

In Chad, the famine of 1913 and 1914 was inseparable from war.[46] Even when French soldiers were not intentionally starving people, conquest and "pacification" contributed to famine by bringing about social disorder and diverting food from the African population. Military operations had first claim on resources. The campaign to pacify the northern Borkou and Ennedi regions was the biggest drain on money, food, and transportation.[47] In the summer of 1913, the French army asked nobles from the south of Chad to assemble 120 tons of millet for soldiers. As an afterthought, Sultan Gaourang II of Baguirmi added 10 tons of grain for the poor of the capital Fort-Lamy (N'Djamena).[48] In one devastated district in central Chad, between 60 and 120 tons of grain were collected in 1914 for soldiers fighting in Borkou-Ennedi.[49] The French consistently prioritized military provisioning ahead of subsistence.

As soldiers first, Chad's administrators saw the famine primarily as an operational obstacle. Famine reduced tax receipts, dispersed the nomads the army relied on for transportation, and killed pack animals. This rendered what should have been a simple military operation in Borkou-Ennedi into one requiring "meticulous organization," a euphemism for the violent appropriation of resources.[50] When World War I began in the summer of 1914, it exacerbated supply issues by cutting off access to markets in German Africa and redirecting men, animals, and food for operations against German forces in Kamerun.[51] Military provisioning joined violence and drought first to trigger a food crisis and then to hinder relief.

The Ouaddaï region in eastern Chad, conquered only in 1909 and not pacified until 1911, exploded in violence under the stress of famine. What the French called bandits were in fact former soldiers of the Wadai Empire who had until recently resisted French occupation. They descended from secluded mountain hideouts to steal food and livestock before retreating with their spoils. French officers criticized the strong young men who eschewed work in favor of "reliv[ing] the troubled times of three years ago, to pillage, to assassinate, and to give themselves up to orgies in the midst of general misery." These bandits were driven, the French thought, by a force greater than mere hunger. They stole in excess of what they needed. They gratuitously killed livestock and burned villages guarded by defenseless old men.[52] From this point of view, cruel Africans unleashing a primal will to violence were not subjects to care for, but enemies to overcome.

The large size of the armed groups exposed the weakness of the early French presence in Chad. In one clash, a French force of 25 African soldiers killed 168 bandits. The soldiers' French commander was disgusted upon entering the enemy camp to find hundreds of kilos of stolen meat rotting wastefully. When one of the most troublesome ringleaders, Djibrin Djougourdi, was killed along with 86 of his men in March 1914, a group of 300 to 400 remained at large.[53] Near Abéché, the capital of the Ouaddaï, French troops fought at least three pillaging bands, one of which was 200 men strong.[54] In August 1914, the French estimated that 1,100 bandits had been killed and 1,700 head of cattle returned to their owners.[55] Conflating large-scale resistance with crime was a way of imposing French rule of law on the chaos of conquest.

Famine was seen as a tragic feature of this desolate landscape. The military governor Colonel Étienne Largeau wrote bluntly that "a crisis unforeseen and of an intensity that in the memory of the old men has never been known in the basin of Chad stopped dead the general prosperity in the last months of the year 1913." According to Chadian informants, there had been two killing famines over the previous century, and neither had been as severe. The autumn harvest failed. Watercourses dried up. Pastures were ruined. Cattle succumbed to epidemic disease. Granaries that had been full before the conquest lay empty because the French could not afford to restock them. Farmers began migrating in search of resources in October. By the beginning of 1914, the situation was "almost unbearable."[56]

French soldiers in Chad played up the disarray.[57] Until pressed, Governor Clozel of Upper Senegal and Niger gave the impression that the crisis in his colony was limited. Governor Largeau of Chad, on the other hand, stressed that famine stretched across the territory into neighboring Nigeria and Darfur. Clozel emphasized orderliness. Largeau blended observation with rumor to communicate chaos:

> At each post, in front of the kitchens of the African riflemen, one finds every day the corpses of oldsters or children who had died of privation during the night. Mothers offer their children to travelers to save them from hunger. . . . After having eaten the hyenas and the jackals, the starving resorted to devouring cadavers, and then to killing to satiate their hunger. In a hut in Abéché a man and a woman were found butchering the body of a young man they had murdered. They were cooking pieces on the fire. . . . Everywhere is reported similar cases of cannibalism.[58]

Clozel marginalized famine. Largeau sensationalized it.

An emphasis on disorder framed French shortcomings as helplessness instead of callousness or incompetence. Possibilities for emergency provisioning were severely curtailed by low river levels, banditry, mass death of transport animals, and resistance to forced labor. The owners of pack animals fled or bribed French agents to avoid the seizure of their property. Obtaining transportation was no longer a "requisition" but "the hunt."[59] For these reasons, it was impossible to import grain from the colony's more favored southern districts. Civilized countries, Largeau explained, escaped famine thanks to high-capacity means of transportation that facilitated free exchange, such as roads, railroads, and waterways. In their absence, his administration was powerless. With the grain he had, Largeau fed his personnel first and then distributed the leftovers.[60] His administration held itself to the standard of the possible. The more difficult the situation, the less could be expected from even the most competent and humane.

Largeau implied that adhering to modern European norms was impossible and inappropriate in Chad. Famine was correlated to a rise in slavery, a standby of the Sahelian subsistence repertoire. Children were kidnapped or were exchanged for the going rate of three kilos of millet by parents who preferred to sell them than to watch them die. Largeau, under the circumstances, approved. He predicted that after the famine, the children would be tracked down and brought home: "The damage done by the slave traders will be repaired and all that will remain is the service that they involuntarily rendered by rescuing a few human lives from death."[61] French civilization's abhorrence of slavery, a major justification of colonial conquest, was of small value here.

The military commander of the Ouaddaï district, Lieutenant-Colonel Jean Hilaire, reported that Abéché was nearly deserted by spring of 1914. Only merchants and aristocrats rich enough to buy food at famine prices remained. The town's authorities buried people found dead in the streets: 125 in April, 76 in May. Hilaire attributed the reduction in mortality not to a decreased rate, but to depopulation as the sick and the elderly died and the healthy fled. Wells dried up. Watering gardens was prohibited. Medical clinics shut down. The army took its animals to better pastures, depriving the region of transportation.[62] Violence was ubiquitous as starving refugees resorted to theft.[63] Some small distributions of millet and meat had little effect. In the summer of 1914, Hilaire estimated the mortality in his district at an extraordinary 150 thousand.[64]

The market price of millet rose from 10 centimes per kilo in early 1913 to a peak of 3 francs.[65] In summer of 1914, wild vegetation and hoarded grain released onto markets cut millet prices in half to 1.50 francs per kilo. This was still fifteen times the price of the previous year.[66] The administration distributed what grain it had, but the shortage of seed and labor compromised planting. Many surviving farmers were too sick to care for their fields. Nonetheless, by the beginning of September, an abundance of wild famine foods and some quantity of newly harvested millet reduced the price of a kilo to 20 centimes. Those driven to violence by hunger ceased their criminal activities, though "professional brigands" continued to ply their trade. The French declared the famine over.[67]

Looking back from fifteen years later, Jean Hilaire estimated the population of the Ouaddaï had dropped from seven hundred thousand to four hundred thousand.[68] These figures are unlikely to be accurate, but they give a sense of scale and of what it was like to witness such a famine. Many districts lost at least 50 percent of their inhabitants. In some places, including Abéché, the population fell by 90 percent. Villages across the territory simply disappeared. One example among many was Koutoul, a village east of Abéché, which in 1913 counted 54 men, 96 women, and 111 children. In May 1914, its population numbered 4 men, 5 women, and 6 children "in such a condition that they will probably not make it to the next harvest."[69] Livestock herds were decimated.[70] Nonetheless, Largeau believed that the French presence had been salutary, asking, "What would have become of the Ouaddaï if a cataclysm of this magnitude had occurred when the improvident Sultans surrounded themselves with thousands of idle people?"[71] For French administrators steeped in civilizational supremacy, European rule was by definition beneficial for its subjects, irrespective of outcomes.

There exists little information about relief plans for Chad and even less about execution. The general idea was to move grain from southern regions less affected by drought to Sahelian and Saharan districts. Administrators claimed that Baguirmi exported 370 tons, and that Salamat furnished 300 tons to Ouaddaï alone. Fort-Lamy received 30 tons of grain in February 1914 and 25 more in March. This was advanced to the well-off and distributed free of charge to indigents.[72] Given the documented difficulty of transportation and the priority of military provisioning, it is likely that much, even most, of earmarked aid never reached the needy. Largeau estimated that 1,500 tons of grain would be needed for soldiers, administration personnel, and their families in Ouaddaï alone, but he confessed the impossibility of obtaining it. Hilaire complained that the number of camels at his disposal had dropped from over 2,000 to 242. The surviving animals could not be mobilized because a "hecatomb" would ensue.[73] As in Upper Senegal and Niger, aid that looked impressive on paper was likely less so on the ground.

As acute mortality diminished in 1914, it was self-evident to French officers that the famine had been caused by drought and the improvidence of Chadians who wasted precious grain brewing beer when shortages were imminent. Administrators had little to say about how to deal with future famines. Some mentioned restocking precolonial granaries, accompanied by pessimistic caveats about budgetary and logistical challenges. A few others proposed to combat the monoculture of millet by introducing drought-resistant crops.[74] One administrator suggested drawing up evacuation plans for the populations of the most vulnerable areas.[75] Nobody followed up.[76] In Chad, observers of the famine felt no formal responsibility for prevention or relief. Candid descriptions of starvation were not signs of care. Rather, they justified its absence.

Famine in Colonial Memory

The famine of 1913 and 1914 was a major event with profound consequences for the inhabitants of the Sahel. It passed with little commentary or reflection from French people. Unlike the Algerian famine of 1867, the Sahel famine was not a topic of public discourse in France. Unlike famines in Indochina around the same time, it did not provoke discussions of reform. During the famine, administrative communications gravitated toward one of two rhetorical tendencies: a bureaucratic formalism that conveyed order and mastery, and a sensationalism that played up disorder and helplessness. Each, in its own way, shielded administrators from responsibility or criticism, one by a brute imposition of bureaucratic order, the other by insisting on order's impossibility. These differences cannot be explained solely by variations in how the famine was experienced. It is necessary to take the perspectives and priorities of reporting administrators into account.

In the vastly different context of interwar France, the contrast between these ways of seeing and remembering became even more pronounced. In 1933, the French Ministry of Colonies took a belated interest in the 1913 famine. Sensitive about food issues after two politically embarrassing famines in Niger and Indochina in 1931, the ministry ordered the African administrations to provide mortality estimates for the earlier crisis. Chad submitted a dossier of reports from the famine years that remains in French archives. If a response from French West Africa was ever submitted, it immediately went missing. It was not in Ministry of Colonies archives when in 1938, German and Italian newspapers brought up the 1913 famine in their propaganda. As part of a campaign to discredit French colonialism, the Fascist newspapers accused France of having allowed three hundred thousand to four hundred thousand Africans to starve.[77] Finding that it had no information whatsoever about a massive famine which may or may not have occurred, the ministry felt the need to investigate.

In 1938, two functionaries, Director of Political and Administrative Affairs Vidaud and Inspector-General of Medical and Sanitary Services Pezet, were dispatched to Dakar, Senegal, to consult the archives of French West Africa. The research trip yielded no definitive answers. The paucity of sources, Vidaud and Pezet reported, did not allow them to estimate mortality with any confidence. Invited to give their personal opinions in the event that their research was inconclusive, they inferred that if the famine had been as grave as the German and Italian articles claimed, it would surely have left a more substantial documentary trail.[78]

The story of the famine as told by Vidaud and Pezet was simple enough to require just a few paragraphs. It was the triumphant narrative of a responsible and competent colonial administration overcoming misfortunes of climate and the apathy of Africans. Whether or not this was intentional obfuscation, colonial reporting and archiving practices allowed and encouraged such an interpretation. As they were meant to, Vidaud and Pezet drew politically expedient conclusions from the routine reports for Upper Senegal and Niger, the only ones they consulted. They reasoned that if the famine had been serious, administrators would not have failed to record it. In fact, it was the explicit function of *rapports d'ensemble* to exclude information that ran counter to the arc of colonial progress. Vidaud and Pezet's investigation followed the contours imposed by the rules regulating the production of colonial documentation. Routine reports rarely dealt with famine directly and minimized its impact when the topic did come up.

If the colonial functionaries moonlighting as historians in 1938 had been slightly more rigorous, they would have found substantiating evidence of the mortality cited in the German and Italian newspapers. Estimates of the death toll were scattered in sources that Vidaud and Pezet did not consult, including those from Chad sent to Paris in 1933. The famine also left traces through less formal channels—personal recollection, rumor, and the culturally transmitted experience of observers and victims. French colonial administrators did in fact have a memory of the famine, a vague sense that a major calamity had occurred, but one lacking detail or focus. This was how the Ministry of Colonies knew to ask about the crisis in its 1933 request for information.

After the famine of 1931 in Niger, a commission of inquiry convened by the Ministry of Colonies complained that no written accounts of the earlier 1913 famine existed to guide administrators in Africa. In the absence of formal documentation, the commission interviewed witnesses who remembered the widespread misery of 1913. Monsieur Itier, who had been posted in the remote Nigerien outpost of Zinder, recalled that the famine had struck with no warning and no measures had been taken to avoid it.[79] Monsieur Beyries, at the time an inexperienced administrator in the Goundam district of Upper Senegal and Niger, not far from Timbuktu, had also been caught lacking. He was given thirty tons of millet with which to feed one hundred thousand subjects, barely enough to distribute a few rations to children. He claimed to have seen cases of cannibalism.[80] An administrator named Nemos guessed that up to a million people may have died.[81] A few years later, a circular from 1940 advised colonial governors to take precautions to avoid the repetition of a war famine.[82] Administrators knew about the 1913 famine, even if official recording procedures wrote it out of institutional memory.

Vidaud and Pezet's conclusion that the famine had not happened was the logical outcome of colonial communication practices meant to provide plausible deniability for overwhelmed and underequipped administrators. On the other end of the rhetorical spectrum from cold, dry reports were eyewitness memoirs that appeared in the 1930s. The generic conventions of memoir, as opposed to bureaucratic formalism, allowed direct, emotional observation. Lieutenant-Colonel Jean Hilaire, who had commanded the Ouaddaï district of Chad in 1914, published *From the Congo to the Nile* in 1930. From a self-centered point of view common in colonialists and encouraged by the genre of memoir, Hilaire portrayed himself as protagonist, as though the famine had happened primarily to him. This style of storytelling required exaggerating rather than hiding African suffering. Starvation served as the backdrop against which Hilaire demonstrated his own manly charisma, physical and mental endurance, and benevolent paternalism.[83] In contrast, Denise Moran's 1934 memoir *Tchad* portrayed the 1913 famine as an embarrassment. Moran witnessed the famine while accompanying her husband, a colonial administrator, on his tour of duty, and what she saw horrified her. Her book described the same abject scenes as Hilaire's, but her intention was to spark reform. Hilaire's text was a heroic epic, Moran's an exposé.

Lieutenant-Colonel Hilaire had participated in the French conquest and pacification of the Wadai sultanate completed in 1911. When the famine struck in 1913, he was posted in France. In Hilaire's telling, Colonel Largeau, the military governor of Chad, recognized that he was the only man who had the hands-on experience and strength of character to lead Ouaddaï through the famine. In early 1914, Hilaire was reluctant to forego the glory of fighting in the European trenches. Largeau enticed him to return to Africa with a stark portrayal of his beloved Ouaddaï. The population had been halved by death and migration. The "indifferent," "inhuman" command had taken no action to avert or relieve starvation. People killed each other for scraps of food. Cannibalism, stamped out by French civilization, had reappeared. Human meat, thinly disguised as hyena, was bought and sold within sight of the French headquarters.

Hilaire was moved by this plea. When he arrived in Ouaddaï, he confirmed that Largeau had not exaggerated. Fields were abandoned, villages deserted, corpses scattered. The odor of death permeated the air. Starving people begged for millet, which Hilaire dared not give because careless refeeding often proved fatal. In an unforgivable breach of duty, his predecessor had taken advantage of desperate subjects. This officer of Turkish origin had "noisily" converted to Catholicism but without bothering "to encumber himself with the most elementary scruples, humanitarian or otherwise, of our Western morality." He sold millet requisitioned at 5 centimes per kilo back to farmers at 2.50 francs, fifty times the original price.[84] Drought and inhumanity had reduced Ouaddaï to a hellscape.

The scene was set for Hilaire to come to the rescue. Heroically overcoming drought, war, and the budget, Hilaire managed to feed the population at reduced rations until "finally, around mid-July, the sky burst in life-saving torrents! I was, by unanimous acclaim, crowned 'Grand Sultan,' 'He who finally made it rain!'"[85] Hilaire's memoir dramatized the harm wrought by famine to portray himself as a hero of empire, appealing to readers' taste for adventurous exoticism. Through a pseudo-mystical understanding of the Ouaddaï born of personal experience, coupled with an impeccable moral compass, a humanitarian sensitivity, and a forceful charisma, he had been able, he claimed, to "save" the people under his command.[86]

Hilaire bounded his altruism with a paternalist, masculine strength rooted in racial and civilizational chauvinism. In the memoir, he remarked on a supposedly amoral precolonial state of nature with the topical metaphor of the strong "eating" the weak. During the famine, these primitive voracious urges manifested symbolically and literally as banditry, murder, and cannibalism. Hilaire was forced by circumstances to violence. "With death in my soul, I had to show myself implacable, crack down without weakness, without pity, against crimes that were all in all only delirious gestures of necessity, of panic. I was forced to make terrifying examples, more terrifying even than the hunger that armed these criminals."[87] Hilaire's prose was saturated with a sentimentality at odds with his violence. His feelings of care, even of fatherly love for the starving led to pitiless repression.

Hilaire's boast of having "saved" Ouaddaï while freely admitting, indeed accentuating, overwhelming suffering appears paradoxical. In both his memoir and his administrative communications, he estimated that hundreds of thousands had died, the population of the Ouaddaï nearly halved. Yet, far from being embarrassed, he touted his own role with pride. Hilaire's actions and their integration into a narrative of personal heroism were not primarily intended to help people. Rather, they fulfilled the psychological and cultural needs of the author and his readers. Any material reduction in the suffering of subjects was fortunate but incidental. In a situation beyond human control, it was nonsensical to make judgments about the efficacy of relief. Without institutional structures that channeled feelings into coordinated administrative policy, and without even the sense that famine was within the realm of human action, there could be no expectation that pity for victims should lead to less suffering. The impossible fight against the hostile forces of African nature was admirable regardless of outcomes. Hilaire's memoir differed sharply in tone and function from Vidaud and Pezet's formal investigation. Yet both, in their own ways, served to relieve France of responsibility.

Memoirs did not necessarily have to be so self-aggrandizing. Denise Moran's descriptions of famine were similar to Hilaire's in content but had a different narrative and moral valence. Moran was influenced by the authors André Gide and Albert Londres, who she believed had successfully shamed French people overseas into better behavior by exposing colonial abuses. Following their style of activist journalism, Moran's 1934 book reconstructed a desolate world governed by the self-interested violence of French soldiers in the absence of the rule of law. She recalled how the hungry had raided anthills for grain, gnawed at wild plants, and abandoned the elderly with only termites for food. The administration's horses remained well fed through the famine, so people sifted through manure for undigested millet grains. Children were traded for sheep or clothing or they were simply abandoned.

For many, the only recourse was to appeal to the humanity of administrators, a risky survival strategy. "Here was an entire language: 'we are yours, you must save us, we can no longer do anything for ourselves, have pity on us.'"[88] Officials responded with annoyance and violence more often than with care. They were warriors, more interested in fighting bandits than providing relief. Soldiers made an example of criminals by taking heads, hands, and ears as trophies. This brutality was justified because "starving people have no conscience." Of the French army's killing of hundreds, Moran wrote sarcastically, as if in response to Hilaire, "Glory to the vanquishers of the famished!"[89]

Out of disaster, a myth of lazy, improvident, and ignorant natives was born. And yet, Moran contended, Chadians knew how to survive far better than scornful French officers. Farmers had traditionally stored grain in clay containers housed in raised straw structures. The administration had ordered these replaced. In Moran's district, the eight new granaries were corrupted with termites and worms. Then two were flooded. The grain in the remaining six spoiled. In another district, when people opened the granaries to stave off famine, they were punished.[90] In 1914 and 1915, the administration of Chad collected taxes as usual and recruited soldiers from the depleted African population to fight in World War I. Moran was not surprised when the region broke out in revolt.[91] For Jean Hilaire, the famine was a source of pride; for Denise Moran, it was a shame.

In their 1938 inquiry, Vidaud and Pezet said they found no evidence of famine. This evidence, though, did exist, in archives and in the testimony of witnesses. The researchers' conclusions say more about the communication and recording practices of the French colonial state than about the famine itself. The consulted reports functioned, as they were intended to, to convey a positive story of colonial development. The horror of famine was for the most part relegated to the unofficial, less authoritative domain of eyewitness mem-

ory, memoir, and rumor. In the Sahelian context of a skeletal, weak, thin colonial administration, relations between the French and their subjects were
governed as much by interpersonal relations, sentiment, and force as by rule
of law or bureaucratic order. Official reports were poor instruments with
which to capture or even acknowledge this reality.

Care between Politics and Pity

"I saw in a dream Friday night that a time will come when under the blast of
an oppressive wind men and women will die in great numbers, and this year
numerous sicknesses will strike them." The anonymous African who authored
these lines implored readers to resist the curse by wearing amulets, drinking
magical texts dissolved in water, and donating cowrie shells, clothing, sheep,
or goats to the poor and to "those who know." If these things were not done,
"the wind will turn red and scorching." The holy man pleaded, "Oh servants
of God, do not abandon God for the perishable earth. Know that we are entering the end of the world in which a terrible famine will come and a devastating wind will descend upon your homes until it has destroyed you."[92] The
French interpreted this tract, which circulated in Upper Senegal and Niger in
1913, as the work of a confidence artist taking advantage of hungry, scared
people. They took note only because it was seen as a security threat. But the
prophecy also contained hints of a world concealed by French sources, a world
that included a moral economy to support the poor. Uninterested in this world,
the French could not recognize that its end was upon them.

The French deemed the famine over after the fall harvest of 1914. But no
society so unsettled could revert to normality overnight, even under the best
of circumstances, which the war years were not. Labor and resources needed
for recovery went instead to the European war effort.[93] Many African subjects
associated famine with French rule.[94] Shortly after the outbreak of World War
I, rebellions against colonial authority erupted across French Africa. Military
recruitment was the primary trigger, but the famine was also significant. As
some local administrators argued, the number of recruits demanded by Paris
and Dakar in the aftermath of the famine provoked "serious dissatisfaction
among our black subjects."[95] Recruitment on top of starvation proved intol-
erable for many, who vindicated the warnings of these administrators by rising up.

The famine also formed part of a longer and wider history of hunger in
the French Empire. Colonial administrators took as a given that famine was
inevitable, and interventions could only be reactive. One historical task, then,

is defining the relationships of administrators to people in need and the reactions those relationships demanded. In the Sahel, administrators and soldiers improvised a range of responses defined at one extreme by an orderly, formalistic, bureaucratic control over people and territory, and at the other by an apolitical, unmediated humanitarianism. These approaches served different needs by obscuring the utility and truth of the other. Bureaucratic discourse superimposed its own order onto reality, overwhelming the facts of human suffering not only by dissimulation, but by creating an illusion of hegemony that left no room for the pain of colonial subjects. Emotional descriptions of famine that acknowledged suffering concealed the role of the colonial state in both its causes and its potential remedies. Without political responsibility or administrative capacity, pity did not lead to less suffering. Sentiment could, in fact, substitute for relief. By severing administration from humanity and emotion from capability, the French hid the necessary connections between these modes of care.

PART TWO

The Politics of the Belly

CHAPTER 4

The Science of Hunger in the International Sphere, 1890–1939

In 1913, starvation struck the Sahel from Senegal to Sudan, killing hundreds of thousands of people.[1] The event garnered little attention from Europeans. In 1931, a far smaller famine in western Niger, a fraction of the same area, caused between fifteen thousand and thirty thousand deaths. This time, the famine was scandalous. In a period of less than twenty years, colonial famine, which once received only cursory attention, became a major preoccupation of policy makers throughout the French Empire. For the first time, colonial officials deemed it essential not only to rule their subjects, but also to feed them.

Why did famine shift so quickly from a marginal tragedy to a central problem of French colonial policy? One answer lies in the emergence of new forms of knowledge and changing ideas of internationalism. Until World War I, French colonial administrators shared a view that famine was the unavoidable result of incompetent races interacting with difficult environments. Under these conditions, the colonial state's role was consistently thought of as reactive, conditional, and voluntary. In the interwar years, the development of a new science of nutrition gave French administrators novel concepts through which to understand famine and new tools with which to address it. At the same time, an emerging vision of the French Empire as a participant in an international humanitarian project profoundly altered ideas of what colonialism was supposed to accomplish. In principle, the purpose of the French

Empire became the well-being of its constituents. Among its most basic responsibilities was ensuring subsistence.

The question of what the colonial state should do about famine was closely linked to developments in scientific knowledge of the human body and its relationship to food. In the nineteenth century, the study of food in the colonies fell under the scope of tropical hygiene, a medical discipline concerned primarily with the maintenance of white bodies under the strain of unhealthy colonial conditions.[2] Beginning in the late nineteenth century, the dietary health of colonial subjects became a matter of scientific investigation. Scientists in Europe and the colonies devoted themselves to understanding what came to be known as deficiency disease, in the process discovering vitamins and inaugurating the modern science of nutrition. French medical experts studying the deficiency disease beriberi in Indochina were more concerned with physiology than with medicine, treating colonial subjects as experimental subjects first and only incidentally as patients.

In the wake of the First World War, nutrition took on unprecedented importance in the administration of the French Empire. The new attention to diet was motivated not so much by a concern for subjects, but by the economic imperative to maximize labor power. In their efforts to fight depopulation and improve worker efficiency, doctors and administrators in French Equatorial Africa (Afrique Équatoriale Française, AEF) began treating diet as an economic problem as well as a physiological one. In the 1920s, experts in AEF applied nutritional thinking not only to individual bodies but also to collective races.

A decade later, nutrition became a framework for understanding and managing not just workers or races but society in general. Fulfilling nutritional needs became a foundational component of social order. Nutrition science came to encompass economic, cultural, and ecological elements of life. Scientific involvement in colonial administration deepened as biologists and physicians in France and the colonies took a more active role in formulating and implementing policy.[3] Famine in the French Empire ceased to be understood as an accident of nature. Instead, it became a public health issue and therefore the responsibility of French administration.

In Europe during the interwar years, especially after the onset of the Great Depression, the well-being of individuals became a matter of increasing concern for states. The laissez-faire approaches to social problems of the nineteenth century gave way to debates about the role of state and society in the welfare of citizens. While nation-states were being reimagined as the guarantors of the quality of life of their citizens, international organizations such as the League of Nations expanded this project to include the entire world.[4] Food and its relationship to bodies and populations became a basic concern at the national and global levels. Experts drawing on internationalism and nutrition put forth a vision of society centered around human physiology. Their ambitious goal was nothing less than the rationalization of global ecology, economy, and biology into a single system to facilitate the unobstructed flow of vital nutrients from agricultural production, to distribution, to metabolism.

Europeans began to reconsider the nature of political responsibility in their empires. Reformers newly interested in the well-being of colonial subjects saw that subsistence was logically prior to any other civilizing aims. Under increased scrutiny from humanitarians, journalists, and international organizations, French colonial functionaries reformulated their understanding of famine in light of developments in nutrition science. Researchers and administrators began to address the problem of colonial famine as a broadly social one, revising previous ideas of famine as a natural disaster characterized by simple calorie shortage. Famine was reconceived as an extreme point on a spectrum of nutritional health. Starvation was no longer a categorically different state from undernutrition or malnutrition; rather, these formed part of a range of conditions united under the framework of nutrition science.

Nutrition science vastly complicated the problem of famine. New understandings of how hunger worked provoked a serious rethinking of the purpose and purview of the French Empire. States were now supposed to use all the tools at their disposal to ensure that each individual ate a proper diet, including the newly discovered elements necessary for the body's biochemical functions: vitamins, minerals, and amino acids. Famine was at once medical, economic, ecological, and political. But while new ideas about nutrition began to figure prominently in colonial discourse, they did not in most cases radically transform policy. The expansive way of understanding the problem of diet was applied to the colonies, but the extensive, and above all expensive, solutions offered in Europe were not. Ultimately, the science of nutrition saddled the French colonial state with responsibilities that it was unable and unwilling to fulfill.

Tropical Hygiene

As early as the beginning of the nineteenth century, experts associated with what was called more or less interchangeably tropical, naval, or hot hygiene were concerned with diet. These experts—mostly physicians, surgeons, and pharmacists attached to European navies—founded national and international professional organizations, schools, and journals focused on health issues specific to tropical climates. The internationalism of these professional networks was supposed to mirror the universality of science itself.[5] Famine was not at this time considered a medical problem and was not a topic of study for hygienists. Even so, the discipline of tropical hygiene and its international networks paved the way for the reconceptualization of colonial famine between the world wars.

In the nineteenth century, the science and medicine of food in the French Empire focused on the health of the colonizers rather than that of the colonized. It was widely accepted that those who suffered from colonization were the Europeans who braved dangerous and unhealthy lands rather than the indigenous populations who were supposed to be the beneficiaries of the project.[6] White bodies, so well adapted to the temperate climates of Europe, were thought to undergo physiological changes in tropical climates, impairing bodily processes and diminishing resistance to disease. The basic concern of tropical hygiene was the acclimatization of European bodies to tropical conditions.[7] This was to be achieved in large part through the management of diet. Hygienists generally held that Europeans could benefit from dietary practices indigenous to tropical milieus rather than the other way around.[8]

Georges Treille, professor of naval hygiene and exotic pathology, was a major figure in French tropical medicine in the late nineteenth century. He was among the first medical professionals to leave the navy for the colonial health service after its creation in 1890, which made his betrayed colleagues so mad they retaliated by sending him a medical book with a bomb hidden inside.[9] The device malfunctioned, permitting him to write in 1899 that tropical hygiene was a "general science, a total science," and must be practiced at the level of the individual as well as that of public administration to ensure bodily security in the tropics. Diet, according to Treille, was the foundation of the science of hygiene, as "nutrition" was the most important organic function. Channeling vitalist strains of medical thought, he saw the general program of tropical hygiene as the identification of the rules for choosing and preparing food that would help maintain "vital energy" in a "cosmic milieu" that had a depressing influence on the physiological forces of Europeans.[10]

Treille argued that Europeans had to "indigenize" their bodies to suit the climate. Minimum standards for dietary elements such as protein and carbohydrates were established under European conditions and were therefore useless in radically different tropical climates. Instead of adhering to European norms, Treille recommended choosing foods that would reduce strain on the vitally important digestive organs "which distribute life in its two forms, heat and energy."[11] Though hygienists debated the finer points of colonial diet such as the amount of meat it was advisable to consume and whether alcohol was acceptable in moderation or should be strictly avoided, the focus on white health was taken for granted.[12]

Beriberi and Vitamin B in Indochina

The science of food in the colonies as it pertained to indigenous people first focused on deficiency disease. When colonial medical experts turned their attention to indigenous diet in the late nineteenth century, they concentrated on soldiers, workers, and prisoners almost exclusively. Soldiers and workers performed services directly for Europeans. It was in the interest of doctors and administrators to keep them not only alive but also as productive as possible. Unlike the general population, these groups were under direct French supervision. Their health conditions and dietary habits could be easily observed. They often lived on fixed rations, making them especially prone to deficiency diseases, as well as making it easier for experts to monitor and control their diet.

One of the earliest sustained investigations of indigenous nutritional health focused on beriberi. The disease, as colonial physicians did not yet know, is caused by a deficiency of vitamin B1, or thiamin. The observation of soldiers, workers, and prisoners, who were often fed rations composed almost exclusively of polished rice, led tropical health experts to a preoccupation with beriberi. In rice, thiamin is contained almost entirely in the germ and in the pericarp, the thin layer between the husk and the grain, both of which are eliminated in the processing of white rice. For this reason, rice-eating populations suffered from beriberi at extremely high rates.

Physicians had speculated that beriberi was related to food since at least the early nineteenth century, but it was Japanese surgeon Kanehiro Takaki who first demonstrated the correlation. Between 1883 and 1887, he was able to drastically reduce the prevalence of the disease in the Japanese navy by replacing sailors' diet of white rice with a more varied one that included meat, milk, and vegetables. Takaki believed that beriberi was a protein deficiency addressed by the more varied foods.[13] This view would be revised after the discovery of vitamin B, but the practical efficacy of diet in treating beriberi was widely accepted.

In the 1890s, Dutch colonial experts building on Takaki's research directly implicated white rice in the development of beriberi. Dutch doctor Christiaan Eijkman experimented on chickens in Java to demonstrate that a diet of unprocessed rather than polished rice vastly reduced the risk of the disease. Eijkman would win the 1929 Nobel Prize in Medicine for this work.[14] Turning Eijkman's insights about chickens to people, physician Adolphe Vorderman used data on prisoners in the Dutch East Indies to study the relationship between diet and disease. Vorderman realized that the different rations used in different prisons made for a natural experiment in which inmates could be divided into three groups: one group subsisting on polished rice, one on whole rice, and one on a mixed diet of both. In the group eating whole rice, the rate of beriberi was one in ten thousand. In the group eating polished rice, it was one in thirty-nine.[15] The Dutch work showing that beriberi was strongly correlated to white rice diets sparked a lively international debate about what exactly that relationship was.

After the experiments in the Dutch East Indies, most scientists accepted that beriberi was somehow related to rice consumption. They could not agree, though, on whether the disease stemmed solely from poor diet, was a contagious infection or a toxin triggered by the consumption of rice, or was actually caused by eating rice via, perhaps, a parasite.[16] Those who advocated the "dietary theory" were hard-pressed to explain the correlation. Some experts attributed beriberi to diets low in phosphoric acid, others to a lack of fat or protein. Whatever the precise mechanism, it became clear to colonial health professionals from observation of indigenous people and experiments on animals that removing the husk of rice vastly increased the risk of beriberi.[17]

In the French Empire, beriberi was often observed among people who lived on fixed rations. Nowhere was it more prevalent than in the prisons of Indochina. The island prison of Poulo Condore off the coast of Cochinchina was one of the main sites of observation. Prison regulations mandated a varied diet that included protein, vegetables, and fish sauce as well as rice. But the quality of the food was poor and the regulations were routinely ignored.[18] Several "epidemics" of the disease were recorded. Between October and December of 1897, 550 prisoners died, 405 of them from beriberi. Officials attributed the epidemic to a poor diet of rice and salt fish, as well as to poor hygienic and moral conditions. One doctor observed that promising prisoners an early release helped rid them of the disease.[19] In 1900, the prevalence of beriberi among prisoners on Poulo Condore was 391 per 1,000, with a death rate of 193 per 1,000. Prison authorities ordered a general improvement of diet and sanitation, and the outbreak was brought under control.[20] In the summer of 1906, 105 inmates, about a fifth of the prison population, died of beriberi. Prison officials thought they were dealing with a contagious parasite. They disinfected the camp and treated patients with purgatives and arsenic. When this failed, officials gave heed to observations from other French and Dutch colonial prisons and replaced the polished rice in prisoner rations with whole rice. This had both curative and prophylactic effects.[21] Following this episode, whole rice was definitively substituted for white rice, substantially reducing the occurrence of beriberi on the island.[22]

While the empirical effects of dietary treatment became increasingly accepted in the tropical medicine community, the disease mechanism remained mysterious. A commission set up to collect and analyze findings on beriberi at the 1910 meeting of the Society for Exotic Pathology in Paris agreed that a diet composed primarily of white rice was a necessary condition of the disease, though commission members continued to disagree on the cause.[23] Participants at the Far Eastern Association of Tropical Medicine in Hong Kong in 1912 came to a similar conclusion.[24] The next year, experts at the Third Biennial Congress of the Association of Tropical Medicine stated the dietary case more strongly, concluding that "beriberi results from insufficiency in the diet of certain chemical substances not yet determined" that existed in unhulled or partially hulled rice but not in polished rice.[25] Despite disagreement over what the disease actually was, dietary prophylactic and therapeutic measures such as the consumption of whole rice, mung beans, and other "replacement foods" were almost universally accepted as a remedy.[26]

The key to the mystery was the "chemical substances not yet determined." In 1912, Polish-born scientist Casimir Funk, who was influenced by Eijkman's work in the Dutch East Indies, reported that he had cured pigeons suffering from beriberi using a substance isolated from the residue of rice processing that he called a "vital amine."[27] It took a few years for this discovery to affect French colonial expertise. In 1920, a short notice appeared in a French colonial medical journal stating that "accessory dietary factors," or "vitamins," were necessary to avoid "deficiency disease." The fact that the quotation marks were in the original highlights the newness of these concepts. Three factors were identified, tellingly described in relation to the diseases they prevented: an anti-rickets factor, an anti-beriberi factor, and an anti-scurvy factor. The anti-beriberi "growth factor B" could be found in plants, in eggs, and, crucially, in the germ of cereals such as rice. When in the 1920s vitamin B was recognized to be several distinct vitamins, B1 was initially called "aneurin" for its anti-neuritic, or anti-beriberi, properties.[28]

This was a tremendous physiological discovery, but its impact on French colonial medicine remained limited. Even after the elusive element found in whole but not in polished rice had been identified, debate continued through the 1930s over whether vitamin B deficiency caused beriberi or merely exacerbated it.[29] On a practical level, basic measures for fighting the disease had been known empirically for some time before the discovery of its etiology. Cases continued to occur among prisoners and workers not from lack of knowledge but from lack of will.

In Indochina, officials recorded a huge rise in cases of beriberi through the first four decades of the twentieth century.[30] There are several possible reasons for the increase, including more widespread use of machine-processed rather than hand-processed white rice, increased concentration of plantation workers under European supervision, and an administration progressively more effective at recording statistics. As more women went to work on European-run plantations, the understanding of their susceptibility to beriberi changed. In the early twentieth century, women were thought to be less vulnerable to the disease than men. By the 1930s, physicians believed that that post-partum women were at particular risk.[31] This suggests that the increase in cases reflected better observation as much as more beriberi. What is clear is that knowledge of the cause and cure did not necessarily lead to more effective care. Professor of medicine Charles Richet's embarrassed 1933 confession that "The day we want to, we will make it disappear" indicates that if new scientific knowledge was an essential ingredient in the expansion of state responsibility for food, it was not by itself sufficient.[32] It was not until a decade after the discovery of vitamin B that the French were motivated to discuss the implications of nutrition science for colonial rule in a systematic way. This impetus came not from medical progress or humanitarian sentiment, but from colonial economics.

Nutrition and Human Capital in French Equatorial Africa

Understandings of vitamins were initially limited to their role in preventing specific deficiency diseases, but soon came to occupy a central place in physiology and public health. Soldiers and prisoners continued to be a focus of dietetics in the colonies, but the major developments in colonial nutrition came in the realm of labor. In the 1920s, a new field of analysis relating to workers linked the emerging knowledge of nutrition to colonial administration. Medical experts concerned with labor began to apply physiological insights to the management of collectivities. While administrators never fully followed through on the proposals of experts, the moment marked an acknowledgment that the problem of hunger, conceived in increasingly complex ways, came under the purview of both science and administration. Experts, including physicians and pharmacists attached to the military, the colonial medical service, and metropolitan institutions, all became involved in colonial policy through their study of nutrition, sometimes in an official capacity, sometimes lobbying from the outside.

Nutrition broadened from a science of individuals to a science of collectivities through the concept of race. In the 1920s, physicians and scientists thinking about labor productivity applied biochemical knowledge to the management of races, not only as aggregates of individuals but as unitary objects of analysis that opened up new possibilities for diagnosis and policy. Colonial experts began to think about nutrition in terms of the improvement of races as well as the healing of bodies. Hygienists had long expressed fears of the degeneration of white people in hot climates. Now, experts reversed this logic to attempt the regeneration of "black" and "yellow" races.[33] Diet as it related to racial collectivities was a bridge between the strictly medical idea of nutrition as therapy and prophylaxis for deficiency diseases and the understanding of nutrition as public health that emerged in the 1930s and took the population as its object.

In the 1920s, health and humanitarian concerns were secondary to how diet related to economic production. Experts saw nutrition as a new solution to the intractable problem of capitalism that labor is attached to bodies. Health or quality of life benefits were side effects of the maximization of labor potential.[34] The idea of "human capital," which was central to Minister of Colonies Albert Sarraut's economic development program (mise en valeur), was a major impetus for changes in food policies as administrations became concerned with both the quantity and the quality of labor. This was reflected in anxieties about worker inefficiency and general depopulation.[35] Officials measured success not in medical or humanitarian terms, but by the metric of aggregate labor power.

One might expect that nutritional concerns would have arisen in the colonies of the Sahel, the site of the huge famine of 1913, but this was not the case. Instead, diet was of special interest in areas where the colonial administration and private European firms extracted value directly from indigenous labor, such as Gabon and Congo in French Equatorial Africa, rather than primarily through tax revenue as in the Sahel. The medical interest in workers' nutrition in AEF coincided with two economic developments. The first was a labor shortage related to an intensification of the lumber trade in the Gabon estuary following the collapse of global rubber prices after World War I. The second was the massive, and massively brutal, construction of the Congo-Ocean Railway between 1921 and 1934.[36] This period marked the first systematic interest in the alimentary dynamics of collectivities in the modern French Empire.

Like many colonies, French Equatorial Africa had little coherence as an administrative unit. Many parts of Chad, for example, had more in common with Sahelian Niger and Soudan than with the Congolese and Gabonese rain forests they were grouped with. The French approach to colonization in AEF, officially created in 1909, was different than in French West Africa (Afrique Occidentale Française, AOF). The first official French incursions into equatorial Africa were undertaken in the 1870s and 1880s by the celebrity explorer Pierre Savorgnan de Brazza. In 1898, the French legislature began doling out the territory that would become AEF as concessions to private companies. Soon, 80 percent of the colonies of Gabon, Middle Congo (contemporary Republic of Congo), and Ubangi-Shari (contemporary Central African Republic) was in the hands of private firms. Though the reign of the companies was somewhat curtailed in the early twentieth century, they remained economically dominant until the 1930s. The companies were coercive, controlling inhabitants using private militias backed by the colonial state. They were even allowed to collect taxes in the manner of governments.[37] The organization of territory into private sovereignties that viewed inhabitants primarily as a labor force had momentous human consequences. The population of AEF declined drastically from the 1880s, regaining its precolonial strength only in the 1930s.[38]

For French people, AEF became synonymous with depopulation. The Antillean-born novelist René Maran, the first Black person to win the prestigious Prix Goncourt literary award in 1921, witnessed many evils as an administrator in Ubangi-Shari, but was particularly affected by population decline.[39] In the early 1920s, Protestant missionaries working in Gabon likewise reported a decrease in population and a reduction in adherents due to the lumber trade and "general famine." Inhabitants abandoned villages and fled to the forest to escape harassment by soldiers demanding food, taxes, and labor.[40] Employees of the lumber companies and the railroad died "in very great numbers, and those that return home are in a pitiable state." Bananas, once ubiquitous, had become "almost mythological."[41] Famine became "a chronic and incurable sickness."[42] According to missionaries, Gabonese blamed the crisis on irrational administrators, and some wondered if all white people needed their brains examined.[43] Administrators, in turn, blamed hunger on the destruction of crops by elephants and other wild animals, as well as farmers distracted from food production by cash cropping or other business opportunities.[44] The problem of food supply was deemed "the most urgent." Officials hoped that despite their tendency to waste days in idleness and nights in dancing, natives could be forced to feed themselves on pain of severe punishment.[45]

In 1925, Governor-General of AEF Raphaël Antonetti delivered a speech in Brazzaville advocating "measures to protect the indigenous population, and to protect it, I regret to say, as much from its indolence, its improvidence, as against the natural elements that we have too often blamed." He was reacting to the fact that in coastal areas of Gabon, Africans had pivoted from food production to the lumber trade, forcing them to rely on imports to survive. Those who still grew food sold it all at once to the lumber workers and spent the money, Antonetti claimed, on parties. Within a few weeks, they were on the verge of starving to death. A sudden drop in the price of timber, he noted, would plunge the entire population into a state of dearth. Since Africans did not have the maturity to avoid famine, "that chronic sickness of the forest populations," it was the duty of administrators to protect "these big children." Antonetti informed officials that their first responsibility was food supply. Even the collection of taxes, the fulfillment of contracts, and the freedom of commerce should be subordinated to subsistence. Dearth, Antonetti threatened administrators, would be considered a crime. Though such an attitude admittedly countered the "modern spirit," he thought that the suspension of liberal doctrine was justified in a situation next to which "what we call 'the dark ages' seems a joyful dawn."[46] Even as Antonetti scolded subordinates and subjects, his own leadership of the Congo-Ocean railroad construction project contributed to hunger in a major way.[47]

French officials blamed the shortage of good quality workers for public and private enterprises on famine and poor diet. Medical practitioners in AEF and France felt that the colonial health service should have a "preponderant voice" in the solution.[48] As with colonial nutrition in general, deficiency disease was the entry point into the broader problem of diet and labor in AEF. Whereas in Indochina the interest in deficiency disease had been primarily physiological, medical experts writing about AEF considered the problem one of labor. In 1922, for example, a consortium of French firms working a forest concession in Gabon had been nearly put out of business by beriberi, which afflicted 192 of 750 workers. Because food containing vitamin B was unavailable, the sick were treated with palm oil, boiled bananas, and arsenic (kept on hand primarily to treat trypanosomiasis, or sleeping sickness) in an attempt to "accelerate general nutrition."[49]

The problem of deficiency disease among workers led experts to the problem of general depopulation in AEF, always from the perspective of the "labor question." They sought to address what they saw as a "crisis of quantity and quality" of unskilled labor. They complained that AEF struggled to produce workers of even average physical health. The medical officers charged with examining the fitness of potential workers eliminated 40 to 50 percent of candidates for "physiological misery." Men were generally frail and poorly developed, with no muscle strength and in a "defective state of nutrition."[50] Administrators and medical experts who saw the population of AEF as a labor reservoir were anxious to preserve their human capital. Poor diet had to be addressed, they believed, because it contributed to declining birth rates, high infant and adult mortality, cannibalism, and sleeping sickness—all threats to a labor pool that was rapidly shrinking.[51] One physician emphasized the stakes of the crisis, warning, "It is the economic future of the country that is at risk."[52]

The poor physiological condition of workers was uniformly attributed to inadequate food. Like Africans themselves, Africans' diets were seen as insufficient in quantity and poor in quality. They were especially deficient in protein and fat. Other health problems stemmed from this principal cause, as poor diet led to increased vulnerability to diseases such as the dreaded sleeping sickness. Mass starvation was an increasing concern. Without drastic action, experts warned, it was a question of when rather than if the Black races would go extinct.[53]

The first urgent steps required little by way of nutritional sophistication. The French administration simply had to supply the calories that Africans could not or would not obtain for themselves. Once the danger of imminent extinction was averted, the focus could turn to development. This required addressing qualitative as well as quantitative dietary deficiencies by bringing economics and agriculture into line with the physiological insights of scientists. Both short-term rescue action and long-term food policy required chemical analyses of local foods to ascertain what vitamins, minerals, and other elements were missing from the diet. The more optimistic experts believed that once the deficiencies were known, the problem could be easily solved through better cultivation of protective foods and the enrichment of common products such as table salt with the missing dietetic elements.[54]

Embedded in this discourse on the quality and quantity of the labor pool was a particular conception of race. In France, race had long coexisted uneasily with a republican universalism that privileged voluntary association over hereditary descent.[55] The perplexities of race were compounded by the enduring influence of Jean-Baptiste Lamarck, the French naturalist who died in 1829 and theorized that characteristics acquired during an organism's lifetime could be transmitted to offspring. Many French scientists held fast to Lamarckian transformism through the 1930s even as it was supplanted elsewhere by Mendelian inheritance.[56]

In the years between the world wars, debates about race became increasingly polarized. Some biologists and social scientists thought race signified nothing of importance, while others believed it to be the basis of biological and social existence. Reacting to the scientific racism of right-wing researchers, which related individual and civilizational capacity to essential biological characteristics, a strain of European biologists and anthropologists insisted that race was a biologically arbitrary designation. They argued that groups commonly referred to as races were in fact unified by culture, language, nationality, or nothing at all.[57]

Nutritionists now added a new possibility: human differences could be explained by diet. Nutrition provided a new approach to the French obsession with racial decline that emerged after the Franco-Prussian War ended in 1871.[58] In contrast to a British Malthusianism that stressed the dangers of overpopulation in relation to food supply, French patriots and savants fretted about the declining quantity and quality of the French population.[59] Though this concern was originally with the French race as compared to the German one, the Lamarckian-tinged understanding of the degeneration and regeneration of biological collectivities influenced colonial thinking.[60]

Expanding an earlier focus on individual physiology, nutrition in AEF took the "black races" as its target. Medical authorities interpreted depopulation as a problem of racial degeneration. The successes of using food to cure deficiency diseases such as beriberi and scurvy suggested the possibility of rejuvenating races in danger of extinction. Rejecting rigid race essentialism, French physicians studying AEF turned to diet to perfect the character of Africans by making them more active, more provident, and, most crucially, more productive. This view of a nutritional basis for the physical and mental characteristics of races was transitional between nutrition as a problem of individual deficiency disease and nutrition as a problem of public health.

Observations of colonial subjects who served as soldiers in France during World War I gave experts evidence that racial degeneration could be counteracted with better diet. One researcher found that Indochinese and Malagasy soldiers who were fed European diets became bigger, stronger, happier, and more alert than their poorly fed compatriots at home. The soldiers' level of activity, and therefore their economic productivity, became far superior to that of natives in their natural conditions. These changes were not permanent, however: "Leaving sickly and puny, those who were able to adapt . . . returned vigorous and healthy; then, several years later, seized by misery, they reverted to the same physical degeneration as before."[61] Such observations were very promising for physicians looking for ways to improve races that had often been considered immutable.

An understanding of race as malleable allowed French experts to formulate the problem of depopulation in AEF as one of racial degeneration due to malnutrition. Arguing that races that had been understood as inherently incapable of work were in fact perfectible, they turned to scientifically informed diet to make Africans more productive. This project was articulated in the language of business. If the French invested calories, protein, and vitamins in the colonies, they could hope for remuneration in the future. If the autochthonous races remained incapable of generating wealth, there was no economic hope for the empire. Proper nutrition was an economic imperative, and medical experts applied themselves to achieving it with the least possible outlay of capital. Administrators and doctors felt that advances in nutrition made investing in racial improvement a bargain. The discovery of vitamins suggested that a healthy diet need not necessarily be composed of expensive foods such as meat and wine, but that it sufficed to complement ordinary indigenous diets with small and cheap doses of the accessory factors they lacked.[62] French colonials thought of Africans as, in the phrase of investigative journalist Albert Londres, "banana engines."[63] These were cheaper than gasoline engines, but they still needed to be fueled.

Proposed solutions to worker inefficiency and depopulation drew on nutrition science. One doctor revived an ancient observation that animals that ate meat were warlike and violent, while herbivores were pacific. He reasoned that introducing more meat into African diets would make Black races more robust and energetic. This presented a problem, as fresh meat was expensive and preserved meat lost a large proportion of its accessory factors. Both issues could be overcome by transporting the unused animal blood discarded by European butchers to Africa. Blood was cheap, was easily preserved without losing its vitamins, and had a remarkable effect on nutrition. It increased vivacity and appetite in animals, and there was no reason to think it would not do the same for humans. This would, in several generations, transform Black men into capable laborers who could finally extract value out of persistently unproductive colonies. Possibly expecting ridicule, this physician insisted that there was nothing utopian about his proposal, which was founded on rational observation and experimentation.[64]

In their anxiety about labor shortage, colonial administrators and private firms in AEF listened carefully to what experts said about diet and depopulation. In 1923 the new Academy of Colonial Sciences in Paris formed a commission led by the vice director of the Pasteur Institute, Albert Calmette, a former naval physician whose illustrious career was launched from Indochina.[65] Calmette was recognized as one of France's most important scientists for his role in developing the bacillus Calmette-Guérin vaccine against tuberculosis.[66] Anticipating the much larger Commission of Inquiry in the Overseas Territories of the late 1930s, Calmette's team sent questionnaires on indigenous diet to administrators, physicians, and scientists throughout the French Empire. These researchers were among the first to include famine in a spectrum of alimentary health ranging from normal nutrition to malnutrition to starvation. When the study ended in 1924, the conclusions were dire. Subjects throughout the empire rarely enjoyed a "normal" diet. Even in relatively prosperous areas, native imprudence combined with natural disaster to cause famine, as in the 1913 catastrophe that "cost Chad half its population." In Madagascar, most of the island's races were on the verge of regression and extinction. Even in Asia, where the quantity of food was sufficient, diets often lacked essential elements such as vitamins and protein.[67] The alimentary situation was bad everywhere France ruled, but nowhere was it worse than in Equatorial Africa. The uniquely desperate state of AEF led Calmette's commission to declare the region "in danger" and beg the French government to rescue it at any cost.[68]

Calmette's study resonated with colonial administrators' concerns about the economic viability of the empire. Minister of Colonies Édouard Daladier

circulated the study to the colonial governors, along with instructions directing them to formulate a "veritable dietary policy" that took account of qualitative as well as quantitative needs.[69] Each colony was charged with conducting
laboratory analyses of indigenous staples to determine the specific nutritional
deficiencies to be addressed.[70] To make sure that colonial pharmacists had the
requisite expertise, they would be required to undertake training in laboratories specializing in nutrition during leaves in France. Once the particular deficiencies in vitamins, minerals, carbohydrates, or other dietetic factors were
established, administrations could take appropriate measures. Daladier suggested introducing condiments such as protein-rich Vietnamese fish sauce or
fortifying salt and sugar with the missing vitamins or minerals.

Daladier acknowledged that the "strongest arms" belonged to those who
ate meat, as it was rich in the protein needed for the growth and maintenance
of muscle tissue. However, nutrition science suggested other and cheaper ways
to strengthen arms. Inexpensive protein was seen as a promising way to regenerate human capital. Great hope was placed in plans to intensify local fishing industries, as well as in educational programs to promote cooking
techniques that retained this food's considerable nutrients.[71] The National Museum of Natural History started a program in Paris to train Cameroonians in
proper fishing and cooking techniques, who would then serve as teachers for
their compatriots.[72] With such programs, the colonial state would assure "the
physiological development of the races" even in environments that did not
naturally provide for a healthy diet.[73] These proposals reflected a new preoccupation with proper nutrition, though still primarily in the context of labor.

In the mid-1920s, Minister Daladier established a set of rules to protect the
health of laborers on public and private enterprises, to "assure the conserva-
tion of a labor force all the more precious as it becomes less abundant." The
regulations included a system for triaging workers based on fitness for hard
labor and provided for travel to and from work sites. They required the inoc-
ulation of workers against common diseases, and mandated hygienic services
such as water purification and waste evacuation. They even attended to
"moral" considerations, recommending diversions such as wrestling matches
and footraces on days off. Food occupied a central place in these rules. Rations had to be served in kind based on standards set for soldiers, sufficiently
nourishing to allow for the most difficult work. The motivations for these
regulations were explicitly economic. An abundant and healthy diet was the
essential condition for obtaining maximum labor output. Before returning
home, workers were to be examined by a doctor one final time, as healthy
men were essential for the regeneration of their race. Healthy and abundant

races would in turn facilitate future recruitment and assure an easier exploitation of colonial resources.[74] Food policy emerged as a way to maximize labor for colonial administrations and businesses.

Daladier's food policy for the most part remained a dead letter. Medical conditions on the work sites of the Congo-Ocean railroad show that even the most basic solutions were beyond the reach of both the colonial administration and private firms.[75] The governor-general of AEF mandated a minimum daily ration that included a carbohydrate staple, fish or meat, oil, and salt, with the expectation that fresh fruits and vegetables would be distributed whenever possible. In practice, the lack of supplies meant that the minimum ration was rarely met. Supervisors complained that "parasites" such as friends and wives appropriated nutrients meant for employees. Improper preparation made the food both unappetizing and less nutritious. Worker diets were severely deficient in calories, protein, and vitamins. As construction progressed, local food shortfalls were addressed by importing polished rice. Workers suffered increasingly from beriberi, blindness due to vitamin A deficiency, and a condition known only as physiological misery, which referred to men too emaciated to work.[76]

The more conscientious among French observers recognized the humanitarian implications of equating life with labor. One doctor warned, "It is dangerous to consider this continent a reservoir of men."[77] Lieutenant-Colonel Gaston Muraz, head of the Gabon Medical Service for part of this hungry period, wrote about his experiences in 1933. Influenced by the investigative journalism of Albert Londres, whom he had met in Equatorial Africa, Muraz insisted on the importance of total honesty in exposing the inhumanity of colonialism.[78] He described harrowing scenes of famine radiating for hundreds of miles from the epicenter of the Congo-Ocean work sites. He commented that in attempting to construct a nervous system around the new railroad, the French had forgotten that "in a black world the *bellies* of individuals must be full so that the whole organism can realize its potential."[79] The first one hundred kilometers of the railroad, Muraz estimated, cost seventeen thousand lives.[80] Of these, he believed that 13 percent were directly related to poor diet, not accounting for diminished resistance to infection. He added that in the eight years since the Academy of Colonial Sciences had declared AEF "in danger," so little had changed in terms of diet that the warning was more apt now than when it was first issued.[81]

The French administration in AEF failed to act effectively in the face of this decade-long food crisis, but the sense of responsibility for the alimentary health of subjects was growing stronger. In 1933, the administrator-ethnographer Henri Labouret wrote that it was not enough that workers on public and private enterprises benefit from a normal diet. The scope must be expanded to "the whole of colonial populations."[82] While journalists and reformers continued to write about how unscrupulous administrations and firms perpetuated chronic hunger in AEF through the 1930s, scientists and physicians expanded their focus to the international sphere.[83] From its use as a tool for the improvement of races to maximize labor power, nutrition developed into a principle of social organization at the level of population.

International Gastrotechnics

In the 1920s, French administrators and scientific experts saw nutrition as a way to increase the economic productivity of the colonies. In the 1930s, there emerged a global vision of nutrition focused on the well-being of humanity. Europeans who had thought of colonial subjects as individuals governed by physiology or as homogenous races ruled by biological and ethnographic characteristics began to see them as societies, best understood through social scientific analysis and population dynamics. Colonial populations, considered as holistic and internally differentiated social formations, became the target of nutritional analysis and policy for the first time.

As nutrition expanded the purview of state power over food outward to encompass population, it also focused it inward to incorporate human biochemistry. The social no longer stopped at the skin but was articulated seamlessly to internal bodily processes. This profoundly altered conceptions of what was subject to social forces and what was insulated from them. These new domains of state power had significant implications for the French Empire's sense of responsibility for hunger and famine.

The physiological discoveries that revolutionized modern nutrition science were global, incorporating experimental knowledge and analysis from around the world. In the international organizations of interwar Europe, these discoveries were elaborated into new ways of thinking about public health. Following the discovery of vitamin B in 1912, physiological knowledge was integrated into technopolitical practices. Nutrition became an expansive discourse shared by natural scientists, social scientists, politicians, and administrators. The broadest conception of nutrition implied a global program for the organization of society centered on individual biological needs, encompassing economic, medical, ecological, and cultural elements of life. Nutrition became a plan for the management of populations as well as for the care of individuals, the basis of the body and of the body social.

As scientists learned more about human metabolism, food consumption was increasingly seen as a problem of state management. During World War I, nations faced the logistical challenges of feeding armies of unprecedented size. In the process, they demonstrated the possibility of directing the production and distribution of food on a larger scale than ever before. The French biologist André Mayer wrote of the war, "We learned that science, which permits us domination over nature, permits us also domination over the machinery of states, over their material organization."[84] The logistics of modern warfare made it possible to imagine using state power to manage food in a way previously unthinkable.

If the Great War brought food under the technical control of states, it was the Great Depression that politicized it. The reduction in living standards that accompanied the crash intensified anxieties about the health of Europeans just as nutrition science was gaining credibility. Diet came to be understood not only as a medical issue affecting individuals, but as a social problem related to income inequality, public education, and state welfare programs. The nutritional efficacy of the free market came to be doubted since consumer demand did not necessarily correspond to biological needs. Experts proposed planning global agriculture around the principles of nutrition for a more rational production and distribution of nutrients. Government food policy would no longer be merely reactive, invoked only in emergency situations. It would be systematic, encompassing political economy, agronomy, medicine, and culture.[85] Nutrition even theoretically penetrated the intimacy of domestic life as private economic choices and optimum cooking practices became a matter of administrative and scientific concern, what one expert called "gastrotechnics."[86] The new knowledge of nutrition made the consumption of food a question of social welfare and public health.

Nation-states were understood to have an essential role to play in bringing society and biology into harmony, but malnutrition was not confined by political borders. The scope of the problem required an international framework to establish best practices and coordinate policy. In the 1920s and 1930s, a number of international organizations were formed to organize research on nutritional themes. The focus was originally on Europe, but as transnationalism became a defining part of the nutritional project, participants looked increasingly to tropical, subtropical, and hot countries. The work associated with the largest of the interwar international organizations, such as the League of Nations, the International Institute of Agriculture, and the Red Cross, had a significant impact on scientific opinion and state policy.

Nutrition as a global framework oriented around individual physiology became a driving force of the League of Nations' work. The league devoted increasing energy to the nutrition problem through the 1920s, leading to the influential 1935 report *Nutrition and Public Health* by the Franco-British duo Étienne Burnet and Wallace Aykroyd. Both researchers would go on to study nutrition in their respective countries' empires, Burnet in Tunisia and Aykroyd in India. Their report put the physiology of individuals at the center of a holistic vision of global society.[87] The authors conceptualized nutrition as a public health problem requiring a multidisciplinary approach much broader than the medical care of individuals. They laid out an ambitious program for further research that included questions of a scientific nature, such as determining the precise role of protein in human growth, and social tasks such as establishing usable dietary standards and assessing the nutritional state of children. The report, though expansive, was concerned exclusively with Europe and "countries with a western civilization." It acknowledged that the problem of nutrition was especially acute in Asia, Africa, and tropical countries generally, but non-European regions could not be considered due to the lack of data.[88]

After the publication of Burnet and Aykroyd's 1935 report, the League of Nations established the Mixed Committee, an international, interdisciplinary group of experts charged with looking into the dietetic and economic aspects of "the nutrition problem." According to the Mixed Committee, malnutrition was rampant all over the globe and among all social classes. Reflecting new tenets of nutrition as an organizing principle of social and biological life, the committee considered malnutrition not merely a humanitarian problem but one that threatened the fundamental structure of nations. It was thus the duty of public authorities everywhere to formulate a "nutrition policy" to orient society toward the fulfillment of individual physiological needs. The crux of this policy would be the management of the production, distribution, and consumption of protective foods, the foods high in vitamin and mineral content that enabled people to fulfill their physical and mental potential and to resist disease.

Like Burnet and Aykroyd, the Mixed Committee insisted that improving nutrition required state guidance. Nutrition policy should be directed toward two mutually dependent aims: consumption, or "bringing the foods which modern physiology has shown to be essential for health and physical development within the reach of all sections of the community," and supply, or rationalizing agriculture and commerce for the production and distribution of healthy food.[89] Proper family nutrition involved both adequate income and adequate education on how to purchase and prepare a healthy diet. Malnutrition, the committee argued, was linked to income inequality, so any effective nutritional policy must include social insurance and income redistribution programs.[90] While insisting that the protection of free markets was a priority, the committee also recommended supply-side interventions to increase the production of protective foods.[91]

At the level of the individual, the Mixed Committee advocated for the "optimum diet" rather than mere "minimum nutrition." The optimum diet would provide for "the full development of the individual for efficiency without exhaustion and for his resistance to disease." Though eliminating deficiency disease would be a more ostentatious achievement, the committee argued that the greater social good would come from eliminating the less acute but more widespread forms of malnutrition that caused inferior physical development, nervous instability, poor endurance, fatigue, diminished resistance to infection, and premature aging.[92] This was a critical step in the understanding of nutrition as the basis of individual and social health rather than simply the prevention or cure of specific diseases.

Experts in nutrition advocated for strong welfare states, but action could not be confined to individual nations. The nature of the problem implied internationalism, and the international point of view brought new solutions into focus. Only international experts had the scope of vision needed to organize the work undertaken by states into a coherent global plan. This interdisciplinary and international coordination was supposed to mirror the scale and complexity of the nutrition problem itself. It was up to national governments to integrate universities, armies, banks, food regulations, and even cinema and radio into their nutritional policies. The League of Nations would then orchestrate national initiatives into a harmonious global plan.[93]

At the meeting of the International Scientific Congress on Nutrition (Congrès Scientifique International de l'Alimentation) of 1937, whose distinguished participants included Nobel laureates, French ministers, and the nutritionist Étienne Burnet, experts emphasized scientific optimism and global interconnection. In the previous hundred years, they enthused, the relationship of humans to food had changed radically as biochemical knowledge progressed. The biologist André Mayer declared in his opening remarks, "The science of nutrition, like all the sciences, renders us, in the words of Descartes, 'masters and possessors of nature.' But here, it is a question of our own nature."[94] Using nutrition to control nature required attending to its economic and social implications, involving agriculture, livestock farming, manufacturing, food preservation, and logistics. The purpose of the congress was to find ways to integrate physiological and social policies for the health and economic benefit of all.

Étienne Burnet posited that nutrition was as much a social science as a natural one, a project of global social justice as much as one of public health. Quoting his own report with Aykroyd, Burnet emphasized the synergy between, and even the identity of, scientific and social thought. The Great Depression had made the link between health and economics undeniable: "The global crisis has called attention to the gap that almost everywhere separates nutritional needs, determined by physiology, and their means of satisfaction permitted by economic conditions." In a discussion that was supposed to focus on the physiological aspects of nutrition, he asked, "What obligations does it impose on governments? What are the effects of the economic crisis, of partial famines, of unemployment?"[95] For Burnet and like-minded thinkers, scientific questions automatically implied social and ethical ones, and these at an international scale.

The nutrition problem was totalizing and universal. It followed that its solutions must be as well. This was where international organizations had a role to play. Though managing diet at a global scale would have seemed "superhuman" to previous generations, modern science provided both the scope of vision and the social engineering tools to accomplish the task. The organizers of the 1937 International Conference for the Protection Against Natural Disaster proclaimed that by uniting technical knowledge with "humanitarian and philanthropic" notions of international solidarity, it would finally be possible to "tear from nature the veil of mystery with which it has jealously concealed, for thousands of years, the causes and rhythms of its most deadly attacks against the human species." In an even bolder formulation, the conferees sought "to correct the imperfections, the errors, of Nature."[96]

If the project of rationalizing nutrition was superhuman in Europe, it was doubly so in the disadvantaged colonies. The former French colonial administrator Georges Hardy saw the situation as so desperate that he adapted the gastronome Jean Anthelme Brillat-Savarin's famous phrase "Tell me what you eat and I will tell you what you are" into "Tell me *if* you eat. . . ."[97] But participants in international conferences felt that modern science and European generosity were up to the task. The physician Charles Richet, son of the Nobel Prize–winning eugenicist of the same name who would be imprisoned at Buchenwald as a resistance fighter, claimed at a 1937 panel on "Diet in the Colonies" that it was the first time that experts in colonial nutrition had assembled to demonstrate a "European solidarity" vis-à-vis "the European colonial empire."[98] Without denying the work yet to accomplish, Richet related the story of colonialism as one of ineluctable progress. The colonial situation one hundred years earlier could have been summarized by a single word: famine. The efforts of soldiers, administrators, and physicians, he asserted, had suppressed such crises. As successful as the heroes of empire had been at improving nutrition throughout the world, it was now the task of imperial nations to build on their progress by articulating and executing a coherent dietary policy, for "without proper nutrition, no civilization is possible." The "white race" had duties as well as rights in the colonies. The most important of these was to guarantee that every subject had enough to eat.[99]

The conceit of internationalism was that it could coordinate national policies into a single global project amounting to more than the sum of its parts.

To this end, international organizations developed liaisons not only with national governments but also directly with colonial administrations. The relationship was meant to be mutually beneficial. The organizations received raw data from the colonies and used it to generate studies that would help colonial administrations improve subjects' quality of life. In this way, the colonies were integrated into a transnational flow of dietary knowledge. The Rome-based International Institute of Agriculture (IIA) saw itself as the hub of a network that centralized and analyzed information from all over the world. It worked closely with the League of Nations on nutrition in Europe but was also involved in tropical regions. In 1932, the IIA's president accused the governor-general of AOF of shirking his scientific responsibilities and asked for information on indigenous agriculture. The data would be presented in Rome at the IIA's 1932 conference on the theme of the global Great Depression. In exchange for the raw data, the IIA would share its findings on colonial agronomy.[100]

Another planned event, the International Congress of Tropical and Subtropical Agriculture's March 1939 conference in Italian Libya, showcased the ambition of international science even as it foreshadowed its collapse. The five-day meeting was to unite experts on hot countries to debate problems of agriculture and economics. The event was equal parts scientific conference, vacation, and Fascist spectacle. The itinerary interspersed talks and dinners with side trips to Roman ruins, excursions to desert oases, and tours of laboratories. In the promotional pamphlet, photographs of classical ruins, cutting-edge Italian research facilities, and portraits of King Victor Emmanuel III and Benito Mussolini undermined the spirit of internationalism even while participating in it. It does not appear that the event took place.[101]

In preparation for the conference, the congress sent questionnaires directly to colonial administrations. It asked about family gardens as a way to diversify indigenous diets, and about the role of scientists and doctors in colonial administration. The responses from French West Africa varied in detail. The colony of Dahomey's response dodged the questions by claiming it simply implemented the government-general's regulations fixing the quantity, variety, and quality of agricultural products.[102] The response from Ivory Coast was more detailed, describing typical meals and differentiating food habits by region, ethnicity, and the two occupations of farmer and laborer.[103] Senegal's response was the most comprehensive, with separate reports from the different administrative services.[104] The agricultural service submitted information about crops and livestock, while the health service took a special interest in the nutritional intake of infants. Even the educational service weighed in with a summary of its agricultural training program.[105] This information, however, was never put to use. Adolph Hitler's invasion of Poland shattered the last remnants of interwar international cooperation.

Internationalism helped transform ideas of what states and the global community owed non-Western people. A new focus on responsibility toward humans as humans rather than as citizens or subjects opened up space for international organizations to influence sovereign empires. The international community had a responsibility to guarantee all humans a minimum standard of living. This now included proper nutrition. The well-being of colonial subjects, nominally under the protection of empires, became a concern for an international community of Western-style nations.[106]

The utopian tone of the international conferences contrasted starkly with the reality of nutrition in the colonies. Repeated references to the "mystique of international cooperation," awed wonder at the miracles of modern science, and sentimental celebrations of multicultural esteem gave the proceedings a self-satisfied air at odds with the urgency of the tasks at hand. The participation of Fascist Italy and Nazi Germany in these projects of international harmony is a reminder of just how unrealistic this vision was. Some participants recognized this, arguing that optimistic experts were too quick to consider the global management of food "within the domain of the possible."[107] Yet the formulation of the problem of famine in terms of international nutrition science had a profound impact on governance in the French Empire.

The Full Belly

The rise of international organizations focused on food put pressure on colonial administrators and scientists to address famine, while nutrition gave them a new vocabulary and conceptual tool kit with which to do so. In 1931, famines struck Niger and Indochina. The same year, the Great Depression began to be felt in France and its colonies. Incomes suffered from the collapse of world prices and from tax hikes as colonial administrations struggled to offset plummeting trade duties.[108] Famine and depression forced the French to confront colonial hunger just as nutritional concepts were gaining currency. Reflecting ideas of rational governance, administrators paid more attention to technical expertise, while experts oriented their studies toward policy as well as basic science. This marked the beginning of a modern conception of famine as at once physiological, economic, ecological, and political.

The same nutritional concerns that were being discussed in Europe animated science and policy debates overseas. Famine and hunger in the colonies came to be seen as socially immanent, determined by a complex tangle of factors related to food production, distribution, and metabolism. Policy proposals in the colonies produced only partial or nominal results. They did not amount to the reconfiguration of entire populations, economies, and environments that maximalist nutritional analysis called for. Nutrition did, though, contribute to new expectations for the care of the colonized.

French colonial administrations began to incorporate nutritional concepts into famine policy. At a basic level, this meant considering famine as a preventable problem stemming from state failure rather than as a tragic act of God. The issue took on a new aspect as experts began to see famine in all its social complexity. Where famine had been thought of primarily as lack of food, it was now understood to be a question of geographic and social distribution of food. Famine had been understood to be the result of external shocks such as drought or vermin, but observers now believed the determinants of famine were social and structural. At the level of the individual, starvation was now an extreme form of malnutrition rather than simple calorie deficiency. Following the insights of the new science of nutrition, it was up to enlightened administrations to institute coherent food policies that provided for the qualitative and quantitative food needs of colonial subjects. Many French people took this responsibility to heart. One expert wrote, "In a country where France assumes the protection of everybody, nobody must die of hunger."[109] In AOF, Governor-General Jules Carde called his package of antifamine measures "the policy of the full belly."[110]

Experts now saw starvation and malnutrition as elements of the same problem. Blurring the line between famine as event and condition, observers brought together social, physiological, and environmental approaches, subsuming it under the broader framework of nutrition. Analyses of malnutrition now considered the extreme form of famine, while famine research considered problems of vitamin deficiency and susceptibility to illness.[111] At a social level, famine was no longer categorically separate from dearth and plenty. At the level of medicine, starvation was no longer a problem of a separate order from malnutrition and normal health. Rather, these were now differences of degree. Physicians in Morocco, for example, called for the study of indigenous diet in times of both normality and shortage in search of insights that could be used to prevent famines and improve general quality of life. This would be done by ascertaining individual physiological needs, extrapolating to collectivities, and bringing resources into line with these needs. The doctors argued that the conditions of shortage were related to general living standards. They saw the increase of indigenous agricultural and artisanal production, the introduction and regulation of new marketable products, and the enforcement of a minimum wage as antifamine measures.[112]

Administrators moved beyond the standard of subsistence to account for the range of physiological states between starvation and health, and of social states between famine and plenty. This shift was expressed by Henri Labouret, the influential colonial administrator and ethnographer whose work with the Colonial School (École Coloniale), the National Institute for Oriental Languages and Civilizations (École Nationale des Langues Orientales Vivantes), and the London-based International Institute of African Languages and Cultures advocated for the utility of ethnography in administration.[113] Drawing on his years of experience in Africa, Labouret divided famines in the French Empire into two categories. "Accidental" famine occurred after unexpected shocks such as insect infestation, livestock disease, or war. "Chronic" famine resulted from the economics of afflicted regions. In the case of chronic famine, starvation was caused not primarily by crop failure, but by poor transportation and the weak purchasing power of certain social groups. Labouret distinguished dearth (*disette*) from famine proper. Dearth was a regular and expected seasonal scarcity to which populations learned to adapt. Famine was an unpredictable event, sometimes but not always the result of dearth. Labouret determined several harmful effects of alimentary insecurity, aggravated not only by the insouciance of indigenous people but also by the ignorance of responsible governments. These included low birthrate (*pauci-natalité*), heightened infant mortality, increased frequency of epidemics, and, more generally, the exacerbation of all afflictions.[114] This was very different than the simple distinction between sufficiency and famine, or between life and death, used as a standard in earlier decades, reflecting a more complex understanding of both social and individual health.

Many natural and social scientists no longer accepted previous dismissals of famine as the inevitable outcome of lazy races living in harsh environments, a circumstance that was unfortunate but about which nothing could be done. If some still argued that "Africa is hostile to man, especially to man of the black race which seems the least apt to confront her," this was no longer an excuse, but a problem to solve.[115] Reactivating insights from AEF a decade earlier, colonial experts working in an international context mounted new challenges to biologically essentialist views of human bodies. Unlike in AEF, these experts worked toward the well-being of subjects as well as the augmentation of labor. They argued, against the scientific racism of many researchers and the less scientific racism of many administrators, that bodies were changeable rather than given. They could be improved using the physiological and social principles of nutrition. In 1929, Georges Hardy, director of the Colonial School, the Paris institution that trained overseas administrators, drew on his experience as a functionary in West Africa to argue that what was commonly perceived as innate laziness was in fact due to a vicious circle: subjects ate poorly because they did not cultivate enough and did not cultivate enough because they were weak from malnourishment.[116] Albert Sarraut shared this view, writing in 1931, "The native is undernourished because he does not work, and he does not work because he is undernourished."[117] The characteristics that were often attributed to subject races—improvidence, laziness, physical frailty, and so on—were now considered to be symptoms of malnutrition to which white bodies were equally susceptible if they had the misfortune of living under similar conditions. One Belgian biochemist wrote, "If we ourselves had to settle for a ration of two thousand calories, we would be as lazy as the natives."[118]

The explanation of famine resulting from incompetent races interacting with harsh environments became unsatisfactory. However, colonial experts were reluctant to forego racial categories entirely, even as their evidence increasingly pointed toward the universality of human physiology. Race as an explanatory concept had staying power even if it was ultimately out of place in a nutritional paradigm.[119] Biologists did not dismiss the possibility of physiological characteristics particular to race. Differences in basal metabolic rates, for instance, might help explain other racial differences. Yet the scientists downplayed the importance of these differences, leaning toward social rather than physiological explanations for colonial conditions.[120]

Attempts to split the difference between nutritional and racial explanations of hunger led to some oddly inconsistent theories. In a joint publication, the influential French biologist Lucie Randoin accepted that the metabolic needs of different races were almost identical. Yet she also thought that "blacks" were extremely sensitive to changes in their diet while whites were less so, with "yellow" races occupying an intermediate position. These differences in nutritional adaptability had world-historical as well as physiological implications, explaining why certain races had conquered the world while others had been confined to their home regions by diet.[121] Randoin insisted that variations in diet between the races were due mostly to tradition and taste rather than different biological needs. But she also believed that whites were more resistant to malnutrition than Blacks were.[122] She suggested that these racial disparities in resistance to malnutrition might themselves result from differences in diet. Adhering to a distinctly French Lamarckian transformism that posited the heritability of acquired characteristics, she speculated that cancer and other illnesses could be attributed to the poor nutrition of previous generations. The flip side of this observation was that better nutrition could lead to health benefits that were transmitted through heredity, leading to more perfect races. She cited as evidence the observation that the descendants of Japanese immigrants to California were bigger than Japanese in their home islands. While this awkward analysis never quite reconciled biological race with modern nutrition, the practical takeaway was that science could control and improve colonized people. Randoin would later be a prominent voice in health policy under the Vichy regime.[123]

Nutrition as a framework for understanding populations, races, and bodies suggested solutions to problems that had long been thought unsolvable. Antifamine measures had usually been focused on total food production, informed by the standard of bare subsistence. Policies now moved beyond the metric of calorie availability as an indicator of hunger to account for quality and social distribution of food. In AOF and the Maghreb, Saharan herders such as the Tuareg had since the nineteenth century been considered exceptionally big, strong, and healthy.[124] The legendary vigor of the Tuareg was now attributed to dairy products that gave them an "infinite endurance," while the "apathy and indolence of his immediate neighbor, the black, eater of millet, are proverbial." This difference in energy was accounted for by the essential amino acids that Tuaregs obtained from milk and that were missing from the diets of their sedentary neighbors. The age-old problem of laziness among Black races could be easily solved by requiring every village in AOF to keep a herd of sheep or goats for dairy production.[125] Though this policy was never carried out, it is indicative of how nutritional thinking provided administrators with new tools while saddling them with new responsibilities.

Étienne Burnet expressed a similarly fluid view of race when he wrote that diet could explain problems of individual and social life among indigenous Tunisians. He attributed laziness, for example, to the fact that man, "not being able to adjust his food according to his work, is forced to adjust his work according to his food."[126] Other observers simply denied that negative racial characteristics were real. For Labouret, it was undeniable that the Sahel was especially prone to famine, but racial and environmental determinism could not be squared with empirical observation. The African "who recoils from the labor of the soil," he argued, was a cliché propagated by people who had not taken the trouble to learn about colonial subjects. Contrary to long European tradition, Labouret defended the capacity of African farmers to adapt to their difficult environments through extraordinary effort and specialized knowledge. He argued that what was seen as native laziness and improvidence was in many cases the result of onerous requisitions and the introduction of market crops to the detriment of food production.[127] Not all observers bothered to modify their rigid notions of race. Some continued to blame malnutrition and famine on the physiology and psychology of indigenous people, even as they embraced the social and economic solutions offered by modern nutrition.[128] But an increasing number of colonial experts were convinced that racial stereotypes, to the extent that they described reality, resulted at least partly from diet rather than innate biology.

The Guernut Commission of 1937, an unprecedented inquiry into colonial living conditions, represented the height of the reformulation of famine as a nutritional problem. Many of its experts understood nutrition not as mere epiphenomenon, but as an organizing principle of the social, leading the commission to conclusions that would have been impossible a mere decade previously. Colonial subjects were, in general, malnourished. They ate diets poor in vitamins and protein. This led not only to deficiency diseases, but also to poor average health and decreased resistance to infections. These shortcomings, caused by the monotony of regional diets overly reliant on carbohydrates, afflicted not just individuals but entire populations. To improve the health of the colonized, it was necessary to tailor diets to local conditions to ensure both nutritional balance and economic viability. Colonial administrators could work toward these goals by distributing milk to schoolchildren, encouraging the production of protective foods, and propagating the basics of culinary hygiene.[129] By the 1930s, colonial famine was seen as a problem that could be addressed by science and administration. It was now a responsibility of nations, international organizations, and colonial administrations.

The Limits of Nutrition

Nutrition science implied new responsibilities toward colonial subjects, but many experts remained at a loss as to how these might be fulfilled. For all the soaring rhetoric about how new knowledge could guide colonial administration, physiologists, doctors, and social scientists complained that without experimental data and reliable statistics, even a preliminary diagnosis of colonial nutrition was impossible. The restructuring of society to facilitate the flow of nutrients from the soil through the metabolic process appeared very distant. While experts called continuously for collaboration between administration and science, they had little of substance to offer. Their research was often descriptive rather than analytic, and prescriptions were speculative and vague.

Much research on colonial diet in the 1920s and 1930s ignored nutritional developments entirely. Doctors continued to study the diets of soldiers and other convenience samples based on old-fashioned ideas of calories consumed in relation to work expended, the balance of albuminoid, fatty, and carbohydrate elements, and the adaptation of diet to climate.[130] Ethnographers compiled dietaries for indigenous groups, along with studies of cooking methods and cultural practices surrounding consumption.[131] Chemists analyzed foods such as Vietnamese fish sauce, soy sauce, and "soybean cheese" (tofu), but colonial laboratories and technicians lacked the equipment and training to measure vitamins and minerals.[132]

No less eminent a nutritionist than Étienne Burnet admitted the impossibility of serious nutritional analysis in Tunisia, where he worked at the Pasteur Institute of Tunis.[133] The colony's indigenous population alternated between abundance and partial famine, but the extent and degree of undernutrition was unknown. Burnet deplored the lack of data about a range of concerns, including agricultural production; import and export of different foods; consumption at the level of individuals, families, and social groups; the relationship between diet and health for different age cohorts; the relationship between diet and income; and the chemical content of staple foods, to name just a few. As agricultural and customs statistics were not yet "oriented toward nutrition," there was no way of analyzing the relationship between production, commerce, and consumption. No experiments on the metabolism of Tunisians had been done to determine the links between food, climate, work, and health. Burnet's complaints showcased the ambition of nutrition science even as they highlighted its shortcomings. He gave vent to incredulity and frustration when he wrote, "We can be astonished and regretful that, in a country that can be said to be still primitive, but not barbaric, that has suffered chronically from more or less protracted and serious dearths, and that has been protected for over fifty years by a great European nation, we have not yet sought to establish scientifically the conditions of diet and of their relation with the economic situation and public health."[134]

Burnet sought to address the absence of data by undertaking what he called the first nutritional study in Tunisia in 1937. He and his colleagues weighed the food of thirty-seven families from a range of locations and socioeconomic classes over one week. Though Burnet's own research stressed the balanced diet, this study measured only quantity, not quality, of food. The results were not encouraging: six of the families consumed less than one thousand calories per person per day. Burnet admitted that this simple "provisional sketch" of Tunisian nutrition was of limited practical use. Even so, his findings indicated the uneven distribution of the benefits of nutritional discoveries and economic development. While advanced countries were moving toward diets based on protective foods completed by high-calorie "energetic foods," Tunisians struggled to eat enough calories. Disparities existed within families as well as across class and geography. Women and infants ate especially poorly, with consequences for public health and the reproduction of labor. During famines, people were reduced to eating hedgehogs, crows, locusts, and wild vegetation, foods for which chemical analyses had yet to be performed. Based on these impressions, Burnet proposed well-worn solutions such as better transportation, grain reserves, and culinary education.[135] This was far from the expert-guided reorganization of the Tunisian economy that he himself had called for.

Two French physicians and their Malagasy assistant ran into a similar dearth of data about Madagascar. They calculated that on average Malagasy ate only 1,367 calories per person per day, compared to a baseline 2,500 calories they deemed necessary for the hot climate. Most Malagasy, they added, ate far too little animal protein for a "balanced" diet. However, the researchers admitted that since they had not actually been to Madagascar, they could not account for calorie distribution and real usage. Since these general averages were unsuitable for making policy, they proposed a special administrative service to study Malagasy nutrition properly.[136]

Based on these impressionistic studies and others like them, European participants in international scientific networks made suggestions. The most concrete of these was that colonial administrations should rely more heavily on specialists to formulate policy. Scientists and doctors should be permanently integrated into governing institutions. Ethnographers, physicians, pharmacists, chemists, and agronomists should conduct detailed inquiries on food consumption and quality of life in all territories in which people were undernourished. The results of these inquiries should be shared internationally to serve as a map of the "nutritional geography" in European possessions. Colonial functionaries would then be able to make informed policies. These might include planting larger surface areas, introducing new food products, and expanding culinary education. Administrations could develop cooperative organizations to administer famine reserves and hire specialists to guide food policy. Experts agreed on the need for studies on the physiology of indigenous races, the composition of diets, and the nutritional health of subjects. They recommended studies on the production and transportation of meat and fish to fight widespread protein deficiency, and the replacement of white rice with whole rice to counter beriberi.[137]

The existing famine policy was judged by most experts to be entirely unsatisfactory. In 1937, Henri Labouret gave an overview of the practical measures taken to fight famine in the French Empire. They did not amount to much and ran counter to what experts now knew about nutrition. Labouret opposed new laws requiring granaries in Niger: "This institution, which has been considered a universal panacea against famine and shortage, was in reality founded on . . . ignorance of real local conditions." He pointed out that granaries had not prevented the Niger famine of 1931. In Madagascar, administrators had tried to improve crop yields by building dikes, draining swamps, and digging wells. Malagasy farmers, however, were suspicious of these measures that interfered with their own ecological practices, so they refused to cooperate.[138] An expert on Algeria proposed irrigation, grain reserves, and the relief of Malthusian population pressure by sending Algerians to Niger, a questionable proposition given the famine that had occurred there six years previously.[139] None of these ideas were new, and no data to ensure better execution materialized. When experts shifted their focus from the promise of nutrition science to its actual impact, the hunger of subjects was more visible than ever against ambitious new standards and hopes.

The Physiology of Famine

In the interwar period, developments in nutrition science and internationalism drastically changed expectations for famine relief and prevention in the French Empire. Before World War I, responsibility for colonial famine was consistently reactive rather than systematic, conditional rather than automatic, and voluntary rather than obligatory. The discovery of vitamin B in 1912 launched a new science of nutrition that gave French administrators new means to address a problem that had been considered intractable. Old explanations of famine as the inevitable result of improvident races interacting with unfavorable natural conditions became untenable. Races and environments came to be seen as mutable and controllable by scientifically informed administrations. At the same time, an internationalist ethos centered around organizations such as the League of Nations motivated empires to care for colonial subjects while providing an institutional framework to share expert knowledge. Attention to hunger and famine intensified in the 1930s as the Great Depression brought well-being to the center of European and global politics. In the French Empire, the new science and sociology of nutrition was applied first to individuals, then to races, and finally to populations. At their most ambitious, nutrition thinkers sketched a techno-utopian vision of a holistic global society managed by international institutions and optimized for the fulfillment of metabolic needs. This maximalist program implied something like a global welfare state. Together, these developments engendered new norms for preventing and alleviating famine as critical elements of the duties of sovereignty and of humanity.

The French Empire was ill-equipped to implement the sweeping social and economic reforms called for. European confidence in the ability of international organization to transform society was grandiose, but the paucity of knowledge about nutrition in the colonies illustrated just how far out of line rhetoric was with reality. Norms of proper colonial governance now took account of new standards of nutrition and public health, but colonial administrations still struggled to ensure mere subsistence. This gap between norms and realities would itself become a historical force. When famine struck the western districts of Niger in 1931, administrators were held personally responsible for the first time.

CHAPTER 5

The Scandal of Starvation in Niger, 1931

When the new governor of Niger, Louis-Placide Blacher, took up his post in Niamey on Christmas Day 1930, starvation was not among his most pressing concerns. Just the previous year, in 1929, a French functionary had declared the colony safe from famines. In a rare invocation of the famine of 1913, he called the catastrophe "a lesson too costly for Niger to permit itself to forget." A seemingly strong economy, growing population, and reserve granaries had convinced him that such events were relegated to the past.[1] In 1929, the functionary judged "the specter of famine" to be very distant.[2]

In 1930, the autumn harvest failed. In 1931, mortality spiked. By the Niger administration's own estimate, between fifteen thousand and thirty thousand people starved, and a further thirty thousand became refugees. The true toll may have been greater.[3]

The 1931 Niger famine was a historical inflection point in a way previous ones were not. The natural triggers, locusts and drought, were familiar. But the place of famine in French colonial thinking had changed. The event marked the first time that the French Empire explicitly took responsibility for the subsistence of its subjects. By 1931, changing ideas of scientific control, humanitarian ethics, and welfare politics had begun to generate new obligations. New norms of well-being and a new confidence in the technical control of people and environments converged through the crisis, initiating a mutually reinforcing interplay of motivation and means. Famine prevention was acknowledged as a raison d'être of the colonial state. But if expectations were different, the outcome was the same. Retrospective declarations of responsibility and expressions of shame had little bearing on the ordeal itself.

When famine struck in Niger, components of a heightened responsibility for colonial subsistence were circulating in Europe and the international sphere. Such ideas were not often shared by local administrators caught up in the quotidian concerns of managing large, diffuse, and sometimes uncooperative populations with minimal resources and personnel. Unlike in French Equatorial Africa, where an interest in subsistence and nutrition emerged organically with regard to workers, officials in Niger oversaw primarily independent farmers and pastoralists. The Niger administrators did not have the same incentives to maximize human capital. Responsibility for famine in Niger was imposed from above and limited by the isolation of the colony. Blacher and his subordinates were stunned when they were censured for having failed to prevent a famine, an occurrence they saw as natural and inevitable.

Two investigations, one carried out in Niger by Inspector of Administrative Affairs Bernard Sol and the other in Paris by the senior administrator Gaston Joseph, were tasked with determining the causes of the famine and establishing whether any administrators should be held personally responsible. These investigations were unprecedented. They divulge a major change in attitudes about state responsibility for starvation. Yet this shift in responsibility was not matched by a corresponding shift in capability. Personal blame did not address the political and economic roots of hunger. In fact, it distracted from the structural exposure of colonial subjects to chronic undernourishment and frequent food crises. Though after 1931 famine became a focal point of official colonial discourse, practical action remained reactive, disorganized, and superficial.

The documents compiled by the investigations permit a detailed account of the famine's unfolding, the botched recovery, and the mentalities that help explain Blacher's ineffective handling of the crisis. Interpreting Niger society through frameworks of race, gender, and ecology that naturalized famine as an inescapable fact of life, administrators failed to diagnose the impending crisis and then failed to react to mitigate mass starvation. As in 1913, Niger had few settlers and journalists to witness the famine. Nonetheless, the highly localized crisis reverberated beyond its territorial confines just as the Great Depression began to be felt in France. The reactions to the famine, including the two official investigations and the intervention of the Human Rights League, linked it to the long-term development of ideas regarding state responsibility for well-being. The crisis focused and merged new concepts in international humanitarianism, the physiology and sociology of nutrition, and the state's role in the economy into a coherent formal obligation to provide subsistence. In doing so, the Niger famine materialized a latent contradiction between heightened responsibility for hunger and the incapacity of colonial administrations to fulfill that responsibility. From 1931 on, the gap between expectations and realities would be an important part of the history of French colonial famine.

An African Famine Zone: Environment, Race, Gender

In the Zarma language, the 1931 famine was called "the year of the locust larvae," "sending away one's wife," or else "machete" followed immediately by "machete junior."[4] In some ways, the crisis echoed the "great famine" of 1913. There were differences—the earlier famine was vastly more extensive, and it was triggered by drought and war rather than drought and locusts. But in their unfolding and in how they were experienced, the two famines probably looked and felt alike. The economy of Niger was still composed primarily of subsistence farming and herding. The French still collected taxes and requisitioned products and labor from colonial subjects. African survival strategies of migration, wage labor, pawning, and foraging were similar across the two famines. The mentalities and capabilities of French administrators in the Sahel had not changed significantly in the eighteen-year gap. Very little information about either famine was transmitted through official channels. It was not in the 1931 famine itself but in the French reaction once it had passed that the event took its singular place in the history of imperial hunger.

In 1930, drought and locusts ravaged the staple millet crops throughout the colony of Niger. Despite the heroic efforts of farmers who replanted over and over, the 1930 autumn harvest was far below average. That summer, the three westernmost districts of the colony—Niamey, Dosso, and Tillabéry—suffered mass starvation.[5] Louis-Placide Blacher arrived in Niamey for the first time in the last week of 1930. With no experience as head of a colony and no experience in the Sahel, the governor was immediately confronted with a perilous situation. Hearing talk of possible shortages, Blacher convened a "native food office" on January 10, 1931. These offices, mandated in French West Africa (Afrique Occidentale Française, AOF) in 1930, consisted simply of local administrators who gathered to discuss food supply. Blacher's food office concluded that the fall harvest would be reached without undue difficulty.[6] On January 14, less than three weeks into his tenure, Blacher met with a group of notables including Seydou Zarmakoy of Dosso, a veteran of Verdun and respected leader of the Zarma.[7] According to the zarmakoy's later testimony, he took the opportunity to request 150 tons of millet from Blacher, warning the governor that

FIGURE 6.   Niamey from the air in 1930 or 1931. Photo by Walter Mittelholzer. ETH-Bibliothek Zurich, Image Archive.

Zarma farmers were already nearing the end of their reserves and there would "without any possible doubt" be a famine. Blacher never followed up on this request, later claiming that the zarmakoy had asked for only a hundred tons of millet and had not spoken the word "famine."[8]

Over the following months, district officers confirmed that the harvest had been insufficient, that the period until the next harvest would be difficult, and that there was significant malaise among the population. Millet prices soared. At the end of April 1931, Blacher traveled to the neighboring colony of Dahomey to visit Nigerien laborers working on a new railroad. While he was there, he bought twenty-four tons of millet from the Dahomey administration, which would arrive in Niger at the end of June. It was Blacher's only effort to combat shortage before people started dying. District administrators described the situation as "critical."[9]

In May, European functionaries saw the first physical signs of hunger when refugees trickled and then flooded into Niamey. For the central authorities in the colonial capital, this was "the first official witnessing of a dearth that, judging by its consequences, had been rife in the region for several months already."[10] The physicians of the health service reported cases of physiological misery due to prolonged undernutrition. Still, Blacher dismissed the "adventurous solutions" of alarmist functionaries who began talking of large-scale food distributions. The only action came not from Blacher, but from Garnier, the administrator commanding Niamey. He authorized the distribution of one thousand to two thousand grain rations of five hundred grams daily, giving priority to children. The distributions were strictly supervised to guard against healthy men hoarding food at the expense of women and children, but the fear of rewarding laziness soon outweighed the desire to save lives. The distributions were suspended and the refugees were expelled from Niamey when their sheer numbers made it impossible to distinguish between the "truly indigent" and well-off grifters.[11]

It was only at the end of June, when the first deaths of children and the elderly were reported, that the word "famine" appeared in official records. This grim acknowledgment finally prompted Blacher to action. On July 1, he convened a committee of senior administrators to explore options.[12] Even then, most functionaries insisted that the misery was limited and the refugees were merely lazy people looking for government handouts. Blacher himself was as concerned with following bureaucratic rules as with feeding people. Though he later acknowledged "the emotion he [felt] as a human being and the painful sentiments that agitate[d] him," he was operating not in the capacity of a feeling human, but as the head of a colony who must adhere to "the strictest legality." The lone dissenter on the committee was Monsieur Nemos, new to Niamey but a veteran of the 1913 famine, who argued that human lives should not be subordinate to financial rules. Blacher countered with chapter eight, article six, paragraph two and chapter fourteen, article two, paragraph four of the budget regulations. Though the committee estimated that it would cost three hundred thousand francs for a robust rescue effort, the two budget articles allowed only forty-five thousand francs for indigents and public emergencies. Even these funds were not fully mobilized. Fear of disrupting the local grain market and rewarding improvidence led the committee to authorize only forty thousand francs. Administrators used this money for free food aid for women and children in the towns of Niamey and Dosso, reinstating the distributions that had been begun and then suspended by Garnier. The committee considered and rejected tax relief. The two investigations later saw the July 1 committee as a missed opportunity. Gaston Joseph wrote, in understated fashion, "The assistance measures taken were disproportionate to the scale of the disaster."[13] The more fiery Bernard Sol accused Blacher of convening the meeting as mere cover, an "umbrella opened in case things went bad."[14]

Unwilling to begin large-scale distributions on its own account, the Niger administration offered to act as intermediary between starving farmers and grain merchants. On July 4, 1931, as mortality escalated, Governor Blacher learned that the Bordeaux firm Morel and Prom held two hundred tons of millet in Timbuktu. He instructed his district officers to ask their subjects if they wanted to purchase any of this stock. He offered to advance the money from the colony's budget, but he added that the conditions for reimbursement should be worked out in advance, with the names of village notables who would guarantee the debt specified in the terms. Blacher ended up ordering eighty of the two hundred tons on sale.[15]

The grain bought from Morel and Prom did not arrive until after the fall harvest. Never having invested in transportation, the administration was unable to import food in a timely manner. Niger was isolated, especially in the summer when the Niger River was essentially unnavigable. There were few trucks to transport food by road, and the closest that supplies could be brought by rail was eight hundred kilometers from Niamey. Under these circumstances, the delay in stocking grain proved fatal.

Looking back on this sequence of events, the investigator Bernard Sol was incredulous that it would take the administration until summer to even acknowledge a "disaster no longer menacing but unleashed."[16] Administrators distributed whatever grain was available, but this was an "obviously token gesture." In the district of Niamey alone, the administration reported nearly five thousand deaths and fifteen thousand refugees out of a population of forty thousand.[17] The French had to content themselves with making preparations to avoid the return of famine the next year, watching helplessly as tens of thousands of people died.

How was it possible that even as starving refugees arrived in the capital the French administrators did not acknowledge that a famine was underway? One answer can be found in French understandings of Niger and its people. This area of Africa, the thinking went, was naturally prone to famine because of the harshness of the Sahelian environment. African racial characteristics and social organization only exacerbated these ecological challenges. Finally, ideas of how families functioned in Niger joined negative characterizations of African environments and races to produce the fatal misdiagnosis. The experience of starvation unfolded along gendered and generational lines. The French interpreted the gendered symptoms of famine as the normal functioning of an African society that regularly abandoned unproductive individuals to their own devices.[18] Following a script that naturalized African suffering as unexceptional, Blacher and his colleagues failed to see a famine that was occurring literally in front of their eyes.

European ideas about the Sahel and its people were almost uniformly negative.[19] Administrators with experience in the Sahel reported that seasonal dearth was endemic in Niger and helped account for the people's apathy and fatalism.[20] British administrators across the border in Nigeria acted according to similar understandings of the Sahel as a land of endemic seasonal hunger.[21] Even US scientists with no political interest in the area held this view. A scholarly article published in 1926, titled "A Famine Zone in Africa: The Sudan," blamed endemic hunger in the Sahel on unfavorable rainfall distribution and the alleged incompetence of the natives.[22]

The Niger administration shared this understanding of the Sahel as a land of chronic food shortage and undernourishment. In fact, the extremely rapid turnover of administrators—Tillabéry cycled through six district officers between 1930 and 1932—meant that functionaries were particularly reliant on transmitted knowledge rather than personal observation. The lack of experience was made worse when Seydou Zarmakoy traveled to Paris in June to participate in the Colonial Exposition of 1931, just as mortality was beginning to accelerate. In the absence of experienced leaders, Blacher and his colleagues relied on stereotypes.

For administrators, the seasonal hunger common to many peasant societies was the most salient characteristic of the regional economy. Each year, farmers endured what the French called the *soudure*. Literally translated as "soldering" or "joining," it referred to the period that stretched from the exhaustion of the previous crop to the harvesting of the next crop.[23] According to Blacher, the population of Niger was permanently undernourished because even good harvests did not provide a "normal" amount of food. The result of this chronic shortage was that inhabitants, particularly the Zarma, were obliged to endure "alimentary restrictions" each summer as a matter of course. They had adapted to supplement their insufficient grain harvests with wild leaves and roots, traditionally gathered by women, and with food imports. Informed by stories of Africans competing with insects over wild vegetation in the seasonal gap before the harvest, administrators saw nothing unusual in the presence of extreme privation.[24] Believing that seasonal hunger—a structural fact of the subsistence agricultural cycle all over the world—was environmentally and racially determined, administrators did not view it as a problem. Even when the reality of famine was undeniable, it was considered "the ordinary and ineluctable consequence of certain natural disasters."[25]

Governor-General of French West Africa Jules Brevié later pointed out that it was absurd to characterize Niger as a land of chronic shortage when there had been a long tradition of exporting grain south to Nigeria.[26] Nonetheless, widely held views of the harshness of the Sahel contributed to the normalization of African hunger and the reluctance of Blacher's administration to acknowledge an emergency in 1931. Ecological and social phenomena such as locusts, drought, harvest shortfalls, the splintering of families, and even physical starvation were interpreted not as evidence of an impending or actual famine, but as the ordinary conditions of African life.

When Blacher took up his post shortly after the bad harvests of 1930, he was concerned enough to convene the native food office. His administrators reassured him that inhabitants had experienced yearly shortage for all time and had adapted to deal with it.[27] Afterward, one official admitted that he "knew, along with everyone else, that the harvest was deficient, that locusts had appeared, that drought had occurred, but none of this was out of the ordinary and in any case could not suggest the eventuality of a famine."[28] Yet another testified, "Nobody spoke of famine: we expected a shortage, but this is habitual at the moment of the *soudure*. Moreover, all Sahelian regions experience a difficult three-month period each year, and it is very hard to appreciate in advance the exact degree of these difficulties."[29] What may intuitively appear to be unmistakable signs of an emergency, French administrators interpreted as normal.

For the Niger administrators, the task was not to judge whether people were hungry because they were always hungry. Rather, it was to distinguish between ordinary and extraordinary hunger. Blacher explained that in a region where people were routinely undernourished, it was "very difficult to determine the moment they arrive at the limits of their physiological resistance."[30] Mass mortality was a problem, but nonlethal hunger and even the death of people deemed unproductive were normal and acceptable conditions requiring no special intervention. For Blacher, the famine of 1931 was "the unforeseen outburst of an endemic evil, one maintained by the state of chronic shortage which the stricken regions have always suffered."[31] There was, he argued, no way to have predicted that dearth would lead to famine. Even as experts were building more subtle understandings of the physiology and sociology of famine and malnutrition, many administrators continued to see alimentary issues in terms of the simple line between life and death.

The image of the Sahel as a desolate land of drought and want dovetailed with conceptions of Zarma racial characteristics and family values to make extreme hunger look ordinary to French eyes. If the Sahelian natural environment was difficult, the Zarma were particularly ill-equipped to deal with it. Colonial ethnography, especially the impressionistic pseudo-ethnography practiced by many administrators, habitually reduced complex, stratified cultures to simplistic essential attributes. An ethnographic sketch of the district of Niamey from 1921 compared the Zarma unfavorably to neighboring ethnic groups, conceding that the Zarma were intelligent but also calling them lazy, poor farmers, proud, greedy, and cowardly.[32] These moralistic generalizations were still widely accepted ten years later.

During and after the 1931 famine, administrators blamed the Zarma race for its own suffering. Most administrators accepted that the racial characteristics of pride, laziness, and improvidence prevented the Zarma from taking any rational action to combat famine. Indeed, French functionaries observed that the Zarma were so apathetic that they were incapable even of instinctive animal reflexes of desperation, which explained why the famine did not cause rebellions against French authority.[33] Administrators complained that Zarma chiefs, paralyzed by "this indifference, this apathy, this improvidence, this extraordinary fatalism," had failed to warn the French of impending famine.[34] The chiefs, administrators claimed, were repeatedly asked about the food situation and repeatedly held that though there would be a dearth, it would be of a routine nature and would not require any special interventions.[35] This was demonstrably false since the zarmakoy had warned of a coming crisis in January 1931, and a council of notables that convened on March 13 was unanimous in its warnings. Bernard Sol later mocked the administrators for whining, "'But the chiefs said nothing. It was those selfish and nonchalant chiefs,'" adding, viciously, "He who pretends not to see is worse than blind."[36]

French administrators believed that Zarma starved at an especially high rate, even in territory they shared with other races. Governor Blacher reported that at the height of the famine, the Zarma did not fish, they did not hunt the abundant game, and chiefs could not be bothered to collect government grain meant for distribution.[37] The specific inability of the Zarma to deal with famine was attributed to memories of the Songhai Empire of the fifteenth and sixteenth centuries, which endowed its descendants with delusions of grandeur antithetical to honest farm work. The militant Zarma had historically lived by rapine, instilling atavistic instincts in the race that persisted into the present day. Mass migration and the seeking of wage work, famine strategies common all over the world, were explained as expedients intended to avoid agricultural labor that were well suited to the lazy and irrational Zarma temperament.[38]

The Zarma possessed neither the foresight nor the work ethic to handle the difficult ecology of the Sahel; they simply "[suffer] the fait accompli."[39] This natural lethargy, the French thought, was compounded by the effects of chronic undernourishment, rendering the Zarma physically as well as mentally incapable of surviving hardship. Blacher explained how these "underprivileged regions" prone to "unfavorable natural phenomena" interacted with "a population without any moral resilience, undernourished for many generations, cultivating entirely insufficient areas of land" in such a way as to all but ensure a vicious cycle of starvation.[40] Inspector Sol, scorning race essentialism, looked to nutrition rather than inherent character to explain African behavior. If the Zarma were lazy, this was not an inescapable product of timeless culture or immutable racial attributes, but an issue of policy. Allowing sarcasm to inflect his tone, he accused, "It seems not to have occurred to anybody to establish a cause and effect between this situation of apathy, indolence, laziness . . . Undernourished people cannot deploy a vigorous energy."[41]

Perceptions of the severe Sahelian environment and degenerate races were two of the factors that determined how the French reacted to the famine. Another component of their interpretive framework involved gender and families. The extent to which women and children dominated French descriptions of the famine is striking. This can be attributed partly to a longstanding humanitarian interest in the suffering of women and children, but it probably had more to do with the different ways men and women acted when unable to procure food. Zarma men, many of whom engaged in seasonal migratory labor in the Gold Coast (contemporary Ghana) and Nigeria, took advantage of these preexisting connections to leave the famine area in search of wages.[42] Women tended to stay home with their children and parents to gather wild vegetation, or they fled to Nigerien towns. For these reasons, the suffering of women and children was more visible than that of men. It is their experiences that dominated the French view of the famine. Regional reports were full of descriptions of children with swollen bellies and of women gathering pseudo-edible grasses and leaves.[43] Administrators noticed a rise in abortions and premature births among women who were unable to feed their children or themselves.[44] There was, in contrast, relatively little focus on the hunger of men.

Just as it was disproportionately women and children who remained in the countryside and villages, the refugees who fled to the capital of Niamey, and into the direct eyesight of central administrators, were primarily women, children, and the elderly. Every resident of Niamey would have been aware of the situation in May as two thousand to three thousand women and children presented themselves each morning to the medical service, which supplied rations to those judged the most needy until the distributions were suspended.[45] When starvation began to lead to mortality in June, it was again women and children who died most publicly in the countryside and the towns. The fact that the French saw the suffering of women, children, and the elderly while that of able-bodied men occurred out of sight is critical for understanding administrators' delay in reacting to the famine. These gendered and generational observations were interpreted according to scientific and anthropological understandings of the Sahel and its inhabitants.

According to the French, the Zarma had adapted family structures and values to their environment by strategically shedding economically unproductive members in times of stress. Administrators interpreted the exodus of men in search of food and money as the routine abandonment of dependents.[46] Women, in turn, abandoned their children to increase their own chances of survival. One doctor voiced a typical view: "With an astonishing sense of its duties, the great majority of the fathers of families abandoned wives and children to go searching for millet, and has not reappeared. The women left alone demonstrated the most monstrous egoism by letting their children, even those at the breast, die of hunger while they themselves succeeded in procuring some food."[47] At least one report mentioned that migrants to British territories were sending remittances to their families. But the view that Zarma men were uninterested in providing for their wives, children, and parents had a strong impact on French famine policy. For administrators who thought of African families as social units designed to deal with environmental distress by jettisoning unproductive members, the influx of women, children, and disabled and old people was seen as nothing more troubling than the normal functioning of African families. In fact, it was a symptom of the most urgent desperation.

Intertwined ideas about the Sahelian natural environment, Zarma racial characteristics, and African families constituted the framework through which the Niger administrators filtered the signs of famine. Major aid distributions were not begun until July, when the sheer number and public visibility of starvation deaths forced even the most stubborn to acknowledge the crisis. Yet, Blacher knew that the harvest would be deficient in December of 1930. In May 1931, he witnessed hungry refugees converging on Niamey from the surrounding countryside. The refugees, who numbered in the thousands, consisted almost entirely of women, children, and the elderly.[48] In a town with a normal population of two or three thousand, the effect must have been striking.[49] For functionaries who mostly stayed in the administrative centers, taking brief tours to rural areas easily accessible by car, the starving women and children fleeing to towns were the first concrete signs of hunger. Blacher did not see this as evidence of famine, but rather "a matter of useless mouths rejected by their villages."[50]

Acute crisis exposed a contradiction between the humanitarian and civilizing elements of colonial ideology: "To not come to the aid of these people would be proof of inhumanity. But it is also encouraging their laziness to do so."[51] When the administration began to take measures in July, aid was limited not only by the resources at hand, but also by the fear of rewarding men who had failed in their responsibilities to provide for their families.[52] In the view of

Blacher, "It is unacceptable that a man of working age has not made arrangements for his nourishment and that of his family, and that he not make an effort to ameliorate his critical situation."[53] Administrators provided free charitable relief only to women and children, and large-scale aid to men only on credit. Limiting free aid to women and children whose families had been verified to be indigent eased the burden on the budget and avoided supporting Zarma men who, by abandoning their families, had caused the refugee crisis in the first place.[54] Advancing seed only to men reinforced their role as providers, even as it excluded women from the resources needed for survival and recovery.[55]

It was not until the beginning of July, six months after reports of bad harvests and two months after the appearance of the first refugees in the towns, that Blacher convened a committee of functionaries to come up with a plan. Later, when asked why this committee was not convened in May as the first famine victims began arriving in Niamey, Blacher answered, "This first manifestation did not catch the attention overmuch, we were expecting alimentary difficulties and the presence of slightly more beggars than usual in the capital, elderly for the most part, did not at first appear to be a very troubling symptom."[56] Other administrators shared the view that the refugees were simply the useless and the lazy taking advantage of government handouts.[57] One functionary testified that even in July, Blacher "did not have, at that moment, the sentiment of the gravity of the situation . . . for him, the natives that presented themselves for the distributions were the disadvantaged, the unfortunate, the starving."[58] As with observers of previous famines in the French Empire, the Niger administrators would not make the connection between famine and the material impact of French colonialism. They preferred to blame uncivilized races living in difficult environments.

The Coercion of Markets

Race, environment, and gender did their work in conjunction with a theory of progress that advanced freedom of commerce as the answer to famine. As Western European countries modernized in the eighteenth and nineteenth centuries, the rise of economic liberalism, improvements in transportation, and an agricultural sector increasingly oriented toward exchange shifted the location of responsibility for subsistence from the state to the market. "For centuries, the state or the monarch had been viewed as the ultimate provider of the people in times of direst need, and though this expectation had often passed unfulfilled, it had never been emphatically denied as it was by the early nineteenth century."[59] The defeat of French famines through market liberalization and the denial of direct state responsibility for subsistence remained key components of French national myth through the twentieth century. This myth formed part of the justification for assuming a civilizing role in the colonies.

Colonial officials, like the modernizing administrators of enlightenment France, denied that famine prevention and relief were ultimately their responsibility. Taking the story of the French defeat of famine as a universally applicable model, colonial administrations espoused liberty of commerce as the definitive solution to famine. The compulsory granaries mandated in French West Africa in 1915, aid distributions, price and export controls, and other illiberal policies were necessary deviations from this ideal, unfortunate detours on the road to liberalism paved by France.[60] This version of the story of France's victory over famine elided both the historical specificity of these developments and the persistence of state interventions in French food markets into the twentieth century.[61] The inheritance of a pure laissez-faire ideal, divorced from its historical context and decoupled from the interventions that oriented market mechanisms toward the aim of subsistence in France, allowed colonial administrators to place responsibility for the minimum provision of food on markets. Inefficiencies were attributed to a racially determined inability to engage with markets rationally. In 1931, the Niger administrators were reluctant to intervene in a situation that was caused, in their view, by a combination of accidents of climate and African improvidence, and that could be resolved only by the free play of markets.

The selective and inconsistent deployment of the rhetoric of economic liberalism camouflaged the Niger administration's true role in a famine that was probably induced and inarguably permitted by its own actions. The proximate causes of harvest shortfalls were drought and locusts, but the underlying conditions that converted crop shortage to famine were political and economic. French officials rhetorically embraced liberty of commerce while simultaneously engaging in coercion, implementing incoherent and mutually disruptive policies that neutralized the potential protections of markets, administrative interventions, and local subsistence arrangements alike. Forced labor, grain requisitions, compulsory cash cropping, and taxation all operated to extract wealth from land and people with little thought to economic growth or the management of risk. The insistence that only liberty of commerce could prevent famines let administrators deflect blame from their own extractive policies onto subjects' supposed economic irrationality.

Jules Brevié, who was governor of Niger from 1922 to 1929 before becoming governor-general of AOF, exemplified how the language of liberty of commerce joined with the language of civilization and race to justify almost any policy or outcome while cushioning the administration from the consequences.

When Brevié became the first civilian head of the new Colony of Niger in 1922, he remembered the administration's inaction before the 1913 famine. Anyone who witnessed "the pathetic, starving masses that crowded the gates of our posts to receive a fistful of millet and the cadavers of children and elderly that filled the villages" learned firsthand the importance of "methodical preventive action." This action, according to Brevié, must include phasing out the harmful and illegal system of administrative grain requisitions and reestablishing the traditional African practice of maintaining granaries.

Ultimately, though, famine prevention could be achieved only through "liberty of commerce," which, "following the general law, will itself create the organ that is indispensable for all subsequent transactions: the market."[62] But Brevié acknowledged it was liberty of commerce that had depleted granaries in the first place as farmers sold rather than stored surpluses. Reconstituting the granaries required prohibiting growers from capitalizing on high prices in British territories, a solution obviously at odds with liberty of commerce. At the same time that Brevié criticized labor requisitions and crop quotas as anachronistic in a modern empire, he excused them as evils necessary to protect improvident people from starvation. In 1929, he wrote that Africans claimed a "right to laziness" with the same fervor that their French counterparts claimed a "right to work."[63] In 1936, he had not resolved the contradiction that it was the races who lived "closer to a state of nature, in a ferocious familial individualism" who were more likely to stock reserves, while relatively civilized races such as the Zarma had lost this primitive instinct and sold their surpluses.[64] If Africans were not forced to grow and store food, he claimed, they would die.

During and after the 1931 famine, Governor Blacher shared the view that coercion was not contrary to civilization but, rather, justified in its name.[65] Perhaps thinking of the International Labor Organization's forced labor convention signed by France in 1930, Governor-General Brevié reminded Blacher late in 1931 that coercion was permissible only in extreme circumstances.[66] For Blacher, African circumstances were always extreme. Only a "wise coercion that must be measured in all cases" could save Africans from their own laziness.[67] Economically irrational subjects needed to be coerced into making the correct choices in the free market. The seemingly incompatible principles of liberty of commerce and state intervention were reconciled through race, giving administrators recourse to either approach as convenient.

The rhetoric of race and markets concealed the fact that many of the consequences administrators attributed to African irrationality were the results of French policies. In particular, the three extractive practices of forced labor, taxation, and grain requisitions contributed to a high risk of famine. The forced labor system in AOF required ten days of unpaid work from each subject or up to several months of paid work, with the possibility of purchasing exemptions.[68] It is not clear how many men from western Niger were fulfilling labor requirements during the critical agricultural cycle before the famine. In the winter of 1930–1931, there were between 900 and 1,200 men from the districts of Niamey, Tillabéry, and Dosso assembled in the capital for the construction of administrative buildings. Among other jobs, they were finishing work on a new governor's palace. These laborers were completing an obligatory six-month stint, earning a food ration and one franc per day. In addition, the districts of Niamey and Tillabéry were required to provide laborers for barges on the Niger River.[69] Finally, an unknown number of men were sent to Dahomey to work on railroad construction. According to Governor-General Brevié, there were 1,000 men from the three districts fulfilling labor requirements, while Nigerien scholar and politician André Salifou has estimated a total of 1,600 forced laborers.[70]

After the famine, Governor Blacher noted that forced labor had been a significant drain on the agricultural workforce, monopolizing months of the highest-quality labor that might otherwise have been devoted to growing millet. The men chosen as laborers were the healthiest, strongest, and most capable. He explained that although these men represented only a small proportion of the working population, any labor at all was sorely missed when normal yields barely met minimum needs. Food was always stretched as thinly as possible. In retrospect it was obvious to Blacher that taking even a small number of men from their fields would plunge total production below the subsistence threshold.[71] Before and during the famine, though, when all hands were needed to combat drought and locusts, his administration proceeded with worker recruitment even during the labor-intensive periods of sowing and harvesting. After the famine, administrators continued to requisition workers, ignoring the higher proportion of total labor each man represented from a population diminished by mortality and migration.[72]

Governor-General Brevié denied that recruiting workers from a population he estimated at half a million contributed to the famine.[73] Whether or not it was by itself decisive, the reallocation of labor away from agriculture worked in combination with other extractive practices such as taxation. Subjects were responsible for a regressive capitation or head tax, the Muslim tithe levied by African chiefs, and a livestock tax.[74] The famine occurred immediately following a 35 percent hike of the capitation tax from eleven francs to fifteen francs in 1930.[75] The livestock tax remained steady at five francs per head as the value of cattle dropped from between four hundred and six hundred francs to thirty-five francs, representing a huge proportion of each animal's value.[76] Crucially, taxes had to be paid in cash, contributing to a reorientation of peasant production from subsistence agriculture to cash cropping and wage work.[77] To earn money to pay taxes, farmers had to sell either crops or labor power. Instead of being stored, surpluses were marketed to British territories, including to a new class of laborers and merchants from Niger operating in Nigeria and the Gold Coast. This had the dual effect of taking labor away from subsistence agriculture and exposing peasants to the fluctuations of labor and food markets at a time of global depression.

As the west of Niger fell into famine, tax collection remained the administration's priority. In response to one official who reported difficulties collecting taxes from famished farmers, Blacher urged him to spur lazy people to work harder, chiding, "I would like you to show yourself less tolerant and that on the contrary, you apply yourself to the collection of the taxes owed by your subjects." There is little doubt that tax increases and aggressive collection contributed to the erosion of people's ability to obtain enough food. The administrative inspector Bernard Sol was harsh in his judgment of Blacher's ruthlessness. "The administrators said: famine! The response was: taxes!"[78]

Alongside forced labor and taxation, a third practice that increased the risk of famine was the requisitioning of grain to feed soldiers and other government employees. Grain requisitions, which could reach a thousand tons a year for the military alone, were determined according to administrative needs rather than people's capacity to provide.[79] During and after the famine, the individual burden increased since grain quotas were assessed collectively according to population and were not reevaluated to account for mortality and emigration.[80] Even when the administration sought to establish harvest estimates to assess contributions fairly, these estimates were, according to Inspector Sol, "absolutely fantastic . . . nothing other than numbers haphazardly strung together, as distractedly established as they would be distractedly read in the capital," numbers that made sense only if one "had never seen a millet field in this region."[81]

Farmers were remunerated for requisitions, but the fact that they were compulsory allowed the administration to set prices so far below market rates that requisitioning functioned in essence as an additional tax.[82] After the deficient autumn harvest of 1930, the administration requisitioned millet at twenty-five to thirty-five centimes per kilogram while the market rate was one franc per kilogram or more.[83] A total of 540 tons of millet was requisitioned from the three afflicted districts. The administration of Tillabéry alone requisitioned 225 tons at thirty centimes per kilogram.[84] When the administration advanced grain to peasants during the famine a few months later, it did so at the prevailing market price of seventy-five centimes to one franc per kilogram and even higher.[85] The policy of distributing rescue grain only on credit forced farmers to buy their own grain back from the administration at several times the price at which they had been compelled to sell it. The irony was not lost on Inspector Sol: "This is not requisitioning: it is plundering."[86]

The combination of forced labor, taxation, and grain requisitions severely curtailed the capabilities of farmers to obtain enough food for survival, either from their own harvests or in the market.[87] The temporal rhythm of the agricultural cycle, coupled with taxes, requisitions, and debt service, meant that by the time starvation set in, producers had already sold their crops to meet their obligations. Farmers sold grain immediately after, or even before, it was harvested and spent the money on taxes and debts. This cyclical process negated any protective advantages of growing food instead of any other type of crop.[88] Farmers grew millet, but they did not have any when they needed it, nor did they have money to buy some. Town-dwelling artisans and merchants seem to have survived by buying food, but very few farming families had cash on hand.[89] Some grain was put on the market by merchants, "profiteers without scruples and without a heart" setting up shop to take advantage of famine prices. This was out of reach of all but the wealthiest, selling for as much as 4.25 francs per kilogram.[90] As one administrator noted dryly of famine victims, "The law of supply and demand plays against [them]."[91] On top of harvest shortfalls, the cadence of agriculture and administrative extraction helps explain how farmers who grew food found themselves without any.

In the years after the famine, taxes and requisitions hindered recovery. In 1931, the Great Depression, which had until then spared France and its empire, made itself felt. Prices for agricultural products, livestock, and labor collapsed. The devaluation of the British pound when it came off the gold standard in September of 1931 was especially harmful given the increasing reliance of farmers, herders, and laborers on British colonial markets to earn money for taxes and debt payments.[92] In the famine districts, the taxes for 1931 could not be collected in their entirety until 1932. In 1933, subjects were responsible for the taxes for 1932 and 1933 simultaneously. In the district of Dosso, the inhabitants were 1.34 million francs in debt for millet advanced to them during the famine. By comparison, the yearly tax receipts for the district were around 260,000 francs. The Dosso administration expressed concern that it would be "impolitic" to enforce payment stringently when a significant portion of the population had died or fled. Doing so, it was feared, would provoke a new exodus and ruin the economic recovery.[93] But by 1933, farmers were again exporting food for cash to pay accumulated back taxes and service the debt incurred when they had "eaten their last chicken and their last grain of millet." The glut of grain and livestock on the export market in a global depression lowered prices to a fraction of those paid in 1930.[94] Farmers faced an impossible choice between selling their grain to pay taxes, reimbursing the administration for aid advanced during the famine at five times the prevailing export prices, or restocking their still-empty granaries.[95] Taxes usually won out: "They talk of nothing but taxes, they work for nothing but taxes."[96]

Investigating the Famine

Blacher and his administrators governed under the influence of certain beliefs about race, nature, gender, and markets that to them were axiomatic. They interpreted everything they saw through a framework that naturalized colonial hunger as inevitable and permanent, and that deemphasized the role of administration in controlling it. This way of seeing and understanding increased the risk of famine and prevented an effective response.

The Niger administrators took for granted that famines could not be helped. But what seemed self-evident to them now clashed with new obligations toward hungry people prevailing in Paris and Geneva. When officials in France learned of the famine, they launched the official investigations conducted in Niger by Bernard Sol and in Paris by Gaston Joseph. Sol worked for the colonial inspection service, the administrative division tasked with, among other things, investigating abuses. Joseph was a respected high functionary and ethnographer at the Ministry of Colonies. The investigators were instructed to establish the causes of the famine and determine "responsibilities incurred."[97] Compared to the 1913 famine that struck the Sahel a mere eighteen years earlier, was many times more deadly, and passed virtually unnoticed by the French, the scrutiny of the 1931 famine stands out. What accounted for such a drastic shift in priorities over such a short period of time?

As famine was underway in Niger, the purpose and capabilities of states, including colonial ones, were elsewhere being reconsidered. New theories about the connections between governments, environments, and people, most plainly embodied in the League of Nations, influenced thinkers and practitioners in a wide variety of roles. These ideas, existing but diffuse in the 1920s, converged and sharpened through the 1931 famine into a clear expectation that French colonial administrations guarantee subsistence. In the discussion surrounding the famine, disparate ideas of scientific control of bodies and populations, humanitarian care, and welfare politics coalesced into a generalized responsibility to prevent and mitigate famines. No longer an unavoidable tragedy, famine became a solvable problem and a sign of extreme state failure. Though they did not know it, the Niger administrators were being held to new standards.

The famine exposed a disjuncture between the upper echelons of the colonial hierarchy and the local administrations tasked with translating expectations into concrete policy. It was easier for the minister of colonies to demand the eradication of hunger than for the governors and district officers to achieve it. From their point of view, being asked to stop a famine was equivalent to being asked to make it rain during a drought. The Niger administrators handled the famine as administrators always had. They were surprised to learn of their new job responsibilities after the fact. As Governor Blacher pointed out more than once, people had been starving in French Africa for a long time and administrators had never before been held responsible. He cited the 1913 famine, "said to be so deadly that the bodies piled up in the villages because they could not be buried," as evidence of the frequency and inevitability of famines in the Sahel.[98] In fact, he reminded his superiors, when free aid had been distributed in Senegal during a recent shortage, functionaries had been censured for ignoring the budget.[99]

New standards of care found organized expression in national and international institutions while colonial administrators on the ground were left behind. The Human Rights League, founded in 1898 for the purpose of defending Alfred Dreyfus, the Jewish army captain falsely convicted of treason, was one of the more powerful organizations promoting humanitarian causes in the interwar years. One of the league's tactics was intervening with government authorities in situations of injustice and escalating, if needed, by making the injustices public. The league was involved in bringing the 1931 famine to the attention of colonial authorities. As was common for local administrators protective of their autonomy, Blacher had tried to keep news of the famine quiet, to "sort it out within the family."[100] A functionary in Niamey who was unsatisfied with the administration's handling of the famine, later identified as a Monsieur Valtaud, broke ranks to inform the Human Rights League of what he saw as criminal mismanagement.[101] The league was an outlet for information that might otherwise have been stifled, as in 1913, in formal bureaucratic channels. It also served as a disinterested outside observer to hold administrators to account. Its role was similar to that of the press in earlier Algerian and Indochinese famines, but at a time when norms of good governance were changing.

In April 1932, the Human Rights League wrote to the minister of colonies asking for information about the famine and related abuses. Reflecting a traditional humanitarian preoccupation with women and children, the league's most forceful charge was that administrators had allowed women to sell children they were no longer able to feed.[102] The administration dismissed these "monstrous" stories, countering that they were surely misinterpretations of cases where administrators or charitable individuals rescued abandoned children. Deftly parrying the accusation, the Niger administration told of the wife of an employee in Niamey who had organized a "veritable nursery" to feed orphans.[103] The administration concluded that no transactions involving children had taken place and that the Human Rights League had decontextualized and misinterpreted the facts.[104] The famine had been a "veritable nightmare," but Niamey had not become a "slave market."[105] Official denials, though, do not necessarily indicate that the selling and pawning of people did not occur.

In addition to airing concerns about selling children, the Human Rights League accused administrators of enabling, and possibly participating in, theft and grain speculation.[106] The colonial administration acknowledged that speculators had hoarded food until famine drove up prices, but it denied that this had been coercive; farmers had sold their grain freely for cash. Minister of Colonies Albert Sarraut maintained that the causes of famine were strictly environmental, not economic.[107] Finally, the league accused the chief administrator of Niamey, Garnier, of beating and briefly jailing dozens of children, some blind or otherwise disabled, caught stealing money and clothing from Europeans. Garnier, far from denying the violence, argued that it had been warranted to keep order amid social disintegration. It was particularly justified since, he claimed, the subsistence of children was guaranteed by the Niamey administration.[108] Despite these easy deflections, the fact that the administration felt the need to engage with the league at all suggests that an era of increased scrutiny limited the colonial state's ability to act with impunity in cases of famine.

The Human Rights League's correspondence brought the famine to the attention of the Ministry of Colonies for the first time. Blacher had not reported the crisis up the chain of command until August 6, 1931, when mortality was at its peak. The government-general in Dakar had not forwarded the information to Paris. Governor-General Brevié, who had been in France during the worst of the famine, claimed that he had not known about it until November, when he returned to Dakar. When he learned, he did not inform his superiors either.[109] Two brief allusions to the famine buried in some routine paperwork from Niger reached Paris in May 1932. The ministry's clerks would perhaps have passed them over without comment had the Human Rights League not intervened the previous month. Though he closed ranks to defend the Niger administration against the league, Albert Sarraut was angry at having been kept in the dark. He ordered an inquiry to check the league's estimate of fifteen thousand starvation deaths and thirty thousand refugees. If such a thing had occurred, Sarraut wrote, it would be "unpardonable" and implicated the administration directly. He ordered investigators to verify if the famine had in fact occurred and to determine if and which administrators had been negligent. If need be, he was prepared to "sanction without weakness."[110]

On July 6, 1932, the ministry tasked Bernard Sol of the colonial inspection service, already on mission in neighboring Upper Volta, with carrying out the inquiry in Niger. He built up a body of evidence, consulting administrative documents and touring the districts of Niamey, Dosso, and Tillabéry by car to interview witnesses. He completed his final report at the end of summer. In it, he rebuked Governor Blacher and the rest of the Niger administration in the strongest language. In a reversal of French stereotypes of Africans, Sol charged French officials with laziness and improvidence as famine loomed. He excoriated them for not knowing what was going on in their own districts and for ignoring those warning signs of emergency that did reach their desks. He expressed astonishment that the frequency of shortages in the area was taken as a reassurance of normality rather than an exacerbating factor demanding careful vigilance. Blaming improvident subjects for failing to plan for the future was disingenuous since it was precisely the job of the administration to ensure good decision making. He justified illiberal interventions in private choices by reminding that "to colonize is to constrain." Sol methodically laid out the evidence of imminent famine, including ample reports of drought and locusts, harvest shortfalls, and the quintupling of millet prices. He wondered incredulously, "What would it have taken to attract the attention of the authorities?" Inspector Sol concluded that Africans had been "abandoned, more or less totally, to their own devices."[111] Just as Blacher and his subordinates chastised Zarma men for deserting their wives and children, Sol condemned administrators for shirking their paternal responsibilities toward their colonial subjects. For Sol, unfavorable environmental and racial attributes exacerbated rather than mitigated the irresponsibility exhibited by administrators.

The violence of Sol's attacks on the Niger administrators expressed and helped crystallize a new understanding of famine as political and social. Sol made a distinction between the "material fact of dearth" caused by natural factors and famine proper, which he attributed to administrative malpractice. Four things, in his view completely avoidable, allowed natural disaster to become famine: lack of reserves, abusive requisitions of grain and labor, heavy taxation, and the hoarding of food by speculators. Listing drought and vermin as the natural triggers of food shortage, the investigator asked, "Was it necessary for a famine to follow? Yes, if we accept that our administration is nothing but a witness to mark the blows; no if we maintain that its role is different."[112]

Minister of Colonies Albert Sarraut concurred with Sol that the effects of natural phenomena could be controlled through administrative action. The excuse of famine resulting from the incompetence of Black races no longer held water. For Sarraut, the aim of the colonial project was precisely the improvement of human beings so they could better confront the world they lived in. It was the duty of administrators to "bring the native to shake off his enslavement to the contingencies of natural conditions" and lessen "the precarity of his individual situation exposed to the accidents of everyday life."[113] It was precisely the job of colonialism to save Africans from nature, including their own nature.

The second inquiry, which convened in Paris in the spring of 1933, was more sympathetic in its judgment of Blacher's team. Led by Gaston Joseph, a pillar of the Ministry of Colonies' central bureaucracy, it heard testimony from functionaries and expert witnesses, including veterans of the 1913 Sahel famine. Asked to establish personal responsibilities, Joseph's commission discovered that nearly all the administrators involved had been at fault. They had been too trusting of indigenous chiefs, had not been rigorous in touring their districts, and had failed to inform their superiors of warning signs. Individual errors, though, were made in the context of "errors of design that cannot be borne in particular by the personnel in service in the colony at the moment that the consequences of these errors brusquely manifested in disaster." The overreliance on dissimulating and sycophantic indigenous chiefs, the dearth of personnel to govern the million and a half subjects living in Niger, and the lack of transportation in an isolated colony twice the size of France were not personal shortcomings but structural facts. It was not entirely correct to blame those who had the misfortune of being in charge when natural forces "independent of the will of man" put pressure on a dysfunctional administration. Blaming Blacher, Garnier, and other administrators only distracted from the truth that "to fully respond to the human aims of colonialism, it is urgent to devote substantial funds." Unlike Inspector Sol, Joseph believed in the "goodwill of all, and that the personnel of the colony cannot be accused of not having strived to do their duty completely, as they conceived it."[114] The report, gentler in tone than Inspector Sol's, nonetheless offered a devastating critique of the state of French colonialism from a different angle. What greater indictment of a system than when the best intentions lead to the most disastrous results?

Louis-Placide Blacher, Joseph's commission concluded, lacked the "intuition" born of experience that alone could have warned him of the coming famine.[115] It also found a possible mitigating circumstance in Blacher's biography and dark skin. Born in St. Pierre, Martinique, in 1883, Blacher benefited from the French citizenship granted to inhabitants of the "old colonies" in 1848.[116] He graduated from the Colonial School in Paris with a degree in law. In 1918, he was assigned to accompany the Senegalese politician Blaise Diagne, who had been elected to the French Chamber of Deputies in 1914, on his legendary mission through West Africa to recruit tens of thousands of soldiers for the Great War.[117] Until the deputy's death in 1934, Diagne remained a mentor and confidant to Blacher as he rose through the ranks of the colonial service.

Perhaps taking heart from his friend Diagne's advice to speak his conscience rather than exchange cooperation for leniency, Blacher wrote a vigorous defense against Bernard Sol's accusations.[118] In it, Blacher expressed indignation at the inspector's efforts "to present me as having failed in my duties toward the black populations I am called to guide, and with whom I feel an attachment of the most profound solidarity." A member of Gaston Joseph's commission, Jules Marcel de Coppet, long-time socialist, future governor-general of AOF, and close friend of André Gide, interpreted this as evidence that "color prejudice" may have inhibited Blacher's leadership.[119] This sentence, Coppet wrote, was "the only allusion in the voluminous dossier to the fact, singularly important in our view, that Monsieur Blacher is a man of color (*homme de couleur*)." Coppet admitted that it was irregular even to mention a "particularity of this nature." At the risk of appearing impolite by drawing attention to distinctions between French citizens, he did so anyway to point out that many whites in the colonies felt giving authority to a Black man damaged "the prestige of the conquering race." In fact, Coppet went on, colonial subjects paradoxically exhibited prejudice against people of color as well: "As strange as it might appear, natives do not accept to be placed under their authority." Coppet wondered if, envious of Blacher's successful career and resentful of his skin color, his white subordinates had engaged in a "conspiracy of silence" regarding the critical food situation. This "hypothesis," he thought, would go a long way in explaining Blacher's otherwise inexplicable behavior.[120] There was little evidentiary support for Coppet's hypothesis of a conspiracy of silence against Blacher, who never denied that he was aware first of crop shortfalls and then of starvation.[121]

Blacher himself, while sharing chauvinist presuppositions about African races and civilizations, expressed solidarity with his African subjects. In a telling exchange during one session of Joseph's commission, Blacher explained how, after leaving service in Niger, he had a conversation with Jules Brevié in Dakar. Blacher had said to the governor-general, "I found myself in difficulties for which I was not responsible, but they will blame me for them nonetheless. They will say that a *nègre*, Governor of the Colonies, permitted thousands of *nègres* to die of hunger." Brevié, brushing aside the implications of racism and stubbornly adhering to the French republican ideal of color blindness, had reassured Blacher by invoking the famine of 1913. Brevié had asked rhetorically, "Did they blame Monsieur Clozel for the famine in the Soudan?" At this point in the session, Gaston Joseph interjected, "We are no longer in that era and the time is over when we could consider disasters of this kind normal occurrences that the metropole did not need to know about— this is no longer tenable and we should be pleased about it."[122]

A republican universalist insistence that race had no place in matters of law hid the multiple ways it functioned in colonial administration, from prejudice against Black authority figures to the systemic exposure of Africans to famine.[123] Blacher's personal identification and solidarity with Black Africans coexisted with a racism embedded in imperial institutions and culture. Race, intertwined with ideas of ecology and gender, was an inescapable characteristic of colonial governance even for the Black leaders of the empire. Race naturalized the suffering of subjects and neutralized efforts to help.

As often happened in the French Empire, the inquiries into the famine absolved the overarching colonial project without addressing the conditions that led to suffering. By blaming individual administrators or claiming that the ideal of proper colonial governance had not been fulfilled in the particular case, such inquiries framed famine and other failures as exceptional.[124] The unprecedented inquiries into the famine led by Bernard Sol and Gaston Joseph do not seem to have had lasting consequences for the personnel implicated. Blacher left Niger in December 1931, after one year of service, to take up the governorship of Dahomey. After the two inquiries found him negligent in his duties, he was fired from his new job. This, however, was only a temporary setback. In April 1934, a socialist deputy expressed displeasure that Blacher could be appointed governor of French Somaliland after inquiries had resulted in his removal from the governorship of Dahomey.[125] Blacher ended his career as governor of Guinea. At the fall of France in 1940, he faced a choice between declaring for the Vichy government or remaining loyal to the republic. Rather than joining his Guianese colleague Félix Eboué, governor of Chad, in declaring for Charles de Gaulle's Free French—an act that would immortalize Eboué as a symbol of French republican patriotism, antifascism, and antiracism— Blacher promptly retired and claimed his pension from Vichy. He returned to Paris where he lived with his wife, the Swiss artist Béatrice Appia, on the Avenue Constant Coquelin in the seventh *arrondissement* of Paris.[126]

Aftermath

In the summer of 1931, it dawned on the Niger administrators that they were helpless to stop the mortality in front of them. They turned their attention to preventing its return the following year. This was no easy task. Agricultural labor power had been vastly diminished by death, migration, and the physical weakness of those who remained. There was a shortage of seed as people ate whatever they could get their hands on. Locusts returned to several villages. Faced with disarray, the administration set three goals: keep people alive, equipped, and strong enough to work their fields; prevent additional migration; and encourage the repatriation of refugees. The overall aim was a return to the "status quo ante."[127]

To ensure that subjects had enough millet to eat and to plant, the administration's main tool was short-term advances in kind. It first tried to distribute grain on an individual basis to entice refugees back from British territories, but subjects gamed the system by showing up to collect aid and then returning to Nigeria or the Gold Coast. Some who stayed in Niger extorted the French by threatening to emigrate unless they got millet or money.[128] Allergic to the threat of people getting more than they deserved, the administration henceforth loaned grain and cash only to villages, which were held collectively responsible for the debt.

The sources relating to the amount of aid distributed in 1931 and 1932 are inconsistent. It is often unclear whether the amounts discussed were requested, approved, shipped, or distributed. When grain was made available, it is not evident who actually ended up with it, or if it was still in usable condition if and when it arrived at its destination. For example, grain was usually distributed through African notables who may or may not have passed it on to the intended beneficiaries. In some cases, the quantities quoted appear implausible. Also, what the French counted as aid could be misleading. In Tillabéry, for example, administrative distributions in 1931 amounted to the following: thirty tons of millet that had been requisitioned in the fall of 1930 were advanced in April and May of 1931 at the cost of 75 centimes to 1 franc per kilogram, roughly three times what the administration had paid for it; two tons of grain from the stock earmarked for the administration's own use was advanced to farmers to be repaid in kind after the harvest; thirty-five tons of millet ordered from Morel and Prom in the French Soudan, which arrived after the 1931 harvest, was sold at the extravagant price of 1.89 francs.[129] Selling farmers their own grain at a markup and acting as an intermediary for price-gouging merchants stretched the definition of aid.

Even if the numbers are accepted at face value, the French themselves admitted the inadequacy of aid during and after the famine. African leaders in the district of Dosso estimated that 864 tons of millet, not including seed, would be needed to bridge the *soudure* before the 1932 fall harvest. According to one estimate, the district administration distributed 140 tons of millet in 1931, almost entirely on credit.[130] According to another, by the end of the year Governor Blacher had approved a total of 221 tons for Dosso, about one-quarter of the requested amount.[131] Théophile Tellier, who replaced Blacher as governor of Niger in December 1931, claimed to have distributed a total of 3,000 tons of grain at a cost of between three million and four million francs.

Even this possibly inflated quantity was acknowledged to be only a small proportion of the investment needed for full recovery.[132]

Administrators in Niger retained strict control of stocks. Subjects were expected to feed themselves from the 1931 fall harvest and from wild vegetation for as long as possible. Stocked grain was not released until May 1932, when the administration began advancing it little by little on a monthly basis according to the perceived needs of the population. Families were also obligated to keep grain reserves. Required quantities were fixed at sixty kilograms of millet per adult and forty kilograms per child, judged the minimum amount necessary to keep individuals alive until the harvest.[133] Administrators reversed the prefamine policy of encouraging cash cropping to refocus on food production. In particular, they promoted secondary crops such as beans, manioc, corn, and rice to supplement the staple cereals.[134] A small amount of grain was distributed for free to farmers who were once again struck by locusts. Otherwise, the plan was to assess the quality of the harvest and distribute food to those judged at risk. This grain would be sold at the lowest possible price "by way, naturally, of payment in cash."[135]

According to French functionaries, the efficacy of these measures was stubbornly undermined by the people they were supposed to benefit. If Africans could sustain serious effort over several years, they could grow enough for dietary needs, constitute emergency reserves, and eventually provide surpluses for export. But administrators were not convinced that improvident African farmers could understand how grain advances worked or even the concept of planning ahead. "It remains to be seen if the Zarma population, owing to its essentially lazy character, will understand the goal to be attained and will not see in this advance merely a gift of food repayable in a distant and abstract future." Farmers who were advanced seed had to be coerced into planting it rather than fleeing with it. Cultivated surface areas fell far short of what should be expected from hard-working people. The French considered this to be pure laziness on the part of the Zarma, who were "soft [molle] beyond all conception."[136] During the recovery as well as during the famine, administrators were guided by deep-seated and convenient stereotypes of Africans as having no work ethic and no foresight.

Emergency measures such as grain distributions were necessary to fight acute starvation and prevent its return in the short term. But for administrators who took reform seriously, a thorough overhauling of the colony was in order. A palpable change in how Niger administrators talked about subsistence became obvious in the years following the famine. For the first time, colonies faced direct pressure from the chain of command to manage the risk of starvation. Dakar and Paris required all colonies in French West Africa to submit contingency plans to be implemented in case of food emergencies. They also demanded comprehensive long-term famine prevention plans that went beyond reactive emergency aid. These plans were supposed to account for racial attributes, which would no longer be accepted as an excuse when disaster struck. The crux of Governor Tellier's plan for Niger, submitted to the government-general in the summer of 1932, consisted of the creation of native provident societies (sociétés indigènes de prévoyance, SIPs) and the careful supervision of obligatory reserve granaries. Tellier believed that if SIPs had been operational the previous year, the famine would have been far less severe. In the future, they would help farmers share environmental and market risk. The SIPs would distribute high-quality seed and tools, teach farmers advanced agricultural techniques, and serve as guaranteed buyers for members' crops. They would function as marketing boards, buying and aggregating grain to sell little by little over the course of the year, thereby avoiding the seasonal glut at the harvest that kept prices low. Following the new directives to account for racial characteristics in famine planning, Tellier argued that "moral" education was essential to the success of the institutions. Functionaries needed to convince improvident subjects that contributing to the provident societies was for their own future good, not merely an extra tax to be defied. The governor weighted the SIPs heavily in his famine prevention plan. But due to lack of funds and personnel, the program would initially be limited to a few model societies that might eventually pave the way for more.[137] After the famine, SIPs were made obligatory, not just in Niger but throughout AOF. Their number increased from 35 in 1930 to 102 by 1935.[138]

Together with native provident societies, the other major element of Governor Tellier's long-term plan was a reform of the granary system along the lines of precolonial practices. The reserve granaries in the west of Niger were empty in the wake of the famine, as they had been for several years before. To help reconstitute them, Tellier issued a circular to the district officers about the history of granaries in Niger and how they had traditionally worked. "From time immemorial, the native has put aside a reserve of grain that the family selects according to age-old custom and keeps carefully for use as seed, even in the event of famine." Along with familial seed reserves, the governor wrote, Africans had kept food reserves collectively. Though the custom had been lost under the French, it could be used as a model for new granaries at the village level. Villages would be required to have on hand between forty and sixty kilograms of millet or eighty kilograms of rice paddy per person. Though families and villages would be responsible for the granaries' upkeep, final authority over when to open them would belong to the governor.[139] Beyond the SIPs and the revamped granary system, experiments in cooperative community farms, irrigation, and

FIGURE 7. "Granaries in a village of the district of Dosso," Niger, 1937. ANOM, 61COL 591.

FIGURE 8. "Granaries in a village in the district of Konni," Niger, 1937. ANOM, 61COL 591.

bounties for killing locusts made Tellier optimistic about the colony's future. As commercial crops once again took secondary importance to food, he urged the development of livestock for export. These measures were all part of what Tellier called a policy of "healthy foresight" that looked beyond immediate needs and counteracted the inertia of the natives.[140]

The Niger administration began paying attention to quality as well as quantity of food. Tellier's policies encouraged farmers to grow rice, manioc, and maize to remedy an overreliance on millet. Planting alternative crops would stagger the timing of harvests and hedge against crop-specific natural disasters. These foods also possessed nutritional qualities that could improve daily diets.[141] Beans could provide protein, and peanuts could help augment the fat intake that experts estimated was deficient in nine out of ten African diets.[142] The rationalization of African farming in accordance with the principles of nutrition and agronomy became a key element of the colony's food policy.

As a complement to the technical concerns of agriculture, the French deemed it urgent to improve administrative communication and execution. This was especially important given the findings by the famine investigations that each level of the administration, from African village and canton chiefs to Governor Blacher and Governor-General Brevié, had failed to report the famine up the chain of command. District officers would now be required to complete a monthly report to the governor detailing the state of crops and food stocks. They would include an estimate of the likelihood that subjects would have to deplete grain reserves. As the logistical nightmare during the famine made plain, material as well as information needed to flow freely. Tellier proposed bringing the entire network of roads in the colony to a state of "permanent viability." This would enable the administration to transport rescue grain in emergencies even when the Niger River was impassable. As importantly, it would allow markets to distribute food rationally and even out grain prices across the territory.[143] Tellier's reasoning left out the fact, observed before the 1931 famine, that markets were as likely as not to draw food away from vulnerable places and people. Commodities were attracted by purchasing power, not need.

Vanquishing famine in Niger required controlling the natural environment as well as its inhabitants. A 1937 report presented the "drama of poor Africa" in its ecological setting. Farmers, it argued, practiced a monoculture in millet, which exhausted the soil. This in turn forced them to clear new fields through deforestation while former plots were left to erode into uselessness. This pattern progressively degraded the environment. If administrators could teach Africans the techniques of crop rotation and fallow, they could follow in the footsteps of the eighteenth-century physiocrats who, with the cooperation of forward-thinking royal administrators (*intendants*), eradicated famine in France. The report painted a potential Sahelian landscape of living hedgerows to delineate pasturage from crops, irrigation and wells to ensure a consistent water supply across seasons, and fields of cereals genetically engineered for drought resistance. Careful management of the environment would not just preserve the fertility of existing farmland, but also could reclaim land from the desert. The Niger River valley could be made into a breadbasket, an "African pampa."[144]

To this end, Niger set up two experimental farms to research seeds specifically engineered for local conditions. Inspired by Soviet successes in plant genetics, the farms petitioned Paris for a geneticist to engineer robust crops with short growing cycles, though it is not clear whether one was sent. To combat locusts, the administration hoped to hire entomologists to collaborate with the Rome-based Conference for Anti-Locust Research. This international initiative identified "gregarization areas" where immature insects gathered and could be destroyed before they formed the killer swarms that caused famines. Rural reform was tested out in a "colonization center" comprised of forty-seven families who pursued a lifestyle modeled on that of French peasants. The administration reported that the colonists enjoyed an elevated standard of living. They even ate meat several times a week, a rare luxury for protein-deficient farmers.[145]

Ambitions for social and environmental renewal never materialized at scale. It is indisputable that French administrators and experts devoted more attention to subsistence after the Niger famine, but the results of French food policy are hard to measure. No repetition of the 1913 or 1931 famine occurred under French rule. On the other hand, France never achieved the kind of society called for by interwar reformers to provide long-term structural protection from malnutrition and food crises.

From 1913 to 1931

The Sahelian famines of 1913 and 1931 tell a story of stasis. They reveal an incoherent colonial state incapable of conveying information across territory or through time, an administration institutionally unsuited to building on itself, sustaining policies, or accreting and incorporating past experience. Every time the French confronted famine, they approached it as novel, as though they had never seen it before. Administrators had little besides personal recollections, word of mouth, and whitewashed narratives of success as guides. Recurring famines were interpreted, paradoxically, as both inevitable within an unchanging African nature and as aberrations or detours within an overarching trajectory of civilizational progress that was so slow it could appear static. Together, these understandings shrouded the fact that far from eliminating the conditions that made famine possible, colonialism sustained them.

Administrative explanations for the two famines were so similar they appear interchangeable: monoculture of millet, improvidence and laziness of African farmers, poor transportation, insufficient cultivation, and an unforgiving environment prone to drought. Yet in the years between the crises, almost nothing was done to address these perceived problems. When faced with famine in 1931, Blacher had no instructions, no protocols, and no precedents to follow. In the 1933 investigative hearings, Gaston Joseph was incredulous that there was no report on the 1913 famine that killed hundreds of thousands and might have held lessons for 1931.[146] Blacher, bereft of institutional knowledge, primed by stereotypes of race and gender, and constrained by rigid administrative rules, was paralyzed.

From the perspective of people in Niger, the two famines probably looked and felt nearly identical. But they took on different meanings for French colonial history. In the intervening years, ideas of technical control and humanitarian responsibility had changed expectations about what states were supposed to do for colonial subjects. Famine was inevitable in 1913 but unacceptable in 1931. The Niger famine helped formalize these responsibilities even as it exposed the chasm between normative standards and colonial realities. Retroactive expressions of shame, anger, and incredulity had no effect on the famine itself, which unfolded much as previous famines had. However, the tension between the newly shouldered responsibility for subsistence that emerged through the 1931 famine, and the administrative incapacity to live up to that responsibility, would help define the decade of the 1930s.

CHAPTER 6

Taking Responsibility in the French Empire, 1931–1939

The spectacular International Colonial Exposition of 1931 showed off the glories of the French Empire for millions of Parisians and tourists curious about what Europe was up to overseas. Visitors to the exposition's campus in the Bois de Vincennes park promenaded through scaled-down models of Malagasy huts, Maghrebi mosques, and the ancient Cambodian temple Angkor Wat. They were charmed by demonstrations of music, dancing, art, and handicrafts from all over the world. Ethnographic exhibits taught viewers about the myriad peoples inhabiting Greater France and other European empires. There were photographs of railroads, dams, and other grand feats of modern engineering. Placards displayed statistics on colonial trade. Ideally, as they were having fun, guests absorbed a few facts about the benefits of imperialism for indigenous development and French commerce alike. Perhaps some would even be moved to invest in colonial business ventures.[1]

While Parisians reveled in colonial exoticism, colonial subjects starved. As the Zarma leader Seydou Zarmakoy joined in the Paris festivities, famine was devastating his people. The 1931 Niger famine was a turning point in a way previous and larger famines had not been. It did much more than bring attention to a single dysfunctional administration. The shock spurred technical experts and political reformers to take stock of the empire in light of new ideas that had emerged after the Great War regarding the role of science, technocracy, and humanitarianism in colonial governance. The 1931 famine forced administrators to articulate the relationship between famine and the colonial state at a moment when these new discourses were circulating, in the process crystallizing new norms for prevention and relief. Through the Niger famine, these diffuse threads coalesced into an explicit responsibility for the subsistence and nutritional health of colonial subjects.

The Niger famine was not the only important food crisis of 1931. The same year, a famine in central Indochina introduced another dimension to the problem of hunger—security. The famine associated with the anticolonial Nghe Tinh soviets helped elevate subsistence as a central point of contention between the French colonial state and those who believed it should be reformed or replaced. Alimentary politics became a terrain on which French colonialists battled liberal humanitarianism at home, anticolonial nationalism overseas, and communism everywhere. The ethical dimensions of hunger were inseparable from questions of social order. Whether national or imperial, capitalist or communist, sovereign states were expected to guarantee the subsistence of their constituents. The association of famine prevention with colonial security and sovereignty, reinforced through the Nghe Tinh uprising, would have explosive consequences in 1945, when famine and revolution once again joined forces to threaten French dominance in Southeast Asia.

The convergence of technical, ethical, and political aspects of hunger through the 1931 crises in Niger and Indochina made famine a focus of the decade's debates on colonial reform. Food as a basic requirement for human life gave it powerful symbolic force in the reevaluation of colonial priorities. Famines provoked a sense of urgency and shame that other kinds of failings did not. The rhetoric of three of the most influential colonial officials of the interwar years, Albert Sarraut, Marius Moutet, and Jules Brevié, exemplified the new centrality of colonial famine. New thinking about food was accompanied to varying degrees by public infrastructure projects, agricultural reforms, education efforts, and increased spending on emergency aid. Subsistence and nutritional health were key concerns of *mise en valeur,* the development ideology most closely associated with Minister of Colonies Albert Sarraut. French alimentary policy in the 1930s was aimed at addressing the two characteristics long believed to cause famine in colonial settings—deficient races and harsh environments. These approaches continued to be tinged by a civilizational and racial thinking that expected only laziness, improvidence, and irrationality from colonial subjects.

Attention to how non-Europeans ate peaked with the 1937 Guernut Commission, a sweeping inquiry into the "quality of life" and "legitimate aspirations" of French colonial subjects. An initiative of the short-lived antifascist coalition government known as the Popular Front, the commission was the most serious attempt to rethink colonial governance before the Second World

War. Comprised of notables including politicians, humanitarians, scientists, colonial administrators, and, for clout, celebrities such as future Nobel laureate in literature André Gide, the Guernut Commission embodied the multidisciplinary technocratic ethos of the interwar years. Hunger was at the heart of the project. The commission requested scientific and social scientific research to guide colonial food policy. The centerpiece of the inquiry was a series of questionnaires sent to technical experts, administrators, and subjects throughout the colonies. It was one of the first times the concept of "quality of life" was used to evaluate colonial governance, and one of the first times officials bothered to ask what colonized elites thought and wanted. The qualifier "legitimate," though, meant the French retained final judgment over which "aspirations" counted. The Guernut Commission showed just how seriously France took its new role of guiding the full human development of subjects, at the base of which was their nutritional health. But it also revealed how spectacularly the French Empire was failing in this mission. The Guernut Commission's inquiries found active food emergencies throughout the empire.

The 1931 famines in Niger and Indochina and the Guernut Commission of 1937–1938 anchored a decade of transformation in conceptions of colonial hunger. The threat of anticolonialism, a reformist press, French activists that could vote (if they were men), and heightened interest in the quality of life of the colonized began to approximate, weakly, elements of the system that Amartya Sen has posited as the best protection against famine—democracy.[2] What emerged was not a single policy position shared by all, but a collective sense that some sort of policy was needed. The grounds of this obligation remained indeterminate, neither fully political nor fully humanitarian. Clearly the welfare state coming fitfully into existence in France would not encompass the colonies, but neither was it acceptable to continue providing famine relief only as charity. This tension increasingly brought French leaders to the uncomfortable truth that to fulfill its basic responsibilities, France would have to give subjects a political voice and spend money. The problem of how to provide welfare state-like protections in the absence of welfare states was unsolvable. But the contradiction between the utopian promises of nutrition science and the partial, dissonant actions on the ground was a driving force in the interwar empire.

Famine and Security in the Nghe Tinh Soviets

In the early 1930s, two commentators put forth contrasting accounts of the French presence in Indochina. One, Henri le Grauclaude, argued optimistically that French management of the colony's natural environment had made life better for millions of Indochinese. The other, the militant journalist Andrée Viollis, disparaged the immorality of a colonialism that yielded subjugation and suffering rather than liberation and well-being. This antithesis between a technopolitics that promised limitless progress and a lived reality of poverty and oppression was a structuring dynamic of the French Empire in the decade before World War II.

In 1933, Le Grauclaude, an obscure writer specializing in popular histories of Southeast Asia, published a book grandly titled *The Waters, Disciplined, Have Routed Famine*. The text opened with a series of excerpts from ancient Annamite sources. In 1290, "many people were forced, in order to procure something to eat, to sell their rice fields and even their children, girls and boys"; in 1596, hunger propelled pirates to "pillage the villages day and night"; in 1741, the population subsisted on the flesh of snakes and rats. More surprisingly, at least for believers in the civilizing mission, hunger continued to reign under French rule. In 1895, starving peasants ransacked fields, ate the bamboo palisades surrounding their villages, and once again sold their children. In 1932, just a year before the book's publication, a single district had lost nearly five hundred people to starvation. The archives of the Empire of Annam, reports of the early years of French occupation, and contemporary administrative documents were quite consistent. "From all these pages fell the same words with the sound of a death knell: 'drought, poverty, . . . drought, famine . . . , drought, piracy and banditry.'" And yet, the author noticed an interesting pattern. Famine continued to strike Annam but not Tonkin. This dubious observation led Le Grauclaude to conclude that France had definitively defeated famine in the Red River Delta.[3]

In flood-prone Tonkin, water, which could "easily become the worst of things when it stops being the best," had for thousands of years frustrated the legendary patience of "the Asiatic." The obsession with floods was embodied for all to see by the ever-present work crews monitoring water levels on the dikes, supervised by foremen distinguished by red bands on their left arms. Fulfilling the legacy of Rome, ancestor of colonizing nations and builder of aqueducts, modern French engineers had blunted water's teeth and claws. The ancient enemy was harnessed against another old foe: drought. A recently built pumping station above Hanoi cost 1.324 million piastres and used three 300-horsepower motors to draw water from the Red River to an elevated reservoir at a rate of eight thousand liters per second. The water was then dispersed by gravity to the paddies through a sixty-kilometer network of canals. Rice yields doubled. Farmers who had scraped by half-naked and undernourished were now appropriately clad and had full, healthy faces. Under the genius of the French, the volatile energy of the Red River was made to serve rather than harm human beings.[4]

Andrée Viollis saw the same scenes with different eyes. Born with the Third Republic in 1870, Viollis began her career in journalism as a Dreyfusard and continued to champion left causes until her death in 1950.[5] Alongside colleagues such as Albert Londres and André Gide, she pioneered a new form of subjective, emotional reportage that drew on the eyewitness authority of travel writing to expose the dark side of colonial triumphalism.[6] In 1931, fresh from interviewing Mahatma Gandhi in India, she accompanied French Minister of Colonies Paul Reynaud on a tour of Indochina as a correspondent for the big newspaper Le Petit Parisien.[7] The pieces she published from Indochina depicted picturesque and politically innocuous exotica such as the beauty of landscapes, the uncut fingernails of court ladies, the "discreet and impenetrable" demeanor of Chinese merchants, and the luxurious silk robes of mandarins.[8] But in May of 1933, a series of trials of Vietnamese nationalists resulted in unreasonably harsh punishments, inflaming the French left. Viollis was inspired to publicize the uglier observations from her trip. She published an exposé in the Catholic journal l'Esprit then expanded the article into the 1935 book Indochine S.O.S.[9] Prefaced by the celebrated novelist André Malraux, himself the founder of an anticolonial newspaper in Saigon in 1925, the book became a bestseller.[10] The bitingly critical travelogue included an account of the famine associated with the anticolonial Nghe Tinh uprising that killed several thousand Vietnamese. It was one of the only descriptions of colonial starvation to reach a wide French public since the Algerian famine of 1867.

In early November of 1931, outside the city of Vinh in Annam, Viollis encountered three thousand to four thousand shriveled and desiccated "human creatures" covered in festering wounds. They were packed so closely into a wooden enclosure that they seemed to form a single indistinguishable mass. They lacked all features of humanity, "no age, no sex, nothing but a mortal misery which, through thousands of black mouths, unleash horrible animal cries." Well-fed, white-uniformed guards controlled the crowd with blows as their wives observed the spectacle with fascination. The famished held out baskets to be filled with rice, then rushed off with their ration clutched protectively to their bellies. Seeing Viollis' horror, a French official pointed out that faced with bad harvests, indigenous improvidence, and communism, there was little the authorities could do other than set up thirty-seven such distribution centers to feed eighty thousand registered indigents. A nearby doctor overheard this conversation and led Viollis to a second enclosure. This one contained those deemed beyond help, deformed by edema and waiting to die. Minister of Colonies Reynaud pulled up in his car. His presence made the crowd restive, so he and Viollis were whisked away to lunch: fish, chicken, foie gras, and champagne. As they ate, entertained by traditional singing and dancing, hungry masses stared.[11]

When Viollis returned to Vinh a few weeks later, she discovered that the rice distributions had been a performance for the benefit of the minister, discontinued as soon as he was gone. The scenes of suffering were much the same. "One [woman] left her husband, the other her son, dead on the side of a road; a third tries to slide the nipple of a flaccid and blackened breast between the lips of an infant wrinkled like an eighty-year-old man." At a medical clinic, patients died under the care of six overworked and underfunded physicians. This was in contrast to several round-cheeked, lively-eyed orphans running around the clinic's yard, who had been "adopted" by staff. They hoped, to Viollis's shock, to "sell" these children to whoever could afford to keep them. A doctor urged sarcastically, "Don't look so tragic! Here we lose quickly enough the prejudices of France. Maternal love is a luxury. Not to croak, that's the point!"[12]

For Viollis, responsibility for the famine fell unequivocally on the French administration. It neglected irrigation, failed to transport rice from Cochinchina, and aggressively collected taxes from impoverished people. "Lack of pity or lack of organization? A crime in any case." Viollis thought it absurd to have suppressed precolonial granaries without replacing them, and she denounced the dangers of monoculture in rice. But she was as disturbed by emotional shortcomings as by material ones. After visiting a nun named Sister Ignace, who worked tirelessly to distribute rice and even seemed sympathetic to the communist soviets, Viollis was offered fresh oranges as they would go to waste at the mission. How, Viollis wondered, could food go to waste during a famine, especially when in the hands of a generous and compassionate person like Sister Ignace? "So? Thoughtlessness? Accustomed to seeing natives suffer and die, and not completely considering them human beings?"[13] For Viollis, a colonialism that failed to value the lives of the colonized could not help but perpetuate misery.

The opposing analyses of Le Grauclaude and Viollis exemplified the tension between norms and realities. People like Viollis, through writing and activism, helped instill in interwar French political culture a sense that new standards for the well-being of subjects were not being met. Much was lost in the translation of ambition to practice. The French fell far short of constructing the thriving technostate envisioned by boosters such as Le Grauclaude. Acute famine at a time of heightened expectations forced this contradiction to the surface.

The Nghe Tinh insurgency and famine brought together two important dynamics of the 1930s French Empire: the discrepancy between new standards of well-being and the persistence of misery, and the escalating conflict between

colonialism and anticolonial nationalism. The famine merged social responsibility and state security into a single problem.[14] The Nghe Tinh uprising occurred at a moment of elevated French sensitivity to Vietnamese anticolonialism.
The Yen Bai mutiny of February 1930, a botched attempt by the Vietnamese
Nationalist Party to incite revolution, had put French forces on alert. This uprising of indigenous soldiers in northern Tonkin had been easily defeated. But the
conditions it was responding to remained. French analysts trying to understand
what had gone wrong connected anticolonialism to hunger. One tract blaming
Yen Bai on famine—"because we must call it by its name"—invoked the description of seventeenth-century French peasants in Jean de la Fontaine's fable
"Death and the Woodcutter." "Sometimes no bread and never any rest. / His
wife, his children, soldiers, taxes, / Creditors and forced labor (corvée) / Make
him the perfect picture of a wretch." If one replaced "bread" with "rice," the
verse was as apt a description of modern Indochina as early modern France.
For this anonymous writer considering the mutiny, no amount of repression
could stop hungry people from rising up.[15] After Yen Bai, left-wing activists and
propagandists from Indochina to France to the Soviet Union leapt on the opportunity to condemn a French imperialism that produced nothing but violence and famine.[16]

The Nghe Tinh soviets further tightened the link between anticolonial nationalism and famine. On May Day 1930, the provinces of Nghe Anh and Ha
Tinh in Annam erupted in pandemonium. Thousands of demonstrators armed
with spears, clubs, and machetes gathered and marched, waving red flags and
beating drums. This was no isolated protest but the launch of an audacious
movement, at the heart of which was the creation of state-like peasant associa-
tions called soviets. Under the auspices of the newly formed Indochinese Communist Party (ICP), the soviets implemented egalitarian policies including tax
abolition, rent reduction, land redistribution, and debt forgiveness.[17] Social reforms were backed by the liberal use of violence against those identified as enemies, especially Vietnamese who were wealthy or who were suspected of
collaboration. The French repression of the movement was particularly brutal,
featuring mass killings of demonstrators, the destruction of villages, the incar-
ceration and torture of thousands, and aerial bombing of civilians. Amid the
disruption of the fighting, several thousand Vietnamese starved to death.

By the close of 1931, starvation and violent French repression put the experiment to an end. But the association of food, security, and sovereignty
would have a lasting effect. The Nghe Tinh movement marked one of the first
times activists explicitly framed nationalism as a contest over social justice and
well-being.[18] Subsistence was vital to this new type of anticolonialism. The soviets were probably not a response to famine; they were more likely among

its causes rather than its effects.[19] Nor did the French intentionally perpetuate the famine as some Vietnamese nationalists claimed, unless negligence and misplaced priorities can be construed as intention.[20] But after Nghe Tinh, the question of subsistence was bound up in competing visions of political order. The conflict between the soviets and the French over who could ensure subsistence was a small-scale preview of the cataclysmic famine of 1945 that coincided with the declaration of Vietnamese independence.

The Nghe Tinh famine was as important a field of conflict as the territory itself. Before the uprising, hunger was an omnipresent topic as revolutionaries built support by distributing literature and holding clandestine meetings. Propagandists built common cause against imperialism and capitalism through physical suffering. In overtures to reluctant Vietnamese Christian priests, communists tried to connect at somatic, emotional, and ideological levels: "He who has not eaten and lacks clothing, who is not lazy but lacks work, who is beaten down by tax upon tax, feels that there is nothing left but to die." In its abhorrence of suffering, the cadres claimed, "The humanitarian thought of the Communist Party is no different from that of Christ."[21] Once launched, the soviets organized "hunger marches" against rich merchants and Catholic missionaries who hoarded food.[22] When demonstrators targeted the centers of colonial power, their demands included famine relief.[23] Revolutionaries expropriated food from the administration and wealthy landowners, both European and Vietnamese, for distribution to the needy. Farmers formed syndicates to oversee and redistribute rice harvests equitably.[24] Through these highly organized efforts, the soviets took upon themselves the ethical and organizational functions unfulfilled by the French protectorate.

For the French, fighting communism and fighting famine were synonymous. Resident-Superior of Annam Yves Châtel cracked down on the soviets with relentless violence, but violence alone was not enough. Because starving people were "so many recruits for the agitators," famine relief was a duty of security as well as of humanity. The communists gave rice to the hungry. The French, needing to convince people of the material advantages of colonial rule, "could not on this point prove themselves inferior to their enemies."[25] Though Châtel wanted one hundred thousand piastres for aid, he asked only for thirty thousand out of respect for the budget. He pointed out that taxes in Nghe Anh and Ha Tinh had been collected aggressively to counter a communist antitax campaign. Thirty thousand piastres amounted to less than the hardship exemptions that would otherwise have been granted.[26] At a time when people flooded the market with livestock and religious heirlooms to earn cash for taxes, rice distributions could achieve the double goal of relieving the masses and foiling the communists.[27]

When Governor-General Pierre Pasquier ignored his request, Châtel again blended the languages of humanitarianism and security. Even as he pitched famine relief as a countermeasure to communist violence and propaganda, Châtel wrote apologetically, "I use the word 'famished' like a journalist, but I have learned precisely the lamentable situation of the people we must feed, and I judge that above all, humanity should drive our action."[28] In the end, he got twenty-five thousand piastres for aid. Provision was contingent on people accepting "submission cards" indicating their loyalty to the Hue court and to France, further tying subsistence to security.[29] Châtel claimed that between official aid and private charity, thirty-six thousand rations were distributed daily.[30] Other officials remembered that nearly forty rice distribution centers of the kind described by Viollis were set up to service "lazy beggars" and "feeble oldsters" whose villages rejected them pitilessly.[31] Food aid, distributions of milk to children, and hydraulic works to improve rice yields and provide emergency salaries were seen as indispensable counterinsurgency tactics.[32]

Once the French reestablished authority in Nghe Anh and Ha Tinh by means of machine guns, airplanes, and soup kitchens, they reflected on how a meticulously organized movement with deep social roots could have arisen in the heart of French Indochina. Among the most prominent explanations was hunger. A French official tasked with investigating the causes of the Nghe Tinh movement insisted that "misery in this country, denied by certain functionaries and missionaries, is great and real." Farmers were at the mercy of drought and usurers as land was consolidated in the hands of the hated wealthy. While the French and the mandarins sat on their hands, the ICP "found the ground already prepared." Through psychological manipulation of nationalist sentiments and dreams of a better life, party cadres enticed followers to the "pure Muscovite doctrine." The communists sold themselves as the only power attending to the "well-being of the people and the amelioration of its condition." They earned widespread support by redistributing money, land, and food to people "who had nothing under the sun." Arms were of limited use against such tactics, as "security forces will arrest men, they will not imprison thoughts." The French, the investigator wrote, could have avoided rebellion if they had simply had greater contact with the natives, shored up mandarin power, distributed rice, provided education, and arrested troublemakers at the first sign of dissent—in short, if there had existed the welfare and police apparatus of a modern state. If the French wanted to best the communists in the fight over social provision, they had to govern with "an iron hand in a velvet glove."[33]

The French acknowledged that the suffering of a population that rarely ate its fill was a cause of the Nghe Tinh uprising. Pauperism, though, was often still considered an entrenched fact of Asian rural life unrelated to colonial policies. Some believed French success in public health had actually tightened the Malthusian trap by allowing the population to increase in relation to food supply.[34] Publicly, most officials and many journalists in Indochina and France minimized misery and concealed the severity of the famine. They falsely insisted that Russian agents and the Comintern, not homegrown revolutionaries, were responsible for the soviets.[35] It was convenient for administrators to blame exogenous forces such as drought, locusts, or outside agitators for causing famine. It allowed them to downplay the failures of colonial governance. But other observers saw the soviets for what they were: a direct defiance of French rule, rooted in material misery, egalitarian ideology, and patriotic nationalism. Even the professional cadres of the ICP, who had judged historical conditions immature for revolution, were caught off guard when local activists launched the movement. Once the soviets were established, agents had to scramble to bring them under Party control.[36]

Eyewitnesses and a robust press did not allow the official French account to stand unchallenged. It would be very odd indeed, one newspaper writer opined, if Governor-General Pasquier had donated five thousand piastres to a charity for starving indigents if indigents were not starving. In language remarkably similar to that of Viollis, the writer shared the "inexpressible and poignant distress" of people "assembled in the vast courtyard of a pagoda, under an implacable sun, among the buzzing flies." These three thousand "poor beasts, who retained nothing human but the face" received a meager ration sufficient only to "prolong their agony."[37] Another reporter likened the callousness of administrators to that of Marie Antoinette when she invited the hungry of France to eat cake.[38] Ngac Van Dong, a member of the consultative chamber representing the people of Tonkin in the colonial government, submitted a document to the visiting Paul Reynaud. In it, he begged the minister to look beyond the capitalists, businessmen, and mandarins. Only then could he see the truth that French functionaries did not suspect or admit: famine was endemic. Peasants were worse off under the French protectorate than under the Nguyen dynasty. Millions of proletarians survived on one meal, even half a meal, per day, composed of some sad greens on a bed of rice cut with corn. Parents sold children.[39]

The revolts of Yen Bai and Nghe Tinh had repercussions in France as well as in Indochina. The journalist Louis Roubaud thrilled readers with a deeply reported account of Vietnamese clandestine anticolonial fighters, unveiling the sophisticated organization of militant nationalists.[40] A network of left-leaning activist intellectuals including Andrée Viollis, André Gide, André Malraux, and Félicien Challaye formed the Committee for Indochinese Amnesty and Defense, a pressure group that worked to procure a blanket pardon for Vietnamese imprisoned for participating in the rebellions at Yen Bai and Nghe Tinh.[41]

The group was unsuccessful due largely to the dedicated opposition of Albert Sarraut.[42] The future minister of colonies, Marius Moutet, entered the debate not in his capacity as a government official but as a member of the Human Rights League. He attributed the Nghe Tinh soviets to the distortion of a colonialism that was meant to uplift subjects but amounted in practice to simple racial domination. Disrespecting the rights of man and unwilling to grant those of citizenship, France found itself bombing villages and killing women and children. Such contraventions of human rights gave rise to "inexpiable hatred." Moutet warned presciently that France would lose Indochina unless the hopes awakened by its own civilizing rhetoric were taken seriously. The origins of the Nghe Tinh soviets should thus be sought not in communist agitation, but in the deep misery pervading Indochinese society. Accordingly, Moutet proposed a sweeping program of social and political reforms, culminating in time with a liberal democracy animated by respect for human rights and racial equality.[43] As minister of colonies in 1936, Moutet would partially grant the amnesty for the revolutionaries that had been refused by Sarraut. The wide sweep of French responses to Nghe Tinh, ranging from Châtel's urgent requests for relief funds to the call for an Indochinese social democracy by a leading politician, show how famine came to embody basic questions of security, responsibility, and political purpose in the French Empire.

Norms of Care: Sarraut, Moutet, Brevié

The famines of 1931 in Niger and Indochina forced a rethinking of subsistence in the French Empire. Famine became newly conspicuous in the rhetoric of the senior administrators who set policy at the most general level and served as the empire's public face. Via these high functionaries, ideas that were scattered throughout imperial and international discourse in the 1920s began to coalesce into norms of governance. The impact of the senior administration came not so much from handing down specific policies as from setting a tone for the colonial project and modeling a stance toward the colonized. The senior administration's ideologies were not hegemonic. Local administrators often ignored or resisted meddling from distant bureaucrats. Nonetheless, the reformist attitude that permeated the empire in the 1930s found its clearest and most far-reaching articulation in the voices at the top of the colonial hierarchy. Two ministers of colonies, Albert Sarraut and Marius Moutet, and the governor-general first of French West Africa and then of Indochina, Jules Brevié, were the first senior figures to speak of colonial famine in a new idiom of care.

Albert Sarraut was one of the most influential thinkers on French colonial-ism in the interwar years.[44] The scion of an entrenched republican family from the South of France, he was a dedicated member of the centrist Radical Party and a Freemason. Elected deputy in 1902, he began his long association with the empire with two stints as governor-general of Indochina in the 1910s. There, Sarraut tried to reform the education system and cracked down vio-lently on Vietnamese dissidents. He became minister of colonies in 1920, hold-ing the post for over four years, an impressive tenure considering the usually rapid turnover. In 1921, he proposed an enormously ambitious and expensive plan to invest in colonial infrastructure and education. He estimated the cost at 3.5 billion francs over a decade.[45] The Sarraut plan's price tag doomed it from the start, but the tome he wrote in its support, *The Development of the French Colonies* (*La mise en valeur des colonies françaises*), laid the groundwork for his colonial philosophy.[46] The gist was that France should invest heavily in the eco-nomic development of the colonies to reap both financial and cultural re-wards. Sarraut remained a fixture in the French governments of the 1920s and 1930s, holding various high posts including minister of colonies in 1932 and 1933 as well as two brief tenures as prime minister. At the fall of France, he voted full powers to Philippe Pétain, then was deported by the Germans in 1944. He survived the ordeal to become heavily involved with the overseas French Union under the Fourth Republic.

A generally reformist presence who insisted on the "value of humanity" in colonialism, or colonialism as a humanitarian pursuit, Sarraut was a firm impe-rialist and virulent anticommunist.[47] He associated empire not just with the progress of non-Europeans, but with the greatness of France and the struggle against international bolshevism. Colonialism for Sarraut was not a political choice so much as a universal human instinct, a natural law, and an organizing principle of history.[48] Colonialism was an internationalism, the only way to harmonize differently endowed places and races into a "planetary *mise en val-eur*," a single global society held together by functional complementarity and reciprocal obligation.[49] What good was the inventive scientific genius of white Europeans without the vast material riches of Africa and Asia? Was it fair for the productive capacities of backward regions to go unrealized while the ex-ploding global population demanded more and more food? In accordance with a natural division of labor in global society, no race had the right to isolate itself from common human life, to withhold its contribution from the "universal patrimony."[50]

For Sarraut, the League of Nations was indispensable for orienting human-ity's common riches toward a grand future. France, though, had a unique role to play. Without French care, backward races under natural conditions of competition would go extinct. The French, with their history of the Rights of Man, were the first to reject a social Darwinist survival of the fittest to value humanity per se. Influenced by a somewhat gentler social Lamarckism still popular in France, along with a belief in white and French superiority, Sarraut argued that only a firm French hand could guide the evolution of the colored races and harmonize the world around the principle of "human solidarity."[51]

Human solidarity appears to have been an adaptation of the doctrine of solidarism proposed by French parliamentarian and Radical Party theorist Léon Bourgeois at the turn of the century. Bourgeois was contributing to a debate made famous by the sociologist Émile Durkheim about how societies cohered. Durkheim posited that there were two pure types of social solidarity: primitive societies cohered because they were homogenous, while advanced societies cohered because they were internally differentiated according to a complementary division of labor.[52] In the colonial context, these types corresponded to homogenous races and civilized societies. Bourgeois, who would go on to win the 1920 Nobel Peace Prize for his involvement with the League of Nations, argued that societies emerged naturally, amounted to more than the sum of their parts, and implicated individuals in involuntary "quasi-contractual" relations engendering mutual social debt.[53] For Sarraut, humanity in its entirety constituted one such natural social whole. Empire was the political formation that corresponded to the objective social reality determined by a natural global division of social functions.

Human solidarity was Sarraut's answer to the self-evident contradictions of empire. By expanding French solidarism to the entire world, Sarraut sought to redeem a colonialism that had been launched in a spirit of violence and self-interest, a colonialism that had produced the slave trade, the extermination of the "redskins," and the "methodical decimation" of the Herero people of German Southwest Africa. He understood this reformed colonialism as "correcting the injustices of nature" to bring about a universal improvement in moral and material well-being.[54] Human solidarity was what transformed an act of "spoliation" into a work of "human right."[55] In a phrase he liked so much he recycled it repeatedly, Sarraut explained that the empire was the proving ground for the nation's commitment to humanity, that France "must be able to look even its colonial policy in the face, like a mirror of its conscience, and not feel shame or remorse for a shocking contradiction, for a brutal antinomy between what it does afar and what it does on its own territory."[56] His vision of the world was similar to the global society imagined by interwar nutritionists but with human solidarity replacing physiology as its organizing principle. This was unconvincing to many anticolonial thinkers, for whom Sarraut's *mise en valeur* became synonymous not with human solidarity but with exploitation, misery, and hunger.[57] The Martinican poet Aimé Césaire later wrote that Sarraut's ideas of non-European peoples anticipated Adolf Hitler's. Nguyen Ai Quoc, soon to reemerge as Ho Chi Minh, hounded Sarraut in the left-wing press for years.[58]

Until 1931, if Sarraut considered famine at all it was with pride at how colonialism had "imposed on nature the discipline of a rational production, and on indolent man that of nourishing work."[59] The famines in Niger and Annam shook his flattering conception of European rule and shocked him into prioritizing subsistence as a basic precondition of civilization. After 1931, Sarraut expressed a new kind of alimentary responsibility that both encompassed death from calorie shortage and drew on nutritional sociology: "It is necessary not only that all threat of famine be eliminated, but also that the state of chronic undernourishment [*sous-alimentation*] of the inhabitants end." The reconstitution of healthy human reserves depleted by hunger was consistent with *mise en valeur*, as strong, productive bodies were the empire's most valuable economic resource.[60] Accordingly, the state had an urgent duty to protect subjects from "the scourge of hunger" that diminished individual capacity for labor, degenerated races, and threatened human capital.[61]

As minister of colonies in 1932 and again in 1933, Sarraut declared that famine would henceforth be considered man-made rather than natural. He warned his functionaries that the 1931 Niger famine was an unpardonable "administrative failure," technically anachronistic and repugnant to the civilizing mission.[62] The colonies, he knew, suffered from unfavorable environmental conditions. Administrators were often frustrated by the passivity of natives who "an ancestral habituation has enslaved totally to nature." But this situation was not an excuse; it was a challenge. The whole point of civilization was to "liberate man from the tributes that his fatalism has led him to pay resignedly to the forces bigger than himself."[63] It was precisely this rejection of apathetic submission to nature that qualified Europeans to rule others. French rationality and technical prowess could and should transform the natural and social conditions that caused famines, reworking subjects' relationship to nature from one of passive subservience to one of active control.

The fight against famine came to be foundational to Sarraut's ideas of global cohesion through a natural division of labor. Compared to the grandiosity of this proposed world-historical transformation, his prescriptions were a little tired. His plan for eliminating hunger involved modifying natural conditions through improved transportation, irrigation, and laboratory-derived agricultural techniques, all adapted to the particular environments and civilizational stages of famine-prone regions. People as well environments could be improved by instilling in them foresight and diligence. Colonial administrations would teach farmers to stock reserves, prohibit premature consumption of food stores, and distribute grain equitably in times of need. These tasks would be gradually devolved to indigenous cooperatives, which had the dual merit of teaching solidarity and overcoming the dearth of European personnel. Sarraut accused administrators of sins of commission as well as of omission, ordering them to be more careful in ascertaining how much taxes, food, and labor subjects could safely contribute to the state without risking starvation. Forced labor and obligations in kind were to be phased out, little by little, in favor of a free market, cash system. At the same time, he instructed administrators to intervene to prevent too sharp a shift from alimentary to commercial production. Finally, Sarraut ordered administrators to draw up detailed rescue plans specifying the provenance of emergency food and logistics for distribution. Perhaps chafing at Governor Louis-Placide Blacher's lack of communication during the 1931 Niger famine, Sarraut reminded subordinates that they had a strict duty to report food problems up the chain of command. In these ways, administrators would do their part in fulfilling the destiny of Europe and the world: "Improving the condition of humans is the veritable end of our science, and, in the name of human solidarity, the highest aim of colonization."[64]

Marius Moutet, another prominent interwar colonial commentator, shared many of Sarraut's ideas of development from a different political perspective. Man of the left and dedicated member of the Human Rights League, Moutet was motivated more by a tradition of activism linked to the Dreyfus affair than by Sarraut's solidarism and anticommunism. Yet both men had famine at the heart of the programs for their ministries. In 1935, several left-of-center factions in France frightened by Hitler committed to an international Popular Front strategy that prioritized antifascism over doctrinal disagreements.[65] The three participating parties—the Radicals, the socialist French Section of the Workers' International (Section française de l'internationale ouvrière, SFIO), and the French Communist Party (Parti communiste français, PCF)—dominated the elections of May 1936. They formed a government under Léon Blum, replacing a temporary caretaker government entrusted to Albert Sarraut. The election sparked a burst of activism and legislation in France as excited workers and intellectuals pounced on the opportunity to empower labor and erect social protections.

As the Popular Front's minister of colonies, the socialist Moutet channeled this hopeful energy overseas. At a 1936 conference uniting the governors-general of the empire, Moutet shared his vision of an "altruistic colonialism" based on the physical, economic, and intellectual "quality of life" (*niveau de vie*) of the masses. He contrasted this to an extractive "selfish colonialism" that put France's interests above those of the colonies. His ideal empire was a "complex ensemble acceptable for everyone," rooted in a market system that would "sustain and improve" (*faire vivre et mieux vivre*) every member of the polity. This ambition of creating healthy, affluent, and intellectually fulfilled subjects had a logical progression: to achieve "political liberties," it was necessary first to secure the "primordial liberations" from famine and disease.[66]

In assessing the needs of the colonized, Moutet's attention was drawn ineluctably to food. When he became minister in 1936, he wrote candidly, "I could have nothing else for my first concern than the study of what I am forced to call, without wanting to use euphemisms, the famine dossier."[67] For him, as for Sarraut, the 1931 Niger famine had been an unacceptable example of administrative apathy and a turning point in imperial history. Like Sarraut, Moutet made it clear that starvation would henceforth be considered the fault of administrators. "In what concerns one famine which several years ago ravaged one of our African colonies and led to inquiries and reports," he discovered in the governor a "state of mind I would prefer not to see." "Real colonials," he challenged, always took the initiative and must cease to think of famine as "an inevitability against which nothing can be done." Moutet modeled this active stance when in one of his first acts as minister he required colonial administrators to submit information on famine to be studied and archived by the ministry.[68]

Without suggesting concrete policies, Moutet had thoughts about how to approach famine. Influenced by ethnographers such as Henri Labouret, he argued that a successful colonialism should be "animated from the inside by the natives that benefit from it." Rejecting general purpose solutions, he required administrations to devise famine prevention systems tailored to specific contexts. All colonized people, Moutet explained, had some tradition of emergency food storage. Emphasizing that he did not advocate a regression to precolonial civilizations, he nonetheless wanted to "discover the spring [*ressort*] that made them move" and harness its power for modern antifamine programs. It was inefficient to reinvent reserve granaries from scratch and impose them exogenously when they could be rooted in local tradition. Technical measures such as popularizing locust-resistant seeds or diversifying crops would be useless without a "living native policy."[69]

Moutet's ministry envisioned an alimentary "five-year plan" to begin in 1938.[70] Again invoking the 1931 Niger famine as motivation, the plan had few details, serving more as a statement of intent than an actionable strategy. Due to the Popular Front's fall in 1938 and the outbreak of World War II the next year, the five-year plan was abandoned almost as soon as it was begun. However, it did ensure that Moutet's successors inherited an approach to food policy that sought to remedy not just insufficiency, but also malnutrition and the reduction of labor power it caused.

Ministerial instructions for administrators in Africa from 1938 reflect this focus, pointing out that most subjects were protein deficient because of an almost exclusively vegetarian diet. Preserved meat or fish being financially unfeasible, protein deficiency could be overcome by popularizing milk and vegetables rich in nitrogen. Saharan camel herders were living proof that milk was a first-rate food, providing albuminoids essential to life, cholesterol to fight infections, and a high concentration of calcium (*chaux*) and digestible phosphates. Coupled with vegetables such as beans, peanuts, and Indochinese soy, milk could substitute for the "nitrogenous," or protein, content of meat and fish. In addition, the ubiquitous millet should be replaced by protein-rich corn and whole rice, which, when properly prepared, contained minerals, essential amino acids, and vitamins proven to remedy "colonial avitaminoses." Mangos, avocados, and breadfruit were other nutrient-rich alternatives to expensive animal foods.[71] In the 1930s, nutrition became the normal paradigm for official thinking about food.

Jules Brevié, governor-general of French West Africa (Afrique Occidentale Française, AOF) from 1930 to 1936 and of Indochina from 1937 to 1939, was a third high-ranking official who grappled with new responsibilities for famine. He was later disgraced for running the ministry of colonies for Vichy, but in the 1930s he was responsible for implementing Sarraut and Moutet's reforms in two of France's most important colonial holdings. Though the 1931 Niger famine occurred under Brevié's leadership, he had been in France at its height and managed to emerge from the scandal unscathed. In its wake, he joined Sarraut in accepting famine control as an obligation. Brevié wrote to the governors of French West Africa that alimentation was "at the very base of the life of our subjects" and thus constituted a "legitimate preoccupation" of colonial administration. Reflecting his own experience of the 1931 famine, which he had learned about only after the fact, he instructed his subordinates to keep superiors informed of imminent or actual shortages and to make methodical plans rather than rely on "hasty improvisations." These plans should respect liberty of commerce. Echoing nearly word for word his convictions from a decade earlier, when he was governor of Niger, Brevié still believed that "it is by the free play of supply and demand that, little by little, will be created . . . the indispensable organ of the economic development of the region: the local market."[72]

Brevié accepted that it was his administration's job to control famine, primarily by protecting freedom of commerce. But he was skeptical that famine's natural roots could be easily overcome. His response to Moutet's 1936 request for information espoused the environmental and racial determinism his superior was trying to stamp out. Brevié considered vast geographic areas with low population density, poor communication, and limited means of transportation as intractable barriers to the elimination of famine. Environmental improvements such as irrigation and subterranean, water-efficient crops would take years to make an impact. Moutet called for a living native policy; Brevié countered with crude chauvinism. African society, he explained, had long proved incapable of the organizational scale necessary to feed widely dispersed people over extended periods of need. Reviving long-forgotten granaries would, in any case, be no easy matter. In a discordant critique for a champion of the free market, Brevié complained that Sahelian farmers sold food to pastoral nomads instead of storing it (though he conceded that nomads, too, had to eat). Early warning of crop shortages could give time to mount a response, but here, too, Brevié was pessimistic. "The faculties of man, even cultivated," did not grant the power to foresee harvest yields. For Brevié, the conditions that produced the Sahel famines of 1913 and 1931 persisted in 1936 with little hope of improvement. His feeling that "before the inclemency of the climate, we are unarmed" contrasted sharply with the spirit of Moutet's inquiry.[73]

Brevié believed that the only feasible preventive measure was a granary system managed by local administrators. Instead of the prevailing practice of requisitioning grain in fixed amounts at fixed prices, he wanted administrations to pay market rates and buy only in proportion to farmers' resources. Letting markets rather than administrators determine prices would also correct for the improvidence of Africans who lacked the foresight to sacrifice immediate profit for protection from future harm. Selling to the state, however, would not be a choice. Blending liberty of commerce with colonial authoritarianism, Brevié's solution to famine was to coerce irrational farmers into economically sound decisions.[74]

In an admission of helplessness that would have been unpalatable to Sarraut or Moutet, Brevié argued that the failure of granaries to prevent the famine of 1931 should not be considered an indictment. Successive poor harvests could overwhelm any preparations whatsoever, as when crops failed over 1.35 million square kilometers of the Sahel between 1912 and 1914. Encompassing between eight million and nine million mouths to feed, this area was the size of France, Belgium, Holland, Switzerland, Austria, Czechoslovakia, and Germany combined. Brevié, chiding his superiors for unreasonable expectations, claimed that one had to have witnessed ordeals such as the 1913 famine to understand the impotence of those in charge.[75]

Most consequentially, Brevié laid out the costs of famine prevention. He calculated that to be reasonably safe through the months of the *soudure*, the four million inhabitants of the French Sahelian zone, not including children, required reserves of one kilogram of millet per day per person. This would require an initial expense of one hundred million francs, a sum exceeding the combined budgets for all the colonies of AOF. Brevié wrote provocatively that as famine was undeniably a public calamity, he would not hesitate to request the financial support of the national government just as a French department would. But even without the urgency of acute famine, Franco-colonial solidarity demanded investment. Brevié proposed a fund capitalized by France to finance famine prevention and improve diet.[76] This symbolic proposal, counter to the near-sacred principle of colonial self-sufficiency, was intended as a rebuke to ministers who demanded miracles without means.

Despite these reservations, Brevié was a willing booster of the Popular Front's famine policies when he became governor-general of Indochina in January 1937. Among his first concerns was the chronic undernourishment that "makes the heart bleed." The French, Brevié admonished, had failed to secure "the bare minimum that is the right to life." It made no sense to "raise the social level of the masses if they remained condemned to suffer from hunger."[77] Following Minister of Colonies Moutet's instructions, Brevié planned for the creation of native food offices. Composed of five to six individuals, at least one of whom would be French, the offices were tasked with gathering information about harvests, stocks, and deficits, advising the administration on food policy, and providing technical education to farmers, including the basics of plant genetics.[78]

The implementation of the native food offices confirmed, once again, the gulf between new norms and persistent realities. Yves Châtel, who had been head of Annam during the Nghe Tinh soviets, was now resident-superior of Tonkin. He claimed that barring unforeseen catastrophe, famine was no longer a risk in his region. Chronic undernutrition caused by Malthusian overpopulation had taken famine's place "in the hierarchy of social evils." Between land reclamation projects to relieve population pressure and an emergency fund created in 1935—like similar funds, quickly forgotten—Châtel felt confident about the safety of his subjects.

However, when he relayed Brevié's instructions to create native food offices to his subordinates, they complained that they had no money for the new organizations, struggling even to provide emergency aid.[79] Following Châtel's advice, local administrators cynically sidestepped the problem of funding by simply renaming existing mutual aid cooperatives "native food offices."[80] Knowing full well that the unfunded offices would be useless in emergencies, Châtel suggested that administrators rely on the "altruistic sentiments" of the inhabitants instead.[81] Soon, a shortage motivated concerned Vietnamese notables to ask for emergency export controls. The French demurred, referring them instead to the new institutions, already demoted to "native food sections" of the mutual aid cooperatives. Complaints from both subjects and administrators make it clear that these merely nominal, unfunded institutions fulfilled the letter but not the spirit of reform.[82] It is no wonder that when the Guernut Commission took a closer look at the alimentary situation of the colonies, it found that that several years of relatively enlightened rule had failed to achieve the goals set by reformers such as Sarraut and Moutet.

The Apotheosis of Reform

The rise and fall of French governments was far removed from the physical experience of hunger. But when Jewish socialist Léon Blum led the Popular Front to electoral victory in May 1936, the impact echoed. French labor greeted Blum's election with a massive wave of strikes. The actions forced the negotiation of the Matignon Agreements, a generous program of worker protections including a forty-hour workweek and paid vacation. Most of these gains were cut back by 1938. Their application to the colonies would have been dismissed as absurd. Nonetheless, this socially conscious stance permeated the French imperial polity. The Popular Front was decidedly not anticolonial, but it inspired more attention to the living conditions of colonized people than any previous French government. The empire-wide inquiry led by Henri Guernut was singular in its scope and detail. As in France itself, though, the hopes of Popular Front-affiliated colonial reformers soured quickly into disillusion.

The short time the Popular Front was in power saw more interest in famine from a wider range of observers than ever before. Upon becoming minister of colonies in 1936, the socialist Marius Moutet declared famine prevention his single biggest priority. One of his first acts was to ask the colonial leadership to report on the nutritional condition of subjects. The information compiled was not the empirical data that scientists begged for, but the interested impressions of administrators. Still, the application of new standards of well-being to colonized people contributed to a new dynamic in imperial history. Radical party politician Justin Godart, sent to assess the situation in Indochina, was persuaded that as a precondition of any reform, everyone had to eat their fill. "In Indochina, *there are people who are hungry*. France cannot tolerate this, cannot be responsible."[83]

The governor-general of AOF, Jules Brevié, dismissed the Popular Front's antifamine ambitions as fantasy. The Indochinese response to Moutet's 1936 request for information was more positive and less candid. It claimed that famine had been rare since the French conquest. The French administration, taking its cue from the autochthonous Annamite government on which it was superimposed, had always prioritized hunger. Though it was true that the administration had suppressed the granaries of the kings of Annam, this was not because it lacked compassion. In the context of a cash economy, good transportation, and advanced hydraulic engineering, granaries were unnecessary. Indeed, the recently completed trans-Indochina railway linking Saigon and Hanoi, along with new dikes and increasing polyculture, had definitively eliminated the risk of famine.[84] This genre of instinctively self-flattering and self-protective analysis from colonial administrators afraid of getting in trouble was not helpful for real reform efforts.

After digesting the various responses, Moutet shared his conclusions. These reflected recent thinking in nutrition and public health. Famine, he explained, was an acute manifestation of habitual alimentary deficiency. If it struck public opinion more forcefully than chronic malnutrition, this was because it was more dramatic but not more harmful. The fight against famine, then, was primarily a fight against malnutrition and only secondarily against "accidental" famines triggered by disasters. As well as blaming the laziness of natives, Moutet directly implicated administrators who prioritized taxes above "well-being" and "living conditions." Tending to nutritional health, he insisted, was both a humanitarian duty and a political obligation tacitly accepted in the very act of colonization. It was, furthermore, a precondition for anything "great," or even "useful," to be accomplished overseas—subjects could not be civilized if they were malnourished or dead. Moutet instructed administrators to subordinate all policies and to orient all actions to the goal of proper diet. His proposals of agricultural cooperatives, polyculture, population redistribution, granaries, and improved transportation would not have been out of place decades earlier.[85] However, the idea that nutrition and public health were fundamental to colonial governance helped cement new norms of care.

Moutet's 1936 request for information was a precursor to a much more ambitious project. The Commission of Inquiry in the Overseas Territories, inaugurated January 30, 1937, was the prewar peak of a governing philosophy that applied modern living standards to colonial subjects. Colloquially named for Henri Guernut, the left politician and lifelong human rights activist who spearheaded the project, the commission sought to generate the data deemed necessary to assess and improve quality of life in the colonies. Guernut had been the secretary-general of the League of the Rights of Man and had, with Moutet and Viollis, participated in the Committee for Indochinese Amnesty and Defense. The Guernut Commission institutionalized this activist energy, coupling it to the machinery of the state. The commission was composed of forty-two politicians, experts, and public figures. They included professors from the Museum of Natural History and the Academy of Medicine, former colonial administrators such as Robert Delavignette and Henri Labouret, people of letters such as André Gide and Andrée Viollis, and the president of the Human Rights League Victor Basch, who would be assassinated by Vichy militants in 1944.[86] Even if some of these dignitaries lent their names more than their labor, their support gave the project standing.

The Guernut Commission sent questionnaires to French and indigenous figures overseas, solicited expert analyses, and centralized existing records and studies. In doing so, it compiled the most thorough set of data on colonial living conditions in the history of the French Empire. The fall of Léon Blum in June of 1937, then of the Popular Front in April 1938, deprived the commission of political support. It was dissolved before completing its work.[87] However brief, the formalization and institutionalization of new responsibilities provoked a flurry of activity. As much as technical advances, the framing of colonial governance in terms of quality of life and legitimate aspirations, accompanied by the sense that superiors and the public cared and were watching, pushed administrators to take famine seriously.

In his inauguration speech, Moutet promised that the Guernut Commission, politically independent and composed of the most qualified experts, would usher in a "new colonial doctrine." What good, he asked, was the authoritarian power of a colonial state uniting the legislative, executive, and judicial functions of government if it did not rest on a foundation of knowledge? To build this foundation, the commission's experts would go beyond questions of basic science, instead orienting their research toward the "development [développement]" of colonial populations. Scientific rigor would be guided by "that spirit of humanity" exemplified by the great novelist Gide. Without humanitarian grounding, any technical action involving "not a malleable and inert material, but men who expect everything of us" would be sterile. The commission would be guided by the triple mission of "an inventory, a program, a doctrine: in other words, what has been done, what must be done, and in what spirit it should be done." Moutet's eventual, radical goal was the extension of the Declaration of the Rights of Man and Citizen, the principles of individual liberty, and the protections of judicial rights to the overseas territories.[88] Modern science guided by a humanitarian conscience would make good the revolutionary promises of French civilization.

The Guernut Commission's work was structured around the twin problems of the quality of life and the legitimate aspirations of colonial subjects. Previously concerned primarily with simple biological life, the French now considered cultural and psychological fulfillment as part of their remit in the colonies.

Ironically, diagnosing the state of the empire in relation to these heightened norms exposed severe shortcomings according to the standard of the merely biological. Subjects could not aspire to much if they were starving. Preliminary research indicated that among the legitimate needs and aspirations of colonized people, the improvement of the "material conditions of existence" had logical priority. By shedding light on famine, which had "remained too long in shadow," the commission would contribute to an "alimentary policy that is obviously at the base of any truly colonizing action."[89] Subdividing its work into domains of investigation including "housing" and "migration," the commission gave the symbolically significant designation "inquiry number one" to its investigation "On the Alimentation of the Natives."[90]

The Guernut Commission presented its work as a decisive juncture in the history of French colonial famine. Famines had been too long accepted as the "ordinary and ineluctable consequences of certain natural calamities." The famines of 1931 in Niger and Annam underscored the need for a new approach.[91] The "extremely complex" problem required a division of labor corresponding to its scientific and social facets. The commission directed doctors and scientists to collect field data and conduct laboratory benchwork to ascertain the role of diet in the "human economy," paying special attention to vitamins and other chemical factors. This biochemical side of the project was managed by Émile Marchoux of the Pasteur Institute, a distinguished physician and microbiologist who had experience in the colonies and had trained with Émile Roux, one of Louis Pasteur's most important collaborators.[92] Marchoux's team sent out questionnaires on housing and sanitary conditions but emphasized both the importance and the difficulty of obtaining data on food consumption. Experts of the colonial health service were asked to observe roughly thirty families from different social situations through the agricultural year, weighing the food of each family member. They were charged with calculating the energetic value of diets with the help of a table converting grams of food categories such as flour, fish, fat, and starch to calories. There was a long list of questions regarding food availability and preparation. Did families eat vegetables such as beans, tomatoes, and eggplants? How much? Did they consume vitamin-rich peppers? If meat was eaten, was it fresh? Smoked? Spoiled? Was geophagy practiced? What was the albumin, hydrocarbon, fat, and vitamin content of typical diets? Did the inhabitants appear malnourished? What were the desiderata of the natives regarding diet? Perhaps anticipating resistance to the extra work these instructions entailed, the commission promised unspecified rewards for the medical functionaries who did the most thorough job completing the forms.[93]

For the social aspect of the alimentation problem, the commission sent questionnaires to district officers, functionaries of the agricultural service, and indigenous notables. Each recipient answered questions about the diet of indigenous families, divided into the categories of poor, comfortable, and rich.[94] The form intended for administrators included questions on demography, race or tribe, economic activities, household budgets, and the impact of social and economic change. How, for example, did the introduction of industrial agriculture affect the amount of money and labor families devoted to food production? The questionnaire sent to the agricultural service asked about climate, farming and husbandry practices, peasant budgets, and the effect of cash cropping on subsistence. The questionnaire for indigenous elites was the most detailed. Respondents were asked to establish a seasonal agricultural calendar, a description of the division of labor within families, and sample household budgets. They were to indicate the main food sources in their region, including staple crops, secondary crops, and poisonous emergency foods eaten during droughts. The descriptions of food were to be accompanied by drawings. Respondents were also asked to provide information on eating habits such as mealtimes and intrafamily disparities in access to food between men, women, and children. They were asked to give full sample menus chosen from throughout the agricultural year. For the purpose of scientific analysis, they were to record precise measurements of different ingredients.[95] Not everyone was convinced by this methodology. Some agreed with the Vietnamese ethnographer Nguyen Van Huyen of the French School of the Far East in Hanoi, who complained that the commission bombarded people with a hundred questions without giving adequate time to answer and without controlling for differences in climate, mores, and other variables.[96] There was no doubt, though, that the exercise, inadequate as it may have been, was unprecedented.

The questionnaires were standardized, but responses varied significantly. Some respondents took the job seriously, meticulously answering each question for both families and individuals divided by class, sex, age, and other variables. Others did the bare minimum. There were no standardized methodologies for weighing food, averaging quantities (of calories, francs, hectares, or whatever else), defining social classes, or choosing statistically representative cases. Some respondents chose to describe recipes for popular dishes, others the method for making millet beer. Despite these inconsistencies, the attention to food at the scale of the entire empire was novel. Most paperwork at the ministerial level tended to generalize, homogenize, and render information into easily manipulated numbers. Guernut's questionnaires, on the contrary, were notable for their detail.

Responses conveyed the color of daily life, rarely seen in official paperwork, sometimes literally in the form of drawings. Teacher Marcel M'vet informed the commission that in the subdivision of Oyem in Northern Gabon, rich families ate three meals a day, usually consisting of peanut soup, fish or meat, and chocolate. This was sometimes accompanied by manioc, fruit puree, and either a lemon beverage or wine. Poor families had no fixed mealtimes. They ate a tedious diet of thin soup, manioc, and fruit. With this, they drank only water. On average, individuals consumed twenty to forty grams of peppers, one to two kilograms of manioc, three hundred to four hundred grams of peanuts, and twenty to twenty-five grams of salt per day. Meat and fish were eaten in variable amounts depending on class. Under no circumstances did anyone, rich or poor, eat with their fingers. Those who could afford it used European-style cutlery. Those who could not served meals in banana leaves and ate with carved wooden spoons. At mealtimes, men gathered communally and women waited on them. Though men and women ate separately, they partook of the same diet. The exception was pregnant women, for whom antelopes, chimpanzees, and certain fish were taboo.[97] Another functionary in the region contradicted M'vet on this point, reporting that women were denied meat almost entirely, out of "masculine egotism."[98]

In contrast to such careful weighing and measuring, a functionary in the Congo explained that he was unable to report on mealtimes or weigh ingredients as the natives possessed neither watches nor scales. He focused instead on descriptions of agricultural and cooking techniques. Thus the commission learned about *endjouni*, small fish cooked in oil and eaten during the dry season; *m'vouia*, a sauce made of greens and meat; and *ndouga*, wild tubers eaten in lean times.[99] In some areas of French Equatorial Africa (Afrique Équatoriale Française, AEF), purchasing food was considered shameful. Every household was expected to grow enough food to offer a meal to guests, even in times of dearth. The accountant Félix Jean-Tchicaye from Pointe-Noire, which had suffered terrible violence and hunger during the Congo-Ocean railroad construction, was convinced that commerce and transportation had rendered true famine impossible. Even so, his response included a request for metropolitan aid to improve agriculture and husbandry so people could "eat their fill."[100]

In the Red River Delta of Indochina, the questionnaires confirmed the existence of huge wealth disparities. Absolute sums varied by region, but in general rich families earned at least twenty times as much as the poorest, permanently indebted families, sometimes much more. Disparities in wealth led to disparities in diet. Sample budgets showed that poor families spent 70 to 85 percent of their income on food. They were forced to settle for poor-quality rice cut with corn or roots supplemented with salt and vegetables when available. Soy or fish sauce was the sole protein source. This poor-quality diet was insufficient in quantity as well. In the *soudure* before harvests, poor families typically subsisted on just one daily meal consisting of rice bran or other marginal foods normally

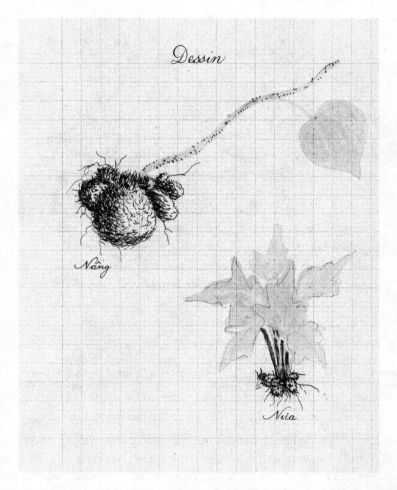

Dessin

Nẵng

Nia

FIGURE 9. "Venomous plants consumed in times of dearth," Cochinchina, 1938. Drawing by Le Luan Phan. ANOM, GGI 53486.

reserved for pigs. These families ate meat only on feast days or the anniversary of an ancestor's death. Rich families spent two to three times as much per meal as poor ones. The extra expenditure that comfortable families could afford let them vary their diets based on good-quality rice with meat and fats. Rice stocks saw them through shortages comfortably. Some favorite regional recipes included turtle boiled with fat, vinegar, soy, saffron, mint, fish sauce, and chilis; coagulated duck blood; pork cooked in the style of dog meat and seasoned with cardamom; and fish with mustard, onion, ginger, and fish sauce. The well-off enjoyed wine, beer, and in the summertime, lemonade. The poor endured a hungry existence in dark and unsanitary hovels. They labored from before dawn

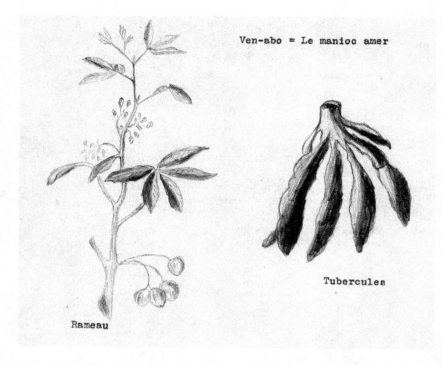

Ven-abo = Le manioc amer

Tubercules

Rameau

FIGURE 10.   "Bitter manioc," Gabon, 1938. A venomous food eaten after rinsing in running water for three to four days. Drawing by Jean-François Ondo and François Engohang. ANOM, 61COL2853.

until late at night with only a short break to swallow something cold on the paddy dike.[101] One respondent, a Vietnamese teacher, commented, "Truly, it is hard to imagine that so much activity, struggle, and will could lead to such an atrocious result: misery."[102]

In addition to distributing questionnaires, the Guernut Commission solicited in-depth expert studies. One study on the "quality of life of agricultural workers" in Tonkin concluded they were no better off in 1938 than they had been in 1920. In a telling comparison highlighting a new universality of living standards, the report contrasted abject Tonkinese peasants with their better-off counterparts in Europe. Old-fashioned racial generalizations coexisted with new sociological understandings of colonized people as forming complex, stratified societies. Annamites were lazy and unambitious, taking advantage of incessant funerals, weddings, and ritual ceremonies to constantly skip work. Whenever they had a little money, they blew it all in spending binges. Such tendencies to see subjects as undifferentiated masses ruled by innate racial qualities persisted alongside new analyses of social dynamics. There was a growing recognition that famines did not affect a region or a race indiscriminately; certain people within a society were made vulnerable by economic status, gender, age, or any number of other social variables. The report thus divided rural people into the categories of agricultural laborer, sharecropper, peasant owning enough land for subsistence, and peasant owning too little land to subsist solely from its produce.[103] Analyzing colonial people as internally differentiated populations rather than homogenous races suggested that modern forms of social management were appropriate in non-Western settings.

In Tonkin, according to the quality-of-life report, rich and poor alike suffered from overpopulation. Colonization schemes offering land for settlement in sparsely populated areas in the highlands or in Cochinchina had seen only limited success. Annamites were loath to leave their ancestral homes, among other reasons because they were afraid of the unfamiliar ghosts that haunted foreign lands. More effective was the recruitment of peasants as temporary labor on Cochinchinese plantations, where wages were withheld so workers could not break contract or waste earnings before traveling home to their families. To address widespread usury, an agricultural credit fund loaned to landowners at 12 percent interest. For nonlandowners, the administration of Tonkin had earlier in 1938 founded agricultural cooperatives to store and distribute seed communally. These institutions allowed for shared rice storage and marketing, thereby avoiding postharvest gluts and earning farmers a "more just" remuneration.[104]

These were, experts warned, temporary expedients that did not address the root cause of overpopulation. The Red River Delta was one of the only places in the French Empire that consistently invited a Malthusian analysis of population growth in relation to the capacity for food production. Densities of one thousand people per square kilometer, one observer wrote, saw miserable masses "swarming like ants" on land that could not feed them.[105] The demographic and ecological pressures of six million farmers cultivating land appropriate for just two million could only be definitively relieved by industrialization.[106]

Among the Guernut Commission's more novel procedures was to solicit *vœux*, desiderata, from settler and indigenous notables. Though some remained skeptical about the value of the opinions of people they considered backward, it was one of the first times the French thought to ask subjects—though only elite ones—what they wanted.[107] In Indochina, where floods and shortages were ongoing, most respondents asked for things that the administration insisted already existed, such as reserve granaries, aid distributions, antispeculation measures, mutual aid societies, credit unions, flood management, and emergency requisitioning of hoarded food.[108] Some respondents pointed out this discrepancy, as did French and Vietnamese officials who openly admitted that emergency reserves existed only on paper.[109] The *vœux* proposed a variety of plans, some better conceived than others. But taken together, the criticisms amounted less to specific policy preferences than to an appeal for a change in posture toward suffering. This spirit was captured in the translated response of retired functionary and self-identified "simple soul" Monsieur Cat Van Tran: "We have never done enough for the poor class. The problem is very arduous, but should we not search for a solution?"[110]

Many Vietnamese respondents demanded worker protections equal to those just passed by the Popular Front in France. The Guernut Commission affirmed the legitimacy of these requests while maintaining that French "social law" was inappropriate for the lagging level of social evolution in Indochina. Attenuated versions of European institutions and laws could improve quality of life while providing civilizational training. For example, rather than instituting a national minimum wage, a "vital" wage could be fixed by region. Instead of unions, "amicable" trade societies would "prepare the ground" for future labor organization without giving ignorant and gullible natives the power to bargain collectively. These proposed labor protections would not apply to agricultural workers, the vast majority of the population.[111] Reformers such as those in the Hanoi chapter of the Human Rights League militated for the application of French social legislation (*legislation de prévoyance sociale*), including a minimum wage, as protection against the "excesses of an all-powerful capitalism." But the Popular Front's nascent welfare state would never extend overseas.[112]

Instead of empowering colonized workers in the manner of French ones, the Popular Front sought to make colonial paternalism somewhat gentler and vastly more ambitious—a disposition similar to what Franco-Tunisian philosopher Albert Memmi later called "charitable racism."[113] A dossier compiled for the Guernut Commission by the government-general of Algeria displayed a heightened technical and social responsibility for subsistence. Many subjects and administrators would have been surprised to learn that "of all public calamities, famine is today the one that the genius of man can most efficiently foresee and combat."[114] Algeria's leaders saw themselves as participating in an international nutritional program in concord with the League of Nations and non-league nations such as the United States and Japan, motivated by "a more social understanding of politics." Improving indigenous diet required the coordinated management of economics, social and cultural life, and the environment. Social policies should be structured around the physiological aspects of nutrition, including the calculation of healthy rations, proper cooking techniques, and attention to health problems stemming from under- and malnutrition.[115]

Famine was still considered the product of improvident people interacting with harsh environments, but these ingredients were thought to be subject to rational control. Algerian functionaries believed nature could be, if not completely tamed, at least nudged toward human ends. Modern science as yet had no defense against extreme temperatures, but the caprices of precipitation could be rendered irrelevant by irrigation. The other input, people, was more complicated. Relegated to undesirable farmland Europeans did not want, caught in a vicious cycle of debt, and constitutionally incapable of economic reason, indigenous Algerian farmers lived at the edge of death. Experts now looked for the causes of famine in underlying conditions rather than in abrupt disasters. Shortage was sporadic, but poverty and precarity, "neighbor to misery," were constant. The quintupling of the population in the last century had upset the Malthusian balance between bodies and resources, "physiology and economy," inviting famine to install itself as "mistress of the home." But like the Algerian environment, the "ancestral character" of Algerian people could be improved by rationalizing the economy around food.[116]

In thinking about famine, Algerian officials drew heavily on nutrition science. "Alimentary hygiene," one wrote, had recently emerged as a principal branch of preventive medicine and public health. Organic chemists had learned that diet was key to the health of mothers, children, and those afflicted with diseases such as rickets, pellagra, and beriberi. Its implications, though, were even broader, as a proper diet was discovered to be necessary for normal human development. In fact, deficiency disease was not a major problem in Algeria. Most people had access to vitamins from fruit, milk, eggs, cereals, and oil. Of all the avitaminoses, only rickets was prevalent. However, habitually deficient diets led to symptoms such as physiological weakness, gastrointestinal distress, and susceptibility to infection. Fighting malnutrition (*malnutrition*) in Algeria was less about treating deficiency diseases than managing infections exacerbated by poor diet and promoting overall nutritional health.[117]

The idea that bodies and environments could be controlled and oriented toward a holistic society centered on dietary health had been taking hold for several years. What was new about the Guernut project was the effort to remedy the absence of data that nutritionists had complained was the limiting factor in social transformation. To establish this foundation of knowledge about the needs, resources, and "nutritional state [*état de nutrition*]" of native Algerians, a study of diet and "normal conditions of existence" was executed in seventy-three of Algeria's communes. The study found that out of 3,507,428 inhabitants divided into 694,845 families, 142,294 families were "very poor," with an annual revenue of less than one thousand francs. An additional 222,824 were "poor," with an annual income of between one thousand and two thousand francs. Even families categorized as "well-off," earning an income between two thousand and four thousand francs, were counted as nutritionally deprived. A full 85 percent of native Algerians were undernourished or malnourished. The researchers concluded that the dominant characteristic of the Algerian diet was its insufficiency, which stunted the potential of the race.[118]

The effects of malnutrition for the unfortunate 85 percent began in infancy. Algerian mothers breast-fed for up to two years. This, experts believed, depleted their milk of nutrients essential to human growth. Once weaned, infants were fed rancid boiled herbs, indigestible bread, and polluted water. Children who managed to survive this early diet struggled to fulfill their "vital needs" during the crucial growth period of adolescence. Poor adults lived on a diet consisting almost exclusively of carbohydrates and fats. This protein-deficient regimen fell far short of the optimum diet, barely providing a "maintenance ration." Daily consumption for the poorest 50 percent of Algerians averaged 1,375 calories. This was less than half the standard of 3,000 calories for a man of average size and activity calculated by the League of Nations in 1932. Stunted development resulted in physically and morally degenerate individuals. Thus closed a vicious circle: "The organism presents a state of marked deficiency that makes very difficult the fight against meteorological conditions in a country where atmospheric variations are brusque and intense."[119]

The Guernut Commission prompted a surge of activity in colonial food research. It is difficult, though, to distinguish between projects that made a difference in people's access to healthy food and those that did not. New data could be oriented toward welfare, but it was also crucial to a politics of representation that lent the gravitas and authority of numbers to the French Empire's stories about itself. A published pamphlet entitled "Diet of the Natives in Algeria" insisted that France's civilizing successes were self-evidently "inscribed in figures." "The rational management of alimentation has become a new task of states," the pamphlet explained. Algeria's fulfillment of this responsibility was advertised through the visual display of quantitative information. Graphs showing decreasing mortality rates among Algerians established the overall statistical context. One chart showed huge increases in agricultural loans, from ten million francs in 1929 to over one hundred million in 1936. Another displayed the amount of aid distributed during shortages in 1937 as a percentage of total budget, and another the volume of water passing through new irrigation networks.

These impressive numbers said little about who received this aid, who benefited from irrigation, and the practical effects of either on nutritional health. Some proposals, such as a 1937 regional minimum wage for agricultural workers meant to guarantee "subsistence" and "quality of life," may have been effective had they been enforced.[120] Others, such as the Consultative Commission for Indigenous Diet, which was established in 1937 as a counterpart to the 1936 National Committee for the Study of Diet in France, seem to have provided little benefit. Intended to unite administrators and University of Algiers savants to think about nutrition policy, there is no evidence that the indigenous diet commission met more than once.[121] Many of the grandest plans inspired by the Guernut Commission existed primarily, perhaps only, in graphs, tables, and correspondence between colonial administrators and the Parisian authorities on whom their careers depended.

Among the most consequential and least surprising findings of the Guernut Commission was that proper nutrition was expensive. The need for subventions from France to bolster inadequate colonial budgets was a refrain among the administrators, technicians, and subjects consulted by the commission. The problem of famine was a problem of money: "Budgetary difficulties in our overseas possessions are certainly not the only cause of famines, but they create a situation that greatly favors them."[122] The work of the Guernut Commission implied that France would need to face up to Albert Sarraut's challenge of fifteen years earlier to "accept the logical consequences" of its principles.[123] This logic was starkly antithetical to the economic imperative that colonies be self-sufficient.

Famine in a Time of Reform

The years of the Guernut inquiry, 1937 and 1938, were also years of widespread food emergencies. It is possible that the commission happened to coincide with a period of exceptional privation in places as far-flung as the Maghreb, West Africa, and Indochina. It is more likely that once French people began looking for famines, they were distressingly easy to find. Judging from these crises, several years of instructions and threats had had little effect on the prevalence of hunger. But now more than ever, with the quality of life of colonial subjects front and center, famine was shameful. The economic logic of administering an empire attuned to the needs of subjects reached its necessary conclusion: colonial administrations demanded money from France to make good their alimentary responsibilities.

As Henri Guernut gathered his data, a food crisis was unfolding across all three French territories in North Africa. The commission dispatched Senator Théodore Steeg, who had been head of the Algerian and Moroccan administrations (as well as prime minister for a few weeks in 1930) and would succeed Moutet as minister of colonies in early 1938. It was the first time that a French official was sent specifically to address an active famine overseas. Steeg reported that Algeria, Morocco, and Tunisia were bankrupt. A combined expenditure of nearly half a billion francs on food aid, credit for farmers, famine camps, and other emergency measures had depleted all three budgets. Famine was most intense in southeastern Morocco. There, the French protectorate subsidized Muslim aid societies to house the destitute. To keep the starving from moving around, the administration set up cordons composed of refugee camps to head off (*refouler*) Moroccans fleeing to cities or to neighboring Algeria. This spatial management, a direct extension of the geographic segregation policies of nineteenth-century Algeria, was meant to control the spread of typhus and other infectious diseases. Administrators hoped it would also stop thousands of refugees from seeking starvation wages in the cities, undercutting the urban proletariat and drawing them into starvation as well. At the camps, refugees were fed, given medical care, and returned by truck to their tribal lands, where they received food distributions.[124] To counteract the ripple effects of famine through an interconnected economy, the administration subsidized urban artisans and merchants affected by the collapse of rural demand. The multifactorial interventions famine now demanded, Steeg argued, would be impossible without money from France. If funds were not forthcoming, the consequences for French prestige and security would be dire.[125]

Pleas for money were echoed in a pamphlet published by the protectorate of Morocco. Taking up the new language of quality of life and the old language of gendered humanitarianism, the pamphlet claimed that the French saved thousands from death by distributing food to women and children and providing work for men. Old arguments about the "moral danger" of handouts were bolstered with new arguments about the physiological benefits of hard work. Citing Étienne Burnet's studies of nutrition in Tunisia, the pamphlet explained that physical labor protected against starvation by making metabolism more efficient. Administrative aid workers considered the protective as well as the caloric value of emergency food for the first time. To ensure that Moroccans got the full nutritional benefit from an unfamiliar grain, imported rice rations were accompanied by cooking instructions. Previously, famine relief had always been granted according to the minimum quantity of food that would keep people alive at the lowest price. Cereals were the only food offered. Now in Morocco, distributions of vitamin-rich vegetables supplemented carbohydrate staples. Doctors, recognizing that mortality in mobile and malnourished populations was as likely to be caused by epidemics as by starvation, vaccinated hundreds of thousands of Moroccans against typhus. Burnet hailed the campaign as the largest collective prophylaxis effort since the Great War. Looking ahead, the protectorate hoped to stave off future famines by transforming the Moroccan environment through irrigation and reforestation. Dealing with the complex emergency in Morocco, then, required coordinated interventions related to economics, nutrition, medicine, public health, culinary science, ecology, logistics, and other domains of expertise. However, even short-term rescue efforts would falter without metropolitan subventions. The protectorate lent its official voice to Steeg's call for money.[126] There is no evidence it was heard.

Indochina, too, experienced a food crisis in 1937. Though reserve funds and granaries had been mandated repeatedly for fifty years, none were in operation when drought, typhoons, and floods put the "tragically eloquent figure" of eight hundred thousand Tonkinese at risk of starvation. Resident-General of Tonkin Yves Châtel improvised. He appropriated whatever money he could find and hoped not to be disciplined for misallocating budget funds. He eventually received emergency aid from Governor-General Jules Brevié, but only a third of the 822,690 piastres requested.[127] As Châtel had foreseen just months earlier in his instructions regarding native food offices, administrators relied on private charity. Buddhist benevolent societies, professional organizations, expatriate Vietnamese in France, and even the Chinese government donated money for food and clothing.[128] Administrators in Indochina set up public fundraising drives and charity balls, efforts that "could only with difficulty be presented as a brilliant success, the height of the art of foresight, for to govern is to foresee."[129] Reflecting a blurred division of state and civil society and a gendered division of labor, Madame Colombon, the wife of a functionary, was appointed to coordinate fundraising efforts.[130] With these charity funds, the administration negotiated with private companies for bulk discounts on food. As of September 1937, two hundred thousand tons of rice had been ordered.[131] Châtel was hostile to free distributions, arguing that "pure liberality" allocated resources arbitrarily. It would be more equitable, he thought, to require work in exchange for rice. The point was not to extract labor but to apply a work test for aid. Remuneration would be provided regardless of physical fitness so that the elderly, women, and children as well as able-bodied men could survive. Through work, subjects would learn to search within themselves for their own salvation instead of relying on the state.[132] The implementation of this plan was marked by confusion. Administrators complained of not receiving their full allocation of rice, making it impossible to comply with instructions.[133]

For the first time since the 1867 Algerian famine, metropolitan France intervened. European officials and settlers made overtures in the name of Indochinese subjects to Minister of Colonies Marius Moutet and the French legislature. They employed a hybrid language of responsibility incorporating elements of political obligation but appealing primarily to sentiment. This strategy drew more from the traditions of natural disaster philanthropy and international aid than the modern welfare and public health approaches embraced by the Popular

Front. Muddying the distinction between politics and charity, a petition to the French legislature claimed the status of humanitarian crisis for the famine. Unlike earthquakes or other natural catastrophes, food shortage did not enthrall spectators with flames, explosions, and terrifying cries. Nonetheless, its quieter victims deserved compassion too. The petitioners reminded lawmakers that Indochina had never before asked France for aid. It did so now "in the name of humanity and of the solidarity the great protector peoples owe their humble protégés."[134]

The petition appealed to the precedent of French disaster aid for colonies. But it also pointed to the charity France had given after natural disasters in foreign countries such as Italy and Japan, and the half-million francs Chiang Kai-shek's government had just donated to Indochinese famine victims. It invoked Indochina's sacrifice in blood and money during the Great War, and noted the charity the people of Indochina had offered after floods in France, cyclones in Guadeloupe, and earthquakes in Japan.[135] By connecting the food crisis to other instances that had mobilized global philanthropy, petitioners made claims in the terms of a global economy of international humanitarian aid. Only as an afterthought did they make political demands as a constituent part of the French Empire. The French legislature responded by voting three million francs to relieve the hungry. This was a great deal less than the 350 million francs requested by Tonkin alone. But as the petition itself asserted, it was the first direct famine aid of its kind under the Third Republic.

Interest groups lobbied Moutet for even more. The three million francs were "ridiculously insufficient" for a situation rapidly deteriorating into hopelessness. Painting pathetic scenes that "official reports do not and will never mention" to move the "pitying and generous heart" of France, throwing in ominous warnings of security threats from Vietnamese nationalists and Japanese imperialists, the suppliants stressed that the future of Indochina was at stake.[136] Another heartfelt petition appealed to the "pity" of the chamber of deputies on behalf of the "rice-eating populations of Tonkin."[137] Even at the beginning of the welfare era, calling on sentimental humanitarianism was a better bet than making political claims for the relief of colonial suffering. The care of the colonized remained rooted in pity as much as in law.

French philanthropy mobilized. A charitable organization was founded to raise money for Indochina and Algeria. The philanthropists again blurred public and private by choosing the politician Albert Sarraut as president of the charity. They counted the omnipresent Gide and antifascist ethnographer and politician Paul Rivet as members.[138] The aid legislation and charitable campaign were not without controversy. There were complaints that the money was misused, distributed as loans instead of as free donations, or was bolstering administrative budgets rather than rescuing the needy. The effort in Indochina was spearheaded by European politicians and planters, who benefited disproportionately from French generosity even as they used images of starving Vietnamese to open hearts and coffers. One settler in Cochinchina affiliated with the fascist group Cross of Fire (*Croix de feu*) sought to discredit the humanitarian republicanism of the Popular Front. He informed the Guernut Commission that after inviting journalists to photograph the moving spectacle of food distributions, administrators then sold the rice for their own profit. One bought a refrigerator with the proceeds.[139] The local administration denied these accusations.[140] Another whistleblower wrote an open letter to his representative in the French Chamber of Deputies, complaining that charity funds were being disbursed only as loans. The writer chided that "when a man is dying of hunger and thirst on the road, one does not dare make him sign a promissory note as a precondition for sliding a few drops of water between his dried lips."[141] The dynamics of aid showed that talk of quality of life and legitimate aspirations did not itself create mechanisms through which to claim provision. The response to shortages in 1937 and 1938 resembled the charity drives during the 1867 Algerian famine more than the welfare empire aspired to by the Guernut Commission.

The dearth of 1937 in Indochina, only a few years removed from the Nghe Tinh soviets, raised concerns of security and communism. The local and international left claimed credit for providing aid. A Vietnamese-language article from 1938 detailed how the Hanoi chapter of the SFIO distributed rice when the administration would not.[142] The mayor of Hanoi warned that Annamites, like the European masses, would soon "declare, with greater and greater force, that each has a right to life and to a nourishing diet [*ration alimentaire*]." The municipal police had dispersed crowds of thousands of peaceful protestors demanding food, but how long before they claimed their rights violently? If they had "our ideas," wrote the mayor, they would take by force the bags of food flouted in front of their eyes in carts and depots. Under these circumstances, the mayor argued, charity was merely symbolic. It conferred honor upon donors without doing much to lessen suffering. Good intentions alone, wrote the mayor, were not enough to capitalize aid funds. He proposed raising taxes to augment Tonkin's emergency funds tenfold, from three hundred thousand piastres to three million.[143] His advice was not heeded, but his words correctly predicted nationalists' claim of a right to subsistence.

As philanthropists gathered donations in 1937, Indochinese administrators proposed a permanent public fund to avoid the need for such ad hoc measures in the future.[144] They did so again in 1938, when the government-general of Indochina decreed the creation of a "supply service." Responding to complaints about irregularities in rescue provisioning, the new service emphasized precise accounting and a transparent paper trail so that "improvisation" could be replaced with "organization."[145] As Hanoi had no public granaries, arrangements were made with the chamber of commerce in Haiphong to store fifteen hundred tons of emergency rice.[146] This was another in a long list of plans mandating reserves in cash or in kind for all or parts of Indochina, including in 1907, 1912, 1930, 1935, 1937, and 1938. Each plan was preceded by debates about what form the reserves should take. Each time, the same concerns about the character of the Annamite race, the overpopulation of the Red River Delta, the need for better hydraulic infrastructure, the role of mandarins, and the poverty of budgets were repeated. Each time, the plans were immediately abandoned. There is no evidence of their operation during any subsequent emergencies.

Through the entire colonial period, the French resorted to disjointed, ad hoc measures. They scrabbled together funds from overburdened budgets while appealing to public charity. Interwar discourse encouraged greater responsibility for famine, but administrations bereft of institutional memory and money fell short in their new tasks. As one functionary put it in 1930, coherent antifamine policy had been sabotaged by the vicissitudes of an Indochinese administration short on funds and personnel, lacking coordination and continuity and incapable of learning from past experience. Again and again, "the repetition of the same errors lead to the same failures."[147] Far from solving these problems, the Guernut Commission made them stand out all the more.

In French West Africa, drought and locusts threatened to plunge the region back into crisis in 1937. The AOF administrators, having been inundated with instructions and threats after the 1931 Niger famine, were more vigilant than they had been before. The government-general ordered administrators to inspect crops and estimate food availability in January 1937.[148] Native provident societies (sociétés indigènes de prévoyance, SIPs) appear to have been equipped and operational.[149] Farmers had managed to restock family granaries without government intervention.[150] Crediting Moutet's recently initiated five-year plan, the Niger administration prided itself on succeeding where Governor Louis-Placide Blacher had failed. In the face of locusts and a rainfall deficit nearly identical to that of 1930, the colony launched a "battlefield mobilization" of chiefs, administrators, and technicians. The sultan of Zinder and the zarmakoy of Dosso took commanding roles in this "agricultural crusade." Administrators claimed that despite farmers' resistance to government granaries, they held reserves of over one hundred kilograms of grain per person. Fearing that distributing food for consumption would encourage improvidence, the SIPs instead gave farmers seed for fast-growing millet, corn, and beans. These measures, administrators reported, staved off starvation under the same conditions that had caused famine in 1931. Indeed, during the emergency, grain reserves per capita increased.[151]

Officials declined to estimate mortality for any of the food emergencies of 1937. It seems likely that none reached the severity of the 1931 Niger famine. In North Africa in particular, the large expenditures may have mitigated what might have otherwise been more serious famines. But there is also evidence that administrators exaggerated the success of their interventions. In AOF, contentions of meticulous preparation were contradicted by Governor-General Brevié's pessimistic report to Marius Moutet from just a few months earlier, which emphasized the difficulties of famine prevention. When money was spent on agricultural projects, it did not necessarily decrease famine risk. For example, the Office du Niger irrigation and colonization scheme in the French Soudan boosted cotton production but also increased food precarity for the semivoluntary participants.[152]

One fictionalized recollection suggested that seemingly benevolent policies that were attractive on paper suffered from problems of implementation. As the story goes, the governor of Niger ordered his subordinates to requisition grain for newly compulsory reserves. An experienced officer pleaded with the governor to reconsider. If the plan went forward, the officer warned, "the peasants will starve to death next to their full granaries." The governor insisted on requisitioning the millet mandated by his superiors in Dakar, who were anxious to avoid a repetition of 1931. The consensus among the district officers was that the operation was dangerous. The old colonial hand resigned in disgust. His post went to a young and ambitious newcomer who would at least pretend to follow orders. The new officer's subjects were distraught: "Will we have to dig through anthills like in 1931? Or eat dogs?" The young administrator's solution to the impossible task was as cynical as the orders themselves. An African chief had already stocked granaries with the receipts from the traditional tithe. Through some creative accounting, the granaries were found to hold the exact amount of grain required by Dakar. The officer bought the chief's cooperation by recommending him for the Legion of Honor and repainted the granaries with the administration's symbol. Alas, an inspector from Niamey discovered that not only did the granaries belong to the chief and not the administration, but they contained less grain than they were supposed to. The inspector sent a report to Niamey, where, at the moment that the chief clerk was about to read it, a gust of air blew it out the open window. Back in the district, the rains arrived and famine, no thanks to the maladroit young administrator, was avoided.[153] This short story suggests that the grand plans devised by distant bureaucrats had a tenuous connection to reality.

Well-being in the French Empire

In the decade of the 1930s, French people paid more attention to famine in the colonies than ever before. But this attention did not translate into the kind of solidarity or technocratic action that colonial reformers envisioned. The 1931 catastrophes in Niger and Annam pushed senior administrators to amalgamate ideas related to nutrition, international humanitarianism, and security into an explicit norm of governance. The French Empire was now unequivocally responsible for the subsistence and dietary health of subjects. The Popular Front's Guernut Commission was the climax of the interwar history of rising standards of care. However, French administrations were ill-suited to achieving the sweeping social and economic reforms this norm implied. The Guernut Commission represented both the height of humanist imperialism and a rupture in the imperial project. It helped unveil the full cost of an empire oriented toward the well-being of subjects. This was not a cost the French were willing to pay. Though rhetoric now included new ideas of balanced diet and nutritional health, famines persisted. When the Guernut Commission discovered active food emergencies all over the empire in 1937, underprepared and overwhelmed functionaries relied on charity. The dynamic of identifying needs, taking responsibility for them, and failing to follow through would reach a breaking point during World War II. Following a famine in Tonkin in 1945, nationalists could credibly claim that the French had failed in the most basic duty of states: ensuring that people had enough to eat.

CHAPTER 7

Losing Control in Vietnam, 1945

In 1956, the author Tran Van Mai looked back on the famine of 1945 that cost between one million and three million Vietnamese lives. Compelled by the conviction that "human lives and human rights must be respected above all else," his purpose was to present an objective account of the catastrophe. The famine, Tran Van Mai explained, had been orchestrated by the French to sabotage the nationalist movement. Rice requisitions in 1943 and 1944 were not merely poor planning; they were deliberately calculated with "the intent of murder." As prices rose beyond the means of ordinary people, the French commandeered rice at a fraction of market value, committing "robbery in broad daylight." People starved outside government warehouses, unable to reach the food hoarded within. The French head of Tonkin, Tran Van Mai alleged, made his murderous intent explicit: "The more of them die, the better!"[1]

For Tran Van Mai, the French bore ultimate responsibility for the famine crime. But they were not alone in their guilt. Rich Vietnamese ignored compatriots dying in full view of their stocked granaries. When the French administration organized belated relief, corrupt mandarins filled their own pockets rather than the bellies of the starving. Wealthy villagers refused to allot public funds for aid, fearing it would be seen as communistic. Ironically, this cruelty thrust needy people further into the arms of the communists. But Tran Van Mai was unimpressed with the nationalist Viet Minh, a venal power easily bribed by speculators. Finally, he turned his critical eye inward. He recalled how on coming across a lifeless body, "I was not moved as much as I wanted to be. I tried to take control of my mind, to kindle a flicker of humanity in my bronze-cold heart."[2]

Tran Van Mai was liberal with blame, but in his telling the French were the clear villains. Historians are more ambivalent. There is debate about the relative responsibilities of the colonizing French and the occupying Japanese, about the role of food availability decline versus failures in food entitlements, and about the influence of policy as opposed to acts of God such as typhoons and Allied bombs. Some scholars emphasize the importance of Japan's food extraction policies as it treated Indochina as a rice basket for its own empire, the Greater East Asia Co-Prosperity Sphere.[3] Others implicate France more directly, citing the decisive impact of French requisitioning, forced conversion to inedible industrial crops, and a monetary policy that quintupled the currency in circulation and caused runaway inflation.[4] Each of these arguments illuminates different elements of the confluence of forces that led to mass starvation.[5]

Establishing the relative weight of its multiple causes or apportioning blame are important ways to approach the famine of 1945. Another is to study it from the perspective of international relations. Up close, the famine was the intensely personal struggle for survival so movingly described by Tran Van Mai. At a broader scale, the famine formed part of an international struggle over the shape of the postwar global order.[6] Feeding populations had become a constitutive element of sovereignty, and France seized on famine relief as a strategy to reestablish its great power credentials after the humiliation of military defeat.

This contest over sovereignty and famine was a key juncture in a historical process in which the French Empire took increasing responsibility for subsistence and failed to fulfill this responsibility. Until the interwar years, French colonial administrators saw famines as tragedies to be relieved by charity. In the 1930s, they accepted famine prevention as a political obligation. In Indochina at the end of the Second World War, ensuring subsistence was not just an obligation, but a right that the French sought to secure in competition with other claimants. As a marker of legitimacy in relation both to colonial subjects and the international sphere, famine control became a political asset that outweighed its financial costs. The Great Famine of 1945 not only contributed to the material conditions of the Vietnamese revolution; it was also at the center of the struggle over the right to rule during World War II and the lead-up to the First Indochina War. The fight for sovereignty was in part a fight over subsistence.

As early as the 1884 Berlin Conference that tried to impose order on the scramble for Africa, European powers debated what constituted colonial sovereignty. The negotiators settled on the principle of "effective occupation" as the standard for recognizing European nations' rights in the territories they claimed. In theory, effective occupation entailed not just military control over a territory and its population, but also the assumption of responsibilities including the protection of "existing rights."[7] No usable definitions of these requirements were elaborated, and no oversight mechanisms were set up. But at least in the abstract, some form of respect for the well-being of colonized people was present at this important moment of modern colonial history. After World War I, the League of Nations formalized norms of colonial care by monitoring the new "mandates," the German and Ottoman territories transferred to countries on the winning side of the war.[8] Imperial powers submitted only reluctantly to league oversight in the mandates. The question of where exactly sovereignty was located—whether in the territory itself, the mandatory nation, or the league—was never fully resolved. In formal colonial territories in which empires were unequivocally sovereign, imperial nations guarded their autonomy jealously against an encroaching international community that set itself up as the guardian of humanity.[9] One way that empires protected their prerogatives was by persuading the international community they were responsible colonialists.

The association of sovereignty and famine control that had been building over the previous decades intensified during the jockeying for power as World War II was winding down. Though both French propaganda and the retrospective narratives of Vietnamese nationalists imposed a false continuity on their control of the territory, Indochina was up for grabs.[10] The responsibility, and the right, to alleviate famine became intertwined with sovereignty itself— became part of the content of the concept—both internally, facing the people, and externally, facing the international community.[11] The Vichy administration, the French republic, imperial Japan, nationalist China, the Japanese-backed Empire of Vietnam, the Viet Minh, the Allied powers, and the United Nations all sought the prerogative to provide famine relief, and, thereby, to have a say in the future of the region.

Famine and the Endgame of World War II

The reformism that permeated the French Empire in the 1930s built to an inescapable obligation to deal with the famine of 1945. In the Vietnamese-speaking areas of Indochina, the weight of responsibility for hunger shifted away from a neo-Confucian benevolent governance that was increasingly incapable of bearing it and toward a modern technopolitics that had yet to be realized. An influential strain of nationalist thought sensed that traditional Confucianism was moribund. Only by rejecting it could the Vietnamese people actualize its potential.[12] This thinking involved a move away from the Sino-Vietnamese tradition of famine relief rooted in state paternalism, the patriarchal family, and mandarin noblesse oblige toward something resembling the ideal of the welfare state. New forms of care embraced by both imperialists and anticolonial nationalists made it more difficult for the French to blame famine on Vietnamese racial characteristics, Malthusian overpopulation, and corrupt mandarins. Subsistence was now universally considered an essential component of sovereignty. The question now was who was capable of securing it.

After France fell to Germany in 1940, the collaborationist Vichy regime sent naval officer Jean Decoux to take control of Indochina. This control was strictly curtailed by imperial Japan. Though French sovereignty was maintained in principle, in 1942 Admiral Decoux was compelled to sign treaties that essentially amounted to tribute. As part of the economic plan for the Greater East Asia Co-Prosperity Sphere, French Indochina would supply Japan with a minimum of one million tons of rice and a quarter million tons of corn each year.[13] To fulfill this obligation, the Japanese required the French to requisition rice at below-market prices. At the same time, they made farmers, especially in Tonkin, switch from subsistence food production to commercial crops such as cotton and jute. Thousands of Japanese troops stationed throughout Indochina enforced compliance. A shipping shortage prevented the full amount of food from being exported, but there is no doubt that Japanese demands contributed to the famine.[14]

Decoux's accommodationist position preserved French pseudo-sovereignty in Indochina until March 9, 1945. That day, the Japanese troops he had been forced to accept in Indochinese territory violently overthrew his administration. It was replaced by the Empire of Vietnam, a nominally independent state under Emperor Bao Dai affiliated with the Co-Prosperity Sphere. Japan surrendered to the Allies in August. Anticolonial leader Ho Chi Minh seized the opportunity he had been awaiting for years. In 1941, he had formed the Viet Minh, a communist-dominated anticolonial coalition based at the remote frontier with China. Prepared to step into the power vacuum at the end of the war, Ho persuaded Bao Dai to abdicate and declared the independence of the Democratic Republic of Vietnam (DRV) on September 2, 1945.

While Vichy was formally in control of Indochina, French republican loyalists continued to take directives from Charles de Gaulle's Free French. Thus, there were two overlapping and competing French claims to sovereignty in Indochina, one Vichy and one republican. The French republic was reestablished in France when Paris was liberated by Allied armies on August 25, 1944, just as the food situation in Indochina was giving cause for alarm. With the Vichy regime no longer in power in Europe, Admiral Decoux's administration operated autonomously while the provisional republic sought to circumvent his authority. After the Japanese *coup de force* of March 9 ousted Decoux, the republic held the sole French claim to Indochina but had no formal presence in the territory. It was not until March 1946 that the Chinese army, which had occupied the northern half of Indochina after Japan's surrender, restored the territory to France. Immediately finding itself in a power struggle with the forces of independent Vietnam, France had to fight to reestablish authority.

Before it was overthrown, the Vichy administration, reflecting both ideological affinity and political strategy, allied itself with the conservative Vietnamese mandarin class. Confucian hierarchy resonated with Vichy's traditionalist preoccupation with work, family, and homeland as the basis of social order.[15] The Vichy administration blended this conservatism with a concern for nutritional health. Upon taking power, Decoux paid special attention to the Red River Delta, where high population density, he believed, deprived people of the "indispensable vital minimum." Only about 20 percent of the population enjoyed "well-being" (*bien-être*). Decoux intended not only to palliate immediate "human misery," but also to ensure long-term flourishing through equitable wealth distribution.[16] Among his solutions to endemic undernutrition was a proposal to create, once and for all, the emergency reserves that he complained had been repeatedly foiled by budget technicalities.[17]

These long-term ambitions were overwhelmed by reality. As early as 1943, administrators in the provinces of the Red River Delta were worried about rising rice prices. At the request of the mayor of Haiphong, private companies opened canteens (*restaurants populaires*) providing daily subsidized meals to between seven hundred and one thousand employees. The administration sold rice from municipal stocks to city residents at below-market price. This had security benefits as well as humanitarian ones, as a "policy of the belly" to ensure the "daily ball of rice" would keep the masses sympathetic to the French.[18]

These small measures proved feeble, however, in the face of typhoons, spiraling inflation, and Japanese extraction. In early 1945, French administrators in the delta began reporting deaths from "physiological misery." The administration purchased and distributed corn and manioc, and advanced cash to farmers. It pressured businesses to expand employment, coordinated with private charities to open soup kitchens, and formed aid committees to collect donations and organize relief.[19] One such aid committee in Thai Nguyen opened a public soup kitchen in February 1945 that distributed salted rice to between seven hundred and eight hundred indigents daily. A flood of refugees, however, put unsustainable pressure on this charity. Administrators feared that only a "massive restriction of consumption" would lower prices and avert famine.[20]

Throughout the Red River Delta, the French opened emergency public works that they admitted could supply only minimal relief. These projects paid by the amount of work accomplished, making it impossible for people physically impaired by hunger to earn even starvation rations. While the expense in money could be met through clever accounting, rice for payment in kind was hard to come by.[21] In February of 1945, administrators in Nam Dinh opened dike construction projects paying one kilogram of rice paddy per cubed meter of earth moved. But they confessed that weakened workers would be lucky to move half this amount and doubted that anyone could live off the arrangement.[22] In any case, all French relief measures were abruptly interrupted after the *coup de force* of March 9. The Japanese client state under Bao Dai tried half-heartedly to revive some of the French efforts. Significant relief in the form of grain shipments from Cochinchina did not begin arriving until June, when the harvest had already eased acute starvation.[23]

Catholic missionaries, unencumbered by political jockeying or the constraints of administrative reports, described what the famine looked like. In 1944, church leaders in Hanoi guessed that a million people had already died. Unlike administrators, missionaries openly blamed heavy taxation and cereal requisitions for troops and civil servants, both Japanese and French. British and American warplanes, "sinister birds of death," bombed targets indiscriminately, including the ships and railroads that might have brought relief. On Easter in Hanoi, when the bells joyously rang the hallelujah of the resurrection, the voice of the bombs was heard in reply.[24] The rural populations suffered a "calvary." People went about half naked in freezing weather. Hundreds died of hunger and cold each day.[25] By February 1945, missionaries reported a shortage of mats with which to wrap the thousands of bodies lying unburied in the streets.[26] After March 9, "total anarchy" reigned. The missions suffered from what they called euphemistically anti-French "xenophobia," enduring murder and rapine at the hands of "pirates" and communist "ultra-nationalists." French Christians were accused in the "pagan press" of eating their fill while Vietnamese starved.[27] Normal religious functions were curtailed as the Church's "harvest of the crop of souls" declined with the harvest of the crop of rice. As in previous famines, priests revived the practice of baptizing orphans at death's door.[28] French missionaries, thin but in good health, suffered from a shortage of sacramental wine for mass.[29] It was the deadliest famine in French colonial history.

The Performance of Sovereignty

As famine ravaged Tonkin, the great powers were deciding the fate of the world. The place of Indochina in the emerging global order was not obvious. An article by French businessman Gaston Rueff in the US magazine *Foreign*

Affairs gives a glimpse of what the future looked like from the perspective of October 1944. United States Undersecretary of State Sumner Welles had in 1942 assured the Vichy regime that his country recognized the "sovereign jurisdiction" of France over its colonies. Rueff wondered what this would mean for Indochina. "How will France reestablish her jurisdiction once the Japanese are expelled from the country and Admiral Decoux's puppet government has been ousted? And in what way will she give the native people a fair chance to prepare themselves for self-government?" For Rueff, "white man's rule" rested on white "prestige," which the disgraced French could regain only by joining the fight against Japan. Once Indochina was liberated, he proposed that it be integrated into a new imperial federation in which colonized people would participate at all levels of government. International oversight would "guarantee that the older forms of imperialism have been mitigated and that henceforth serious, consciously-directed and widely-progressive efforts will be made to advance the social and economic well-being of the native peoples and to prepare them for eventual self-government." Rueff proposed an international council comprised of colonial powers, colonies, and independent nations such as Thailand and the United States. The council's role would be strictly supervisory, as "the country which has administrative jurisdiction over a colony must definitely have sovereign rights over that country."[30] The next year, Rueff returned to the theme of the "well-being" of Indochinese people, suggesting that only the industrialization of "underfed" Tonkin and Annam could raise the "standard of living."[31] Rueff's reflections made it clear that questions of sovereignty now implied questions of well-being, international oversight, development, self-determination, and food.

In 1944, it was far from clear who would emerge sovereign in Indochina. While it became plain relatively early in the war that Japan would eventually be defeated, nobody knew what would come out of that defeat. The situation was more complex than Allies versus Axis or colonialists against nationalists. French sovereignty in Indochina was threatened simultaneously by Japanese imperialism, Vietnamese nationalism, a self-determination-minded United States, and a nationalist China preparing for postwar power struggles. In fact, de Gaulle considered Chinese leader Chiang Kai-shek's ambition to establish a "big brother" relationship with Southeast Asia and US President Franklin Roosevelt's ideals of self-determination as greater threats to French sovereignty than the Japanese.[32] The French could count on the British, who themselves hoped to reestablish authority in Japanese-occupied Burma, for imperial solidarity. Roosevelt, though, was critical of colonialism in general and French colonialism in particular. It is likely that he favored the establishment of a multinational trusteeship over Indochina under Chinese leadership.[33] Free French representatives countered criticism of their brand of colonialism with promises of reform, most significantly at the Brazzaville Conference in early 1944. A measure of relief for colonialists came from the Yalta Conference in February 1945, when the United States, United Kingdom, and Soviet Union agreed that no colonial power could be forced to accept formal international supervision. Roosevelt's death in April rendered his personal antagonism to French rule irrelevant.[34] But even with the tentative blessing of the Allies, the questions of whether and how France would regain Indochina remained obscure.

When the Japanese ousted Decoux's administration on March 9, 1945, France lost its already limited de facto sovereignty in Indochina completely. The question became whether it could convince anyone who mattered that it retained it de jure. When the provisional republic was still based in Algiers before the liberation of Paris in August 1944, it had unsuccessfully lobbied the Allies to include French forces in military operations in Indochina, simultaneously begging for material, especially ships, that would make that possible. After Japan surrendered in the summer of 1945, France had no way of reestablishing a physical presence in its colony. It was once again reduced to badgering the Allies, who were not inclined to sacrifice their own hard-earned influence. At the Potsdam Conference in 1944, the Allies had given military jurisdiction over the northern part of Indochina to China and over the southern part to Britain.[35] Embarrassingly, France was excluded from accepting Japan's surrender in its own territory. The French feared that the Chinese would not be easily dislodged. There were rumors that China was promising Vietnamese independence in their occupation zone. As they withdrew, the defeated Japanese were supposedly arming the Viet Minh.[36] The reestablishment of French sovereignty was not seen as inevitable.

In this context, France struggled to secure internal, practical control as well as external recognition. To shore up legitimacy within Indochina, the French searched for ways to appease nationalists without undermining colonial rule. They debated whether to work with moderate Vietnamese intelligentsia against radical anticolonialists, and weighed the pros and cons of governing through Emperor Bao Dai (whose lifestyle inspired Andrée Viollis to call him an "emperor of nightclubs").[37] In 1945, Charles de Gaulle declared that Tonkin, Annam, and Cochinchina would join the re-formed French Empire, now called the French Union, as three separate "countries."[38] These debates and declarations, though, were pointless unless the French could secure international recognition and reestablish an administrative presence on the ground.

During and after World War II, patriotic narratives imposed continuity on France, locating the legitimacy of the nation not in Vichy but in the resistance, the loyal colonies (especially Félix Eboué's French Equatorial Africa), and the figure of General de Gaulle.[39] But in fact, the French were well aware of the fragility of judicial sovereignty in the absence of practical control. The reestablishment of French power in Indochina was by no means taken for granted. French republicans publicly insisted on uninterrupted sovereignty, but they spoke internally of Indochina's potential "return to the imperial community" as though sovereignty had been ruptured and its resumption was in doubt.[40] As the Viet Minh were waiting at the Chinese border for an opportunity to seize power, France was in much the same situation.[41]

This battle for sovereignty was rhetorical and political as much as it was military. A radio station based in Madagascar, the provisional French republic's only way to communicate with Indochinese people, was emblematic of its talking points. The station countered Vichy and Japanese propaganda while rejecting interference from Allied powers. One transmission quoted de Gaulle's insistence that rather than submitting to an international mandate system, "France will be its own mandatory in Indochina" on the basis of humanitarian principles. Making outrageous claims such as "racism is dead," republican propagandists urged Vietnamese to reject the false promises of independence under Japanese overrule in favor of the true liberation of partial autonomy within the French Union.[42]

Famine occupied a central place in the constellation of challenges to French rule, but it was also an opportunity. One way the republic insisted on the Frenchness of Indochina was by making plans to alleviate famine, even though it was in no position to put these plans into action. The French performed sovereignty for an international audience by formulating famine relief measures to be undertaken at liberation, whenever that might occur. Republican agents monitored the famine from liberated Paris and from an organization called the French Colonial Mission in the Far East (Mission coloniale française en extrême-orient) based in British Calcutta, epicenter of its own war famine in 1943. The mission functioned as a shadow imperial government that acted out colonial administration without the actual administrating. The Colonial Mission concluded that French people in Indochina, even devoted fascists, could be counted on to support the republic. Vietnamese intellectuals, on the other hand, were irredeemably obstinate in their desire for immediate independence. The most fertile ground for French propaganda, then, was the rural masses. The mission caricatured peasants as preoccupied entirely by food, uninterested in ideology or international politics. The French in Calcutta believed that peasants in the Red River Delta attributed their hardship solely to Japan, pushing them ever closer to France. Though anticolonial rebellions had broken out in Cochinchina in 1941, the farmers of Tonkin who bore the brunt of Japanese extraction were, the mission thought, inclined to be loyal to

France.[43] Regardless of whether this analysis was correct, it persuaded the French to press their perceived advantage with farmers through famine relief.

From distant Paris and Calcutta, French republicans blamed the Indochinese famine on the Japanese occupation and Decoux's Vichy administration. Already in 1944, secret intelligence reports judged the circumstances dire. The reports alleged that Japan had requisitioned 430 thousand tons of rice in the first half of the year, causing a dangerous shortage in Tonkin and northern Annam.[44] Since the Allies had bombed Indochina's roads and railways, the Japanese islands were the only possible source of food. Japan, though, was more interested in feeding its soldiers than Indochinese farmers.[45] The Vichy French protectorates of Annam and Tonkin had missed the chance to stock rice while transportation was still viable. What was worse, they were complicit in requisitioning food to fulfill treaty obligations to Japan. With starvation looming, Decoux forbade administrators from buying rice on the open market, forcing them to go through the French commercial house Denis Frères. The firm was unable to satisfy rising demand, causing a backlog and contributing to skyrocketing prices.[46]

Even as it denounced the Vichy-affiliated administration, the Colonial Mission in Calcutta took credit for its relief efforts on behalf of France. At times the republican administrators-in-exile criticized Decoux's forced requisitions as the major cause of the famine; at other times they praised the requisitions as effective planning. In 1945 they wrote, with little evidence, that before his ouster, Decoux had transported three thousand tons of rice from Cochinchina to Tonkin monthly. This amount they both criticized as insufficient and lauded as a logistical tour de force. Between requisitions and Cochinchinese imports, Calcutta claimed, France fulfilled up to half of city dwellers' "vital needs" and distributed grain to rural farmers. These measures put pressure on Japan to continue relief after the March 9 coup.[47] Even as it maintained a careful distance from Vichy, the provisional republic was happy to own the relief efforts. Vichy, when it was convenient, was still France.

In 1945, the Colonial Mission, anticipating France's imminent return to Indochina, made advance plans to ship rice from Cochinchina to the famine areas and to redistribute resources within Tonkin. The planners hoped to supply twenty thousand tons of rice within fifteen days of liberation. This would buy time for transportation to be reestablished and for markets to stabilize. Depending on when in the agricultural cycle liberation occurred, authorities might be called to transport several hundred thousand additional tons of rice.[48] In preparation, the mission studied the availability of food in Cochinchina. From Calcutta, the French went so far as to plan for the distribution of specific stocks. For example, they earmarked seventy thousand tons of rice held in Saigon by the Japanese company Mitsui for relief.[49] Some believed this meticulous planning was overambitious. One functionary predicted that even in the event that France managed to return to Indochina, six hundred thousand tons of rice would be required between October 1945 and June 1946, far more than was available even in the best-case scenario. Confused clerks at the Ministry of Colonies in Paris could not follow Calcutta's logic or arithmetic.[50] A Vichy officer had the impression that that the French in Calcutta were well intentioned but woefully misinformed about conditions on the ground.[51]

In August 1945, Japan surrendered. Britain occupied southern Indochina and welcomed the French back to the territory. China occupied northern Indochina but did not allow France to return. The Viet Minh launched the August Revolution. Free French hero Admiral Georges Thierry d'Argenlieu was tasked with reestablishing French administration in the colony, and he had his own plan for famine relief. In September, he proposed gathering two hundred thousand tons of rice from Cochinchina, Cambodia, and the Mitsui stock in Saigon. From this supply, he planned to provide twenty-five thousand tons monthly to Tonkin as soon as the "political situation" allowed for it, ideally beginning in November. The plan was contingent on two "hypotheses." The first was that Britain would renounce its legal right to claim the Mitsui rice as war spoils. D'Argenlieu hoped an appeal to British sympathy could soften a "brutal interpretation" of the law of war. The second very hopeful hypothesis was that hoarders would spontaneously release one hundred thousand tons of rice onto the market after the "reestablishment of order."[52] As it happened, the unfavorable "political situation" made testing the hypotheses moot.

The Ministry of Colonies in liberated Paris agreed that alleviating starvation must be France's first order of business upon its return to Indochina. The ministry added its own unorthodox plan to the mix, which rested on the importation of thirty thousand tons of cotton textiles to stimulate exchange and dislodge and circulate hoarded rice. In addition, the ministry prioritized the urgent restoration of maritime transportation until Indochina's roads and railways could be repaired. As the French had no ships, agents had been sent to the United States and Canada to negotiate the construction of specialized transport vessels. In case these were not ready in time, the agents also asked the United States for a loan of covered landing boats as an emergency expedient.[53] No matter how the French looked at it, they were dependent on the goodwill of the Allies. This raised the question of why Britain, China, and the United States, which were in a better position to do so, did not simply undertake famine relief themselves. In fact, Allied intervention was the outcome that the provisional republic dreaded most.

France was extremely sensitive to the political implications of famine relief. In September 1945, functionaries in Calcutta were alarmed that "the principal claim of anti-French propaganda made by the Annamite government in

Tonkin [DRV] is that the French are responsible for the famine . . . of 1945, a famine that produced two million victims." The Colonial Mission instructed "counter-propaganda" agents to rebut these claims by blaming the famine on the Japanese, the Allies, and the Vietnamese. The propagandists were asked to disseminate the argument that the famine had been caused by Japanese requisitions and the forced production of jute, vanilla, and other inedible commercial crops, and that Allied bombing had impeded transportation and prevented a French response. Perfectly willing to claim affiliation with Vichy when it suited them, the administrators in India asserted that Decoux's administration had taken every measure possible under the constraints of the Japanese. The republican agents claimed that Decoux had been just about to launch a major rescue operation when his administration was overthrown. Calcutta stressed it was imperative to communicate that the famine "became tragic" only at the end of April, after the vicious Japanese and the incompetent Annamites had replaced the French. Even after the fall of Japan, the French saw famine relief as a means to claim sovereign legitimacy as much as a humanitarian duty. They were uninterested in rescue operations unless they could claim credit: "It would be disastrous if the Allies imported rice. This is what the Annamite government is attempting to obtain for propaganda reasons."[54] Admiral d'Argenlieu may even have secured a promise from the British not to send aid from their southern occupation zone to Tonkin.[55] French republicans were less concerned with saving lives than with reestablishing rule.

There is something pitiful about these French relief plans concocted by distant, helpless functionaries with no serious hope of ever executing them, all relying on guesswork and the favors of allies. France's willingness to put on this degrading display attests to the high value placed on famine relief as a sovereign gesture. A 1946 article in the prominent French newspaper Le Monde entitled "The Japanese Are Responsible for the Great Famine of 1945" confirmed how central subsistence had become to geopolitics. Correspondent André Blanchet took issue with anticolonial radicals who claimed France had intentionally caused the famine. He agreed that the famine had indeed been intentionally perpetrated, but not by the French. Rather, it was the Japanese and "Annamite extremists" who engineered the tragedy for their own purposes. Muddying the distinction between Vichy and the republic, Blanchet claimed the French administration had been on the verge of restoring normal conditions when it was interrupted by the coup de force. The Japanese and the Annamites hoarded ever more rice, precipitating a famine that the French would have avoided. Even now, in 1946, Ho Chi Minh spurned French rice shipments as he publicized an exaggerated death toll of two million. Attempts at delivery provoked fire from Viet Minh coastal batteries. The fate of millions of lives, Blanchet stressed, rested on France's ability to regain control.[56]

The United Nations and International Relief

The United Nations Relief and Rehabilitation Administration (UNRRA) was not convinced that the French were up to the challenge of restoring order. The international but US-dominated organization was founded in 1943 to provide emergency relief for war victims. It predated the United Nations, a phrase that originally referred to the nations themselves rather than the organization. UNRRA was integrated into the UN after its creation in 1945.[57] It was one of the major international organizations charged with addressing humanitarian issues among populations affected by the war.

World War II posed a widespread threat to subsistence and triggered major famines in Bengal, Java, China, and the Netherlands. Coordinating food supplies internationally was thus a major priority. Like the French republic, UNRRA kept an eye on Indochina from distant bases such as those in Chongqing, Sydney, and Manila. In the summer of 1944, UNRRA economist Dorothy Grant Jacqueline predicted that in Indochina "there will probably be no food problem." She even hoped that the region could be counted on to supply neighboring countries.[58] Within a few months, people were starving in Tonkin. With UNRRA already involved in famine relief in Europe and China, it made sense for it to extend operations to Indochina. The organization was prepared to transport and distribute emergency aid. It also offered to undertake more embedded interventions such as agricultural surveys, technical consulting, dike repairs, the establishment of agricultural cooperatives, and even the reorganization of labor to improve economic efficiency.[59]

These tasks were not merely technical; they were deeply associated with sovereignty. As an international organization, UNRRA could legally intervene only at the invitation of a sovereign power. In autumn of 1944, UNRRA pressured the provisional French republic to request help in providing essential goods and caring for displaced persons.[60] The French, after ignoring the communication for several months, diplomatically but firmly rejected the offer. They "would welcome the opportunity to consult, from time to time, with the UNRRA" but insisted on its limited remit in France's sovereign territories.[61] Facing French recalcitrance, UNRRA considered unilateral measures such as prioritizing the purchase of Indochinese products or providing technical advice for farmers and fishermen.[62]

When Japan's surrender in the summer of 1945 allowed access to Tonkin, UNRRA's overtures became more urgent. In September, US Lieutenant C. B. Chapman, a medical doctor from UNRRA staff in Chongqing, China, was temporarily attached to the small US Army contingent in Chinese-occupied Hanoi tasked with caring for Allied prisoners of war. He reported that the region was in the midst of an "indescribable catastrophe," that "starvation is widespread," and that "people are dying on streets daily."[63] He estimated that 1.25 million people had already died.[64] Chapman's reports spurred UNRRA to action. Staff in China, Australia, and the United States debated ways to circumvent France's unwillingness to request aid, even exploring the legal consequences of intervening without permission.[65] At the same time, UNRRA invited the French ambassador in Washington to make a formal request for aid, appealing to his humanity with passages from Chapman's reports.[66] Persuaded, the ambassador urged his government to allow UNRRA operations for political reasons as much as humanitarian ones: "If famine ravages Tonkin and Northern Annam, we will be reproached for having refused the help of the UNRRA and we will find ourselves in an extremely delicate situation with both the indigenous populations and the enemies of our colonial policy."[67] It took over two months for the French government to respond to the ambassador's urgent plea.

As it awaited French permission, UNRRA revisited its rules for intervention.[68] The resolution governing its missions stated they should be worked out "in consultation with the government concerned." In Indochina, it was unclear which government was "concerned." This gave UNRRA room to maneuver. An internal memorandum interpreted the phrase to refer to "the government or other authority in administrative control of the area to be helped." It was expected that Tonkin would be returned to France in the near future, but it was the Chinese army that was in administrative control. Thus, a formal request for aid from the Chinese military authorities was determined to be legally sufficient, though it would be "wise" to keep the French informed "in order to preserve good relations." Based on this legalistic reading of UNRRA's mandate, the Chongqing and Manila offices prepared material and transportation.[69] The organization's willingness to intervene in nominally French territory without their authorization accentuated the new association of sovereignty and care. The fact that France could not address the famine gave others the obligation and the right to do so.

The major step of unauthorized intervention was not, in the end, taken. The French finally responded in January 1946. They sought to balance the ramifications of accepting aid and sharing credit with UNRRA and of refusing aid and opening themselves to accusations of negligence. The French response claimed the famine was not as serious as initially feared. It maintained that France's enthusiastic measures—measures that did not in fact exist—were on the verge of success. France appeased UNRRA by formally requesting a token amount of drugs and infant feeding supplies. These would be distributed by French agents and repaid in full by the French government so as not to appear beholden.[70] In this way, France sought to satisfy international opinion while safeguarding French sovereignty. The fact that at the time of this exchange acute starvation was already over and French administration had been restored in the south but not in famine-ravaged Tonkin divulges the cynicism of France's claim to have solved the problem on its own.

France's fear that the famine could empower its enemies was well founded. UNRRA adamantly proclaimed its neutrality with regard to the fraught politics of Indochina, but its involvement could not help but have political implications. In November 1945, Lieutenant Chapman wrote from Hanoi that both French and DRV officials agreed that rice supplies would run out within two weeks. The British army and the Viet Minh reported that stocks existed in Cochinchina. However, French plans for transporting rice from Saigon were impracticable. Vague Chinese promises of aid were not materializing. Chapman confirmed widespread starvation and deficiency disease, asking Chongqing for supplies of "vitamin preparations containing the vitamin B group and vitamin A."[71]

The practical exigencies of humanitarian relief made it necessary for UNRRA to work with whoever held de facto control. Chapman considered the viability of both the French and the Vietnamese revolutionaries as partners. Ho Chi Minh's government and the few French agents whose presence was tolerated by the Chinese treated Chapman's group like "visiting royalty" as they vied for UNRRA recognition. Both sides claimed to transcend political divisions to support the "purely humanitarian work," but Chapman's assessment of the belligerents differed starkly. He accused France of prioritizing politics over well-being. "The French are unconcerned, saying that this is the normal state of affairs in the country and that it can't be helped."[72] Conversely, he was impressed with the DRV's competence. He relayed that there was no need for UNRRA to send medical personnel as "the Ministry of Health in the Revolutionary Government is staffed by French-trained native doctors many of whom are highly intelligent and eager to carry out their work." The region's public health was "ably" managed by Hanoi's Pasteur Institute operating under DRV direction. The institute manufactured vaccine for cholera and other diseases, keeping the epidemics that often accompanied famine in check. According to Chapman's assessment, "It needs some supplies but is doing a remarkable job under the circumstances."[73] The risk of UNRRA partnering with the DRV was a clear threat to French interests. International recognition of the enemy would be a huge blow in the fight for legitimacy.

France's strategy of stringing UNRRA along succeeded in holding off international intervention until the republic could reestablish control. In March 1946, one year after the Japanese *coup de force*, France was able to negotiate China's withdrawal from northern Indochina.[74] Acute mass starvation had passed, and the French were again physically present in the entirety of Indochinese territory. But now they were engaged in an intense war with the DRV. Even as they fought, they sought to reestablish legitimacy by caring for the population. In January 1946, before the return to the north, the republic promised a staggering eight billion francs to partially industrialize Indochina. This project was meant to improve living conditions but without going so far as to inadvertently create a potentially revolutionary "indigenous proletariat."[75] The industrialization plan focused largely on food needs, especially in the Red River Delta where people struggled to maintain the "vital minimum" and suffered from chronic under- and malnutrition. Prone to natural disaster and geographically isolated, the delta's constant precarity often led to famine, as occurred during what was euphemistically called the "recent blockade."[76] Only comprehensive economic development could address these underlying conditions.

First, though, the lingering effects of famine needed to be dealt with. Newly reinstated Minister of Colonies Marius Moutet asked for a detailed relief plan.[77] The most obvious solution was to transport rice from Cochinchina, but this was no straightforward task. In the south, the Viet Minh fought for control of rice harvests and sabotaged French transportation operations. In Tonkin, the French blamed ongoing dearth on war and the revolutionary army's forced relocation of farmers. It was easy to provision cities, where French authority was relatively unchallenged. But Vietnamese control of the countryside hindered French relief and raised the specter of famine refugees flooding Hanoi and Haiphong, "multiply[ing] by 10 or 100 the number of mouths we will have to feed." It was even possible, some speculated, that the Viet Minh would intentionally sabotage dikes to overwhelm the French with needy mouths and achieve a propaganda coup. The stakes were no less than the legitimacy of French rule: "We are making a great effort to assure the provisioning of Tonkin, because we know that otherwise we will be held responsible for famine by Vietnamese opinion."[78] At the same time as France was attempting to claim credit for famine control, the Democratic Republic of Vietnam was doing the same.

The Revolution Has Triumphed over Famine

In January 1946, while China still occupied the north, an American journalist for the *New York Herald Tribune* told of food shortage and bitter cold in Indochina. The French estimated that six hundred thousand had died; Ho Chi Minh thought two million. The French blamed Ho's "illegal" Democratic Republic of Vietnam, which stubbornly refused food aid and engineering assistance for dike repairs. Ho blamed the French, who in eighty years of rule had neglected to teach the population to repair dikes. He compared France's colonial record unfavorably to that of the United States, which had taught Filipinos such skills in a shorter time period. The French complained that the communists refused to allow rice shipments from the south. They nonetheless planned to send some even if the revolutionaries confiscated and distributed the aid themselves. Ho complained that the French withheld Cochinchinese rice. Though it was true that the DRV would not allow French intervention, he said it would be happy to entrust supply operations to a neutral third party such as the United States.[79] This proposal, Ho knew, would be unacceptable to the French who were protective of their flimsy sovereignty. The rhetorical game was intended to expose them as incapable rulers and their intentions as political rather than humanitarian. Ho's flattering references to the United States were no accident as France and the DRV vied for crucial international recognition. Indeed, taking US talk of self-determination more seriously than the Americans did, Ho repeatedly and in vain called on President Harry Truman to support Vietnam's fight against France.

The US newspaper article presented famine relief as a contest for sovereignty. Having accepted responsibility for subsistence in the previous decade, the French Empire was now held to account by nationalists before the international community. Vietnamese claimed the right to rule not in the language of Confucianism but in that of welfare.[80] From this perspective, it was not the colonized who failed to achieve modernity but the improvident colonizers. Nationalists had no shortage of ammunition for anticolonial propaganda. They castigated the French for offenses ranging from excessive taxation, to disrespecting tradition, to encouraging drug abuse. Yet, subsistence trumped other concerns. Famine became a cornerstone of nationalist critiques.

The French republic had not been in control of Indochina during the famine but had to answer for it, nonetheless. Nationalists accused France of hoarding rice while Vietnamese were reduced to salting their food with the ashes of burned bamboo. Vichy agents, some claimed, had ruined hundreds of tons of food with lime instead of letting it fall to the people.[81] The Viet Minh mobilized the masses under the slogan, "Destroy the paddy granaries of the colonialists to avert the danger of famine."[82] During the August Revolution following Japan's surrender, demonstrators held signs reading, "The French occupation cost over two million victims."[83] When Ho Chi Minh publicly read the Vietnamese Declaration of Independence in Hanoi on September 2, it included the line, "From the end of last year to the beginning of this year, more than two million of our fellow-citizens died of starvation." Independent Vietnam was born of the deadliest famine in the history of the French Empire.

In 1945, the Viet Minh published a sourcebook of French documents purporting to reveal the truth of the "so-called civilizing mission."[84] Its editors claimed that France had intentionally orchestrated the famine to kill Vietnamese patriots. As an added windfall for foreign occupiers, firms such as Japan's Mitsui and France's Denis Frères made a fortune through speculation. Hunger forced peasants to labor on plantations and in mines for starvation wages, to the profit of foreign businesses. As capitalists got rich, administrators requisitioned huge amounts of rice. They paid twenty-five piastres per one hundred kilograms while the going rate at the close of 1944 was eight hundred piastres. Peasants were forced to buy back their own rice at an exponential markup. As northerners tried to survive on leaves and banana roots, prices in Cochinchina were so low that farmers left fields fallow and let thousands of tons of grain rot to avoid selling at a loss. French industries burned rice paddy as a cheap substitute for coal. Against French insistence that the famine was Japan's fault, the Viet Minh argued that starvation had already taken hold before the *coup de force*. Besides, pointing to the Japanese was no excuse. It was the colonial state's job to protect its people from foreign powers. Instead, France had willingly carried out Japan's deadly demands.[85]

The Democratic Republic of Vietnam claimed not only a right to subsistence, but also a right to provide subsistence. A pamphlet published in French in 1946, complete with bloodchilling images of the dead and dying by photographer Vo Anh Ninh, contrasted France's failures with the energetic efforts of the DRV. Faced with a relapse of famine in 1946, Vietnam achieved a "miraculous," even "quasi-supernatural," victory over the forces of imperialism and of nature.[86] In decades of rule, France had done nothing about endemic famine in Tonkin and Annam. Given these baseline conditions of precarity, French and Japanese requisitions, forced industrial crop cultivation, hoarding and speculation, Allied bombardment, and typhoons could not help but trigger catastrophe. Out of a population of ten million, two million died.

The revolution inherited a desperate situation. As it rose to power in August 1945, a huge flood destroyed three hundred thousand tons of rice paddy in Tonkin. The drought that followed on its heels destroyed half of what the waters had spared. The November harvest amounted to half the regional average of one thousand tons. The May harvest was months away. At a time when people needed extra food to recover from the prolonged malnutrition of the previous year, the numbers were discouraging. Somehow, they would need to find 530 thousand tons of rice paddy for a "normal" ration, or 330 thousand tons for the "vital minimum." This being impossible, the only way to stave off famine would be to triple the average yield of secondary crops such as potatoes, soy, and maize.

An appeal from President Ho Chi Minh rallied the entire population to the cause. The struggle was not merely for the survival of individuals, but for that of the nation itself. "An entire people coming into consciousness" saw that famine would put an end not only to "physical and material life" but to the hard-earned liberty of Vietnamese citizens. Those spared by hunger joined the "holy war" out of solidarity. Social prejudice disappeared as intellectuals and laborers, rich and poor, realized that their fate was tied to that of the community. The ministries of national economy and agriculture instructed landowners to loan excess land, tools, and livestock to anyone willing to work. Functionaries, students, and soldiers moonlighted as farmers. Private charities sprang up to feed destitute people and provide them with land so that they, too, could contribute to the national cause. Organizations of "soldier-farmers" combined military training with crop cultivation. Frontline fighters planted between battles. Urban merchants and clerks who knew nothing of agriculture planted corn and potatoes in their flower beds. University students sowed the lawns of dormitories. Scout troops planted grassy areas around the sidewalks. Highland minorities, the "new Vietnamese," contributed out of a freshly awoken patriotic honor. At the time of the pamphlet's publication, the May harvest several weeks away was projected to be a bumper crop.[87]

How had the Vietnamese succeeded where the French had failed? "The truth is that the *necessary condition* of victory in this supernatural fight is an entire people's consciousness of their becoming, a race's desire for self-preservation." The people, now citizens, were galvanized by an irresistible need to survive. The forces that prevailed in "the battle of the earth" were the same that had fought colonialism and won recognition for Vietnam: "It is the liberating dynamism of the Viet Minh front, it is the people of Vietnam conscious of its rights, it is the Revolution that triumphed over famine."[88] This account might have been unrecognizable to the many who continued to suffer from hunger, but it shows how decolonization was, in part, a conflict over who could ensure subsistence.

From Indochina to Vietnam

The Great Famine was the culmination of a process in which the French Empire progressively took responsibility for the subsistence of subjects. In a context in which their control over the territory was first limited and then nonexistent, the French performed a simulated sovereignty through the rhetoric of famine relief. Vichy's belated measures were negligible. Republican France was in no position to accomplish anything at all. The plans formulated in Calcutta and Paris were so fantastic it is not obvious whether even their authors took them seriously. This exercise in self-parody did not manage to save lives, but this was only part of the point. The administrators-in-exile were trying to persuade an international audience that France was still sovereign in Indochina, even if nobody was really paying attention to the performance aside from themselves.

Acting out famine relief was a way to buy time for France to reestablish physical control in Indochina. As soon as it was able, France defended its sovereignty with force as well as with food. In 1946, France regained control of the colony and the First Indochina War began. The government of the Democratic Republic of Vietnam that had so impressed UNRRA operatives was forced underground. In 1954, Vietnamese forces would decisively defeat the French army at the battle of Dien Bien Phu. The French would give up Indochina, Vietnam would be partitioned, the Vietnam War would be fought, and in 1975, thirty years after the Great Famine, Vietnam would be independent and unified. Though mortality estimates for both the famine and the wars are unreliable, it is likely they killed around the same number of people.

States were supposed to protect their constituents from starvation. When empires failed to do so, nations claimed that responsibility for themselves. Vietnamese revolutionaries asserted through words and actions that they, not the French, could be trusted to live up to the standards of modern welfare developed in the colonial situation. They seized on famine relief as a way to legitimize their right to govern both internally, vis-à-vis citizens, and externally, facing the international community. A Vietnamese verse from the time of the famine, though, gives a small glimpse at the view from below: "The Japanese laugh, the French weep, the Chinese worry / The Vietnamese, independent, curl up and die all on the streets."[89]

Epilogue
Imperialism without Sovereignty?

> The masses battle with the same poverty, wrestle with
> the same age-old gestures, and delineate what we
> could call the geography of hunger with their
> shrunken bellies.
>
> —Frantz Fanon (1961)

When in the 1970s the Sahel suffered its third
major famine in a little more than half a century, the world was drastically
changed. France had lost the First Indochina War in 1954 and the Algerian War
in 1962. In a 1958 referendum, the people of Guinea had chosen full independence over continued association with France as an autonomous state within
the French Community. By 1960, all the colonies of West and Equatorial Africa were independent. Now, famine was the problem of the countries of Chad,
Mali, Mauritania, Niger, Senegal, and Upper Volta.

The fourth French republic had succeeded in resecuring the empire at the
close of World War II only to come face to face with widespread challenges
to colonial rule.[1] France tried to hold together its crumbling empire with violence and development funds. This involved brutal, and in the end futile, repression of nationalist revolutions in Vietnam, Algeria, Madagascar, and
elsewhere. Like wars of colonial conquest, anticolonial wars were often accompanied by hunger. The Cameroonian independence struggle of the 1950s,
for instance, was marked by severe starvation.[2]

As a complement to force, the French invested in colonial well-being.
Through initiatives such as the Investment Fund for Economic Development
(Fonds d'investissements pour le développement économique et social, FIDES),
France's Fourth and Fifth Republics poured money into programs meant to
achieve standards of nutritional health set but unfulfilled in the 1930s. Among

the first well-funded studies into colonial living conditions was the Anthropological Mission of French West Africa (Mission anthropologique de l'Afrique Occidentale Française). Led by the surgeon and paleoanthropologist Léon Pales, the team included experts in medicine, public health, anthropology, and other domains. The project's findings were published in 1954—the year France was expelled from Vietnam—and included descriptions of diets, chemical analyses of foods, and physiological information about labor capacity.[3] Much of the team's effort was devoted to measuring skulls. Even after the Holocaust, a crude anthropometry that categorized races by physical attributes remained a promising avenue for colonial research. The mission's most striking products were maps of the "comparative raciology" of West African peoples, brightly colored according to variables such as the "cephalic index."[4] In an era of increasingly holistic ways of understanding and providing for needs, colonialists often still thought about the colonized in terms of intrinsic racial characteristics. The contradiction between modern standards of welfare and empires structured on difference was impossible to resolve. Six years after Pales published his study of French West African races, French West Africa no longer existed.

In 1948, three years after the Great Famine in Vietnam, the United Nations recognized in all humans "the right to a standard of living adequate for the health and wellbeing of himself and his family, including food, clothing, housing and medical care and necessary social services." With these words, Article 25 of the Universal Declaration of Human Rights formalized what could be glimpsed at the end of World War II—a shift from a politics of global hunger rooted in colonial civilizing missions to one organized around rights-bearing individuals and sovereign states overseen by the international community. The work of the United Nations Relief and Rehabilitation Administration (UNRRA) during the war famines anticipated the founding of the United Nations Food and Agriculture Organization at the end of 1945, the World Food Programme in 1961, and the proliferation of international nongovernmental organizations (NGOs) in subsequent decades. Famine had evolved from a local tragedy to a global problem demanding awareness, concern, and action.

Having inherited the poverty, lack of infrastructure, and authoritarian governing structures of the French Empire along with its sovereignty, successor states found themselves, as had France, poorly equipped for effective famine management.[5] Unlike France, they were willing to allow the intervention of international organizations to try to save lives they could not. During the Sahelian famine of the early 1970s, NGOs such as the Cooperative for American Relief Everywhere (CARE) and the French Association for Friendship and Solidarity with African Peoples (Association française d'amitié et de solidarité avec les peuples d'Afrique, AFASPA) undertook governing functions usually assumed by states.[6] The physiological and social factors involved in subsistence that had been discovered in the interwar years allowed these organizations to intervene widely and deeply in postcolonial society. NGOs made themselves indispensable to African governments even after the end of acute starvation, arrogating considerable governing power.

Today, the formal equality of sovereignty camouflages the colonial history that led to vast differences in the ability to exercise it. Niger, Mali, and the other countries of the Sahel are as sovereign, have as much sovereignty, as France. Yet they have far less control over their affairs. The sovereignty acquired by colonial successor states is degraded by subordination to international law, humanitarian organizations, and institutions such as the World Bank and the International Monetary Fund.[7] Political accountability falls on states while technical capability is concentrated in the rich parts of the world. This means that significant decision-making control redounds to the international community while responsibility and risk are borne by nations.[8] The split between capacity and responsibility encourages a conceptualization of famine as a technical problem, best managed by international professional experts such as doctors, engineers, and humanitarians. Diagnostic, logistical, and therapeutic tools against acute hunger and related conditions are more powerful than ever. But improved technical ability still does not address the social and political determinants of starvation.

Subsistence is central to the constellation of conditions that postcolonial nations must meet to enjoy the same kind of sovereignty as Western states. If these needs are not met, international intervention by way of NGOs, structural adjustment programs, and military violence can be justified in the language of humanitarianism, development, good governance, and human rights.[9] This humanitarian exception to self-determination resembles a colonial civilizing mission no longer aimed at forming rational subjects who may one day evolve into modern citizens, but at creating states that may one day stand on their own as full members of the international community. Modern humanitarianism is the residue that was left over when the formal political ties binding empire fell away, a form of imperialism without sovereignty.

It is easy to see how the British Empire, with its famine codes and camps, early-warning indicators, and means testing provided a model for technical intervention in food crises. However, humanitarianism is not simply the internationalization of British colonial policy. The history of French colonial famine draws attention to the importance of norms of responsibility as well as techniques of management. At the scale of the event, the "French way of famine" looked a lot like the British way, only more disorganized. Without the guidance of codes, the default French approach to famine relied on camps and means testing to discourage reliance on the state while conceding the bare minimum for survival. This was not simply gratuitous cruelty or racism—though it surely was that too—but in line with a civilizing mission that sought to create provident subjects who could one day ensure their own subsistence through rational decision making.

At a broader scale, the influence of French colonial famine comes into focus. In the nineteenth and early twentieth centuries, French observers dismissed famine in the colonies as inevitable, a tragic act of God or misfortune of nature. Across the diverse landscapes and peoples that made up the empire, colonial officials believed that pity and charity for the suffering were warranted, but that famine lay outside the abilities and responsibilities of the colonial state. After World War I, developments in nutrition science and rational administration suggested new tools for managing food and bodies in the colonies. At the same time, an emerging internationalism profoundly altered expectations of what colonialism was supposed to accomplish. Rather than deflecting responsibility for famine as they had before the Great War, the French Empire came to accept subsistence as an obligation. Developments in the technical control of bodies, populations, and environments came together with new standards of international care to recast famine as a preventable problem within the domain of politics and administration, a basic responsibility of states. Increasingly sophisticated understandings of famine saddled the French Empire with duties that it was unable and unwilling to fulfill, undermining the ideological justifications of colonialism.

Decolonization, though, was not a clean break with the past. The French republican civilizing mission, international humanitarianism, and welfare—forms of care not generally considered as sharing a genealogy—emerged together, in conversation and competition. Colonial and humanitarian approaches to suffering are uncomfortably similar: colonial states substituted governance with charity, while international humanitarianism reproduces colonial inequalities of care. The concepts that society relies on to ensure well-being and liberation contain within them the history of empires. More than exposing the origins of modern international care in the dynamics of dominance and difference that characterized colonialism, this genealogy encourages a reckoning with who is subject to famines and who is not, whose death is normal and whose is not, who is cared for and who is not.

NOTES

Introduction

1. L'Abbé Burzet, *Histoire des Désastres de l'Algérie: 1866, 1867, 1868* (Alger: Imprimerie Centrale Algérienne, 1869).

2. Missions Etrangères de Paris [MEP] 2829: Compte Rendu de l'exercice de 1944–1945.

3. Paul Farmer, "An Anthropology of Structural Violence," *Current Anthropology* 45 (2004): 205–25.

4. J. P. Daughton, *An Empire Divided: Religion, Republicanism, and the Making of French Colonialism, 1880–1914* (Oxford: Oxford University Press, 2006); Eric Jennings, *Vichy in the Tropics: Pétain's National Revolution in Madagascar, Guadeloupe, and Indochina, 1940–1944* (Stanford, CA: Stanford University Press, 2001); Frederick Cooper, *Colonialism in Question: Theory, Knowledge, History* (Berkeley: University of California Press, 2005).

5. An exception is Mike Davis, *Late Victorian Holocausts: El Niño Famines and the Making of the Third World* (London: Verso, 2001).

6. Amartya Sen, *Poverty and Famines: An Essay on Entitlement and Deprivation* (Oxford: Oxford University Press, 1983). For an elaboration of the entitlement approach, see Jean Drèze and Amartya Sen, *Hunger and Public Action* (Oxford: Clarendon Press, 1989). For a short summary of critiques and debates, see Stephen Devereux, "Sen's Entitlement Approach: Critiques and Counter-Critiques," *Oxford Development Studies* 29, no. 1 (2001): 245–63. On the state of contemporary famine research more generally, see Alex de Waal, *Mass Starvation: The History and Future of Famine* (Medford, MA: Polity, 2018); Olivier Rubin, "The Precarious State of Famine Research," *Journal of Development Studies* 55, no. 8 (2019): 1633–53. For a general model of how famines unfold, see Paul Howe, "Famine systems: A new model for understanding the development of famines," *World Development* 105 (2018): 144–55.

7. For a sampling of entitlement analyses of famines, see Sugata Bose, "Starvation Amidst Plenty: The Making of Famine in Bengal, Honan, and Tonkin, 1942–45," *Modern Asian Studies* 24, no. 4 (October 1990), 699–727; Michael Ellman, "The 1947 Soviet Famine and the Entitlement Approach to Famines," *Cambridge Journal of Economics* 24, no. 5 (September 2000): 603–630; Gregg Huff, "Causes and Consequences of the Great Vietnam Famine, 1944–45," *The Economic History Review* 72, 1 (2019): 286–316.

8. Cormac Ò Gràda, *Black '47 and Beyond: The Great Irish Famine in History, Economy, and Memory* (Princeton, NJ: Princeton University Press, 1999).

9. On British colonial famine, see Michael J. Watts, *Silent Violence: Food, Famine, and Peasantry in Northern Nigeria* (Athens: University of Georgia Press, 2013); Megan Vaughan,

The Story of an African Famine: Gender and Famine in Twentieth Century Malawi (Cambridge: Cambridge University Press, 1987); Benjamin Robert Siegel, *Hungry Nation: Food, Famine, and the Making of Modern India* (Cambridge: Cambridge University Press, 2018); Sanjay Sharma, *Famine, Philanthropy, and the Colonial State: North India in the Early Nineteenth Century* (London: School of Oriental and African Studies, 2001); Janam Mukherjee, *Hungry Bengal: War, Famine, and the End of Empire* (Oxford: Oxford University Press, 2015).

10. Tehila Sasson and James Vernon, "Practising the British Way of Famine: Technologies of Relief, 1770–1985," *European Review of History* 22, no. 6 (2015): 860–72; Michael Barnett, *Empire of Humanity: A History of Humanitarianism* (Ithaca, NY: Cornell University Press, 2011); Aidan Forth, *Barbed-Wire Imperialism: Britain's Empire of Camps, 1876–1903* (Berkeley: University of California Press, 2017); Anna Clark, "Humanitarianism, Human Rights, and Biopolitics in the British Empire, 1890–1902," *Britain and the World* 9:1 (2016): 96–115; David Nally, "That Coming Storm: The Irish Poor Law, Colonial Biopolitics, and the Great Famine," *Annals of the Association of American Geographers* 98, no. 3 (2008): 714–41.

11. For this reason, this book does not follow any objective standards for diagnosing famines, such as a set decline in food availability, excess mortality rates, or malnutrition metrics like arm circumference. In a study of conceptions of famine, it is necessary to follow the lead of historical observers who knew famine when they saw it. For an influential model for modern famine diagnosis, see Paul Howe and Stephen Devereux, "Famine intensity and magnitude scales: A proposal for an instrumental definition of famine," *Disasters* 28, no. 4 (December 2004): 353–72.

12. On the limits of a Foucauldian paradigm in colonial empires, see Frederick Cooper, "Conflict and Connection: Rethinking Colonial African History," *American Historical Review* 99, no. 5 (December 1994): 1516–45; Jeffrey Herbst, *States and Power in Africa: Comparative Lessons in Authority and Control* (Princeton, NJ: Princeton University Press, 2000); Peter Zinoman, *The Colonial Bastille: A History of Imprisonment in Vietnam, 1862–1940* (Berkeley: University of California Press, 2001).

13. In one of his celebrated lectures at the Collège de France, Michel Foucault placed the liberalization of the grain trade in the eighteenth century at the very heart of the history of modern governance. Ironically, beginning the story of famine here rather than with the Irish potato famine underscores that colonial famine relief was *not*, in fact, an example of disciplinary or biopolitical management. See Foucault, *Security, Territory, Population: Lectures at the Collège de France, 1977–1978* (New York: Picador, 2004), 29–40.

14. David Arnold, *Famine: Social Crisis and Historical Change* (Oxford: Basil Blackwell, 1988).

15. Steven L. Kaplan, *Bread, Politics, and Political Economy in the Reign of Louis XV,* 2nd ed. (London: Anthem Press, 2015); Steven L. Kaplan, *The Bakers of Paris and the Bread Question, 1700–1775* (Durham, NC: Duke University Press, 1996); Judith A. Miller, *Mastering the Market: The State and the Grain Trade in Northern France, 1700–1860* (Cambridge: Cambridge University Press, 1999); E. C. Spary, *Feeding France: New Sciences of Food, 1760–1815* (Cambridge: Cambridge University Press, 2014); Louise A. Tilly, "La révolte frumentaire, forme de conflit politique en France," *Annales. Histoire, Sciences Sociales* 72, no. 3 (1972): 731–57.

16. Miller, *Mastering the Market,* 12–18.

17. *Report of the Indian Famine Commission* (London, 1880), 36.

18. Cynthia A. Bouton, *The Flour War: Gender, Class, and Community in Late Ancien Régime French Society* (University Park: Pennsylvania State University Press, 1993); George Rudé, "La taxation populaire de mai 1775 à Paris et dans la région parisienne," *Annales historiques de la Révolution française* 28, no. 143 (1956): 139–79.

19. Anne Robert Jacques Turgot, *Lettres sur la Liberté des Grains* (Paris: Institut Coppet, 2015), 14.

20. François Ewald, *The Birth of Solidarity: The History of the French Welfare State* (Durham, NC: Duke University Press, 2020); François Schaller, *De La Charité Privée aux Droits Economiques et Sociaux du Citoyen* (Neuchâtel et Paris: Editions de la Baconnière, 1950). On old regime charity, see for example, Colin Jones, *The Charitable Imperative: Hospitals and Nursing in Ancien Regime and Revolutionary France* (London and New York: Routledge, 1989).

21. The French word *race* encompassed several interrelated meanings. It could refer to peoples, ethnicities, nationalities, or other groupings in addition to collectivities rooted in biological descent. I have translated *race* as "race" with the understanding that the distinction between ethnic and biological characteristics was fluid.

22. On race in France and European empires, see Herrick Chapman and Lara L. Frader, eds., *Race in France: Interdisciplinary Perspectives on the Politics of Difference* (New York: Bergahn Books, 2004); Ann Laura Stoler, *Race and the Education of Desire: Foucault's History of Sexuality and the Colonial Order of Things* (Durham, NC: Duke University Press, 1995); Alice Conklin, *In the Museum of Man: Race, Empire, and Anthropology in France, 1850–1950* (Ithaca, NY: Cornell University Press, 2013); Sue Peabody and Tyler Stovall, eds., *The Color of Liberty: Histories of Race in France* (Durham, NC: Duke University Press, 2003); Emmanuelle Saada, *Empire's Children: Race, Filiation, and Citizenship in the French Colonies* (Chicago: University of Chicago Press, 2012); Tyler Stovall, *Paris Noir: African Americans in the City of Light* (Boston: Houghton Mifflin, 1996); Mame-Fatou Niang and Julien Suaudeau, *Universalisme* (Paris: Anamosa, 2022).

23. I have translated *prévoyance* as either "providence" or "foresight," which I use basically interchangeably. The difficulties of translation stem from overlapping connotations, ranging from fate, prudence, provision, and other shades of meaning related to the management of future risk. The British colonial equivalent of *imprévoyant* was generally "improvident." Ewald, *Birth of Solidarity*, 18, 22, 37–38, 124–25.

24. Diana K. Davis, *Resurrecting the Granary of Rome: Environmental History and French Colonial Expansion in North Africa* (Athens: Ohio University Press, 2007); Melissa Leach and Robin Mearns, *The Lie of the Land: Challenging Received Wisdom on the African Environment* (London: International African Institute, 1996).

25. Alice Conklin, *A Mission to Civilize: The Republican Idea of Empire in France and West Africa, 1895–1930* (Stanford, CA: Stanford University Press, 1997); Jennifer Pitts, *A Turn to Empire: The Rise of Imperial Liberalism in Britain and France* (Princeton, NJ: Princeton University Press, 2005).

26. A note on mortality numbers: it is notoriously difficult to estimate mortality in complex emergencies such as famines. There are definitional issues of what counts as a famine death, as disease may kill more people than starvation per se. Problems arise from classic famine behaviors like mass migration, which makes it difficult to determine mortality from changes in total population alone. Furthermore, the collection of demographic data in the French Empire was rudimentary and always political. Even

many French did not trust their own statistics. Finally, there is the problem of when famines end. Famines continued to have adverse effects long after the French declared them "over." This book does not attempt to establish exact mortality and migration statistics, but instead it relies on primary and secondary sources to give a sense of the scale of famines. On the challenges of reliably estimating famine mortality, see de Waal, *Mass Starvation*, 55–67. On challenges with French colonial demographic data, see Raymond R. Gervais, "État colonial et savoir démographique en AOF, 1904–1960," *Cahiers québécois de démographie* 25, no. 1 (Printemps 1996): 101–31.

27. Bruno Cabanes, *The Great War and the Origins of Humanitarianism, 1918–1924* (Cambridge: Cambridge University Press, 2014); J. P. Daughton, "Behind the Imperial Curtain: International Humanitarian Efforts and the Critique of French Colonialism in the Interwar Years," *French Historical Studies* 34, no. 3 (Summer 2011); Gary Wilder, *The French Imperial Nation-State: Negritude and Colonial Humanism between the Two World Wars* (Chicago: University of Chicago Press, 2005); Martin Thomas, *The French Empire Between the Wars: Imperialism, Politics and Society* (Manchester: Manchester University Press, 2005); Tony Chafer and Amanda Sackur, eds., *French Colonial Empire and the Popular Front: Hope and Disillusion* (New York: St. Martin's Press, 1999).

28. Frank Trentmann and Flemming Just, *Food and Conflict in Europe in the Age of the Two World Wars* (New York: Palgrave Macmillan, 2006); Alice Weinreb, *Modern Hungers: Food and Power in Twentieth-Century Germany* (Oxford: Oxford University Press, 2017).

29. "Blood debt" comes from Gregory Mann, *Native Sons: West African Veterans and France in the Twentieth Century*, (Durham, NC: Duke University Press, 2006). See also Joe Lunn, *Memoirs of the Maelstrom: A Senegalese Oral History of the First World War* (Portsmouth, UK: Heinemann, 1999); Myron Echenberg, *Colonial Conscripts: The Tirailleurs Sénégalais in French West Africa, 1857–1960* (Portsmouth, UK: Heinemann, 1991); Hélène D'Almeida-Topor, "Les populations dahoméenes et le recrutement militaire pendant la première guerre mondiale," *Revue française d'histoire d'outre-mer* 60, no. 219 (1973): 196–241.

30. Paul Dutton, *Origins of the French Welfare State: The Struggle for Social Reform in France, 1914–1947* (Cambridge: Cambridge University Press, 2002); Philip Nord, *France's New Deal: From the Thirties to the Postwar Era* (Princeton, NJ: Princeton University Press, 2010); Susan Pedersen, *Family, Dependence, and the Origins of the Welfare State: Britain and France, 1914–1945* (Cambridge: Cambridge University Press, 1993); Richard F. Kuisel, *Capitalism and the State in Modern France: Renovation and Economic Management in the Twentieth Century* (Cambridge: Cambridge University Press, 1981); Schaller, *De La Charité*; Ewald, *Birth of Solidarity*.

31. Susan Pedersen, *The Guardians: The League of Nations and the Crisis of Empire* (Oxford: Oxford University Press, 2015); Keith David Watenpaugh, *Bread from Stones: The Middle East and the Making of Modern Humanitarianism* (Oakland: University of California Press, 2015); Michelle Tusan, "'Crimes against Humanity': Human Rights, the British Empire, and the Origins of the Response to the Armenian Genocide (Report)," *American Historical Review* 119, no. 1 (2014); Amalia Ribi Forclaz, *Humanitarian Imperialism: The Politics of Anti-Slavery Activism, 1880–1940* (Oxford: Oxford University Press, 2015).

32. Tehila Sasson, "From Empire to Humanity: The Russian Famine and the Imperial Origins of International Humanitarianism," *Journal of British Studies* 55, no. 3 (July 2016): 519–37; Cabanes, *Great War*, 189–247.

33. Simon Jackson, "'Transformative Relief: Imperial Humanitarianism and Mandatory Development in Syria-Lebanon, 1915–1925," *Humanity: An International Journal of Human Rights, Humanitarianism, and Development* 8, no. 2 (Summer 2017): 247–68; Melanie S. Tanielian, *The Charity of War: Famine, Humanitarian Aid, and World War I in the Middle East* (Stanford, CA: Stanford University Press, 2018); Leila Tarazi Fawaz, *A Land of Aching Hearts: The Middle East in the Great War* (Cambridge, MA: Harvard University Press, 2014).

34. Anne Cornet, *Histoire d'une famine: Rwanda 1927–1930* (Louvain-la-Neuve, Belgium: Centre d'Histoire de l'Afrique, 1996); Pedersen, *Guardians*, 239–60.

35. Rob Skinner and Alan Lester, "Humanitarianism and Empire: New Research Agendas," *Journal of Imperial and Commonwealth History*, 40:5 (2012): 729–47.

36. Helen Tilley, *Africa as a Living Laboratory: Empire, Development, and the Problem of Scientific Knowledge, 1870–1950* (Chicago: University of Chicago Press, 2011); Daniel R. Headrick, *The Tools of Empire: Technology and European Imperialism in the Nineteenth Century* (Oxford: Oxford University Press, 1981); Michael Adas, *Machines as the Measure of Men: Science, Technology, and Ideologies of Western Dominance* (Ithaca, NY: Cornell University Press, 1989); Megan Vaughan, *Curing Their Ills: Colonial Power and African Illness* (Stanford, CA: Stanford University Press, 1991); Kapil Raj, *Relocating Modern Science: Circulation and the Construction of Knowledge in South Asia and Europe, 1650–1900* (London: Palgrave Macmillan, 2007).

37. James Vernon, *Hunger: A Modern History* (Cambridge, MA: Harvard University Press, 2007); Josep L. Barona, *The Problem of Nutrition: Experimental Science, Public Health and Economy in Europe 1914–1945* (Brussels: Peter Lang, 2010); Tom Scott-Smith, *On an Empty Stomach: Two Hundred Years of Hunger Relief* (Ithaca, NY: Cornell University Press, 2020); Sunil Amrith and Patricia Clavin, "Feeding the World: Connecting Europe and Asia, 1930–1945," in *Past and Present* (2013), supplement 8.

38. Rudolf Mràzek, *Engineers of Happy Land: Technology and Nationalism in a Colony* (Princeton, NJ: Princeton University Press, 2002); James Scott, *Seeing Like a State* (New Haven, CT: Yale University Press, 1998); Paul Rabinow, *French Modern: Norms and Forms of the Social Environment* (Chicago: University of Chicago Press, 1989).

39. On science and medicine in French colonialism, see Deborah J. Neill, *Networks in Tropical Medicine: Internationalism, Colonialism, and the Rise of a Medical Specialty, 1890–1930* (Stanford, CA: Stanford University Press, 2012); Michael Osborne, *The Emergence of Tropical Medicine in France* (Chicago: University of Chicago Press, 2014); Eric T. Jennings, *Curing the Colonizers: Hydrotherapy, Climatology, and French Colonial Spas* (Durham, NC: Duke University Press, 2006); Richard Keller, *Colonial Madness: Psychiatry in French North Africa* (Chicago: University of Chicago Press, 2007); Aro Velmet, *Pasteur's Empire: Bacteriology and Politics in France, its Colonies, and the World* (New York: Oxford University Press, 2020); Emmanuelle Sibeud, *Une Science Impériale Pour l'Afrique? La construction des savoirs africanistes en France, 1878–1930* (Paris: EHESS, 2002).

40. For population in France, see Dana Simmons, *Vital Minimum: Need, Science and Politics in Modern France* (Chicago: University of Chicago Press, 2015); Joshua Cole, *The Power of Large Numbers: Population, Politics, and Gender in Nineteenth-Century France* (Ithaca, NY: Cornell University Press, 2000). For a classic treatment of population as an object of management, see Foucault, *Security, Territory, Population*.

41. Didier Fassin, *Humanitarian Reason: A Moral History of the Present* (Berkeley: University of California Press, 2011); Luc Boltanski, *Distant Suffering: Morality, Media, and*

Politics (Cambridge: Cambridge University Press, 1999); Thomas W. Laqueur, "Bodies, Details, and the Humanitarian Narrative," in *The New Cultural History*, edited by Lynn Hunt (Berkeley: University of California Press, 1989).

42. Sen, *Poverty and Famines*, 79; Paul R. Greenough, *Prosperity and Misery in Modern Bengal: The Famine of 1943–1944* (New York: Oxford University Press, 1982).

43. On the French Empire after World War II, see Frederick Cooper, *Citizenship between Empire and Nation: Remaking France and French Africa, 1945–1960* (Princeton, NJ: Princeton University Press, 2014); Gary Wilder, *Freedom Time: Negritude, Decolonization, and the Future of the World* (Durham, NC: Duke University Press, 2015).

44. Gregory Mann, *From Empires to NGOs in the West African Sahel: The Road to Nongovernmentality* (Cambridge: Cambridge University Press, 2015); Antony Anghie, *Imperialism, Sovereignty, and the Making of International Law* (Cambridge: Cambridge University Press, 2004); Jessica Lynne Pearson, *The Colonial Politics of Global Health: France and the United Nations in Postwar Africa* (Cambridge, MA: Harvard University Press, 2018).

45. Samuel Moyn, *Not Enough: Human Rights in an Unequal World* (Cambridge, MA: Belknap Press of Harvard University Press, 2018).

1. Bodies and Souls in Algeria, 1867

1. Archives nationales d'outre-mer (ANOM), Fonds Ministériels (FM), F/80/1680: Situation Générale, August 10, 1867.

2. Laurent Heyberger, *Les corps en colonie: Faim, maladies, guerre et crises démographiques en Algérie au XIXe siècle, Approche anthropométrique* (Toulouse, France: Presses Universitaires du Midi, 2019); Djilali Sari, *Le désastre démographique* (Alger: Société nationale d'Edition et de Diffusion, 1982).

3. Jennifer Sessions, *By Sword and Plow: France and the Conquest of Algeria* (Ithaca, NY: Cornell University Press, 2011), 67–124.

4. Osama W. Abi-Mershed, *Apostles of Modernity: Saint-Simonians and the Civilizing Mission in Algeria* (Stanford, CA: Stanford University Press, 2010).

5. Gavin Murray-Miller, "Bonapartism in Algeria: Empire and Sovereignty before the Third Republic," *French History* 32, no. 2 (2018): 249–70; Christina Carroll, "Imperial Ideologies in the Second Empire: The Mexican Expedition and the *Royaume Arabe*," *French Historical Studies* 42, no. 1 (February 2019): 67–100.

6. Benjamin Claude Brower, *A Desert Named Peace: The Violence of France's Empire in the Sahara, 1844–1902* (New York: Columbia University Press, 2009).

7. Abi-Mershed, *Apostles of Modernity*, 98–100.

8. Judith Surkis, *Sex, Law, and Sovereignty in French Algeria, 1830–1930* (Ithaca, NY: Cornell University Press, 2019).

9. For example, ANOM, Gouvernement Général de l'Algérie (GGA), 11K/18: Résumé des faits historiques et politiques accomplis pendant l'année 1866, Cercle de Batna.

10. ANOM, GGA 11K/18: Résumé des faits historiques et politiques accomplis pendant l'année 1867, Cercle de Batna. For a discussion of famine among pastoral nomads, see Sarah Cameron, *The Hungry Steppe: Famine, Violence, and the Making of Soviet Kazakhstan* (Ithaca, NY: Cornell University Press, 2018).

11. Abi-Mershed, *Apostles of Modernity*, 181–83.

12. A rare exception that nonetheless defended the military and criticized Arab laziness is Charles Nicolas Lacretelle, *L'Algérie au point de vu de la crise actuelle* (Lyon, 1868).

13. Lacretelle, *L'Algérie au point*, 39, 75–89.

14. Rebecca Rogers, *A Frenchwoman's Imperial Story: Madame Luce in Nineteenth-Century Algeria* (Stanford, CA: Stanford University Press, 2013), 119; Sessions, *By Sword and Plow*, 318; Charles Robert Ageron, *Modern Algeria: A History from 1830 to the Present*, translated by Michael Brett (Trenton, NJ: Africa World Press, 1991), 37–44; Patricia M.E. Lorcin, *Imperial Identities: Stereotyping, Prejudice, and Race in Colonial Algeria* (London: I.B. Tauris Publishers, 1999), 76–96.

15. Ageron, *Modern Algeria*, 34.

16. Sessions, *By Sword and Plow*, 177–207.

17. James McDougall, *A History of Algeria* (Cambridge: Cambridge University Press, 2017), 78; John Ruedy, *Modern Algeria: The Origins and Development of a Nation* (Bloomington: Indiana University Press, 1992), 76–79; André Nouschi, *Enquête sur le niveau de vie des populations rurales constantinoises de la conquête jusqu'en 1919* (Paris: Presses Universitaires de France, 1961), 362, 375–77.

18. Abi-Mershed, *Apostles of Modernity*, 201–2.

19. Surkis, *Sex, Law, and Sovereignty*, 86–89.

20. McDougall, *A History of Algeria*, 89–97.

21. ANOM, FM, F/80/748: *Moniteur de l'Algérie*, May 1, 1866.

22. ANOM, FM, F/80/747: "Les Sauterelles," *Moniteur de l'Algérie*, June 26, 1866; ANOM, FM, F/80/747: Circulaire du Comité Central, Paris, July 4, 1866.

23. ANOM, FM, F/80/748: Notice sur l'invasion des sauterelles, July 10, 1866; ANOM, FM, F/80/747: *Moniteur de l'Algérie*, June 7, 1866; ANOM, FM, F/80/748: "Les sauterelles," *L'Akhbar*, July 8, 1866.

24. Burzet, *Histoire des Désastres*, 43–45.

25. ANOM, FM, F/80/747: Lettre Circulaire de Monseigneur l'Evêque de Pamiers, July 22, 1866.

26. ANOM, FM, F/80/747: "Les Sauterelles," *Moniteur de l'Algérie*, June 26, 1866.

27. ANOM, FM, F/80/747: "Des sauterelles et des moyens de les détruire," *Moniteur de l'Algérie*, June 12, 1866.

28. ANOM, FM, F/80/747: *L'Akhbar*, June 5, 1866.

29. ANOM, FM, F/80/747: *L'Akhbar*, June 15, 1866.

30. ANOM, FM, F/80/747: *Moniteur de l'Algérie*, May 3, 1866.

31. ANOM, FM, F/80/747: *Moniteur de l'Algérie*, May 3, 1866; ANOM, FM, F/80/747: Conseil de France à Porto-Rico to Maréchal Canrobert, January 20, 1867; ANOM, FM, F/80/748: Canrobert to ministre de l'Intérieur, February 23, 1867. See also ANOM, FM, F/80/750.

32. ANOM, FM, F/80/747: MacMahon to Généraux Commandant les Provinces, May 12, 1866.

33. ANOM, FM, F/80/748: Sous-Gouverneur to Mon Cher Général et Monsieur le Préfet, November 14, 1866.

34. ANOM, FM, F/80/747: *Commission Centrale chargée de la répartition des fonds de secours. Procès-Verbaux des Séances* (Alger: Typographie Bastide, Novembre 1866); ANOM, FM F/80/748: Canrobert to ministre de l'intérieur, February 23, 1867; ANOM, GGA,

1ee40: MacMahon to Napoléon III, June 21, 1866; ANOM, FM, F/80/747: Governor-General's Circular, December 11, 1866; ANOM, FM, F/80/747: MacMahon to Niel, undated.

35. Sessions, *By Sword and Plow*, 39–47.

36. ANOM, FM, F/80/747: Lettre Pastorale de Monseigneur l'Evêque de Tarbes, undated.

37. ANOM, FM, F/80/747: "Circulaire de Mgr. l'Evêque d'Alger," *L'Akhbar*, May 27, 1866.

38. ANOM, FM, F/80/747: Circulaire du Comité Central, Paris, July 4, 1866.

39. On "providentialism" in perceptions of the Irish famine, see for example Peter Gray, "'Potatoes and Providence': British Government Responses to the Great Famine," *Bullàn: An Irish Studies Journal* 1, no. 1 (Spring 1994): 75–90; see also Jacob Viner, *The Role of Providence in the Social Order* (Princeton, NJ: Princeton University Press, 1972); Boyd Hilton, *The Age of Atonement: The Influence of Evangelicalism on Social and Economic Thought* (Oxford: Clarendon Press, 1988).

40. ANOM, FM, F/80/747: Exposé du Comité Central de la Souscription, undated; ANOM, FM, F/80/748: "Les Sauterelles," *l'Événement*, July 12, 1866.

41. ANOM, FM, F/80/747: "Toujours les Sauterelles," *L'Akhbar*, June 10, 1866; ANOM, FM, F/80/747: Note sur les invasions de criquets, July 10, 1866.

42. ANOM, FM F/80/748: "Les Sauterelles: Histoire et Légendes," *l'Événement*, July 12, 1866; ANOM, FM F/80/748: "Les Sauterelles: Histoire et Légendes, suite et fin," *l'Événement*, July 13, 1866.

43. Lettre Circulaire de Monseigneur d'Ire et de Dax, undated.

44. ANOM, FM, F/80/747: "Conférence sur les sauterelles," *Moniteur de l'Algérie*, May 4, 1866.

45. Agnély, *Le Criquet Pèlerin* (Alger, 1866).

46. Caroline Ford, "The Inheritance of Empire and the Ruins of Rome in French Colonial Algeria," *Past and Present* (2015), supplement 10; Patricia M. E. Lorcin, "Rome and France in Africa: Recovering Colonial Algeria's Latin Past," *French Historical Studies* 25, no 2 (Spring 2002): 295–329.

47. ANOM, FM, F/80/747: Cardinal-Archevêque de Bordeaux, July 14, 1866.

48. ANOM, FM, F/80/747: "Circulaire de Mgr. l'Evêque d'Alger," *L'Akhbar*, May 27, 1866.

49. Burzet, *Histoire des Désastres*, 9.

50. F. Robiou de la Tréhonnais, *L'Agriculture en Algérie: Rapport à son excellence M. le Maréchal de Mac-Mahon, duc de Magenta* (Alger, 1867), 15.

51. Davis, *Resurrecting the Granary of Rome*.

52. ANOM, FM, F/80/747: Le Président de la Société d'agriculture d'alger, Arthur Arnould, July 15, 1866.

53. ANOM, FM, F/80/748: Form letter soliciting charity for Guadeloupe, December 18, 1865. See also Christopher Church, *Paradise Destroyed: Catastrophe and Citizenship in the French Caribbean* (Lincoln: University of Nebraska Press, 2017).

54. ANOM, FM, F/80/748: *Moniteur Universel, Journal officiel de l'Empire Français*, Paris, July 2, 1866.

55. ANOM, FM, F/80/747: *Le Courrier d'Oran*, May 2, 1866.

56. ANOM, FM F/80/748: "Les Sauterelles: Histoire et Légendes," *l'Événement*, July 12, 1866; ANOM, FM F/80/748: "Les Sauterelles: Histoire et Légendes, suite et fin," *l'Événement*, July 13, 1866.

57. Agnély, *Le Criquet Pèlerin*, 58.

58. ANOM, FM, F/80/747: *L'Akhbar*, June 17, 1866; ANOM, FM, F/80/747: *L'Akhbar*, June 26, 1866.

59. ANOM, FM, F/80/747: Exposé du Comité Central, undated.

60. ANOM, FM, F/80/748: "Les sauterelles," *L'Akhbar*, July 8, 1866.

61. ANOM, FM, F/80/747: untitled, F. Paysant, May 18, 1866.

62. ANOM, FM, F/80/747: *Le Courrier d'Oran*, May 2, 1866.

63. ANOM, GGA, 1EE40: MacMahon to Napoléon III, May 3, 1866.

64. ANOM, FM F/80/748: "Les Sauterelles: Histoire et Légendes," *l'Événement*, July 12, 1866; "Les Sauterelles: Histoire et Légendes, suite et fin," *l'Événement*, July 13, 1866.

65. Burzet, *Histoire des Désastres*, 30–31.

66. ANOM, FM F/80/748: Lettre Circulaire de Monseigneur d'Aire et de Dax, undated.

67. ANOM, FM, F/80/747: MacMahon to MM. Les Généraux commandant les Provinces, May 12, 1866.

68. ANOM, FM, F/80/747: Circulaire à MM. les Généraux commandant les provinces d'Algérie, July 18, 1866.

69. ANOM, FM, F/80/747: *Commission Centrale chargée de la répartition des fonds de secours*.

70. Nouschi, *Enquête sur le niveau*, 337–78.

71. ANOM, GGA, 1h32: De Wimpffen to MacMahon, May 29, 1866; ANOM, GGA, 1h32: De Wimpffen to MacMahon, January 4, 1867.

72. ANOM, GGA, 11K/18: Résumé, 1866, Cercle de Batna.

73. On Algerian receptions of French medicine, see Hannah-Louise Clark, "Of Jinn Theories and Germ Theories: Translating Microbes, Bacteriological Medicine, and Islamic Law in Algeria," *Osiris* 36 (2021): 64–85.

74. Burzet, *Histoire des Désastres*, 61–62, 66.

75. ANOM, FM, F/80/1791: M. Parenteau-Léon to Minister of War, May 6, 1868.

76. ANOM, GGA, 1ee40: MacMahon to Napoléon III, May 8, 1866.

77. Cormac Ó Gráda, *Eating People Is Wrong and Other Essays on Famine, Its Past, and Its Future* (Princeton, NJ: Princeton University Press, 2015), chapter 1.

78. ANOM, GGA, 1K361: MacMahon to Général Commandant la Province de Constantine, April 14, 1868.

79. ANOM, GGA, 1K361: État indiquant les crimes qui peuvent être attribués à la misère, Subdivision de Sétif, undated; ANOM, GGA, 1K361: Commandant de subdivision de Bône to Général Commandant la Province de Constantine, May 10, 1868.

80. *La Famine en Algérie et les discours officiels: Erreurs et contradictions* (Constantine, Algeria, 1868), 23.

81. Burzet, *Histoire des Désastres*, 92–93.

82. Burzet, *Histoire des Désastres*, 76, 88–104.

83. The phrase "circle of concern" is from Richard Rorty, "Human Rights, Rationality, and Sentimentality," in *Truth and Progress: Philosophical Papers* (Cambridge: Cambridge University Press, 1998), 167–85.

84. Lorcin, *Imperial Identities*, 21–27, 61–75. Justin E. H. Smith, *Nature, Human Nature, and Human Difference: Race in Early Modern Philosophy* (Princeton, NJ: Princeton University Press, 2015), 212; Alexis de Tocqueville, *Letters on Algeria*, in *Writings on Empire and Slavery*, edited by Jennifer Pitts (Baltimore: Johns Hopkins University Press, 2001).

85. ANOM, FM, F/80/646: "Le Rapport du maréchal Niel," *La Gazette de France*, June 7, 1868.

86. ANOM, FM, F/80/1680: MacMahon, Situation Générale, August 10, 1867.

87. ANOM, GGA, 11K/18: Résumé, 1867, Cercle de Batna.

88. ANOM, GGA, 1h32: De Wimpffen to MacMahon, undated.

89. ANOM, FM, F/80/1680: Corps législatif session 1868 n. 172.

90. ANOM, FM, F/80/1680: Exposé de la situation de l'empire, November 26, 1868.

91. *La Famine en Algérie*, 18–19.

92. ANOM, GGA, 1ee40: MacMahon to Napoléon III, March 18, 1867; ANOM, GGA, 1K361: Le Colonel Commandant la Subdivision to Général commandant la province de Constantine, July 27, 1868; ANOM, FM, F/80/1680: MacMahon, Situation Générale, August 10, 1867.

93. ANOM, GGA, 1ee40: MacMahon to Napoléon III, July 6, 1867.

94. ANOM, GGA, 1K361: MacMahon to Général commandant la province de Constantine, June 13, 1868.

95. *Enquête Agricole: Algérie* (Paris, 1870), 426.

96. ANOM, GGA 1K361: Letter to Governor-General, May 24, 1867.

97. ANOM, GGA, 1K361: Rapport hebdomadaire, subdivision de Batna, October 24, 1869.

98. ANOM, GGA, 1K361: letter to Général commandant la province de Constantine, July 27, 1868.

99. ANOM, GGA, 1K361: Général commandant la subdivision de Batna to Général commandant la province de Constantine, May 9, 1868.

100. ANOM, GGA, 1K10: MacMahon to Général commandant la Province de Constantine, June 10, 1867; ANOM, GGA 1K10: MacMahon to Général commandant la province de Constantine, October 14, 1867.

101. ANOM, GGA, 1K361: Colonel commandant la subdivision de Batna, October 7, 1868; *Enquête Agricole*, 110–11.

102. ANOM, GGA, 1K10: MacMahon to Général commandant la province de Constantine, October 14, 1867.

103. ANOM, GGA, 1K361: Colonel commandant la subdivision de Batna, October 4, 1868.

104. ANOM, GGA, 1E92 (71MIOM92): Rapport sur une tournée du commandant supérieur du cercle de Cherchell, Miliana, February 17, 1868.

105. *La Famine en Algérie*, 15, 22.

106. Burzet, *Histoire des Désastres*, 84.

107. ANOM, FM, F/80/646: "Rapport à la commission provinciale de secours" *Moniteur de l'Algérie*, June 27, 1868; ANOM, FM, F/80/1680: MacMahon to Niel, March 9, 1868.

108. ANOM, GGA, 1K361: mesures prises par le Gouvernement, Subdivision de Bône, May 10, 1868; ANOM, GGA 1K361: Note, Commandant-Supérieur, Souk-Ahras,

October 8, 1868; ANOM, GGA, 1K361: Subdivision de Constantine to Gouverneur-Général, February 6, 1868.

109. ANOM, FM, F/80/1680: Commandant de la 2ème compagnie, Blida, February 20, 1868.

110. ANOM, GGA, 1K361: Général commandant la subdivision de Batna to Général commandant la province de Constantine, May 9, 1868; ANOM, GGA, 1K361: Colonel commandant la subdivision de Sétif to Général commandant la province de Constantine, April 24, 1868.

111. ANOM, FM, F/80/646: De Wimpffen, "Rapport à la commission provinciale de secours," *Moniteur de l'Algérie*, June 27, 1868.

112. ANOM, GGA, 1K361: MacMahon to Général commandant la province de Constantine, June 13, 1868.

113. ANOM, GGA, 1K361: Le Général commandant la subdivision de Bône to Général commandant Constantine, May 13, 1868.

114. ANOM, GGA, 11K/18: Résumé 1869, Cercle de Batna.

115. Ageron, *Modern Algeria*, 44–46.

116. Abi-Mershed, *Apostles of Modernity*, 184–85.

117. David Todd, *A Velvet Empire: French Informal Imperialism in the Nineteenth Century* (Princeton, NJ: Princeton University Press, 2021), 51–71.

118. Lorcin, *Imperial Identities*, 37–40, 45–46.

119. ANOM, FM, F/80/1681: Discours prononcé par S. Exc. Le Maréchal de Mac-Mahon, Sénat—Vendredi 21 Janvier 1870.

120. Paul Leroy-Beaulieu, *De la colonization chez les peuples modernes* (Paris, 1874), 501–25.

121. Sessions, *By Sword and Plow*, 121; Abi-Mershed, *Apostles of Modernity*, 159–68.

122. Un ancien officier de l'armée d'afrique, *l'Algérie devant l'assemblée nationale: causes des insurrections algériennes* (Versailles, 1871), 5, 21.

123. *Enquête Agricole*, 407, 431; ANOM, FM F/80/1791: Pascal, "Quelques notes sur l'Algérie," April 27, 1868; ANOM, FM F/80/1791: Martin to Napoléon III, May 15, 1868.

124. ANOM, GGA, 1K361: Chambre de Commerce de Constantine to Gouverneur Général, April 8, 1868.

125. *Enquête Agricole*, 233.

126. On politics and emotion, see Lynn Hunt, *Inventing Human Rights: A History* (New York: Norton, 2007).

127. Philip Nord, *The Republican Moment: Struggles for Democracy in Nineteenth Century France* (Cambridge, MA: Harvard University Press, 1995), 115–38, 207–12; Roger Price, *The French Second Empire: An Anatomy of Political Power* (Cambridge: Cambridge University Press, 2001), 171–87.

128. ANOM, FM, F/80/646: MacMahon to Minister of War, May 9, 1868.

129. ANOM, FM, F/80/646: Circulaire aux généraux commandant les provinces en Algérie, undated.

130. Un ancien officier, 5, 21.

131. ANOM, FM, F/80/646: Deligny, "La Famine en Algérie," *La Liberté*, September 22, 1868.

132. ANOM, FM, F/80/646: "Un Discours Fantastique," *Le Siècle*, Paris, October 20, 1868.

133. Ad. Rocher, "Gazette des tribunaux," *Le Figaro*, May 21, 1868.

134. Édouard Lockroy, "Menus Propos," *Le Figaro*, May 22, 1868.

135. La dame masquée, "Hier, aujourd'hui, demain," *Le Figaro*, April 27, 1868.

136. Aristide Bérard, *l'Algérie: sa situation présente, son avenir* (Paris, 1868).

137. E. Aubert, "Faits Divers," *Le Figaro*, February 13, 1868.

138. Édouard Lockroy, "Menus Propos," *Le Figaro*, March 13, 1868.

139. Francis Magnard, "Paris au jour le jour," *Le Figaro*, July 6, 1868.

140. Charles Daubige, "Fantaisies algériennes A travers champs," *Le Figaro*, November 11, 1868.

141. Édouard Lockroy, "Menus Propos," *Le Figaro*, March 13, 1868.

142. Alphonse Duchesne, "Le Diable à quatre," *Le Figaro*, October 31, 1868.

143. Édouard Lockroy, "Menus Propos," *Le Figaro*, March 28, 1868.

144. ANOM, FM, F80/1746: "Fin du Conflit," *L'Akhbar*, June 3 and 4, 1868; ANOM, FM, F/80/646: "Algérie," *Courrier de Lyon*, June 17, 1868.

145. ANOM, FM, F/80/646: "Algérie," *Courrier de Lyon*, June 17, 1868.

146. ANOM, FM, F/80/646: *Courrier de la Gironde*, Bordeaux, June 11, 1868.

147. ANOM, FM, F80/1746: "Fin du Conflit," *L'Akhbar*, June 3 and 4, 1868.

148. ANOM, FM, F/80/646: Deligny, "La Famine en Algérie," *La Liberté*, September 22, 1868.

149. ANOM, FM, F/80/646: "Algérie," *Courrier de Lyon*, June 17, 1868.

150. Charles Puyau, *de l'Impuissance des bureaux arabes et des réformes à introduire en Algérie* (Alger, 1871); *Enquête Agricole*, 212–13, 357.

151. ANOM, FM, F/80/646: E. Jouen, "La Famine en Algérie," *Le Courrier de Lyon*, June 12, 1868; ANOM, FM, F/80/646: "Une page d'histoire: Le Maréchal Mac-Mahon à Constantine," *L'Indépendant*, September 2, 1868.

152. ANOM, FM, F/80/646: *L'Économiste Français*, Paris, September 5, 1868.

153. Puyau, *de l'Impuissance*.

154. Ch. Cuvier, *Compte Rendu des dons reçus par M. Ch. Cuvier en faveur des victimes de la famine en Algérie* (Strasbourg, 1868).

155. Charles Lavigerie, *Les Orphelins Arabes d'Alger: Leur passé, leur présent, leur avenir* (1875); Bertrand Taithe, "Algerian Orphans and Colonial Christianity in Algeria, 1866–1939," *French History* 20, no. 3 (2006): 240–59.

156. Bertrand Taithe, "Humanitarianism and Colonialism: Religious Responses to the Algerian Drought and Famine of 1866–1870," in *Natural Disasters, Cultural Responses: Case Studies Toward a Global Environmental History*, edited by Christof Mauch and Christian Pfister (Lanham, MD: Lexington Books, 2009), 146.

157. ANOM, FM, F80/1746: L'Archevêque d'Alger to Directeur de l'Œuvre des Ecoles d'Orient, April 6, 1868.

158. ANOM, FM, F80/1746: MacMahon to Lavigerie, April 21, 1868.

159. ANOM, FM, F80/1746: Lavigerie to MacMahon, April 23, 1868.

160. ANOM, FM, F80/1746: L'Archevêque d'Alger to Directeur de l'Œuvre des Ecoles d'Orient, April 6, 1868.

161. ANOM, FM, F80/1746: MacMahon to Lavigerie, April 21, 1868.

162. ANOM, FM, F80/1746: Lavigerie to MacMahon, April 23, 1868.

163. ANOM, FM, F80/1746: Jules Duval, untitled, *L'Économiste Français*, June 20, 1868.

164. ANOM, FM, F80/1746: Lavigerie, Letter to the Editor, *L'Akhbar*, April 28, 1868.

165. ANOM, FM, F80/1746: Lavigerie, *Circulaire Confidentielle de Monseigneur l'Archevêque d'Alger au Clergé de son Diocèse*, Alger, May 7, 1868.

166. ANOM, FM, F80/1746: Minister of War to MacMahon, *Moniteur de l'Algérie*, May 12, 1868.

167. ANOM, FM, F80/1746: "Fin du Conflit," *L'Akhbar*, June 3 and 4, 1868.

168. ANOM, FM, F80/1746: Lavigerie, *Circulaire Confidentielle*, Alger, May 7, 1868.

169. Albert Wolff, "Gazette de Paris," *Le Figaro*, May 18, 1868.

170. ANOM, FM, F80/1746: "Fin du Conflit," *L'Akhbar*, June 3 and 4, 1868; ANOM, FM, F80/1746: Jules Duval, untitled, *L'Économiste Français*, June 20, 1868; ANOM, FM, F/80/646: Perrier, *L'Echo d'Oran*, May 14, 1868; ANOM, FM, F80/1746: "Fin du Conflit," *L'Akhbar*, June 3 and 4, 1868.

171. ANOM, FM, F80/1746: Lavigerie to MacMahon, April 23, 1868.

172. *Enquête Agricole*, 110–11.

173. *La Famine en Algérie*, 25.

174. *Enquête Agricole*, 110, 212–13, 330–32, 350–52.

175. *Enquête Agricole*, 43, 119, 125, 282, 285, 340, 389.

176. Nord, *Republican Moment*, 3.

2. The Mandate of Heaven in Indochina, 1884–1930

1. Pierre-Étienne Will and R. Bin Wong, *Nourish the People: The State Civilian Granary System in China: 1650–1850* (Ann Arbor, MI: Center for Chinese Studies Publications, 1991); Van Nguyen-Marshall, *In Search of Moral Authority: The Discourse on Poverty, Poor Relief, and Charity in French Colonial Vietnam* (New York: Peter Lang, 2008), 13–15.

2. Quoted in Kathryn Edgerton-Tarpley, *Tears from Iron: Cultural Responses to Famine in Nineteenth-Century China* (Berkeley: University of California Press, 2008), 91.

3. James Scott, *The Moral Economy of the Peasant: Rebellion and Subsistence in Southeast Asia* (New Haven, CT: Yale University Press, 1976), 84–85.

4. Edgerton-Tarpley, *Tears from Iron*, 91–93; Hue-Tam Ho Tai, *Radicalism and the Origins of the Vietnamese Revolution* (Cambridge, MA: Harvard University Press, 1992), 171.

5. Alexander Barton Woodside, *Vietnam and the Chinese Model: A Comparative Study of Vietnamese and Chinese Government in the First Half of the Nineteenth Century* (Cambridge, MA: Harvard University Press, 1971); Pham Cao Duong, *Vietnamese Peasants under French Domination, 1861–1945* (New York: University Press of America, 1985).

6. It is unclear whether a national system in the style of Chinese "ever-normal" granaries was ever instituted in Vietnam. Such a system required a centrally planned and constant circulation of grain to even out prices across time and space. The Minh Mang emperor, Gia Long's strict Confucian successor who reigned from 1820 to 1839, believed that ever-normal granaries had existed in the past but were unnecessary in modern times. Woodside, *Chinese Model*, 162.

7. Ngô Viñh Long, *Before the Revolution: The Vietnamese Peasants under the French* (New York: Columbia University Press, 1973), 33–34.

8. P. L. F. Philastre, *Le Code Annamite* (Paris, 1876).

9. Woodside, *Chinese Model*, 137–38.

10. Nguyen-Marshall, *Moral Authority*, 23–37.

11. Christopher Goscha, *Vietnam: A New History* (New York: Basic Books, 2016), 61.

12. Zinoman, *Colonial Bastille*, 39.

13. The main governing body, the *co mat*, translated as "privy council" or "secret council," was comprised of four Vietnamese ministers before 1899 and six after. The French resident-superior presided and approved all decisions. Beginning in 1925, the imperial cabinet was officially headed by the resident-superior rather than the emperor. See ANOM, FM, SG, INDO/AF/8: Governor-general Doumer to Ministre des Colonies, November 12, 1899; Hy Van Luong, "Agrarian Unrest from an Anthropological Perspective: The Case of Vietnam," *Comparative Politics 17*, no. 2 (January 1985): 153–74; Goscha, *Vietnam: A New History*, 84.

14. ANOM, FM, SG, INDO/AF/6: M. Hector, Résident Supérieur en Annam to Gouverneur-Général de l'Indo-Chine, Rapport trimestriel, Hue, October 15, 1889.

15. Ngô Viñh Long, *Before the Revolution*, 63.

16. Ngô Viñh Long, *Before the Revolution*, 84–99; Scott, *Moral Economy*, 109–15.

17. Yves Henry, *Economie Agricole de l'Indochine* (Hanoi: Imprimerie d'extrême-orient, 1932); Duong, *Vietnamese Peasants*, 23–61; Pierre Gourou, *Les paysans du delta tonkinois: étude de géographie humaine* (Paris: Editions d'art et d'histoire, 1936). On economic transformation in an urban context, see Haydon Cherry, *Down and Out in Saigon: Stories of the Poor in a Colonial City* (New Haven, CT: Yale University Press, 2019).

18. Centre des archives nationales No. 1 [Vietnam National Archives Center 1, VNA 1], Résidence Supérieure au Tonkin [RST], N.41/S.67 75780: Lieutenant Ricou, "Au sujet de la disette récente dans le delta," 1906; VNA 1, RST 13967: l'Administrateur délégué à Hanam to M. le Résident Supérieur au Tonkin, Phu-Ly, May 13, 1916.

19. ANOM, GGI 64405: Gouverneur-Général to Ministre des Colonies, July 19, 1905.

20. ANOM, FM, SG, INDO/AF/6: M. Hector, Résident Supérieur en Annam to Gouverneur Général de l'Indo-Chine, Hue, October 15, 1889.

21. ANOM, FM, SG, INDO/AF/6: Annam et Tonkin, rapport sur le 2ème trimestre, 1890; ANOM, FM, SG, INDO/AF/6: Protectorat de l'Annam et du Tonkin, Rapport Politique, 1er trimestre 1890.

22. VNA 1, RST S.67, 74527: Vice-Résident de France to Ministre Plénipotentiaire résident général en Annam et au Tonkin, May 12, 1887.

23. VNA 1, RST U.12 14021: Résident au Tonkin to Gouverneur-Général, August 9, 1890; ANOM: FM, SG, INDO/AF/6: Protectorat de l'Annam et du Tonkin, Rapport Politique, 1er trimestre 1890; VNA 1, RST U.12 14021: Rapport du Kham-Sai to Résident Supérieur, August 6, 1890; VNA 1, RST U.12 14021: Arrêté du Gouverneur Général de l'Indochine, August 10, 1890.

24. VNA 1, RST U.12 14021: Inspecteur Chef du Service des Douanes du Tonkin to Résident Supérieur au Tonkin, Haiphong, November 4, 1890; VNA 1, RST U.12 14021: Arrêté du gouverneur général, December 1890; VNA 1, RST U.12 14021: Arrêté du Gouverneur Général, September 23, 1891.

25. VNA 1, RST U.12 14021: L'Inspecteur Chef du Service des Douanes au Tonkin to Résident-Supérieur, Haiphong, June 17, 1891.

26. VNA 1, RST T.53 78169: Kinh-Luoc to Directeur Affaires Civiles, May 1, 1896; VNA 1, RST T.53 78169: Résident-Maire de Haiphong to Directeur Affaires Civiles,

1896; VNA 1, RST T.53 78169: Arrêté, Gouvernement Général de l'Indo-Chine, n. 732; VNA 1, Résidence de Ha Dong, N.62 3482: M. le Secrétaire Général du Gouverneur Général [J. Fourés] to Résidents Chefs des provinces, Hanoi, April 14, 1896; VNA 1, Résidence de Ha Dong, N. 62 3482: Secrétaire Général to Résidents Chefs des provinces, Hanoi, August 17, 1896.

27. VNA 1, Résidence de Ha Dong, N.62 3482: M. Fourés, Résident Supérieur au Tonkin to Résident de la province de Hanoi, February 26, 1898.

28. ANOM, GGI//20497: Rapport du Résident Supérieur Annam to Gouverneur-Général, January 28, 1898.

29. ANOM, GGI//20497: Rapport du Résident Supérieur Annam to Gouverneur-Général, January 28, 1898.

30. ANOM, GGI//20497: Rapport du Résident Supérieur Annam Briére to Gouverneur-Général Doumer, February 1, 1898.

31. Hoang Cao Khai, En Annam (Hanoi: Edition Annamite-français, 1909). See also Hue-Tam Ho Tai, Radicalism and Origins, 15–20; Goscha, Vietnam: A New History, 92.

32. ANOM, GGI//20497: Rapport du Résident Supérieur Annam Briére to Gouverneur-Général Doumer, February 1, 1898.

33. ANOM, GGI//20497: Rapport du Résident Supérieur Annam to Gouverneur-Général, January 28, 1898.

34. ANOM, GGI//20497: Télégramme Officiel, Gouverneur-Général to Résident Supérieur Annam, February 4, 1898; ANOM, GGI//20497: Telegram from Hue, undated.

35. ANOM, FM, SG, INDO/AF/8: Gouverneur-Général Doumer to Ministre des Colonies, 1899; ANOM, GGI//20497: Telegram from Résident Supérieur to Gouverneur-Général, Hue, February 10, 1898.

36. VNA 1, RST S.67 74525: M. Doan Chien, Tuan Phu to Résident de France à Ninh-Binh, le 13 du 3ème mois de la 18ème année de Thanh, June 11, 1906.

37. VNA, RST S.67 74525: l'Administrateur-Résident de France à Ninh Binh to Résident Supérieur au Tonkin, Ninh Binh, April 10, 1906.

38. VNA 1, Résidence de Nam Dinh [RND], H.42/S/67 3037: Résident Supérieur p.i. to Résidents Chefs de province de Tonkin, October 12, 1905.

39. ANOM, NF 1853: Gouverneur Général de l'Indochine to Ministre des Colonies, October 13, 1905.

40. "La Famine et ses Remèdes," Le Courrier d'Haiphong, May 3, 1906.

41. Nguyen-Marshall, Moral Authority, 24–25.

42. VNA 1, RND, H.42/S/67 3037: Trinh Ngoc Giao, Lu Tai du village de Vu Xa to M. le Tri Huyen, November 10, 1905.

43. VNA 1, RST 13967: Résident Supérieur Annam to Gouverneur Général, April 19, 1916; VNA 1, RST S.67 74525: Résident Supérieur du Tonkin [Fourés] to Résidents Chefs de province au Tonkin, Hanoi, August 3, 1904.

44. VNA 1, RND, H.42/S/67 3037: Do tuc Dat, Huyen de My Loc to Résident Nam Dinh, May 3, 1906.

45. ANOM, GGI 17647: Lettre des Membres du Conseil de Régence to Gouverneur-Général de l'Indochine, December 10, 1910.

46. ANOM, GGI 17647: Résident Supérieur en Annam to Gouverneur Général de l'Indochine, December 16, 1910.

47. ANOM, GGI 46375–46410: Article censuré de l'Avenir du Tonkin, Henri Laumonier, "Théorie et Pratique," September 23, 1916.

48. VNA 1, RST 13967: l'Administrateur Résident de France à Nam-Dinh to Résident Supérieur du Tonkin, April 14, 1916; VNA 1, RST 13967: Hoang-Manh-Tri, Le Tong-Doc to Résident de France à Nam Dinh, 1916; VNA 1, RST 13967: Tran-Ngoc-Quang to Résident de France à Nam-Dinh, Quy-Nhat, April 6, 1916.

49. VNA 1, RST, 13967: circular by Tuan-Phu p.i. de Ninh-Binh, April 29, 1916.

50. VNA 1, RND, H.42/S/67 3037: Ng Duq Luyen, Dong Tri Phu de Nghi Hung Pham to Résident Supérieur à Nam-Dinh, November 9, 1905.

51. VNA 1, RND, D.4, 2338: Notables of the village of Van-Bang to Resident of Nam Dinh, June 2, 1906.

52. VNA 1, RST S.67 74525: Résident Hanam to Résident Supérieur, April 3, 1906.

53. VNA 1, RST H.42/D.647 74773: Les habitants to Gouverneur-Général, Hanoi, October 3, 1905.

54. ANOM, NF 1853: "Lettre d'Hanoi," *Gaulois*, Hanoi, June 12, 1903.

55. ANOM, NF 1853: Gouverneur Général de l'Indochine to Ministre des Colonies, August 31, 1905.

56. ANOM, NF 1853: "Un Typhon," *Le Matin*, Marseille, October 17, 1904.

57. ANOM, NF 1853: *Petite République*, September 12, 1904.

58. ANOM, NF 1853: Gouverneur Général de l'Indochine to Ministre des Colonies, October 13, 1905; ANOM, GGI 64405: Gouverneur Général to Ministre des Colonies, September 24, 1905; VNA 1, Résidence de Nam Dinh H.42/S/67 3037: M. Pham Tong Doc à Nam Dinh to Quan Phu et Quan Huyen de la province, October 22, 1905.

59. Woodside, *Chinese Model*, 137–39.

60. ANOM: GGI 17647: Rapport à M. le Résident Supérieur, Présenté par M. Maron, au nom de la Commission chargée de rechercher les moyens les plus immédiats de remédier à la disette, undated.

61. ANOM, NF 1853: Beau to Ministre des Colonies, October 6, 1904; ANOM, RSTNF 04352: Discours prononcé par M. Beau, Gouverneur Général de l'Indo-Chine à l'ouverture de la session ordinaire du conseil supérieur, December 11, 1905.

62. ANOM, GGI 64405: Gouverneur Général to Ministre des Colonies, September 24, 1905; VNA 1, RST N.41/S.67 75780: Le Résident Supérieur au Tonkin to Messieurs les Administrateurs chefs de provinces, June 24, 1906.

63. ANOM, GGI 64407: Gouverneur Général de l'Indo-Chine to Ministre des Colonies, August 2, 1907.

64. ANOM, RSTAF 46483: Rapport Politique et économique annuel de la province de Nam Dinh, August 1915–August 1916.

65. Hoàng Cao Khai, "Les Inondations au Tonkin," *Bulletin Economique de l'Indochine*, July–August 1915.

66. Hoàng Cao Khai, "Les Inondations au Tonkin."

67. ANOM, NF 1853: "Les Inondations du Tonkin," *L'Autorité*, September 1904.

68. ANOM, GGI 17647: H. Guerrier, planteur à Vinh-yen et à Phuc-ven to Gouverneur Général, August 6, 1917.

69. ANOM, GGI 46375–46410: L'Inspecteur Général des travaux publics de l'Indo-Chine to Résident Supérieur au Tonkin, August 26, 1926.

70. Pierre Duclaux, *L'Annamite et nous* (La Revue de Paris, n. 9 du 1er mai 1909) in *Témoignages et Documents Français Relatifs à la colonisation Française au Viet-Nam* (Hanoi: Association Culturelle pour le salut du Viet-Nam, 1945). For a list of deadly floods in Vinh Yen between 1851 and 1918, see Henri le Grauclaude, *Les eaux, disciplinées, ont mis en déroute la famine* (Hue: Editions de la Presse Populaire de l'Empire d'Annam, 1933).

71. Hoàng Cao Khai, "Les Inondations au Tonkin."

72. Rapport de M. l'Ingénieur principal, Chef du Service de l'Hydraulique Rouen, in *Bulletin Economique de l'Indochine*, July–August 1915.

73. Rapport de M. l'Ingénieur principal.

74. ANOM, GGI 46375–46410: Résident Supérieur au Tonkin to Inspecteur-Général des travaux publics, November 30, 1926.

75. ANOM, GGI 17647: Résident Supérieur en Annam to Gouverneur-Général de l'Indochine, September 19, 1907.

76. VNA 1, RST N.41 / S.67 75780: Le Gouverneur-Général de l'Indo-Chine to Résident Supérieur au Tonkin, June 10, 1906.

77. VNA 1, Résidence de Ha Dong N.6 3485: Résident Supérieur du Tonkin to Résidents Chefs de province du Tonkin, circulaire demandant des renseignements sur les disettes de 1905 et 1906, July 17, 1907.

78. VNA 1, Résidence de Ha Dong N. 6, 3485: M. Dang, Cong-Doc de Ha Dong to S.E. Ve Vu Hau, Résident Chef de la Province, July 19, 1907.

79. ANOM, GGI 64177: Rapport Politique et économique des mois de Juillet-Août 1906.

80. ANOM, GGI 17647: Résident Supérieur au Tonkin to Directeur du Cabinet et du Personnnel du Gouvernement Général à Hanoi, October 19, 1907; ANOM, GGI 17647: Rapport à M. le Résident Supérieur, Presenté par M. Maron, au nom de la Commission chargée de rechercher les moyens les plus immédiats de remédier à la disette, undated.

81. VNA 1, RST N.41 / S.67 75780: Résident Supérieur au Tonkin [Grobeau] to Résidents, chefs de province du Tonkin, June 11, 1906.

82. ANOM, GGI 17647: Arrêté, 1907.

83. VNA 1, RST N.41 / S.67 75780: Paul Lechesne, "Mémoire sur les mesures à prendre pour secourir le peuple d'Indo-Chine en temps de famine et de misère," 1906; ANOM, GGI 17647: Rapport à M. le Résident Supérieur, Presenté par M. Maron, au nom de la Commission chargée de rechercher les moyens les plus immédiats de remédier à la disette, undated; VNA 1, RST D.26 55466: Résident de France à Hoa-Binh (Richard) to Résident Supérieur au Tonkin, October 29, 1910.

84. VNA 1, Résidence de Ha Dong, N.62 3488: Note (sans auteur) sur la constitution des greniers à riz du modèle de ceux du Gouvernement indigène en vue de parer à la famine, undated.

85. VNA 1, RST D.26 55466: Tuan-Phu de Tuyen-Quang, "Constitution d'un fond de réserve destiné à secourir les populations en cas de famine," 1910; VNA 1, RST D.26 55466: Tuan-Phu de Tuyen-Quang, "Repeuplement de la haute région par l'excédent de la population du delta," 1910.

86. Daughton, *Empire Divided*, 61.

87. MEP: *Annales de la Société des Missions-Etrangères,* Mai-Juin 1906; MEP: *Vicariat Apostolique du Tonkin Maritime: Compte Rendu de l'Exercise 1915–1916* (Ninh Binh: Imprimerie Thien Ban, 1916).

88. MEP: *Compte Rendu des travaux de 1907* (Paris: Séminaire des Missions-Etrangères, 1908).

89. Charles Keith, *Catholic Vietnam: A Church from Empire to Nation* (Berkeley: University of California Press, 2012), 44–54.

90. Daughton, *Empire Divided,* 59–118.

91. MEP 704: Mgr. Puginier to Directeurs du Séminaire, April 21, 1887.

92. MEP: Compte Rendu 1887.

93. MEP: Compte Rendu 1890.

94. MEP 704: Mgr. Puginier to Lemonnier, March 27, 1887.

95. MEP: Compte Rendu 1887.

96. MEP 816: Mgr. Puginier to Mollard, August 11, 1887.

97. MEP: Annales de la Société des Missions-Etrangères, Mai-Juin 1906.

98. MEP: *Compte Rendu des travaux de 1906* (Paris: Séminaire des Missions-Etrangères, 1907).

99. MEP 712A: Monseigneur Marcou to MM. Les Directeurs, 1906.

100. MEP: *Compte Rendu des travaux de 1907.*

101. MEP: *Vicariat Apostolique du Tonkin Maritime: Compte Rendu de l'Exercise 1915–1916* (Ninh Binh: Imprimerie Thien Ban, 1918).

102. MEP: *Compte Rendu de l'Exercise 1917–1918* (Ninh Binh: Imprimerie Thien Ban, 1917).

103. MEP: Annales de la Société des Missions-Etrangères, Septembre–Octobre, 1906.

104. MEP: *Compte Rendu des travaux de 1906.*

105. MEP: *Vicariat Apostolique du Tonkin Maritime: Compte Rendu de l'Exercise 1916–1917* (Ninh Binh: Imprimerie Thien Ban, 1917).

106. MEP: *Compte Rendu des travaux de 1905* (Paris: Séminaire des Missions-Etrangères, 1906).

107. MEP 712A: Monseigneur Marcou to MM. Les Directeurs, 1906; MEP: *Compte Rendu des travaux de 1907;* Keith, *Catholic Vietnam,* 83.

108. MEP: *Vicariat Apostolique du Tonkin Maritime: Compte Rendu de l'Exercise 1916–1917* (Ninh Binh: Imprimerie Thien Ban, 1917).

109. MEP 816: Notes et impressions sur la situation en octobre 1889, Mgr. Puginier; MEP 816: Réflexions de Mgr. Puginier, April 7, 1888; MEP: *Compte Rendu des travaux de 1906.*

110. MEP: *Compte Rendu des travaux de 1906.*

111. "La Famine," *L'Avenir du Tonkin,* April 2, 1906.

112. "La Région," in *L'Avenir du Tonkin,* April 6, 1906.

113. C.R., "Prévoyance Officielle contre les Calamités," *L'Avenir du Tonkin,* April 5, 1906.

114. Henri Laumonier, "Courrier de Hanoi," *L'Avenir du Tonkin,* April 1, 1906

115. "La Misère à Nam Dinh," in *L'Avenir du Tonkin,* April 4, 1906.

116. "La Région," in *L'Avenir du Tonkin,* April 3, 1906.

117. VNA 1, RST S.67 74525: Résident Supérieur to Résidents de Nam Dinh and Hanam, February 2, 1906.

118. VNA 1, RST S.67 74525: L'administrateur-résident Hanam to Résident-Supérieur, February 21, 1906.

119. VNA 1, RST S.67 74525: L'administrateur-résident Nam-Dinh to Résident Supérieur, Nam-Dinh, March 30, 1906.

120. Gerard Sasges, "Beast of (a) Burden: State, Enterprise, and the Alcohol Monopoly in Colonial Vietnam," *Journal of Southeast Asian Studies* 43, no. 1 (2012): 133–157; Erica J. Peters, "Taste, Taxes, and Technologies: Industrializing Rice Alcohol in Northern Vietnam, 1902–1913," *French Historical Studies* 27, no. 3 (2004): 569–600.

121. "Nam Dinh," in *Le Courrier d'Haiphong*, May 15, 1906; "La Famine et ses Remèdes,"in *Le Courrier d'Haiphong*, May 29, 1906.

122. "La Région," in *L'Avenir du Tonkin*.

123. "Nam Dinh," in *Le Courrier d'Haiphong*.

124. "En Indochine: Phu Ly," in *Le Courrier d'Haiphong*, May 18, 1906.

125. ANOM, GGI 17647: Le Gouverneur-Général de l'Indochine to Président de la Section Haiphonaise de la Ligue pour la défense des Droits de l'Homme et du Citoyen, May 29, 1906; ANOM, GGI 17647: Ligue Française pour la Défense des Droits de l'Homme et du Citoyen to Gouverneur-Général de l'Indochine, June 2, 1906.

126. ANOM, GGI 17647: La Section de Haïphong de la Ligue des Droits de l'Homme et du Citoyen to M. le Gouverneur-Général de l'Indochine, April 20, 1906.

127. ANOM, GGI 17647: Gouverneur-Général to Chefs des Administrations Locales, May 29, 1906.

128. Goscha, *Vietnam: A New History*, 84.

129. ANOM, INDO / NF / 1746: Commission d'Etude des Moyens d'Accroitre la Valeur Nutritive de l'Alimentation des Indochinois, 1917.

130. ANOM, GGI 46375–46410: Résident Supérieur en Annam to Gouverneur Général de l'Indochine, June 24, 1921.

131. ANOM, GGI 46395: Map of Annam. My thanks to Liz Jacob for her help tracking this down.

132. ANOM, GGI 46375–46410: Résident Supérieur en Annam to Gouverneur Général de l'Indochine, December 9, 1922.

133. ANOM, GGI 46375–46410: Circulaire A.S. de la famine, August 1, 1921; see also ANOM, AGEFOM 858.

134. ANOM, GGI 46375–46410: Circulaire A.S. de le famine, August 1, 1921.

135. Hue-Tam Ho Tai, *Radicalism and Origins*, 146–70, 176.

136. VNA 1, RST S.67 74060: Circulaire, Le Gouverneur Général de l'Indochine [Pasquier] to Messieurs les Chefs d'Administration, March 18, 1930.

137. RSTNF 3893: L. Leuret, Chef du Service de l'Assistance Sociale en Indochine to Gouverneur Général, January 24, 1930.

138. ANOM, RSTNF 3893: Tentative de comité de bienfaisance faite à Hué en Février 1929, February 23, 1929.

139. VNA 1, RST S.67 74060: l'Administrateur H. Colas, résident de France à Phu-Tho to Résident Supérieur au Tonkin, April 7, 1930; VNA 1, RST S.67 74060, Lieutenant-Colonel Dorey, commandant le 2ème territoire militaire, to Résident Supérieur au Tonkin, April 12, 1930; VNA 1, RST S.67 74060: Nguyen Thua Dat, Nghi-vien of Kien An, to Résident de France à Kien An, May 14, 1930; VNA 1, RST S.67 74060: Tuan-Phu

de Ninh-Binh [Ngiêm Xuân Quang] to Administrateur Résident de France à Ninh-Binh, April 18, 1930.

140. ANOM, RSTNF 3893: Résident Supérieur au Tonkin to Gouverneur Géneral de l'Indochine, August 21, 1930; ANOM, RSTNF 3893: Gouverneur Général de l'Indochine to Messieurs les chefs de l'administration locale, March 3, 1930.

141. VNA 1, RST S.67 74060: Procès-verbal de la Commission, July 29, 1930; VNA 1, RST S.67 74060: Arrêté du Gouverneur Général de l'Indochine, 1930; VNA 1, RST, S.67 74060: Note A.S. Création de caisses de Secours, Chef du 1er Bureau, undated; VNA 1, RST S.67 74060: Résident de France à Backan [Massimi] to Résident Supérieur au Tonkin, May 5, 1930; VNA 1, RST S.67 74060: Résident de France à Bac-Giang [Fournier] to Résident Supérieur au Tonkin, May 5, 1930; VNA 1, RST S.67 74060: Résident de France à Nam-Dinh [Chapoulart] to Résident Supérieur au Tonkin, May 6, 1930.

3. The Nature of Famine in the Sahel, 1913

1. André Salifou, "Quand l'histoire se répète: La famine de 1931 au Niger," *Environnement Africain, études et recherches* 1, no. 2 (1975): 25–52. See also Stephen Baier, *An Economic History of Central Niger* (Oxford: Clarendon Press, 1980).

2. See, for example, Yves Henry, *Irrigations et cultures irriguées en Afrique tropicale* (Paris, 1918), 182. On debates about the Sahelian environment, see Monica M. Beusekom, "From Underpopulation to Overpopulation: French Perceptions of Population, Environment, and Agricultural Development in French Soudan (Mali), 1900–1960," *Environmental History* 4, no. 2 (April 1999): 198–219.

3. F. Cooper, "Conflict and Connection"; Herbst, *States and Power in Africa*.

4. Richard Roberts, *Conflicts of Colonialism: The Rule of Law, French Soudan, and the Faama Mademba Sèye* (Cambridge: Cambridge University Press, 2022).

5. A. S. Kanya-Forstner, *The Conquest of the Western Sudan: A Study in French Military Imperialism* (Cambridge: Cambridge University Press, 1969).

6. Mario J. Azevedo, *The Roots of Violence: A History of War in Chad* (New York: Routledge, 1998), 21–46, 65–73.

7. Marielle Debos, *Living by the Gun in Chad: Combatants, Impunity, and State Formation* (London: Zed Books, 2013), 27–42.

8. Rita Headrick, *Colonialism, Health and Illness in French Equatorial Africa, 1885–1935* (Atlanta: African Studies Association Press, 1994), 14, 25.

9. Martin Klein, *Slavery and Colonial Rule in French West Africa* (Cambridge: Cambridge University Press, 1998); Barbara M. Cooper, *Countless Blessings: A History of Childbirth and Reproduction in the Sahel* (Bloomington: Indiana University Press, 2019).

10. Benedetta Rossi, *From Slavery to Aid: Politics, Labour, and Ecology in the Nigerien Sahel, 1800–2000* (New York: Cambridge University Press, 2015), 86; see also Klein, *Slavery and Colonial Rule*, 4–5.

11. Rossi, *From Slavery to Aid*; Stephen Baier, "Long Term Structural Change in the Economy of Central Niger," in *West African Culture Dynamics: Archaeological and Historical Perspectives*, edited by B. K. Swartz and Raymond E. Dummett (New York: De Gruyter Mouton, 1980).

12. The selling of people, again usually girls, would increase in Africa and Indochina during the Great Depression of the 1930s. Martin A. Klein and Richard Roberts, "The

Resurgence of Pawning in French West Africa During the Depression of the 1930s," in *Pawnship, Slavery, and Colonialism in Africa*, edited by Paul E. Lovejoy and Toyin Falola (Trenton, NJ: Africa World Press, 2003), 409–26; Daniel Laqua, "The Tensions of Internationalism: Transnational Anti-Slavery in the 1880s and 1890s," *International History Review* 33, no. 4 (December 2011): 705–26; David Pomfret, "'Child Slavery' in British and French Far-Eastern Colonies, 1880–1945," *Past and Present* no. 201 (November 2008): 175–213.

13. On SIPs in Africa, see especially Robert L. Tignor, "Senegal's Cooperative Experience, 1907–1960," in *The Political Economy of Risk and Choice in Senegal*, John Waterbury and Mark Gersovitz (London: Routledge, 1987); Jane Guyer and Gregory Mann, "Imposing a Guide on the *Indigène*: The Fifty Year Experience of the *Sociétés de Prévoyance* in French West and Equatorial Africa," in *Credit, Currencies, and Culture: African Financial Institutions in Historical Perspective*, edited by Endre Stiansen and Jane I. Guyer (Stockholm: Nordiska Afrikainstitutet, 1999).

14. Yan Slobodkin, "State of Violence: Administration and Reform in French West Africa," *French Historical Studies* 41, no. 1 (2018): 33–61.

15. Archives nationales du Sénégal, Dakar [ANS], 2G14-14: Rapport Politique, 2ème Trimestre, Territoire Militaire du Niger, August 30, 1914.

16. ANS, 2G13-11: Colonie du Haut-Sénégal et Niger. Rapport Politique d'Ensemble, 1913.

17. ANOM, FM 1AFFPOL 159: Rapport Politique Haut-Sénégal-Niger 3ème trimestre 1913, January 15, 1914.

18. ANS, 2G14-8: Lieutenant-Gouverneur du Haut-Sénégal-Niger to Gouverneur Général de l'AOF, Bamako, June 19, 1914.

19. ANOM, AOF 17G/160: Rapport Politique et administratif, 4e trimestre 1913 (Haut-Sénégal-Niger), July 18.

20. ANOM, AOF 17G/160: Rapport politique du deuxième trimestre 1914 (Haut-Sénégal-Niger) Afrique Occidentale et Équatoriale Française, December 26, 1914.

21. ANOM, AOF 17G/160: Situation politique et administrative du Haut-Sénégal-Niger pendant le 4ème trimestre 1914. Afrique Occidentale et Équatoriale Française. Service des Affaires Civiles, Dakar, June 28, 1915.

22. ANS, 2G13-11: Colonie du Haut-Sénégal et Niger. Rapport Politique d'Ensemble, Année 1913.

23. ANOM, AOF 17G/160: Rapport politique du deuxième trimestre 1914 (Haut-Sénégal-Niger) Afrique Occidentale et Équatoriale Française -1ᵉ section, December 26, 1914.

24. ANOM, AOF 17G/160: Rapport Politique du 1ᵉʳ trimestre 1914 Haut-Sénégal-Niger, Dakar, July 30, 1914.

25. On recruitment, see Echenberg, *Colonial Conscripts*; d'Almeida-Topor, "Les populations dahoméenes"; Luc Garcia, "Les mouvements de résistance au Dahomey, 1914–1917," *Cahiers d'études africaines* 10, no. 37 (1970): 144–78; Finn Fuglestad, "Les révoltes des Touareg du Niger, 1916–17," *Cahiers d'études africaines* 13, no. 49 (1973): 82–120.

26. For instructions on categorization and content of *rapports d'ensemble*, see ANS, 2G14-5: Undated template.

27. ANS, 2G14-5: Gouverneur-Général de l'AOF to Service des Affaires Civiles et Musulmanes du Sénégal, November 10, 1915.

28. ANS, 2G14-5: Gouverneur Général de l'Afrique Occidentale Française to Lieutenant-Gouverneurs, June 12, 1914 (W. Ponty).

29. ANS, 2G14-11: Niger, Rapport d'ensemble 1914.

30. ANS, 2G14-11: Niger, Rapport d'ensemble 1914.

31. ANS, 2G 14/18: Rapport d'Ensemble sur la situation générale de la colonie pendant l'année 1914, Formations sanitaires de Bamako, Ambulances de Kayes et Tomboctou.

32. ANS, 2G14-4: Niger, Rapport agricole 1er trimestre, May 11, 1914; ANS, 2G14-14: Rapport Politique, 2ème Trimestre, Territoire Militaire du Niger, Année 1914, August 30, 1914.

33. ANS, 2G14-4: Rapport agricole Niger, 2ème trimestre, Zinder, August 13, 1914.

34. ANS, 15G-105: Lieutenant-Gouverneur du Haut-Sénégal-Niger to Gouverneur-Général, February 5, 1914.

35. The price of millet was around one franc per kilo. ANS, 15G-105: Lieutenant-Gouverneur du Haut-Sénégal-Niger to Gouverneur-Général, February 5, 1914.

36. ANS, 15G-105: Lieutenant-Gouverneur Haut-Sénégal-Niger to Gouverneur-Général, June 11, 1914.

37. ANS, 15G-105: Gouverneur-Général to gouverneurs Conakry, Bamako, Saint-Louis, Service de l'Agriculture et des Forêts, June 20, 1914.

38. ANS, 15G-105: Gouverneur Général to Gouverneur Bamako, June 27, 1914.

39. ANS, 2G 14/18: Rapport d'Ensemble sur la situation générale de la colonie pendant l'année 1914, Formations sanitaires de Bamako, Ambulances de Kayes et Tomboctou.

40. ANS, 2G14-14: Rapport Politique, 1er Trimestre, Territoire Militaire du Niger, Année 1914, May 7, 1914.

41. ANS, 2G14-14: Rapport Politique, 2ème Trimestre, Territoire Militaire du Niger, November 20, 1914.

42. ANS, 2G14-4: Niger, Rapport Agricole 1914, 4ème trimestre; ANS: 2G14-4: Niger, Rapport agricole 3e trimestre, Zinder, November 19, 1914.

43. ANS, 2G14-14: Rapport Politique, Territoire Militaire du Niger, 4ème trimestre, année 1914, February 18, 1915.

44. ANS, 2G14/17: Rapport Médical Annuel 1914, Colonie du Territoire du Niger.

45. ANOM, 61COL662 (1AFFPOL/662): Rapport du Chef de Bataillon Briand, Commandant le Régiment de Tirailleurs du Tchad, sur les opérations dirigées par le Lieutenant Saddler dans le massif de Guerra et qui ont amené la prise de vive force du village réfractaire de Morgue, August 26, 1913. Denise Moran also described destroying or cutting off access to crops as a military tactic in *Tchad* (Montrouge: Gallimard, 1934), 90.

46. Azevedo, *Roots of Violence*, 65–88.

47. ANOM, 61Col662 (1AFFPOL/662): Extrait du Rapport du 1er Trimestre 1914.

48. ANOM, 61COL662 (1AFFPOL/662): Rapport Mensuel Août 1913.

49. ANOM, AEF GGAF, 4(4)d/13: Rapport d'Ensemble pour l'Année, July 13, 1914.

50. ANOM, 61COL662 (1AFFPOL/662): Extrait du Rapport Annuel du Tchad 1913 [signed Largeau]; ANOM, 61COL662 (1AFFPOL/662): Rapport Mensuel August, 1913.

51. ANOM, 61Col662 (1AFFPOL/662): Extrait du Rapport du 1er Trimestre 1914.

52. ANOM, 61Col662 (1AFFPOL/662): Extrait Rapport Tchad 2ème Trimestre 1914.

53. ANOM, 61Col662 (1AFFPOL/662): Extrait Rapport Tchad 2ème Trimestre 1914.

54. ANOM, 61Col662 (1AFFPOL/662): Extrait du Rapport du 1er Trimestre 1914.

55. ANOM, 61COL662 (1AFFPOL/662): Rapport Tchad 3ème trimestre, November 18, 1914.

56. ANOM, 61COL662 (1AFFPOL/662): Extrait du Rapport Annuel du Tchad 1913 [signed Largeau].

57. Many of the documents relating to famine in Chad can be found in ANOM thanks to Albert Sarraut's 1933 request to the African administrations for documents relating to the famine. The response from AOF was lost, necessitating a second request in 1938, but the dossier submitted by Chad survived. ANOM, 61COL662 (1AFF-POL/662): Le Gouverneur Général de l'Afrique Équatoriale Française to Ministre des Colonies, June 24, 1933.

58. ANOM, 61Col662 (1AFFPOL/662): Extrait Rapport Tchad 2ème Trimestre 1914.

59. ANOM, AEF GGAF, 4(4)d/13: Rapport sur les évènements de Mars-Juin 1914.

60. ANOM, 61Col662 (1AFFPOL/662): Extrait Rapport Tchad 2ème Trimestre 1914.

61. ANOM, 61COL662 (1AFFPOL/662): Extrait du Rapport Annuel du Tchad 1913 [Largeau].

62. ANOM, 61Col662 (1AFFPOL/662): Extrait Rapport Tchad 2ème Trimestre 1914.

63. ANOM, AEF GGAF, 4(4)d/13: Rapport sur les évènements de Mars-Juin 1914.

64. ANOM, 61Col662 (1AFFPOL/662): Extrait Rapport Tchad 2ème Trimestre 1914.

65. ANOM, AEF GGAF, 4(4)d/13: Rapport d'Ensemble pour l'Année, July 13, 1914.

66. ANOM, 61COL662 (1AFFPOL/662): Rapport Tchad 3ème trimestre, November 18, 1914.

67. ANOM, AEF GGAF, 4(4)d/13: Rapport d'ensemble pour l'Année, July 13, 1914.

68. J. Hilaire, Du Congo au Nil: Ouaddaï . . . Cinq ans d'arrêt! (Marseille: ASCG, 1930), 91–93.

69. ANOM, AEF GGAF, 4(4)d/13: Rapport d'Ensemble pour l'Année, July 13, 1914.

70. ANOM, 61COL662 (1AFFPOL/662): Extrait Rapport Tchad 4ème trimestre, March 30, 1915.

71. ANOM, 61Col662 (1AFFPOL/662): Extrait du Rapport du 1er Trimestre 1914.

72. ANOM, 61Col662 (1AFFPOL/662): Extrait du Rapport du 1er Trimestre 1914.

73. ANOM, 61COL662 (1AFFPOL/662): Extrait Rapport Tchad 2ème Trimestre 1914.

74. ANOM, AEF GGAF, 4(4)d/13: Rapport d'Ensemble pour l'Année, July 13, 1914.

75. ANOM, 61Col662 (1AFFPOL/662): Extrait du Rapport du 1er Trimestre 1914.

76. ANOM, AEF GGAF, 4(4)d/13: Rapport d'Ensemble pour l'Année, July 13, 1914.

77. ANOM, AOF 17G/160: Note pour M. le Directeur des Affaires Politiques et Administratives, September 30, 1938. On interwar debates about German and French colonial public health, see Neill, "Finding the 'Ideal Diet,'" 182–201.

78. ANOM, AOF 17G/160: Note pour M. le Gouverneur-Général, direction des Affaires politiques et administratives, October 5, 1938; ANS, 1R/7(1): Le Médecin-Général

Pezet, Inspecteur-Général des Services Sanitaires et Médicaux de l'AOF to Gouverneur-Général de l'AOF, Dakar, October 3, 1938; ANS, 1R/7(1): Note Pour Monsieur le Directeur du Cabinet du Gouverneur-Général, Dakar, April 8, 1933.

79. ANOM, 110COL944/3083: Commission d'enquête et d'information sur la famine du Niger en 1931, Procès-verbal de la Séance du 15 mars 1933.

80. ANOM, 110COL944/3083: Commission d'enquête et d'information sur la famine du Niger en 1931, Procès-verbal de la Séance du 15 mars 1933.

81. ANOM, 110COL944/3083: Commission d'enquête et d'information sur la famine du Niger en 1931, Procès-verbal de la séance du 16 mars 1933.

82. ANOM, AOF 17G/160: Circulaire 46, Paris, April 23, 1940.

83. This discussion draws on Edward Berenson's concept of "heroes of empire" who "embodied the era's ideal of manliness, defined as the ability to persist against all odds, to confront physical danger and the perils of the unknown, and to combine strength and fortitude with kindness toward women, 'natives,' and others needing gentle guidance backed by a firm, steady hand." Edward Berenson, *Heroes of Empire: Five Charismatic Men and the Conquest of Africa* (Berkeley: University of California Press, 2011), 10.

84. Hilaire, *Du Congo au Nil*.

85. Hilaire, *Du Congo au Nil*, 203.

86. For a discussion of how anti-empirical, intuitive knowledge influenced imperial agents, see, Priya Satia, *Spies in Arabia: The Great War and the Cultural Foundations of Britain's Covert Empire in the Middle East* (Oxford: Oxford University Press, 2009).

87. Hilaire, *Du Congo au Nil*, 80.

88. Moran, *Tchad*, 92.

89. Moran, *Tchad*, 94.

90. Moran, *Tchad*, 96–97.

91. Moran, *Tchad*, 102–3.

92. ANS, 15G-105: Translated text from 1913 Haut-Sénégal-Niger.

93. ANS, 1R-59: Agricultural excerpt from rapport d'ensemble de l'AOF for 1914.

94. ANOM, 61COL662 (1AFFPOL/662): Rapport Tchad 3ème trimestre, November 18, 1914.

95. ANS, 2G14-8: Lieutenant-Gouverneur du Haut-Sénégal-Niger to Gouverneur Général de l'AOF, Bamako, April 29, 1915.

4. The Science of Hunger in the International Sphere, 1890–1939

1. The title of part II, "The Politics of the Belly," refers not to Jean-François Bayart's seminal study of postcolonial African states, but to a phrase used by French colonial administrators in multiple variations to refer to a new understanding of famine prevention, nutrition, and the management of food as foundational concerns of colonial rule. Jean-François Bayart, *L'État en Afrique: La politique du ventre* (Paris: Fayard, 1989). An earlier version of this chapter was published as Yan Slobodkin, "Famine and the Science of Food in the French Empire: 1900–1939," *French Politics, Culture, and Society* 36, no. 1 (Spring 2018): 52–75.

2. Neill, *Networks in Tropical Medicine*; Osborne, *Emergence of Tropical Medicine*; Jennings, *Curing the Colonizers*. On hygiene in France, see David S. Barnes, *The Great Stink*

of Paris and the Nineteenth-Century Struggle against Filth and Germs (Baltimore: Johns Hopkins University Press, 2006).

3. On medical experts and colonialism, see Tilley, *Africa as a Living Laboratory*; for the case of Senegal, see Mor Ndao, "Colonisation et politique de santé maternelle et infantile au Sénégal (1905–1960)," *French Colonial History* 9 (2008): 191–211.

4. Pedersen, *Guardians*; Clifford Rosenberg, "The International Politics of Vaccine Testing in Interwar Algiers," *American Historical Review* 117 (2012): 671–97; Heidi J. S. Tworek, "Communicable Disease: Information, Health, and Globalization in the Interwar Period," *American Historical Review* 124, 3 (June 2019): 813–42.

5. Until the creation of the Ministry of Colonies in 1894, French colonies (except Algeria) were under the control of the navy, and thus the discipline of exotic or tropical medicine was practiced primarily by naval physicians. When the colonial health service was created in 1890, many prominent naval physicians, including Georges Treille, joined the new service and brought with them the tradition of tropical hygiene.

6. Osborne, *Emergence of Tropical Medicine*, 6, 82–84; Daughton, "Behind the Imperial Curtain," 508–9.

7. Jennings, *Curing the Colonizers*, 8–17.

8. Dantec and Boyé, "Étude d'une labiée à racine tuberculeuse servant à l'alimentation des indigènes du Soudan et pouvant remplacer la pomme de terre aux colonies," *Annales d'hygiène et de médecine coloniales*, tome troisième (Paris: Imprimerie Internationale, 1900), 286–92.

9. Osborne, *Emergence of Tropical Medicine*, 137–41.

10. Georges Treille, *Principes d'Hygiène Coloniale* (Paris, 1899), 151–53.

11. Treille, *Principes d'Hygiène Coloniale*, 217.

12. For example, A. Kermorgant and G. Reynaud, "Précautions hygièniques à prendre pour les expéditions et les explorations aux pays chauds" in *Annales d'hygiène et de médecine coloniales*, tome troisième (Paris: Imprimerie Internationale, 1900), 305–414.

13. Kenneth J. Carpenter, *Beriberi, White Rice, and Vitamin B: A Disease, a Cause, a Cure* (Berkeley: University of California Press, 2000), 10–13.

14. See his Nobel Prize acceptance speech. Christiaan Eijkman, "Antineuritic Vitamin and Beriberi," Nobel Lecture, 1929.

15. A. C. Vorderman, "Rapport sur l'influence de l'alimentation par les diverses espèces de riz sur la fréquence de cas de béribéri, observés dans les prisons de Java et de Madura," trans. Paul Gouzien, *Annales d'hygiène et de médecine coloniales*, tome premier (Paris, 1898), 565–66; Carpenter, *Beriberi, White Rice*, 48–50.

16. Angier, médecin-major de 1ère classe des troupes coloniales, "Le Béribéri. Notes recueillies à l'hôpital de Choquan de 1902 à 1905," *Annales d'hygiène et de médecine coloniales*, tome huitième (Paris: Imprimerie Nationale, 1905), 591–607.

17. For example, see Henry Fraser et A. T. Stanton de l'Institut des Recherches Médicales de Kuala Lumpur, "Étiologie du béribéri," *Annales d'hygiène et de médecine coloniales* (Paris: Imprimerie Nationale, 1910), 777–80.

18. Zinoman, *Colonial Bastille*, 91–97.

19. Andrieux, médecin de deuxième classe des colonies, "Épidémie de béribéri observée à Poulo-Condore en 1897–1898" in *Annales d'hygiène et de médecine coloniales*, tome troisième (Paris: Imprimerie Nationale, 1900), 183–89.

20. A. Kermorgant, "Maladies épidémiques et contagieuses qui ont régné dans les colonies françaises au cours de l'année 1900," *Annales d'hygiène et de médecine coloniales*, tome cinquième (Paris: Imprimerie Nationale, 1902), 277–305.

21. J. Thézé, médecin aide-major de 1ère classe des troupes coloniales, "Sur le Béribéri À Poulo-Condore (Cochinchine) en 1906," *Annales d'hygiène et de médecine coloniales* (Paris: Imprimerie Internationale, 1910), 16–31.

22. Médecin-Colonel Vassal, "Alimentation en Indochine," *La Science de l'Alimentation en 1937* (Alençon: Imprimerie Alençonnaise, 1937).

23. Carpenter, *Beriberi, White Rice*, 85–87.

24. On the Far Eastern Association of Tropical Medicine and international scientific exchange in Southeast Asia, see Claire E. Edington, *Beyond the Asylum: Mental Illness in French Colonial Vietnam* (Ithaca, NY: Cornell University Press, 2019), chapter 3.

25. J. M. J. Vassal, médecin major de 1ère classe des troupes coloniales, "Troisième Congrès Biennal de l'Association de Médecine tropicale d'extrême-orient, tenu à Saigon du 8 au 15 novembre 1913," *Annales d'hygiène et de médecine coloniales* no. 3 (Paris: Imprimerie Nationale, 1914), 747.

26. Dr. L. Mathis, "Contribution à l'étude du béribéri. Considérations sur la tuberculose parmi la population indigène du Tonkin," *Annales d'hygiène et de médecine coloniales*, tome dix-septième (Paris: Imprimerie Nationale, 1914), 483–500.

27. Carpenter, *Beriberi, White Rice*, 98–100.

28. Memorandum du *Committee on Accessory Food Factors*, "Importance des Facteurs accessoires dans l'alimentation" in *Annales de médecine et de pharmacie coloniales, numéro exceptionnel*, Ministère des colonies (Paris: Imprimerie-librairie militaire universelle L. Fournier, 1920), 107–9. By 1927, "vitamin B" was divided into two factors, with the anti-beriberi factor being called B1. It was not until the 1930s that the vitamin was fully isolated in crystalline form and synthesized. Carpenter, *Beriberi, White Rice*, 104–15.

29. Hermant, "Les Maladies transmissibles observées dans les colonies françaises et territoires sous mandat pendant l'année 1928," in *Annales de médecine et de pharmacie coloniales* 29 (Paris: Imprimerie Nationale, 1931), 78–81; Tournier, Médecin Commandant, "Les éléments de la thérapeutique du beriberi," in *Annales de médecine et de pharmacie coloniales* 29 (Paris: Imprimerie Nationale, 1931), 861–75; Sanner, Destribats, et Rarivoson, "Le béribéri à Diego-Suarez. Relation d'une épidémie et des premiers résultats obtenus à Madagascar à l'aide de la vitamine B1 cristalisée administrée par voie parentérale" in *Annales de médecine et de pharmacie coloniales* 36 (Paris: Imprimerie Nationale, 1938), 840–62.

30. Physicians in Indochina recorded 988 cases and 197 deaths in 1916; 3,425 cases and 600 deaths in 1928; and 4,831 cases and 294 deaths in 1930. The prevalence of beriberi declined over the next few years to 2,978 cases with 375 deaths in 1933, apparently under the influence of the obligatory use of incompletely processed rice in all European-run collectivities, including army units and plantations. But in 1936, the number of cases of beriberi reported in Cochinchina alone climbed to 10,465, with 143 deaths, almost all agricultural workers between twenty and forty-five years of age, both men and women. In Annam, the numbers for 1936 were 14,852 cases and 39 deaths. In 1937, the total number of cases reported in Indochina was 25,706, including 6 Europeans, with 250 deaths, breaking down to 12,812 cases in Cochinchina, 7,044 in Cambodia, 2,846 in Annam,

2,919 in Tonkin, and 74 in Laos. In 1938, the numbers for Indochina in total were 26,067 cases and 223 dead. Rousseau, "Les maladies transmissibles observées dans les colonies françaises et territoires sous mandat pendant l'année 1927," *Annales de médecine et de pharmacie coloniales* 27 (1929), 210; Lefèvre, "Les Maladies Transmissibles observées dans les colonies françaises et territoires sous mandat pendant l'année 1930" in *Annales de médecine et de pharmacie coloniales* 30 (Paris: Imprimerie Nationale, 1932), 398–401; G. Ledentu, "Les maladies transmissibles observées dans les colonies françaises et territoires sous mandat pendant l'année 1933," *Annales de médecine et de pharmacie coloniales* 33 (Paris: Imprimerie Nationale, 1935), 689–90; Vogel et Le Rouzic, "Les maladies transmissibles observées dans les colonies françaises et territoires sous mandat pendant l'année 1936" in *Annales de médecine et de pharmacie coloniales* 36 (Paris: Imprimerie Nationale, 1938), 352–520; E. Vogel and M. Riou, "Les maladies épidémiques, endémiques et sociales dans les colonies françaises pendant l'année 1937," *Annales de médecine et de pharmacie coloniales* 37 (1939), 257–552; Grosfilez et Lefèvre, "Les maladies transmissibles observées dans les colonies françaises et territoires sous mandat pendant l'année 1938" in *Annales de médecine et de pharmacie coloniales* 38 (Paris: Imprimerie nationale, 1940), 183–360.

31. Vogel and Riou, "Les maladies épidémiques," 257–552.

32. Charles Richet, "l'Alimentation dans les colonies" in *l'Alimentation indigène dans les colonies françaises*, edited by Georges Hardy and Charles Richet (Paris: Vigot Frères, 1933), 30.

33. Owen White, *Children of the French Empire: Miscegenation and Colonial Society in French West Africa, 1895–1960* (Oxford: Clarendon Press, 1999), 93–123; Jennings, *Curing the Colonizers*, 22–23. For degeneration in Europe, see Daniel Pick, *Faces of Degeneration: A European Disorder, c. 1848–1918* (Cambridge: Cambridge University Press, 1989).

34. On the science of labor, see Anson Rabinbach, *The Human Motor: Energy, Fatigue, and the Origins of Modernity* (Berkeley: University of California Press, 1990).

35. ANOM, 110COL940/3033-3036 (FM, AGEFOM//940): Rapport sur la question de l'insuffisance alimentaire des indigènes dans les possessions françaises, par M. Roubaud, Rapporteur de la Commission, 1925; Albert Sarraut, *La Mise en Valeur des Colonies Françaises* (Paris: Payot, 1923), 94–96.

36. J. P. Daughton, *In the Forest of No Joy: The Congo-Océan Railroad and the Tragedy of French Colonialism* (New York: Norton, 2021); Jeremy Rich, *A Workman Is Worthy of His Meat: Food and Colonialism in the Gabon Estuary* (Lincoln: University of Nebraska Press, 2007).

37. Catherine Coquery-Vidrovitch, *Le Congo au temps des grandes compagnies concessionnaires, 1898–1930* (Paris: Mouton & Co., 1972); Headrick, *Colonialism, Health and Illness*, 18–20.

38. Headrick, *Colonialism, Health and Illness*, 121.

39. René Maran, *Batouala: Véritable Roman Nègre* (Paris: Albin Michel, 1921), 11.

40. Société des missions évangéliques de Paris [SMEP], Congo (Gabon) 1922: Statistiques Ecclésiastiques, Rapport sur l'année 1922, Station de Lambaréné; SMEP, Congo (Gabon) 1922: Statistiques Ecclésiastiques, Rapport sur l'année 1922, Station de Samkita; SMEP, Congo (Gabon) 1922: Statistiques Scolaires, Rapport sur l'année 1922, Station de Ngomo; SMEP, Congo (Gabon) 1922: F. Grébert, "A Talagouga," *Journal des Missions Évangéliques* 4e série, 24e année, premier semestre (Paris: Société des Missions Évangéliques de Paris, 1922).

41. SMEP, Congo (Gabon) 1922: F. Grébert, "À Talagouga," *Journal des Missions Évangéliques* 4e série, 24e année, premier semestre (Paris: Société des Missions Évangéliques de Paris, 1922).

42. SMEP, Congo (Gabon) 1922: Rapport de M. le Missionaire Galley sur son voyage d'enquête (22 mai à 23 septembre 1922); SMEP, Congo (Gabon) 1922: Galley to Allégret, November 22, 1922.

43. SMEP, Congo (Gabon) 1922: F. Grébert, "À Talagouga," *Journal des Missions Évangéliques* 4e série, 24e année, premier semestre (Paris: Société des Missions Évangéliques de Paris, 1922).

44. ANOM, Gouvernement Général de l'AEF 4(1)D/20: Rapport sur la situation politique de la colonie du Gabon à la fin du 3e trimestre 1922; ANOM, GGAEF 4(1) D/20: Rapport sur la situation politique de la colonie du Gabon à la Fin du 4e trimestre 1922; AEF, GGAEF, 4(1)D/21: Note à toutes subdivisions a.s. des plantations à entreprendre durant la saison sèche, June 28, 1922.

45. ANOM, GGAEF 4(1)D/20: Rapport annuel 1922, Colonie du Gabon.

46. ANOM, 61COL662: Gouvernement Général de l'AEF, Discours prononcé par Antonetti, Gouverneur Général de l'AEF, Séance d'ouverture du Conseil de Gouvernement, Session ordinaire de Décembre 1925 (Brazzaville: Imprimerie du Gouvernement Général, 1926).

47. On Antonetti, see Daughton, *Forest of No Joy*, 57–69.

48. Gustave Lefrou, Médecin-Major de 2e classe, "Contribution à l'étude de l'utilisation de la Main-d'œuvre Indigène. Considérations médicales sur le personnel des chantiers de construction du chemin de fer Congo-Océan" in *Annales de médecine et de pharmacie coloniales* 51 (Paris: Imprimerie Nationale, 1927), 5–51.

49. E. W. Suldey, Médecin-Major des troupes coloniales, "Une Épidémie de béribéri au Gabon. Considérations cliniques, thérapeutiques et prophylactiques," *Annales de Médecine et de Pharmacie Coloniales, tome vingtième* 2 (Paris: Imprimerie Nationale, 1922), 176–85.

50. Henri-Joseph Georgelin, Médecin-Major de 2e classe des troupes coloniales, "Notes médicales sur le Gabon: Les facteurs de dépopulation," *Annales de médecine et de pharmacie coloniales, numéro exceptionnel*, Ministère des colonies (Paris: Imprimerie-librarie militaire universelle L. Fournier, 1922), 58–64.

51. ANOM, 110COL940/3033-3036 (FM, AGEFOM//940): Épreuve pour la Discussion: Rapport sur la question de l'Insuffisance alimentaire des Indigènes dans les Possessions françaises, Presenté sur la proposition de M. le Dr. Calmette, au nom de la Commission technique de l'Académie des science coloniales, par M. Roubaud, Rapporteur de la Commission, undated.

52. Georgelin, "Notes médicales," 58–64; Alexandre Gauducheau, Médecin-Major de 1ère classe en retraite, "Comment Combler le déficit alimentaire des indigènes dans les Colonies Françaises," *Annales de médecine et de pharmacie coloniales* 23 (Paris: Imprimerie Nationale, 1925), 289–97.

53. Georgelin, "Notes médicales"; Gauducheau, "Comment Combler le déficit alimentaire."

54. Georgelin, "Notes médicales"; Gauducheau, "Comment Combler le déficit alimentaire."

55. Loïc Wacquant, "Resolving the Trouble with 'Race,'" *New Left Review* 133/134 (January/April 2022). On the history of race in France, see Pap Ndiaye, *La*

condition noire: Essai sur une minorité française (Paris: Gallimard, 2008); David Beriss, "Culture-As-Race or Culture-As-Culture: Caribbean Ethnicity and the Ambiguity of Cultural Identity in French Society" in Chapman and Frader, *Race in France*; Didier Fassin and Eric Fassin, eds., *De la question sociale à la question raciale? Représenter la société française* (Paris: Découverte, 2006).

56. Peter J. Bowler, *Evolution: The History of an Idea* (Berkeley: University of California Press, 2003); Laurent Loison, "French Roots of French Neo-Lamarckisms, 1879–1985," *Journal of the History of Biology* 44 (2011): 713–44; William H. Schneider, *Quality and Quantity: The Quest for Biological Regeneration in Twentieth-Century France* (Cambridge: Cambridge University Press, 1990), 5–6, 73, 87–88.

57. Conklin, *Museum of Man*, 163–70; Emmanuelle Sibeud, "A Useless Colonial Science? Practicing Anthropology in the French Colonial Empire, circa 1880–1960," *Current Anthropology* 53, no. 5 (April 2012): S83–S94; Richard Fogarty and Michael A. Osborne, "Constructions and Functions of Race in French Military Medicine, 1830–1920" in Peabody and Stovall, *Color of Liberty*; Delphine Peiretti-Courtis, *Corps noirs et médecins blancs: La fabrique du préjugé racial, XIX-XXe siècles* (Paris: La Découverte, 2021). For British Africa, see Tilley, *Africa as a Living Laboratory*, 217–59.

58. Schneider, *Quality and Quantity*; Simmons, *Vital Minimum*, 101; Rogers Brubaker, *Citizenship and Nationhood in France and Germany* (Cambridge, MA: Harvard University Press, 1992), 94–104.

59. Alison Bashford, *Global Population: History, Geopolitics, and Life on Earth* (New York: Columbia University Press, 2014).

60. Alice Conklin, "Faire Naître v. Faire du Noire: Race Regeneration in France and French West Africa, 1895–1940," in *Promoting the Colonial Idea: Propaganda and Visions of Empire in France*, edited by Tony Chafer and Amanda Sackur (New York: Palgrave, 2002); Margaret Cook Andersen, *Regeneration through Empire: French Pronatalists and Colonial Settlement in the Third Republic* (Lincoln: University of Nebraska Press, 2015).

61. ANOM, 110COL940/3033-3036 (FM, AGEFOM//940): Roubaud, "Rapport sur la question de l'insuffisance alimentaire," undated.

62. Gauducheau, "Comment Combler le déficit alimentaire."

63. Albert Londres, *Terre d'ébène* (Paris: Le Serpent à Plumes, 1998), 59.

64. Gauducheau, "Comment combler le déficit alimentaire."

65. On the Academy of Colonial Sciences, see Pierre Singaravélou, *Professer l'Empire: Les "sciences coloniales" en France sous la IIIe République* (Paris: Publications de la Sorbonne, 2011), 172–77.

66. On Calmette, see Rosenberg, "International Politics of Vaccine Testing."

67. ANOM, 110COL940/3033-3036 (FM, AGEFOM//940): Roubaud, "Rapport sur la question de l'insuffisance alimentaire," undated.

68. Bibliothèque Félix Houphouët-Boigny de l'académie des sciences d'outre-mer [ASOM], MSS 267, Calmette to académie des sciences d'outre-mer, November 8, 1923; ANOM, 110COL940/3033-3036 (FM, AGEFOM//940): Rapport sur la question de l'insuffisance alimentaire des indigènes dans les possessions françaises, par M. Roubaud, Rapporteur de la Commission, 1925.

69. "Notice annexe sur les mesures d'ordre général à appliquer dans la défense contre les principales causes de dépeuplement et de déchéance des races indigènes," *Annales de médecine et de pharmacie coloniales* 22 (Paris: Imprimerie Nationale, 1924), 468–76.

70. "Instruction du Ministre des Colonies relative à l'Étude Hygiénique de la Ration Alimentaire des populations Indigènes," *Annales de médecine et de pharmacie coloniales* 23 (Paris: Imprimerie Nationale, 1925), 391–92.

71. ANOM, 110COL940/3033-3036 (FM, AGEFOM//940): Conseil Supérieur des Colonies, Secrétariat Général, Conseil Économique, "Rapport sur les productions marines et fluviales de nos colonies," Presenté par M. Gruvel, Membre du Conseil.

72. ANOM, 110COL940/3033-3036 (FM, AGEFOM//940): La Pêche maritime au Cameroun. Commandant Briaud, June,1929. See also Marie Caquel, "L'Impact du protectorat français sur l'industrie du poisson au Maroc," *French Cultural Studies* 26, no. 2 (May 2015): 201.

73. VNA 1, RST 47970: Le Ministre des Colonies to Messieurs les Gouverneurs Généraux et Gouverneurs des Colonies, April 4, 1925.

74. "Circulaire Relatif aux mesures de protection sanitaire à appliquer sur tous les chantiers publics et privés des travailleurs indigènes dans toutes les colonies," *Annales de médecine et de pharmacie coloniales* n. 22 (Paris: Imprimerie Nationale, 1924), 271–75.

75. Daughton, *Forest of No Joy*, 188–213.

76. Lefrou, "Contribution à l'étude."

77. Lefrou, "Contribution à l'étude."

78. Médecin lieutenant-colonel Muraz du Corps de Santé Colonial, Ancien Inspecteur du Service de la Maladie du sommeil en AEF, Directeur des services d'hygiène de Saigon-Cholon, Cochinchine, "L'Alimentation Indigène en Afrique Équatoriale Française," in Hardy and Richet, *l'Alimentation indigène*, 179, 204–05.

79. Muraz, "L'Alimentation Indigène en Afrique Équatoriale Française," 180–81, 201.

80. Muraz, "L'Alimentation Indigène en Afrique Équatoriale Française," 179. The entire 320-mile-long project killed between fifteen thousand and twenty-three thousand people, possibly more. J. P. Daughton, "The 'Pacha Affair' Reconsidered: Violence and Colonial Rule in Interwar French Equatorial Africa," *Journal of Modern History* 91 (September 2019): 493–524.

81. Daughton, "'Pacha Affair' Reconsidered," 177.

82. Henri Labouret, Administrateur en Chef des Colonies, Professeur à l'École Nationale des Langues Orientales Vivantes, et à l'École Coloniale; Directeur de l'Institut International pour l'étude des langues et civilisations africaines, "L'Alimentation des Indigènes en Afrique Occidentale Française," in Hardy and Richet, *l'Alimentation indigène*, 154.

83. Pierre Contet, "Le travail forcé au Congo français, la famine organisée," *Le Populaire (SFIO)* no. 4,182 (July 23, 1934).

84. IIe congrès scientifique international de l'alimentation: Compte rendu des séances et discussion des rapports (Alençon: Imprimerie Alençonnaise, 1937), 9.

85. The most comprehensive treatment of the relationship between nutrition science, social science, and the state in Europe is James Vernon's *Hunger*, which focuses on the United Kingdom. On nutrition in the British Empire, see, Michael Worboys, "The Discovery of Colonial Malnutrition Between the Wars," in *Imperial Medicine and Indigenous Societies*, edited by David Arnold (Manchester, UK: Manchester University Press, 1988).

86. Pozerski de Pomiane, "Enseignement scientifique de la cuisine: La gastrotéchnie," *La Science de l'Alimentation en 1937* (Alençon: Imprimerie Alençonnaise, 1937), 12.

87. On interwar holism, see Bashford, *Global Population*, 159.

88. Étienne Burnet and Wallace Aykroyd, *Nutrition and Public Health* (Geneva: League of Nations, 1935).

89. Final Report of the Mixed Committee of the League of Nations on the Relation of Nutrition to Health, Agriculture, and Economic Policy (Series of League of Nations Publications, 1937), 34.

90. Final Report of the Mixed Committee, 38–41.

91. Final Report of the Mixed Committee, 45–48.

92. Final Report of the Mixed Committee, 82–84.

93. Étienne Burnet, "Société des Nations et Organisation sociale de l'alimentation humaine," in *La Science de l'Alimentation en 1937* (Alençon: Imprimerie Alençonnaise, 1937).

94. IIe congrès scientifique international de l'alimentation, 6.

95. Burnet, "Société des Nations," 33.

96. L. Petitjean, Météorologiste à la Faculté des Sciences d'Alger, "La sécheresse et les Vents de Poussière en Afrique du Nord" at Première Conférence Internationale pour la Protection contre les Calamités Naturelles, Paris, September 13–17, 1937.

97. G. Hardy, recteur de l'Académie d'Alger, Ancien Directeur de l'École Coloniale, "l'Alimentation des Indigènes au Maroc," in Hardy and Richet, *l'Alimentation indigène*, 125.

98. On Richet, see Simmons, *Vital Minimum*, 129.

99. IIe congrès scientifique international de l'alimentation, 59.

100. ANS, 1R/113(158): Institut International de l'Agriculture to Gouverneur-Général of AOF, May 15, 1932.

101. ANS, 1R/113(158): VIIIe congrès international d'agriculture tropicale et subtropicale, Tripoli d'Afrique, March 13–17, 1939.

102. ANS, 1R/113(158): Gouverneur de Dahomey to Gouverneur-Général of AOF, December 31, 1938.

103. ANS, 1R/113(158): Colonie de Côte d'Ivoire, Service de l'Agriculture to 8ème congrès international d'agriculture tropicale, undated.

104. ANS, 1R/113(158): Colonie du Sénégal, Note pour le 8ème congrès international d'agriculture tropicale, Chef du Service de l'Agriculture, Saint Louis, November 17, 1938.

105. ANS, 1R/113(158): Colonie du Sénégal, Service de l'enseignement, note pour le 8ème congrès international d'agriculture tropicale, undated.

106. Susan Pedersen, "Back to the League of Nations," *American Historical Review* 112 (2007): 1091–1117.

107. IIe congrès scientifique international de l'alimentation, 85–87.

108. Catherine Coquery-Vidrovitch, ed., "L'Afrique et la crise de 1930 (1924–1938)," special issue of *Revue Française d'Histoire d'Outre-mer* 63, nos. 232–233 (1976): 375–784; Pierre Brocheux, "The State and the 1930s Depression in French Indo-China," and Irene Nørlund, "Rice and the Colonial Lobby: The Economic Crisis in French Indo-China in the 1920s and 1930s," in *Weathering the Storm: The Economies of Southeast Asia in the 1930s Depression*, edited by Peter Boomgaard and Ian Brown (Singapore: Institute of Southeast Asian Studies, 2001); Richard Roberts, *Two Worlds of Cotton: Colonialism and the Regional Economy in the French Soudan, 1800–1946* (Stanford, CA: Stanford University Press, 1996), 218–20.

109. Gaud et Sicault, "Alimentation indigène au Maroc," *La Science de l'Alimentation en 1937* (Alençon: Imprimerie Alençonnaise, 1937). Sicault was the director of the protectorate's medical service and later worked for UNICEF. Ellen Amster, "The Syphilitic Arab? A Search for Civiliation in Disease Etiology, Native Prostitution, and French Colonial Medicine" in *French Mediterraneans: Transnational and Imperial Histories*, edited by Patricia M. E. Lorcin and Todd Shepard (Lincoln: University of Nebraska Press, 2016).

110. Hardy and Richet, *L'alimentation indigène*.

111. Henri Labouret, Gouverneur honoraire des Colonies, Professeur à l'École Coloniale, à l'Institut d'Ethnologie et à l'École Libre des Sciences Politiques, "Famines et Disettes aux Colonies" at Première Conférence Internationale pour la Protection contre les Calamités Naturelles, Paris, September 13–17, 1937.

112. Sicault, "Alimentation indigène au Maroc."

113. Conklin, *Museum of Man*, 222, 226–27.

114. Labouret, "Famines et Disettes aux Colonies."

115. J. J. Vassal and J. E. Martial, "Alimentation indigène en Afrique Équatoriale Française" in *La Science de l'Alimentation en 1937* (Alençon: Imprimerie Alençonnaise, 1937), 125.

116. Georges Hardy, *Nos Grands Problèmes Coloniaux* (Paris: Librairie Armand Colin, 1929), 18.

117. Albert Sarraut, *Grandeur et servitude coloniales* (Paris: l'Harmattan, 2012), 91.

118. IIe congrès scientifique international de l'alimentation, 62.

119. Conklin, *Museum of Man*, 145–48.

120. IIe congrès scientifique international de l'alimentation, 59–62. On debates about differences in physiology among human groups, see, Georges Canguilhem, *The Normal and the Pathological* (New York: Zone Books, 1991), 164–179.

121. L. Randoin and P. Le Gallic, "Race, hérédité, et alimentation," in *La Science de l'alimentation en 1937* (Alençon: Imprimerie Alençonnaise, 1937).

122. Randoin and Le Gallic, "Race, hérédité, et alimentation," 106.

123. Simmons, *Vital Minimum*, 128.

124. Brower, *Desert Named Peace*, 222–37.

125. J. E. Martial, "Alimentation indigène en AOF" in *La Science de l'alimentation en 1937* (Alençon: Imprimerie Alençonnaise, 1937), 118; Labouret, "L'Alimentation des indigènes," 145.

126. Étienne Burnet, "Alimentation en Tunisie," in *La Science de l'Alimentation en 1937* (Alençon: Imprimerie Alençonnaise, 1937).

127. Labouret, "Famines et Disettes aux Colonies."

128. Sicault, "Alimentation indigène au Maroc."

129. ANOM, Guernut 87: Problème de l'alimentation dans les colonies, undated.

130. Gravellat, Médecin-Major, "Note sur l'Alimentation du Tirailleur en Afrique Occidentale Française," *Annales de médecine et de pharmacie coloniales* 25 (Paris: Imprimerie Nationale, 1927), 80–102; J. E. Martial, "Contribution a l'étude de l'alimentation du tirailleur Sénégalais en Afrique occidentale française," *Annales de médecine et de pharmacie coloniales* 29 (Paris: Imprimerie Nationale, 1931), 517–32.

131. H. Patenostre, Médecin de l'Assistance Indigène de l'AOF, "L'Alimentation chez les Peuls du Fouta-Djallon," *Annales de médecine et de pharmcaie coloniales* 25 (Paris: Imprimerie Nationale, 1927), 51–80.

132. J-C. Peirier, pharmacien Lieutenant-Colonel, and Nguyen Kim Kinh, pharmacien indochinois, "Analyse Chimique d'un Tuong-Dào (sauce de soja)," *Annales de médecine et de pharmacie coloniales* 30 (Paris: Imprimerie Nationale, 1932), 516–23.

133. Burnet, "Alimentation en Tunisie."

134. Burnet, "Alimentation en Tunisie," 79.

135. Burnet, "Alimentation en Tunisie."

136. A. Thiroux, Médecin-Général des troupes coloniales, A. Giroud, Professeur de la faculté de médecine de Paris, and R. Ratsimamanga, licencié ès sciences, assistant à la faculté de médecine de Paris, "Alimentation des indigènes à Madagascar," in *La Science de l'Alimentation en 1937* (Alençon: Imprimerie Alençonnaise, 1937).

137. IIe congrès scientifique international de l'alimentation, 119–20.

138. Labouret, "Famines et Disettes aux Colonies."

139. Le Général H. Simon, "Les Disettes dans l'Afrique du Nord" at Première Conférence Internationale pour la Protection contre les Calamités Naturelles, Paris, September 13–17, 1937.

5. The Scandal of Starvation in Niger, 1931

1. ANOM, AOF 11G/26: Situation économique du Niger, Niamey, May 30, 1929.

2. ANOM, AOF 11G/26: Situation économique du Niger, Niamey, May 30, 1929.

3. One team of scholars has estimated that as many as 150 thousand people may have died or fled. J. Egg, F. Lerin, and M. Venin, "Analyse descriptive de la famine des années 1931 au Niger et implications méthodologiques," (Paris: Institut de Recherche des Nations Unies pour le Développement Social, 1975). See also, Finn Fuglestad, "La Grande Famine de 1931 dans l'Ouest nigérien: Réflexions autour d'une catastrophe naturelle," *Revue française d'histoire d'outre-mer* 222 (1974): 18–33; Alpha Boureima Gado, *Une histoire des famines au Sahel: Etude des grandes crises alimentaires XIXe-XXe siècles* (Paris: l'Harmattan, 1993).

4. Alpha Boureima Gado, *Crises alimentaires en Afrique sahélienne: Les réponses paysannes* (Cotonou: Les Editions du Flamboyant, 2010), 139; Salifou, "Quand l'histoire se répète," 25–52; Diouldé Laya, "Interviews with Farmers and Livestock Owners in the Sahel," *African Environment* 1, no. 2 (1975): 49–93.

5. On similar developments in Northern Nigeria, see Moses E. Ochonu, *Colonial Meltdown: Northern Nigeria in the Great Depression* (Athens: Ohio University Press, 2009), chapter 2.

6. ANOM, AOF, 11G/40: Blacher to Gouverneur-Général de l'AOF, Niamey, August 6, 1931.

7. Finn Fuglestad, "Unis and BNA: The Role of 'Traditionalist' Parties in Niger, 1948–1960," *Journal of African History* 16, no. 1 (1975), 122. On Zarma social structure, see Jean-Pierre Olivier de Sardan, *Les sociétés songhay-zarma* (Paris: Karthala, 1984).

8. ANOM, 110COL944: Commission d'enquête et d'information sur la famine du Niger en 1931; ANS, 2G31-10: Colonie du Niger, Cercle de Dosso, Rapport Economique, 1er trimestre 1931; ANOM, AOF 11G/26: Rapport fait par M. Bernard Sol, Inspecteur des Colonies, concernant la situation alimentaire du cercle de Dosso, dans les anneés 1931–1932, August 10, 1932.

9. ANOM, 110COL944: Commission d'enquête et d'information sur la famine du Niger en 1931.

10. ANOM, AOF 11G/26: Rapport fait par M. Bernard Sol, Inspecteur des Colonies, concernant la situation alimentaire du Cercle de Niamey dans les années 1931–1932.

11. ANS, 17G-210: Blacher, untitled, October 27, 1932.

12. ANOM, AOF 11G/26: Commission pour examiner les possibilités et les modes de ravitaillement de la population indigène atteinte par la crise alimentaire, July 1, 1931; ANOM, AOF 11G/26: Blacher to l'Administrateur Commandant le Cercle de Niamey, July 4, 1931.

13. ANOM, 110COL944: Commission d'enquête et d'information sur la famine du Niger en 1931.

14. ANOM, 110COL944/3083: Exposé de M. le Gouverneur Coppet, Rapporteur de la commission d'enquête et d'Information sur la famine qui a Sévi au Niger en 1931.

15. ANS, 17G-210: Blacher, untitled, October 27, 1932.

16. ANOM, AOF 11G/26: Rapport fait par M. Bernard Sol, Inspecteur des Colonies, concernant la situation alimentaire du Cercle de Niamey dans les années 1931–1932.

17. ANOM, 110COL944: Commission d'enquête et d'information sur la famine du Niger en 1931.

18. Vaughan, *Story of an African Famine*, chapter 5; Drèze and Sen, *Hunger and Public Action*, 55–56.

19. For comparison, see Kent Glenzer, "La Sécheresse: The Social and Institutional Construction of a Development Problem in the Malian (Soudanese) Sahel," *Canadian Journal of African Studies 36*, no. 1 (2002).

20. ANOM, 110COL944: Procès-verbaux des Séances de la Commission d'enquête et d'information sur la famine au Niger.

21. Jeremy Swift, "Desertification: Narratives, Winners, and Losers" in *The Lie of the Land: Challenging Received Wisdom on the African Environment* by Melissa Leach and Robin Mearns (London: International African Institute, 1996); Watts, *Silent Violence*, 93–94.

22. G. T. Renner, "A Famine Zone in Africa: The Sudan," *Geographical Review 16*, no. 4 (October 1926): 583–96.

23. Arnold, *Famine*, 54–55.

24. ANS, 17G-210: Blacher, untitled, October 27, 1932.

25. ANOM, 110COL944: Commission d'enquête et d'information sur la famine du Niger en 1931.

26. ANOM, AOF 11G/40: Observations du Gouverneur-Général sur la Réponse de M. le Gouverneur Blacher relative au Cercle de Niamey.

27. ANOM, 110COL944/3083: Commission d'enquête et d'information sur la famine du Niger en 1931, Procès-verbal de la séance du 18 Mars 1933.

28. ANOM, 110COL944: Procès Verbaux des Séances de la Commission d'enquête et d'information sur la famine au Niger.

29. ANOM, 110COL944/3083: Commission d'enquête et d'information sur la famine du Niger en 1931, Procès-verbal de la Séance du 16 Mars 1933.

30. ANOM, 110COL944/3083: Commission d'enquête et d'information sur la famine du Niger en 1931, Procès-verbal de la Séance du 16 Mars 1933.

31. ANS, 17G-210: Blacher, untitled, October 27, 1932.

32. ANS, 1G-354: Historique du cercle de Niamey, September 15, 1921.

33. ANS, 2G31-100: Rapport politique annuel, cercle de Niamey, 1931; ANS, 2G31-18: Rapport Politique AOF 1931, September 7, 1932.

34. ANOM, FR ANOM 110COL944/3083 (FM, AGEFOM//944): Exposé de M. le Gouverneur Coppet, Rapporteur de la Commission d'Enquête et d'Information sur la Famine qui a Sévi au Niger en 1931.

35. ANOM, 11G/26: Commission pour examiner les possibilités et les modes de ravitaillement de la population indigène atteinte par la crise alimentaire, Procès-verbal, July 1, 1931.

36. ANOM, AOF 11G/26: Rapport fait par M. Bernard Sol, Inspecteur des Colonies, concernant la situation alimentaire du Cercle de Niamey dans les années 1931–1932.

37. ANOM, AOF 11G/40: Le Gouverneur des Colonies Blacher to Directeur du Cabinet, Ministère des Colonies, January 20, 1933.

38. ANS, 2G31-94: Rapport politique année 1931, Colonie du Niger, Cercle de Dosso, January 12, 1932.

39. ANS, 2G31-99: Bulletin Politique, 2ème trimestre, subdivision de Niamey, October 7, 1931.

40. ANOM, AOF 11G/26: Lieutenant-Gouverneur du Niger to Gouverneur-Général de l'AOF, November 13, 1931.

41. ANOM, AOF 11G/26: Rapport fait par M. Bernard Sol, Inspecteur des Colonies, concernant la situation alimentaire du Cercle de Niamey, dans les années 1931–1932.

42. Thomas M. Painter, "From Warriors to Migrants: Critical Perspectives on Early Migrations among the Zarma of Niger," *Africa: Journal of the International African Institute* 58, no. 1 (1988): 87–100.

43. ANOM, FR ANOM 110COL944/3083: Exposé de M. le Gouverneur Coppet, Rapporteur de la Commission d'enquéte et d'information sur la famine qui a sévi au Niger en 1931.

44. ANOM, AOF 11G/26: Rapport fait par Bernard Sol, Inspecteur des Colonies, concernant la situation alimentaire du Cercle de Niamey dans les années 1931–1932.

45. ANOM, 110COL944/3083: Exposé du Gouverneur Coppet, Rapporteur de la Commission d'enquête et d'information sur la famine qui a sévi au Niger en 1931.

46. ANOM, 61COL591: Rapport Politique de 1931, Colonie du Niger.

47. ANS, 2G31-28: Rapport médical annuel, Colonie du Niger, 1931.

48. ANOM, 11G/40: L'Administrateur de 1ère classe des Colonies, Commandant le Cercle de Niamey, to Gouverneur du Niger, June 9, 1932.

49. ANS, 2G31-115: Rapport économique trimestriel 1931, 3e trimestre, October 6, 1931.

50. ANOM, AOF 11G/40: Réponse de M. Blacher, Précédemment Lieutenant-Gouverneur du Niger, October 27, 1932.

51. ANS, 2G31-110: Rapport économique, Colonie du Niger, Cercle de Dosso, 2ème trimestre 1931.

52. ANOM, 11G/40: L'Administrateur des Colonies Commandant le Cercle de Niamey to Gouverneur du Niger, June 9, 1932.

53. ANOM, AOF 11G/26: Lieutenant-Gouverneur du Niger to M. l'Administrateur Commandant le Cercle de Niamey, July 4, 1931.

54. ANOM, AOF 11G/26: Commission . . . pour examiner les possibilités et les modes de ravitaillement de la population indigène atteinte par la crise alimentaire, July 1, 1931.

55. On gender and famine relief in a matrilineal society, see Vaughan, *Story of an African Famine*, chapter 5.

56. ANOM, AOF 11G/40: Observations du Gouverneur-Général sur la réponse de Blacher relative à la crise alimentaire au Niger; ANOM, AOF 11G/26: Lieutenant-Gouverneur du Niger to Gouverneur-Général de l'AOF, November 13, 1931.

57. ANOM, 110COL944/3083: Commission d'enquête et d'information sur la famine du Niger en 1931, Procès-verbal de la séance du 16 Mars 1933.

58. ANOM, 110COL944: Commission d'enquête et d'information sur la famine du Niger en 1931.

59. Arnold, *Famine*, 109.

60. Vincent Bonnecase, "Avoir faim en Afrique occidentale française: investigations et représentations coloniales (1920–1960)," *Revue d'histoire des sciences humaines* 21 (2009): 151–74.

61. Miller, *Mastering the Market*.

62. ANOM, AOF 11G/26: Circulaire n. 32, July 26, 1922.

63. ANOM, AOF 11G/26 (14MIOM2206): Situation économique du Niger, Niamey, May 30, 1929.

64. ANS,1R-7(1): Le Gouverneur-Général de l'AOF to Ministre des Colonies, July 27, 1936.

65. ANS, 17G-210: Circulaire à Messieurs les Commandants de Cercle, 1931.

66. ANOM, AOF 11G-40: Gouverneur-Général de l'AOF to Lieutenant-Gouverneur du Niger, September 14, 1931.

67. ANOM, AOF 11G/26 (14MIOM2206): Lieutenant-Gouverneur du Niger to Gouverneur-Général de l'AOF, November 13, 1931.

68. Babacar Fall, *Le travail forcé en Afrique-occidentale française, 1900–1946* (Paris: Éditions Karthala, 1993).

69. ANOM, AOF 11G/40: Réponse de Blacher, October 27, 1932; ANOM, 110COL944/3083 (FM, AGEFOM//944): Exposé de M. le Gouverneur Coppet, Rapporteur de la Commission d'enquête et d'information sur la famine qui a sévi au Niger en 1931.

70. André Salifou, *Le Niger* (Paris: l'Harmattan, 2002), 130–131; ANOM, AOF 11G/40: Observations du Gouverneur-Général sur la réponse de Blacher relative à la crise alimentaire au Niger.

71. ANS, 17G-210: Blacher, untitled, October 27, 1932.

72. Egg, Lerin, and Venin, "Analyse descriptive de la famine."

73. ANOM, AOF 11G/40: Observations du Gouverneur-Général sur la réponse de Blacher relative à la crise alimentaire au Niger.

74. Olivier de Sardan, *Les sociétés songhay-zarma*, 224–31.

75. Olivier de Sardan, *Les sociétés songhay-zarma*, 165.

76. Salifou, "Quand l'histoire se répète," 25–52.

77. Derriennic, *Famines et domination*, 29–30.

78. ANOM, AOF 11G/26: Rapport fait par M. Bernard Sol, Inspecteur des Colonies, concernant la situation alimentaire du cercle de Dosso, dans les années 1931–1932, August 10, 1932.

79. ANOM, AOF 11G/40: Blacher to Ministère des Colonies, January 1933.

80. Derriennic, *Famines et domination*, 52–53.

81. ANOM, AOF 11G/26: Rapport fait par M. Bernard Sol, Inspecteur des Colonies, concernant la situation alimentaire du cercle de Tillabéry, dans les années 1931–1932 et explications fournies par M. l'Administrateur des Colonies Prud'homme, Commandant le cercle, August 7, 1932.

82. ANS, 17G-210: Blacher, untitled, October 27, 1932.

83. ANOM, 11G/26: Procès-verbal: Commission . . . pour examiner les possibilités et les modes de ravitaillement de la population indigène atteinte par la crise alimentaire, July 1, 1931; ANOM, 110COL944/3083: Exposé de M. le Gouverneur Coppet, Rapporteur de la Commission d'enquête et d'information sur la famine qui a sévi au Niger en 1931.

84. Olivier de Sardan, *Les sociétés songhay-zarma*, 166–67.

85. ANOM, 11G/26: Rapport fait par M. Bernard Sol, Inspecteur des Colonies, concernant la situation alimentaire du cercle de Tillabéry, dans les années 1931–1932 et explications fournies par M. l'Administrateur des Colonies Prud'homme, Commandant le cercle, August 7, 1932.

86. ANOM, AOF 11G/26: Rapport fait par M. Bernard Sol, Inspecteur des Colonies, concernant la situation alimentaire du Cercle de Niamey dans les années 1931–1932.

87. ANOM, AOF 11G/26: Rapport fait par M. Bernard Sol, Inspecteur des Colonies, concernant la situation alimentaire du cercle de Dosso, dans les années 1931–1932, August 10, 1932.

88. This gives a counterpoint to Amartya Sen's findings that peasants and sharecroppers tended to be in a better position than wage earners during famines because the former had direct entitlements to the food they produced. Sen, *Poverty and Famines*, 70.

89. ANOM, 110COL944/3083: Commission d'enquête et d'information sur la famine du Niger en 1931 (Procès-verbal de la Séance du 1 Avril 1933).

90. ANOM, 11G/26: Procès-verbal: Commission . . . pour examiner les possibilités et les modes de ravitaillement de la population indigène atteinte par la crise alimentaire, July 1, 1931; ANOM, AOF 11G/26: Renseignements, July 19, 1932; ANS, 2G31-115, Rapport économique trimestriel 1931, 3ème trimestre, October 6, 1931.

91. ANOM, AOF 11G/26: Commission pour examiner les possibilités et les modes de ravitaillement de la population indigène atteinte par la crise alimentaire, July 1, 1931.

92. ANS, 2G31-8: Rapport Politique vue d'ensemble, Colonie du Niger, 1931.

93. ANOM, 61COL591: Rapport Politique d'Ensemble, Niger, 1933.

94. ANOM, AOF 11G/26: Le Lieutenant-Gouverneur du Niger to Gouverneur-Général de l'AOF, July 25, 1933.

95. ANOM, AOF 11G/26: Lieutenant-Gouverneur du Niger to Gouverneur-Général de l'AOF, August 3, 1933.

96. ANOM, AOF 11G/26: Lieutenant-Gouverneur de la Côte d'Ivoire to Gouverneur-Général de l'AOF, July 25, 1933.

97. ANOM, 61COL 591: Désignation d'une commission chargée de procéder à l'étude des causes de la famine qui a régné au Niger en 1932 et de rechercher les mesures à prendre pour l'avenir, February 20, 1933.

98. ANOM, AOF 11G/40: Le Gouverneur des Colonies Blacher to Directeur du Cabinet, Ministère des Colonies, Paris, January 20, 1933.

99. ANOM, 110COL944/3083: Commission d'enquête et d'information sur la famine du Niger en 1931 (Procès-verbal de la Séance du 18 Mars 1933 and Procès-verbal de la Séance du 20 Mars 1933).

100. ANOM, FR ANOM 110COL944/3083 (FM, AGEFOM//944): Exposé de M. le Gouverneur Coppet, Rapporteur de la Commission d'Enquête et d'information sur la famine qui a sévi au Niger en 1931.

101. There is a brief mention in the sources that Valtaud shared photographs of starving people, though neither the photographs nor any other discussion of their reception remain in the archives. ANOM, 110COL944/3083: Commission d'enquête et d'information sur la famine du Niger en 1931, procès-verbal de la séance du 21 mars, 1933.

102. ANOM, AOF 11G/40: Ligue Française pour la Défense des Droits de l'Homme et du Citoyen to Ministre des Colonies. April 9, 1932.

103. ANOM, 11G/40: Lieutenant-Gouverneur du Niger to Gouverneur-Général de l'AOF, July 5, 1932.

104. ANOM, 11G/40: L'Administrateur des Colonies Commandant le Cercle de Niamey to M. le Gouverneur du Niger, June 9, 1932.

105. ANOM, 11G/40: Secrétaire Général p.i. to Monsieur le Lieutenant-Gouverneur du Niger, June 10, 1932.

106. There is some evidence that merchants and European and African functionaries collaborated to hoard and then market grain in the hopes of turning a profit. ANOM, AOF 11G/26: Renseignements demandés par lettre du 13 Juin 1932, Inspection des Affaires Administratives, July 19, 1932; ANOM, AOF 11G/26: Rapport fait par M. Bernard Sol, Inspecteur des Colonies, concernant la situation alimentaire du Cercle de Niamey dans les années 1931–1932; ANOM, 110COL944/3083: Commission d'enquête et d'information sur la famine du Niger en 1931, Procès-verbal de la séance du 15 Mars 1933.

107. ANOM, 61Col 591: Pour le Ministère des Colonies to Président de la Ligue Française pour la Défense des Droits de l'Homme et du Citoyen, October 12, 1932.

108. ANOM, 11G/40: L'Administrateur Commandant le Cercle de Niamey to Inspecteur des Affaires Administratives, Niamey, June 18, 1932; ANOM 11G/40: Renseignements demandés par lettre 108 c du 28 Juin, 1932, Gouverneur-Général de l'AOF, Inspection des Affaires Administratives, Niamey, June 29, 1932.

109. ANOM, 110COL944/3083 (FM, AGEFOM//944): Exposé de M. le Gouverneur Coppet, Rapporteur de la Commission d'Enquête et d'Information sur la Famine qui a Sévi au Niger en 1931.

110. ANOM, 11G/40: Le Ministre des Colonies to Gouverneur-Général de l'AOF, May 29, 1932.

111. ANOM, AOF 11G/26: Rapport fait par M. Bernard Sol, Inspecteur des Colonies, concernant la situation alimentaire du Cercle de Niamey dans les années 1931–1932.

112. ANOM, AOF 11G/26: Rapport fait par M. Bernard Sol, Inspecteur des Colonies, concernant la situation alimentaire du Cercle de Niamey dans les années 1931–1932.

113. ANOM, AOF 11G/40: Le Ministre des Colonies to Gouverneur-Général, February 22, 1933.

114. ANOM, 110COL944: Commission d'enquête et d'information sur la famine du Niger en 1931.

115. ANOM, 110COL944: Commission d'enquête et d'information sur la famine du Niger en 1931.

116. On citizenship in the French Antilles, see Silyane Larcher, *L'Autre citoyen: l'idéal républicain et les Antilles après l'esclavage* (Paris: Colin, 2014).

117. Lunn, *Memoirs of the Maelstrom*, 73–81.

118. ANOM, 110COL944/3083: Commission d'enquête et d'information sur la famine du Niger en 1931, procès-verbal de la séance du 20 Mars 1933.

119. On Coppet's relationship with Gide, see *Gide & la question coloniale: Correspondance avec Marcel de Coppet, 1924–1950*, edited by Hélène Baty-Delalande and Pierre Masson (Lyon: Presses Universitaires de Lyon, 2020).

120. ANOM, FR ANOM 110COL944/3083 (FM, AGEFOM//944): Exposé de M. le Gouverneur Coppet, Rapporteur de la Commission d'Enquête et d'Information sur la Famine qui a Sévi au Niger en 1931.

121. Emmanuelle Saada writes that in French colonial usage, race "never referred solely to a perceived phenotypic or anthropological difference." Mixed-race people, Japanese, Filipinos, and people from the "old colonies" of the Caribbean could be classified, at least legally, as "European." Saada, *Empire's Children*, 39, 107.

122. ANOM, 110COL944/3083: Commission d'enquête et d'information sur la famine du Niger en 1931 (Procès-verbal de la Séance du 21 Mars 1933). I have left the word *nègre* in the original French to maintain the connotations of the original usage. See Jennifer Boittin, "Black in France: The Language and Politics of Race in the Late Third Republic," *French Politics, Culture, and Society* 27, no. 2 (2009): 23–46.

123. Some indications of Gaston Joseph's personal views on race can be gleaned from his novel *Koffi: The Romance of a Negro*. Written in response to the Martinican novelist René Maran's *Batouala*, it is a defense of the civilizing mission, frank in its cultural and racial chauvinism. See Gaston Joseph, *Koffi: Roman vrai d'un noir* (Paris: Editions du Monde Nouveau, 1922). On the place of Antilleans in France, see Ndiaye, *La condition noire*, 55–56, 221.

124. Daughton, "'Pacha Affair' Reconsidered."

125. ANOM, 61COL591: Chambre des Députés, Commission de l'Algérie des Colonies et des Protectorats, Paris, April 12, 1934. See also Véronique Hélénon, *French Caribbeans in Africa: Diasporic Connections and Colonial Administration, 1880–1939* (New York: Palgrave MacMillan, 2011), 102, 109.

126. Béatrice Appia was the widow of the writer Eugène Dabit, who died while traveling in the Soviet Union with his friend André Gide. ANOM, FM, ee/ii/3020/1: Extrait de registre de l'état-civil, 1938; ANOM, FM, ee/ii/3020/1: Blacher to Chef de Service Colonial, Marseille, December 29, 1940.

127. ANS, 2G31-115: Rapport économique trimestriel, Cercle de Niamey, December, 1931.

128. ANS, 2G31-94: Rapport Politique, Colonie du Niger, Cercle de Dosso, 1931.

129. ANOM, AOF 11G/26: Rapport fait par M. Bernard Sol, Inspecteur des Colonies, concernant la situation alimentaire du cercle de Tillabéry dans les années 1931–1932.

130. ANOM, AOF 11G/40: Le Gouverneur des Colonies Blacher to Directeur du Cabinet, Ministère des Colonies, January 20, 1933.

131. ANS, 2G31-111: Rapport économique annuel 1931, Colonie du Niger, Cercle de Dosso.

132. ANOM, AOF 11G/40: Le Gouverneur des Colonies Blacher to Directeur du Cabinet, Ministère des Colonies, January 20, 1933.

133. ANS, 2G31-115: Rapport économique trimestriel 1931, 3ème trimestre, October 6, 1931.

134. ANS, 2G31-115: Rapport économique trimestriel 1931, 1er trimestre, March 31, 1931.

135. ANS, 2G31-115: Rapport économique trimestriel 1931, 3ème trimestre, October 6, 1931.

136. ANS, 2G31-115: Rapport économique trimestriel 1931, 3ème trimestre, October 6, 1931.

137. ANOM, 61COL591: Lieutenant-Gouverneur du Niger to Gouverneur-Général de l'AOF, Niamey, June 23, 1932.

138. ANS,1R-7(1): Le Gouverneur-Général de l'AOF to Ministre des Colonies, July 27, 1936.

139. ANOM, 61COL591: Rapport Politique d'Ensemble, Niger, 1933.

140. ANOM, 61COL591: Lieutenant-Gouverneur du Niger to Gouverneur-Général de l'AOF, Niamey, June 23, 1932.

141. ANOM, 61COL591: Lieutenant-Gouverneur du Niger to Gouverneur-Général de l'AOF, Niamey, June 23, 1932.

142. ANOM, 61COL591: Rapport Politique d'Ensemble, Niger, 1933.

143. ANOM, 61COL591: Rapport Politique d'Ensemble, Niger, 1933.

144. ANOM, 61COL591: Rapport économique, Niger, 1937.

145. ANOM, 61COL591: Rapport économique, Niger, 1937; ANOM, Guernut 24: Note sur les dispositions à prendre pour éviter le retour de la famine dans les colonies, July 22, 1936.

146. ANOM, 110COL944/3083: Commission d'enquête et d'information sur la famine du Niger en 1931, procès-verbal de la séance du 15 Mars 1933.

6. Taking Responsibility in the French Empire, 1931–1939

1. P. A. Morton, *Hybrid Modernities: Architecture and Representation at the 1931 Colonial Exposition, Paris* (Cambridge, MA: MIT Press, 2003).

2. Amartya Sen, *Development as Freedom* (New York: Anchor Books, 1999), 160–188.

3. Grauclaude, *Les eaux, disciplinées*.

4. Grauclaude, *Les eaux, disciplinées*.

5. On Viollis and colonial humanistic journalism, see Anne Renoult, *Andrée Viollis: Une femme journaliste* (Anger, France: Presses Universitaires d'Angers, 2004); Alice-Anne Jeandel, *Andrée Viollis, une femme grand reporter: Une écriture de l'événement, 1927–1939* (Paris: l'Harmattan, 2006); Frank Harbers and Marcel Broersma, "Impartial reporter or *écrivain engagé*? Andrée Viollis and the transformation of French Journalism, 1918–1940," *French History* 30, no. 2 (June 2016): 218–40.

6. Daughton, "Behind the Imperial Curtain," 503–28.

7. Kimberley J. Healey, "Andrée Viollis in Indochina: The Objective and Picturesque Truth about French Colonialism," *Asian Journal of Social Science* 31, no. 1 (2003): 19–35.

8. Andrée Viollis, "L'adieu de M. Reynaud à l'Indochine," *Le Petit Parisien*, November 20, 1931; Andrée Viollis, "M. Paul Reynaud est à Hanoï," *Le Petit Parisien*, November 9, 1931.

9. Andrée Viollis, "Quelques notes sur l'Indochine," *l'Esprit* (December 1933).

10. Anne Renoult, "André Malraux et Andrée Viollis dans la campagne de protestation contre la répression en Indochine après 1930," *Présence d'André Malraux* 13, André Malraux et le colonialisme (2016): 75–95.

11. Viollis added a footnote in the 1949 edition of the book, as the Vietnamese were fighting their war of independence, that although Reynaud saw such misery with his own eyes, "he who *knew*" did nothing to defend the "natural revolt" of the Vietnamese. "What to think of the conscience of this man?" Andrée Viollis, *Indochine S.O.S.* (Paris: Les Editeurs Français Réunis, 1949).

12. Viollis, *Indochine S.O.S.*

13. Viollis, *Indochine S.O.S.*, 155–62.

14. VNA 1, RST 53 39832: Résident Supérieur [René Robin] to tous chefs, May 1, 1930; VNA 1, RST T.53 39832: Résident Bac Ninh to Résident Supérieur, May 3, 1930.

15. ANOM, NF 2329: Le Malaise Indochinois—Ses causes, ses remèdes: L'Action communiste en Indochine, 1931.

16. ANOM, 3SLOTFOM 128: Les émigrés indochinois de France, "Les massacres en Indochine," undated; ANOM, 3SLOTFOM 128: Secours Rouge International, Section Française, "Arrière les bourreaux!," undated; ANOM, 3SLOTFOM 128: L'Internationale Syndicat Rouge de Moscou, "L'Orient et les colonies," 1930; "La Révolte Indochinoise," *L'Humanité*, January 12, 1931.

17. The Indochinese Communist Party was originally called the Communist Party of Vietnam but quickly changed its name.

18. Martin Bernal, "The Nghe Tinh Soviet Movement, 1930–31," *Past and Present* 92 (August 1981): 148–68.

19. Hy Van Luong questions "the assumption of a strong correlation between agrarian unrest and peasants' economic hardship from natural calamities, economic cycles, and the violation of the subsistence ethic by the lords and the state." Against James Scott's argument that the Nghe Tinh soviets were responses to low rice prices, he argues that the Great Depression did not impact Indochina until at least the end of 1930. Hy Van Luong, "Agrarian Unrest." On the Great Depression and Nghe Tinh, see also Pierre Brocheux, "L'Implantation du mouvement communiste en Indochine française: le cas du Nghe Tinh (1930–1931), *Revue d'histoire moderne et contemporaine* (January–March 1977), 61; Scott, *Moral Economy*; Ngô Viñh Long, "The Indochinese Communist Party and Peasant Rebellion in Central Vietnam, 1930–1931," *Bulletin of Concerned Asian Scholars* 10, no. 4 (1978): 29.

20. Tran Huy Lieu, *Les Soviets du Nghe Tinh* (Hanoi: Editions en langues étrangères, 1960), 41. On Tran Huy Lieu, see Bruce M. Lockhart, "The Nghe Tinh Movement in Communist Party Historiography," *South East Asia Research* vol. 19, no. 4, Special Issue: *Revisiting and Reconstructing the Nghe Tinh Soviets, 1930–2011* (December 2011): 711–35.

21. "La Révolution dans le Nghê-Tinh et le Quang-Ngai," *L'Indochine: Revue Economique d'Extrême-Orient*, Paris, April 20, 1931.

22. Tran Huy Lieu, *Les Soviets du Nghe Tinh*, 42.

23. Ngô Viñh Long, "Indochinese Communist Party," 19, 29.

24. ANOM, GGI 65518: Rapport de la commission d'enquête sur les évènements du Nord-Annam, 1931 (Morché report).

25. VNA 1, Direction de Finances de l'Indochine, [DFI] S.67 18421: Le Résident Supérieur en Annam to M. le Gouverneur Général de l'Indochine, Vinh, June 20, 1931.

26. VNA 1, DFI S.67 18421: Le Résident Supérieur en Annam to M. le Gouverneur Général de l'Indochine, Vinh, June 20, 1931.

27. ANOM, GGI 65518: Morché report, part 2, 90.

28. VNA 1, DFI S.67 18421: Le Résident Supérieur en Annam to Gouverneur Général de l'Indochine, September 21, 1931.

29. William J. Duiker, "The Red Soviets of Nghe Tinh: An Early Communist Rebellion in Vietnam," *Journal of Southeast Asian Studies* 4, no. 2 (September 1973): 186–98.

30. VNA 1, DFI S.67 18421: Le Résident Supérieur en Annam to M. le Gouverneur Général de l'Indochine, September 21, 1931.

31. ANOM, FM INDO NF 267: Au sujet des famines en Indochine, undated; ANOM, FM INDO NF 267: Extrait du rapport n. 752 du résident supérieur en Annam, July 29, 1931.

32. ANOM, GGI 65518: Morché report, part 3, 37–38.

33. ANOM, FM INDO NF 267: Recherches des Causes du Mouvement insurrectionnel, undated.

34. ANOM, GGI 65518: Morché report, part 1, 47–48.

35. "Une Proclamation du gouverneur général aux habitants du Nghê-An et du Hà-Tinh," *L'Echo Annamite*, supplément du 8 octobre; "Le Mouvement révolutionnaire en Indochine," *Le Temps*, Paris, May 13, 1930; "La Situation en Annam," *Le Journal*, Paris, October 31, 1931; Gouverneur-Général Pasquier, "La Politique Française en Indochine," *La Revue du Paçifique*, July 15, 1930.

36. I am indebted to Haydon Cherry for this point.

37. Gouverneur-Général Pasquier, "La Politique Française en Indochine," *La Revue du Paçifique*, July 15, 1930.

38. "La Famine au Nghê-Tinh: Ce qu'en dit la presse, "*L'Eveil Economique de l'Indochine*," August 23, 1931.

39. ANOM, FM INDO NF 267: Ngac Van Dong to Reynaud, November 6, 1931.

40. Louis Roubaud, *Viet Nam: La tragédie indochinoise* (Paris: L'Harmattan, 2010).

41. Renoult, "André Malraux et Andrée Viollis."

42. "Réponse au Bulletin d'informations publié par le Comité d'Amnistie aux Indochinois en Mai 1933," *Contribution à l'histoire des mouvements politiques de l'Indochine française, Vol. 5, La Terreur Rouge en Annam, 1930–1931* (1934).

43. ANOM, FM INDO NF 267: Marius Moutet, "A propos des événements d'Indochine," undated.

44. On Sarraut, see Clifford Rosenberg, "Albert Sarraut and Republican Racial Thought," *French Politics, Culture, and Society* 20, no. 3 (Fall 2002): 97–114; Martin Thomas, "Albert Sarraut, French Colonial Development, and the Communist Threat, 1919–1930," *Journal of Modern History* 77, no. 4 (December 2005): 917–55.

45. Sarraut, *La Mise en Valeur*, 20.

46. See Nicola Cooper's introduction to Sarraut, *Grandeur et servitude*.

47. Sarraut, *Mise en Valeur*, 88.

48. Sarraut, *Grandeur et servitude*, 15–42.

49. Sarraut, *Grandeur et servitude*, 160; on his concept of internationalism, see Albert Sarraut, "The Indivisibility of Peace and the Inseparability of East and West," *Pacific Affairs* 9, no. 4 (December 1936): 509–14.

50. Sarraut, *Grandeur et Servitude*, 70–71, 160.

51. Sarraut, *Grandeur et Servitude*, 50; Sarraut, *Mise en Valeur*, 19.

52. Émile Durkheim, *The Division of Labor in Society* (New York: Free Press, 1984).

53. Léon Bourgeois, *Solidarité* (Paris, 1896), 92–94, 148–54. According to Rabinow, "Solidarism had two main concepts: quasi-contract, the idea that overt and explicit consent was not required for all contracts, because society had prior rights; and social debt, the notion that contract was not voluntary but arose from preexisting obligations to others." Rabinow, *French Modern*, 185. See also Pierre Rosanvallon, *The Demands of Liberty: Civil Society in France Since the Revolution* (Cambridge, MA: Harvard University Press, 2007), 214–16, 239. On the influence of Durkheim in French colonial anthropology, see, Susan Bayly, "French Anthropology and the Durkheimians in Colonial Indochina," *Modern Asian Studies* 34, no. 3 (July 2000): 581–622.

54. Sarraut, *Grandeur*, 69–70, 74.

55. Sarraut, *Grandeur*, 73.

56. Sarraut, *Mise en valeur*, 82; Sarraut, *Grandeur*, 66.

57. Tran Huy Lieu, *Les Soviets du Nghe Tinh*, 8; Hue-Tam Ho Tai, *Radicalism and Origins*, 22–56.

58. Cooper's introduction to Sarraut, *Grandeur*, xix; Aimé Césaire, *Discourse on Colonialism* (New York: Monthly Review Press, 1972), 38.

59. Sarraut, *Grandeur*, 86.

60. ANOM, 61COL591: Le Ministre des Colonies to Gouverneur-Général de l'AOF, January 26, 1933.

61. ANOM, 11G/40: Le Ministre des Colonies to gouverneurs-généraux de l'AOF, de l'AEF, de Madagascar et dépendances, July 25, 1933.

62. ANOM, 61COL 591: Le Ministre des Colonies to Gouverneurs-Généraux et Gouverneurs des Colonies et à MM. les Commissaires de la République dans les territoires sous Mandat.

63. ANOM, 11G/40: Le Ministre des Colonies to gouverneurs-généraux de l'AOF, de l'AEF, de Madagascar et dépendances, July 25, 1933.

64. ANOM, 11G/40: Le Ministre des Colonies to gouverneurs-généraux de l'AOF, de l'AEF, de Madagascar et dépendances, July 25, 1933.

65. Julian Jackson, *The Popular Front in France: Defending Democracy, 1934–1938.* (Cambridge: Cambridge University Press, 1988).

66. ANOM, GGAEF 4(1)d-21: Discours Prononcé par M. Marius Moutet, Conférence des Gouverneurs Généraux, November 5, 1936.

67. VNA 1, RST 75782: Ministre des Colonies to Gouverneurs Généraux et Commissaires de la République, June 24, 1936.

68. VNA 1, RST 75782: Ministre des Colonies to Gouverneurs Généraux et Commissaires de la République, June 24, 1936.

69. ANOM, AOF 17G/160: Le Ministre des Colonies to Gouverneurs Généraux et Commissaires de la République dans les Territoires africains sous mandat, Paris, June 24, 1936.

70. ANOM, 61COL591: Plan Quinqennal, Exécution de la lettre du 27 septembre 1937.

71. ANOM, 17G-160: L'alimentation des Indigènes en Afrique Occidentale Française: Bulletin d'Information et de Renseignements n. 192 p. 1419, May 1938.

72. ANOM, AOF 17G/160: Le Gouverneur-Général de l'AOF to Lieutenants-Gouverneurs des Colonies du Groupe, Dakar, October 10, 1933.

73. ANS, 1R-7(1): Le Gouverneur-Général de l'AOF to Ministre des Colonies, July 27, 1936.

74. ANS, 1R-7(1): Le Gouverneur-Général de l'AOF to Ministre des Colonies, July 27, 1936.

75. ANS, 1R-7(1): Le Gouverneur-Général de l'AOF to Ministre des Colonies, July 27, 1936.

76. ANS, 1R-7(1): Le Gouverneur-Général de l'AOF to Ministre des Colonies, July 27, 1936.

77. ANOM, INDO NF 2279: Le Gouverneur-Général de l'Indochine to Ministre des Colonies, April 16, 1937.

78. VNA, RST, S.67/S.87 75782: Le Gouverneur Général de l'Indochine to Messieurs les Chefs de l'Administration Locale, February 22, 1937; ANOM, Indo NF 55: Gouverneur Général de l'Indochine to Ministre des Colonies, April 27, 1937.

79. VNA 1, RST S.67/S.87 75782: Le Résident Supérieur au Tonkin to Messieurs les Résidents Chefs de province et Commandants de territoire militaire, September 22, 1937.

80. VNA 1, RST S.67/S.87 75782: Résident Supérieur au Tonkin to Gouverneur Général de l'Indochine, May 27, 1937; VNA 1, RST S.67/S.87 75782: Gouverneur Général de l'Indochine to Résident Supérieur au Tonkin, August 9, 1937.

81. VNA 1, RST S.67/S.87 75782: Le Résident Supérieur au Tonkin to Résidents Chefs de province et Commandants de territoire militaire, September 22, 1937.

82. VNA 1, RST M.2/N.01 75357: Vœux addressés à la commission d'enquête d'outre-mer concernant l'alimentation indigène et l'assistance sociale, undated.

83. Justin Godart, *Rapport de mission en Indochine, 1er Janvier -14 mars 1937* (Paris: L'Harmattan, 1994), 65, 177.

84. VNA 1, RST S.67/S.87 75782: Le Gouverneur Général P.I. de l'Indochine A. Silvestre to Ministre des Colonies, Saigon, December 10, 1936.

85. VNA 1, RST S.67/S.87 75782: Moutet to Messieurs les Gouverneurs Généraux des Colonies, February 10, 1937.

86. Thomas, *French Empire*, 287–88; Viollis became an editor of the pro-Popular Front journal *Vendredi* in 1935. On Viollis's attitude toward the Popular Front, see Nicola Cooper, "Colonial Humanism in the 1930s: The Case of Andrée Viollis," *French Cultural Studies* 17, no. 2 (2006): 189–205; J. Jackson, *Popular Front in France*, 116.

87. Catherine Coquery-Vidrovitch, "The Popular Front and the Colonial Question: French West Africa, an Example of Reformist Colonialism" in *French Colonial Empire and the Popular Front: Hope and Disillusion*, edited by Tony Chafer and Amanda Sackur (New York: Palgrave Macmillan, 1999).

88. ANOM, 17G-252: Commission d'Enquête dans les Territoires de la France d'Outre-Mer, Procès-verbal de la Séance Inaugurale, Tenue le Jeudi 8 Juillet, à 15 heures au ministre des colonies.

89. ANOM, GGI 53496: Le Directeur de l'enquête à la Commission d'enquête dans les Territoires d'outre-mer à M. le Gouverneur Général de l'Indochine, Janvier 29, 1938; ANOM, 17G-252: Commission d'Enquête dans les Territoires de la France d'Outre-Mer, Procès-verbal de la Séance Inaugurale, Tenue le Jeudi 8 Juillet, à 15 heures au ministre des colonies.

90. ANOM, 110COL925: Enquête N. 1 sur l'alimentation des Indigènes, December 30, 1937.

91. ANOM, Guernut 24: Note sur les dispositions à prendre pour éviter le retour de la famine dans les colonies, July 22, 1936.

92. ANOM, Guernut 34: letter to M. le Président du Conseil, June 21, 1937.

93. ANOM, GGI 53496: Note pour les représentants du service de santé qui auront à répondre au questionnaire, undated.

94. ANOM, GGI 53496: Note pour les représentants du service de santé qui auront à répondre au questionnaire, undated.

95. ANOM, GGI 53496: Note pour les représentants du service de santé qui auront à répondre au questionnaire, undated.

96. ANOM, GGI 53496: Nguyên Van Huyên, "Une enquête sur l'alimentation annamite," undated.

97. ANOM, 61COL2853: Enquête n. 1-C, Gabon, subdivision d'Oyem, Marcel M'vet, Moniteur Stagiaire de l'Ecole Regionale d'Oyem, May 21, 1938.

98. ANOM, 61COL 2853: Enquête n. 1C, AEF, Moyen-Congo, Subdivision de Divénié, Gilles Akina, Ecrivain auxiliaire, May 31, 1938.

99. ANOM, 61COL2853: En réponse au questionnaire n. 1c (Alimentation des indigènes), Moyen-Congo, Département du Haut-Ogooué, André Tany, Ecrivain-Auxiliaire, undated.

100. ANOM, 61COL2853: Réponses aux questions de l'enquête 1/c sur l'alimentation des indigènes, Félix Jean-Tchicaye, Comptable au centre de sous-ordonnancement, Pointe-Noire, June 28, 1938.

101. ANOM, Guernut 92: Enquête n. 1-c, Province de Nam Dinh, Lê Van Thân, instituteur de 3è cl.; ANOM, Guernut 92: Enquête n. 1-B, province de Nam Dinh, rapport présenté par M. A. Jacquet, ingénieur de 1ère classe des travaux d'agriculture; ANOM, Guernut 92: Enquête n. 1-C, Province de Nam Dinh, Nguyên Ngoc Nhuong, instituteur stagiaire.

102. ANOM, Guernut 92: Enquête n. 1-C, Province de Nam Dinh, Thanh Thê Vy, Instituteur de 8è classe.

103. VNA 1, RST N.01 75357–05: Rapport sur le Niveau de Vie des Travailleurs Agricoles au Tonkin, 1938.

104. VNA 1, RST N.01 75357–05: Rapport sur le Niveau de Vie des Travailleurs Agricoles au Tonkin, 1938.

105. ANOM, Indo NF 55: Pierre Varet, "La lutte contre la faim: hommes et riz au Tonkin," undated.

106. VNA 1, RST N.01 75357–05: Rapport sur le Niveau de Vie des Travailleurs Agricoles au Tonkin, 1938.

107. ANOM, RSTNF 00265: l'Administrateur J. Massimi, Résident de France à Haidong to Résident-Supérieur au Tonkin, undated; ANOM, NF 1858: Le Gouvernur-Général de l'Indochine to Ministre des Colonies, October 15, 1937.

108. ANOM, RSTNF 00265: Note d'ensemble sur les problèmes essentiels évoqués par les vœux d'ordre social, undated. On shortage in Tonkin in 1937, see ANOM, RSTNF 00761; ANOM, RSTNF 4409.

109. ANOM, RSTNF 00265: Vœu de M. E. Chouquet, undated; ANOM, RSTNF 00265: Vœu de M. Hong Tan, Conseiller provincial à Nam-Truc, Nam Dinh, undated.

110. ANOM, RSTNF 00265: Vœu de M. Cat Van Tran, Tri-Phu en retraite demeurant à Sontay, undated.

111. ANOM, RSTNF 00265: Note d'ensemble sur les problèmes essentiels évoqués par les vœux d'ordre social, undated.

112. Godart, *Rapport de mission*, 116.

113. Albert Memmi, *The Colonizer and the Colonized* (Boston: Beacon Press, 1965), 76.

114. ANOM, Guernut 40: Etudes des disettes et famines, undated.

115. ANOM, Guernut 40: Alimentation des Indigènes de l'Algérie, Documents réunis par ordre de M. Georges le Beau, Gouverneur Général de l'Algérie, 1937.

116. ANOM, Guernut 40: Maladies à étiologie alimentaire.

117. ANOM, Guernut 40: Maladies à étiologie alimentaire.

118. ANOM, Guernut 40: Etudes des disettes et famines, undated.

119. ANOM, Guernut 40: Etudes des disettes et famines, undated.

120. ANOM, Guernut 40: Alimentation des Indigènes de l'Algérie, Documents réunis par ordre de M. Georges le Beau, Gouverneur Général de l'Algérie, 1937.

121. ANOM, Guernut 40: Commission Consultative de l'Alimentation des Indigènes, Séance du 19 Juin, 1937.

122. ANOM, Guernut 24: Note sur les dispositions à prendre pour éviter le retour de la famine dans les colonies, July 22, 1936.

123. Sarraut, *Mise en valeur*, 84.

124. ANOM, Guernut 34: Enquête dans les Territoires d'Outre-Mer, Maroc, le problème alimentaire.

125. ANOM, Guernut 34: letter to M. le Président du Conseil, June 21, 1937.

126. Mesures prises pour lutter contre la famine et la maladie, note presentée au Conseil du Gouvernement du 25 Juin, 1937, Résidence Général de la République Française au Maroc.

127. VNA 1, DFI T.4/T.037 12009: Gouverneur Général de l'Indochine to M. le Résident Supérieur en Annam, July 20, 1937; ANOM, Résident Supérieur au Tonkin to Gouverneur Général de l'Indochine, October 31, 1937.

128. The sums reported vary from less than a million francs to over twelve million.

129. The phrase "to govern is to foresee" was used by the nineteenth-century politician and press baron Émile de Girardin, who, for François Ewald, represented a new mode of governance according to a logic of insurance that subdivided and collectivized risk. Ewald, *Birth of Solidarity*, 133. See also VNA 1, RST S.67 74060: Crayssag, "Prévoyance Sociale, Une Caisse de secours pour les sinistrés," in "France-Indochine," May 1937; ANOM, RSTNF 00265: Le Résident-Supérieur au Tonkin to Messieurs les Résidents Chefs de Province et Commandants de Territoire Militaire, undated.

130. ANOM, RSTAF 46483: Dau Van Zu to M. le Ministre de l'Intérieur, November 18, 1937; ANOM, NF 1858: Le Résident Supérieur au Tonkin to M. le Gouverneur Général de l'Indochine, December 2, 1937.

131. VNA 1, RST S.67/S.87 75782: Résident Supérieur au Tonkin to M. le Gouverneur Général de l'Indochine, September 22, 1937.

132. VNA 1, DFI T.4/T.037 12009: Résident Supérieur en Annam to M. le Gouverneur-Général de l'Indochine, June 15, 1937.

133. VNA 1, RST L.6 75778: Procès-verbal de la Réunion du Comité provincial d'Approvisionnement de Haiphong, January 11, 1939.

134. ANOM, NF 1858: Pétition à Messieurs les Présidents et Membres de la Chambres des Députés et du Sénat présentée par les Conseils Provinciaux du Tonkin en faveur des populations sinistrées, undated; ANOM, NF 1858: Théodore Steeg to Monsieur Honel, Député de la seine, March 9, 1938.

135. ANOM, NF 1858: Pétition à Messieurs les Présidents et Membres de la Chambres des Députés et du Sénat présentée par les Conseils Provinciaux du Tonkin en faveur des populations sinistrées, undated; ANOM, NF 1858: Théodore Steeg to Monsieur Honel, Député de la seine, March 9, 1938.

136. ANOM, NF 1858: Le Président du Comité d'initiative des Conseils Provinciaux du Tonkin en faveur des inondés to M. Marius Moutet, November 21, 1937.

137. ANOM, RSTNF 00265: Pétition à Messieurs les présidents et membres de la Chambre des Députés et du Sénat présentée par les Conseils Provinciaux du Tonkin en faveur des populations sinistrées, undated.

138. ANOM, NF 1858: Comité national de secours aux victimes des inondations de l'Indochine, undated.

139. ANOM, NF 2387: M. le Colonel Bernard to Commission d'enquête, October 28, 1937; ANOM, GGI NF 2387: M. V. Belisaire, Chef de la province de Biên Hoà to M. le Directeur des Bureaux, February 19, 1938.

140. ANOM, GGI NF 2387: l'Administrateur Chef de la Province de Thudaumot to Gouverneur de la Cochinchine, February 23, 1938; ANOM, FM, Guernut 24: le Gouverneur de la Cochinchine to Gouverneur Général de l'Indochine, March 11, 1938.

141. ANOM, INDO NF 1850: "Lettre ouverte à Monsieur le Député de la Cochinchine à Paris," *Journal de Paysan*, June 9, 1938.

142. ANOM, RSTNF 4884: Le Chef local des services de police to Résident supérieur au Tonkin, January 26, 1938.

143. ANOM, RSTNF 4549: Maire de la Ville de Hanoi to Résident Supérieur du Tonkin, October 7, 1937.

144. VNA 1, RST S.67 74060: Crayssag, "Prévoyance Sociale, Une Caisse de secours pour les sinistrés," in "France-Indochine," May 1937.

145. VNA 1, RST L.6 75778: Le Gouverneur-Général de l'Indochine [Brevié] to Messieurs les Chefs d'Administration locale, June 1, 1938; VNA 1, RST L.6 75778: Le Gouverneur Général de l'Indochine [Brevié] to M. le Résident Supérieur au Tonkin, 1938; VNA 1, RST L.6 75778: Note pour M. le Chef du 5ème bureau, August 13, 1938.

146. VNA 1, RST L.6 75778: Le Président de la Chambre de Commerce de Haiphong to M. l'Administrateur-Maire de la Ville de Haiphong, September 22, 1938.

147. ANOM, NF 2488: M. Boisson, Inspecteur de 2ème classe, Rapport sur la situation économique de l'Indochine, 1930.

148. ANS, 1R-7(1): Le Gouverneur du Soudan Français to Gouverneur-Général de l'Afrique Occidentale Française, February 5, 1938.

149. ANS, 1R-7(1): Louveau to Gouverneur Côte d'Ivoire, March 3, 1938; ANS, 1R-7(1): Louveau to Gouverneur Côte d'Ivoire, February 26, 1938.

150. ANS, 1R-7(1): Lecorvaisier to Gouverneur Côte d'Ivoire, February 18, 1938.

151. ANOM, 61COL591: Gouverneur-Général de l'AOF, Colonie du Niger, Rapport Économique 1937.

152. Roberts, *Two Worlds of Cotton*, 223–48; Jean Filipovitch, "Destined to Fail: Forced Settlement at the Office du Niger," *Journal of African History* 42 (2001): 239–60.

153. André Thiellement, "Menaces de Famine au Niger" in *Derniers Chefs d'un Empire*, edited by Pierre Gentil and André Soucadaux (Paris: Académie des Sciences d'Outre-Mer, 1972).

7. Losing Control in Vietnam, 1945

1. Tran Van Mai, "Who Committed this Crime?" in Ngô Viñh Long, *Before the Revolution*, 221–27.

2. Ngô Viñh Long, *Before the Revolution*, 237–46.

3. Bùi Minh Dung, "Japan's Role in the Vietnamese Starvation of 1944–45," *Modern Asian Studies* 20, no. 3 (July 1995): 573–618.

4. The currency in circulation increased from 235 million piastres in 1939 to 1.3 billion piastres in 1945. The price of a quintal (100 kg) of rice increased from thirty piastres in 1940 to six hundred piastres in 1945. Nguyên Thê Anh, "Japanese Food Policies and the 1945 Great Famine in Indochina" in *Food Supplies and the Japanese Occupation in Southeast Asia*, edited by Paul H. Kratoska (New York: St. Martin's Press, 1998); Bose, 699–727.

5. Gregg Huff, following the terminology of Michael Ellman, classifies the Great Famine as "Food Availability Deficit II," a situation in which available food declined but not so much that optimal distribution would have failed to prevent famine deaths. Huff, *Causes and Consequences*, 286–316.

6. For a similarly international approach to Algeria, see Matthew Connelly, *A Diplomatic Revolution: Algeria's Fight for Independence and the Origins of the Post-Cold War Era* (Oxford: Oxford University Press, 2002); Jennifer Johnson, *The Battle for Algeria: Sovereignty, Health Care, and Humanitarianism* (Philadelphia: University of Pennsylvania Press, 2016).

7. Anghie, *Imperialism, Sovereignty*, 92–100.

8. Pedersen, *Guardians*.

9. Pearson, *Colonial Politics*.

10. Ken Maclean, "History Reformatted: Vietnam's Great Famine (1944–45) in Archival Form," *Southeast Asian Studies* 5, no. 2 (August 2016): 187–218.

11. Krasner distinguishes between the authority and the control elements of sovereignty. Stephen D. Krasner, *Sovereignty: Organized Hypocrisy* (Princeton: Princeton University Press, 1999). See also Steven Press, *Rogue Empires: Contracts and Conmen in Europe's Scramble for Africa* (Cambridge, MA: Harvard University Press, 2017); Leonard V. Smith, *Sovereignty at the Paris Peace Conference of 1919* (Oxford: Oxford University Press, 2018).

12. David G. Marr, *Vietnamese Tradition on Trial, 1920–1945* (Berkeley: University of California Press, 1981); Hue-Tam HoTai, *Radicalism and Origins*.

13. Bùi Minh Dung, "Japan's Role," 573–618.

14. Jean Decoux, *A la Barre de l'Indochine* (Paris: Plon, 1949), 267; ANOM, Indo, NF 1152: Développements économiques en extrême-orient au cours des 6 mois se terminant le 31/12/1944.

15. Jennings, *Vichy in the Tropics*, 162–98; Nguyen-Marshall, *Moral Authority*, 58–76.

16. ANOM, FM INDO NF 2749: *Programme d'action sociale et culturelle*, 1944.

17. ANOM, RSTNF 3893: Vice-amiral d'escadre Jean Decoux to Messieurs les chefs de l'administration locale, July 4, 1942.

18. ANOM, RSTNF 1387: Rapport d'inspection, Haiphong, May 17, 1943.

19. ANOM, RSTNF 01413: Rapport d'inspection effectué les 24 et 25 février, 1945, Provinces de Hà Nam, Ninh Binh, Nam Dinh, Thai Binh, Hung Yén, Hai Duong.

20. ANOM, RSTNF 01413: Rapport d'inspection effectué les 24 et 25 février, 1945, Provinces de Hà Nam, Ninh Binh, Nam Dinh, Thai Binh, Hung Yén, Hai Duong; VNA 1, RST S.67 74524: M. Nguyên Huu Thu, Président suppléant du tribunal provincial à Thai-Nguyen to M. le Résident de France à Thai-Nguyen, March 1, 1945.

21. VNA 1, RST S.67 74524: L'Ingénieur en Chef de la circonscription du Tonkin (G. Simonet) to M. le Résident Supérieur au Tonkin, March 5, 1945.

22. VNA 1, RST S.67 74524: l'Administrateur Résident de France à Namdinh (Charles Jeannin) to M. l'Ingénieur Chef de la troisième subdivision d'hydraulique agricole à Namdinh, February 22, 1945.

23. David G. Marr, *Vietnam 1945: The Quest for Power* (Berkeley: University of California Press, 1995), 100–40.

24. MEP, 2829: Compte-rendu de l'exercice 1943–44.

25. MEP, 2829: Chaize to Père Procureur, February 11, 1945.

26. MEP, 2829: Au Tonkin, Une mission dans la tourmente, Le Vicariat Apostolique de Hanoi, 1947.

27. MEP, 2829: Chaize to Gros, September 12, 1945.

28. MEP, 2829: Compte-Rendu de l'exercice 1944–45.

29. MEP, 2829: Chaize to Père Procureur, February 11, 1945.

30. Gaston Rueff, "The Future of French Indochina," *Foreign Affairs*, October 1944.

31. Gaston Rueff, "Postwar Problems of French Indo-China: Economic Aspects," *Pacific Affairs* 18, no. 2 (June 1945): 137–55.

32. Xiaoyuan Liu, "China and the Issue of Postwar Indochina in the Second World War," *Modern Asian Studies* 33, no. 2 (May 1999): 445–82.

33. Marr, *Vietnam 1945*, 270–330.

34. Martin Thomas, "Free France, the British Government and the Future of French Indo-China, 1940–45," *Journal of Southeast Asian Studies* 28, no. 1 (March 1997): 137–60; John J. Sbrega, "The Anticolonial Policies of Franklin D. Roosevelt: A Reappraisal," *Political Science Quarterly* 101, no. 1 (1986): 65–84.

35. Marr, *Vietnam 1945*, 260.

36. ANOM, Indo NF 1151: Note à l'attention de M. le Directeur Général de la Direction Générale des Etudes et Recherches, September 17, 1945.

37. Andrée Viollis, *Indochine S.O.S.*, 27.

38. Marr, *Vietnam 1945*, 328.

39. Robert O. Paxton, *Vichy France: Old Guard and New Order, 1940–1944* (New York: Columbia University Press, 1972).

40. ANOM, Indo NF 1150: Note sur la situation en Indochine en Septembre 1944.

41. William J. Duiker, *Ho Chi Minh: A Life* (New York: Theia, 2000), 253–56.

42. Mission Indochinoise d'Information, *Ici Tananarive: L'Empire libre parle à l'Indochine!* (Tananarive, Madagascar: Imprimerie Officielle, 1945), 8, 12.

43. ANOM, Indo NF 1150: Note sur la situation en Indochine en Septembre 1944.

44. ANOM, Indo NF 1152: Développements économiques en extrême-orient au cours des 6 mois se terminant le 31/12/1944.

45. ANOM, Indo NF 2740: Situation économique, 1944.

46. ANOM, Indo NF 1150: Note sur la situation en Indochine en Septembre 1944.

47. ANOM, Indo NF 1267: Direction de l'information et de la documentation, Télégramme Presfrance de New York, undated.

48. ANOM, Indo NF 1152: L'inspecteur des colonies de Raymond, Chef de la Mission Coloniale Française en Extrême-Orient to M. le Ministre des Colonies, Calcutta, June 5, 1945.

49. ANOM, Indo NF 1152: Longeaux to Ministre des Colonies, September 14, 1945.

50. ANOM, Indo NF 1151: Note à l'attention de M. le Directeur Général de la Direction Générale des Etudes et Recherches, September 17, 1945.

51. Jean-J. Bernardini, *Sous la Botte Nipponne* (Paris: la Pensée Universelle, 1971), 24.

52. ANOM, Indo NF 1362: l'Amiral d'Argenlieu, Haut Commissaire de France pour l'Indochine to M. le Commissaire de la République en Cochinchine, September 26, 1945.

53. ANOM, Indo NF 1152: Le Ministre des Colonies to M. l'Inspecteur des Colonies de Raymond, July 26, 1945.

54. ANOM, Indo NF 1152: Note à l'attention de M. le Directeur Général de la Direction Générale des Etudes et Recherches, September 12, 1945.

55. Marr, *Vietnam 1945*, 494.

56. André Blanchet, "Les Japonais sont responsables de la grande famine de 1945," *Le Monde*, March 8, 1946.

57. Jessica Reinisch, "Internationalism and Relief: The Birth (and Death) of UNRRA," *Past and Present* (2011), supplement 6.

58. UNA, UNRRA S-0518-0526, 670: Dorothy Grant Jacqueline, "Brief preliminary survey to be used as a background for the study of relief and rehabilitation problems," July 5, 1944.

59. UNA, UNRRA, S-1220-0000-0041: French Indo-China, Explanatory Note, April 17, 1945.

60. UNA, UNRRA S-0518-0526, 400: Herbert Lehman to Christian Valensi, September 28, 1944.

61. UNA, UNRRA S-0518-0526, 400: Christian Valensi to Herbert Lehman, February 8, 1945.

62. UNA, UNRRA, S-1220-0000-0041: French Indo-China, Explanatory Note, April 17, 1945.

63. UNA, UNRRA, S-1421-0000-0053: Benjamin Kizer, Chunking, to Washington D.C., October 1, 1945.

64. UNA, UNRRA S-1220-0000-0041: Chapman to Powers, September 9, 1945; UNA, UNRRA, S-1545-0000-0038: Memorandum from F.D. Harris, November 28, 1945.

65. UNA, UNRRA, S-1537-0000-0150: Director General Herbert Lehman to Bonnet, November 7, 1945.

66. UNA, UNRRA, S-1545-0000-0038: J Franklin Ray, Jr. to David Weintraub, October 3, 1945.

67. ANOM, Indo NF 1152: Telegram from Bonnet, Washington, October 16, 1945; UNA, UNRRA S-1220-0000-0041: Lehman to French Ambassador, October 3, 1945.

68. UNA, UNRRA, S-1537-0000-0150: J. Franklin Ray to A.H. Feller, November 2, 1945; UNA, UNRRA S-0518-0526, 400: J. Franklin Ray to Benjamin Kizer, November 8, 1945.

69. UNA, UNRRA, S-1537-0000-0150: Alexander B. Hawes to Franklin Ray, November 5, 1945.

70. UNA, UNRRA, S-1545-0000-0038: J. Franklin Ray, Jr. to Roy F. Hendrickson, January 31, 1946; UNA, UNRRA, S-1545-0000-0038: Henri Bonnet to Herbert H. Lehman, January 30, 1946; UNA, UNRRA, S-1545-0000-0110: Minutes of the Twenty-Fourth Far Eastern Staff Meeting, November 28, 1945; UNA, UNRRA, S-0518-0526 723: Lehman to Ambassador for the French Republic, February 2, 1946.

71. UNA, UNRRA, S-1537-0000-0150: C. B. Chapman, Shanghai Branch, to Chief of Mission UNRRA Manila, November 6, 1945.

72. UNA, UNRRA, S-1220-0000-0041: Chapman to Powers, September 22, 1945, Hanoi.

73. UNA, UNRRA, S-1537-0000-0150: C. B. Chapman, Shanghai Branch, to Chief of Mission UNRRA Manila, November 6, 1945.

74. Liu, "China and Postwar Indochina," 480.

75. ANOM, Indo NF 1426: Plan d'industrialisation de l'Indochine, January 1946.

76. ANOM, INDO NF 1426: Comité de l'hydraulique agricole, Saigon, July 16, 1946.

77. ANOM, Indo NF 1267: Moutet to Haussaire Indo Saigon, undated.

78. ANOM, Indo, NF 1362: Haut-Commissaire de la France pour l'Indochine to Bousquet, Ministère de la France d'Outre-Mer, May 27, 1947.

79. ANOM, Indo NF 1269: Stan Swinton, "En Indochine 2 Millions d'individus peuvent mourir de faim ou de froid dans le courant de l'année prochaine," New York Herald Tribune, January 15, 1946.

80. David Marr, Vietnamese Anticolonialism, 1885–1925 (Berkeley: University of California Press, 1971).

81. ANOM, INDO/NF/1192: Traduction d'un appel du parti Dong Minh Hoi distribué le 7.7.45 par la section yunnanaise du parti, July 19, 1945.

82. Nguyên Thê Anh, "Japanese Food Policies," 221.

83. MEP, 2829: Compte rendu de l'exercice 1945–46.

84. Temoignages et Documents Français Relatifs à la colonization Française au Viet-Nam (Hanoi: Association culturelle pour le salut du Viet-Nam, 1945).

85. Temoignages et Documents, IV–39.

86. Coang Van Duc, Comment la révolution a triomphé de la famine (Editions de l'office d'information de la république du Viet-Nam, April 10, 1946), 3–4.

87. Coang Van Duc, Comment la révolution, 12–24.

88. Coang Van Duc, Comment la révolution, 36.

89. Maclean, "History Reformatted," 200.

Epilogue

1. F. Cooper, *Citizenship between Empire and Nation;* Wilder, *Freedom Time.*

2. Meredith Terretta, *Nation of Outlaws, State of Violence: Nationalism, Grassfields Tradition, and State Building in Cameroon* (Athens: Ohio University Press, 2014); Thomas Deltombe, Manuel Domergue, and Jacob Tatsitsa, *Kamerun! Une guerre cachée aux origines de la Françafrique (1948–1971)* (Paris: La Découverte, 2011).

3. Léon Pales, *Le Bilan de la Mission Anthropologique de l'A.O.F.* (Dakar: Direction Générale de la Santé Publique, 1948); Léon Pales and Marie Tassin de Saint Péreuse, *Raciologie comparative des populations de l'afrique occidentale: Cartes de répartition de la stature, de l'indice cormique et de l'indice céphalique en Afrique Occidentale,* Mission anthropologique de l'A.O.F., 1954. See also Barbara M. Cooper, "The Gender of Nutrition in French West Africa: Military Medicine, Intra-Colonial Marginality and Ethnos Theory in the Making of Malnutrition in Niger" in *Health and Difference: Rendering Human Variation in Colonial Engagements,* edited by Alexandra Widmer and Veronika Lipphardt (New York: Berghahn, 2016); Vincent Bonnecase, *La Pauvreté au Sahel: du savoir colonial à la mesure internationale* (Paris: Karthala, 2011), 16.

4. Sibeud, "Useless Colonial Science?" S92; Pearson, *Colonial Politics,*154–63.

5. On African successor states, see Mahmood Mamdani, *Citizen and Subject: Contemporary Africa and the Legacy of Late Colonialism* (Princeton, NJ: Princeton University Press, 1996).

6. Mann, *From Empires to NGOs,* 170–208; Rossi, *From Slavery to Aid,* chapter 5.

7. Achille Mbembe, *On the Postcolony* (Berkeley: University of California Press, 2001); Frederick Cooper, *Africa since 1940: The Past of the Present* (Cambridge: Cambridge University Press, 2005); Adom Getachew, *Worldmaking after Empire: The Rise and Fall of Self-determination* (Princeton: Princeton University Press, 2019); Anghie, *Imperialism, Sovereignty,* 247–54.

8. On a technical-political dualism in humanitarian thinking, see Alex de Waal, *Famine Crimes: Politics and the Disaster Relief Industry in Africa* (Bloomington: Indiana University Press, 1997), 1–4.

9. Partha Chatterjee, "Empires, Nations, Peoples: The Imperial Prerogative and Colonial Exceptions," *Thesis Eleven* 139, no. 1 (2017): 84–96.

Bibliography

Archives

ANOM	Archives nationales d'outre-mer, Aix-en-Provence
ANS	Archives nationales du Sénégal, Dakar
ASOM	Bibliothèque Félix Houphouët-Boigny de l'académie des sciences d'outre-mer, Paris
BNF	Bibliothèque nationale de France, Paris
MEP	Missions étrangères de Paris
SMEP	Société des missions évangéliques de Paris
UNA	United Nations Archives, New York
VNA 1	Vietnam National Archives Center 1, Hanoi

Newspapers and Periodicals

L'Akhbar
Annales d'hygiène et de médecine coloniales
Annales de médecine et de pharmacie coloniales
L'Avenir du Tonkin
Bulletin économique de l'Indochine
Le Courrier d'Haiphong
Le Courrier d'Oran
L'Echo Annamite
L'Eveil Économique de l'Indochine
l'Événement
Le Figaro
Illustration: Journal Universel
Le Journal
L'Indochine: Revue Économique d'Extrême-Orient
Moniteur de l'Algérie
Moniteur Universel
Le Petit Parisien
Le Populaire
Le Siècle
Le Temps

Published Primary Sources

Agnély. *Le Criquet Pèlerin*. Alger, 1866.

Ancien officier de l'armée d'afrique. *l'Algérie devant l'assemblée nationale: causes des insurrections algériennes*. Versailles, 1871.

Bérard, Aristide. *l'Algérie: sa situation présente, son avenir*. Paris, 1868.

Bernardini, Jean-J. *Sous la Botte Nipponne*. Paris, 1971.

Blanchet, André. "Les Japonais sont responsables de la grande famine de 1945." *Le Monde*, March 8, 1946.

Bourgeois, Léon. *Solidarité*. Paris, 1896.

Burnet, Étienne, and Wallace Aykroyd. *Nutrition and Public Health*. Geneva, 1935.

Burzet. *Histoire des Désastres de l'Algérie: 1866, 1867, 1868*. Alger, 1869.

Césaire, Aimé. *Discourse on Colonialism*. New York, 1972.

Coang Van Duc. *Comment la révolution a triomphé de la famine*. 1946.

Commission Centrale chargée de la répartition des fonds de secours. Procès-verbaux des Séances. Alger, 1866.

IIe congrès scientifique international de l'alimentation: Compte rendu des séances et discussions des rapports. Alençon, 1937.

Cuvier, Ch. *Compte Rendu des dons reçus par M. Ch. Cuvier en faveur des victimes de la famine en Algérie*. Strasbourg, 1868.

Decoux, Jean. *A la Barre de l'Indochine*. Paris, 1949.

Direction des affaires politiques et de la Sûreté Générale. *Contribution à l'histoire des mouvements politiques de l'Indochine française, Vol. 5, La Terreur Rouge en Annam, 1930–1931*. 1934.

Durkheim, Émile. *The Division of Labor in Society*. New York, 1984.

Eijkman, Christiaan. "Antineuritic Vitamin and Beriberi," Nobel Lecture. 1929.

Enquête Agricole: Algérie. Paris, 1870.

La Famine en Algérie et les discours officiels: Erreurs et contradictions. Constantine, Algérie, 1868.

Fanon, Frantz. *The Wretched of the Earth*. New York, 1963.

Final Report of the Mixed Committee of the League of Nations on the Relation of Nutrition to Health, Agriculture, and Economic Policy. 1937.

Godart, Justin. *Rapport de mission en Indochine, 1er Janvier–14 mars 1937*. Paris, 1994.

Grauclaude, Henri le. *Les eaux, disciplinées, ont mis en déroute la famine*. Hue, 1933.

Hardy, Georges. *Nos Grands Problèmes Coloniaux*. Paris, 1929.

Hardy, Georges, and Charles Richet, eds. *l'Alimentation indigène dans les colonies françaises*. Paris, 1933.

Hoang Cao Khai. *En Annam*. Hanoi, 1909.

Hilaire, J. *Du Congo au Nil: Ouaddaï . . . Cinq ans d'arrêt!* Marseille, 1930.

Joseph, Gaston. *Koffi: Roman vrai d'un noir*. Paris, 1922.

Lacretelle, Charles Nicolas. *L'Algérie au point de vue de la crise actuelle*. Lyon, 1868.

Lavigerie, Charles. *Les Orphelins Arabes d'Alger: Leur passé, leur présent, leur avenir*. 1875.

Leroy-Beaulieu, Paul. *De la colonisation chez les peoples modernes*. Paris, 1874.

Londres, Albert. *Terre d'ébène*. Paris, 1998.

Maran, René. *Batouala: Véritable Roman Nègre*. Paris, 1921.

Mission indochinoise d'information. *Ici Tananarive: L'Empire libre parle à l'Indochine!* Tananarive, Madagascar, 1945.

Moran, Denise. *Tchad.* Montrouge, France, 1934.

Pales, Léon. *Le Bilan de la Mission Anthropologique de l'A.O.F.* Dakar, 1948.

Pales, Léon, and Marie Tassin de Saint Péreuse. *Raciologie comparative des populations de l'afrique occidentale: Cartes de répartition de la stature, de l'indice cormique et de l'indice céphalique en Afrique Occidentale.* Mission Anthropologique de l'A.O.F., 1954.

Pasquier, Pierre. "La Politique Française en Indochine." *La Revue du Paçifique,* July 15, 1930.

Philastre, P. L. F. *Le Code Annamite.* Paris, 1876.

Première Conférence Internationale pour la Protection contre les Calamités Naturelles. Paris,1938.

Puyau, Charles. *De l'Impuissance des bureaux arabes et des réformes à introduire en Algérie.* Alger, 1871.

Renner, G. T. "A Famine Zone in Africa: the Sudan." In *Geographical Review* 16, no. 4 (October 1926): 583–96.

Report of the Indian Famine Commission. London, 1880.

Robiou de la Tréhonnais, F. *L'Agriculture en Algérie: Rapport à son excellence M. le Maréchal de Mac-Mahon, duc de Magenta.* Alger, 1867.

Roubaud, Louis. *Viet Nam: La tragédie indochinoise.* Paris, 2010.

Rueff, Gaston. "The Future of French Indochina." *Foreign Affairs,* October 1944.

———. "Postwar Problems of French Indo-China: Economic Aspects." *Pacific Affairs* 18, no. 2 (June 1945).

Sarraut, Albert. *Grandeur et servitude coloniales.* Paris, 2012.

———. "The Indivisibility of Peace and the Inseparability of East and West." *Pacific Affairs* 9, no. 4 (December 1936): 509–14.

———. *La Mise en Valeur des Colonies Françaises.* Paris, 1923.

La Science de l'Alimentation en 1937. Alençon, 1937.

Témoignages et Documents Français Relatifs à la Colonisation Française au Viet-Nam. Hanoi, 1945.

Thiellement, André. "Menaces de Famine au Niger." In *Derniers Chefs d'un Empire,* edited by Pierre Gentil and André Soucadaux. Paris, 1972.

Tocqueville, Alexis de. *Letters on Algeria.* In *Writings on Empire and Slavery,* edited by Jennifer Pitts. Baltimore, 2001.

Treille, Georges. *Principes d'Hygiène Coloniale.* Paris, 1899.

Turgot, Anne Robert Jacques. *Lettres sur la Liberté des Grains.* Paris, 2015.

Viollis, Andrée. "L'adieu de M. Reynaud à l'Indochine." *Le Petit Parisien,* November 20, 1931.

———. *Indochine S.O.S.* Paris, 1949.

———. "M. Paul Reynaud est à Hanoï." *Le Petit Parisien,* November 9, 1931.

———. Andrée Viollis, "Quelques notes sur l'Indochine." *l'Ésprit,* December 1933.

Secondary Sources

Abi-Mershed, Osama W. *Apostles of Modernity: Saint-Simonians and the Civilizing Mission in Algeria.* Stanford, CA, 2010.

Adas, Michael. *Machines as the Measure of Men: Science, Technology, and Ideologies of Western Dominance.* Ithaca, NY, 1989.

Ageron, Charles Robert. *Modern Algeria: A History from 1830 to the Present.* Translated by Michael Brett. Trenton, NJ, 1991.

d'Almeida-Topor, Hélène. "Les populations dahoméenes et le recrutement militaire pendant la première guerre mondiale." *Revue française d'histoire d'outre-mer* 60, no. 219 (1973): 196–241.

Amrith, Sunil, and Patricia Clavin. "Feeding the World: Connecting Europe and Asia, 1930–1945." *Past and Present* (2013), supplement 8.

Amster, Ellen. "The Syphilitic Arab? A Search for Civilization in Disease Etiology, Native Prostitution, and French Colonial Medicine." In *French Mediterraneans: Transnational and Imperial Histories*, edited by Patricia M. E. Lorcin and Todd Shepard. Lincoln, NE, 2016.

Andersen, Margaret Cook. *Regeneration Through Empire: French Pronatalists and Colonial Settlement in the Third Republic.* Lincoln, NE, 2015.

Anghie, Antony. *Imperialism, Sovereignty, and the Making of International Law.* Cambridge, 2004.

Arnold, David. *Famine: Social Crisis and Historical Change.* Oxford, 1988.

Azevedo, Mario J. *The Roots of Violence: A History of War in Chad.* New York, 1998.

Baier, Stephen. *An Economic History of Central Niger.* Oxford, 1980.

——. "Long Term Structural Change in the Economy of Central Niger." In B.K. Swartz and Raymond E. Dummett, *West African Culture Dynamics: Archaeological and Historical Perspectives.* New York, 1980.

Barnes, David S. *The Great Stink of Paris and the Nineteenth-Century Struggle against Filth and Germs.* Baltimore, 2006.

Barnett, Michael. *Empire of Humanity: A History of Humanitarianism.* Ithaca, NY, 2011.

Barona, Josep L. *The Problem of Nutrition: Experimental Science, Public Health and Economy in Europe, 1914–1945.* Brussels, 2010.

Bashford, Alison. *Global Population: History, Geopolitics, and Life on Earth.* New York, 2014.

Baty-Delalande, Hélène, and Pierre Masson, eds. *Gide & la question coloniale: Correspondance avec Marcel de Coppet, 1924–1950.* Lyon, 2020.

Bayart, Jean-François. *L'État en Afrique: La politique du ventre.* Paris, 1989.

Bayly, Susan. "French Anthropology and the Durkheimians in Colonial Indochina." *Modern Asian Studies* 34, no. 3 (July 2000): 581–622.

Berenson, Edward. *Heroes of Empire: Five Charismatic Men and the Conquest of Africa.* Berkeley, CA, 2011.

Beriss, David. "Culture-As-Race or Culture-As-Culture: Caribbean Ethnicity and the Ambiguity of Cultural Identity in French Society." In *Race in France: Interdisciplinary Perspectives on the Politics of Difference*, edited by Herrick Chapman and Lara L. Frader. New York, 2004.

Bernal, Martin. "The Nghe-Tinh Soviet Movement, 1930–31." *Past and Present* 92 (August 1981): 148–68.

Beusekom, Monica M. "From Underpopulation to Overpopulation: French Perceptions of Population, Environment, and Agricultural Development in

French Soudan (Mali), 1900–1960." *Environmental History* 4, no. 2 (April 1999): 198–219.

Boittin, Jennifer. "Black in France: The Language and Politics of Race in the Late Third Republic," *French Politics, Culture, and Society* 27, no. 2 (2009): 23–46.

Boltanski, Luc. *Distant Suffering: Morality, Media, and Politics.* Cambridge, 1999.

Bonnecase, Vincent. "Avoir faim en Afrique occidentale française: investigations et représentations coloniales (1920–1960)." *Revue d'histoire des sciences humaines* 21 (2009).

——. *La pauvreté au Sahel: du savoir colonial à la mesure internationale.* Paris, 2011.

Bose, Sugata. "Starvation Amidst Plenty: The Making of Famine in Bengal, Honan, and Tonkin, 1942–45." *Modern Asian Studies* 24, no. 4 (1990): 699–727.

Bouton, Cynthia A. *The Flour War: Gender, Class, and Community in Late Ancien Régime French Society.* University Park, PA, 1993.

Bowler, Peter J. *Evolution: The History of an Idea.* Berkeley, CA, 2003.

Brocheux, Pierre. "L'Implantation du mouvement communiste en Indochine française: Le cas du Nghe-Tinh (1930–1931)." *Revue d'histoire moderne et contemporaine* (January–March 1977): 49–77.

——. "The State and the 1930s Depression in French Indo-China." In *Weathering the Storm: The Economies of Southeast Asia in the 1930s Depression,* edited by Peter Boomgaard and Ian Brown. Singapore, 2001.

Brower, Benjamin Claude. *A Desert Named Peace: The Violence of France's Empire in the Algerian Sahara, 1844–1902.* New York, 2009.

Brubaker, Rogers. *Citizenship and Nationhood in France and Germany.* Cambridge, MA, 1992.

Bùi Minh Dung. "Japan's Role in the Vietnamese Starvation of 1944–45." *Modern Asian Studies* 20, no. 3 (1995): 573–618.

Cabanes, Bruno. *The Great War and the Origins of Humanitarianism, 1918–1924.* Cambridge, 2014.

Cameron, Sarah. *The Hungry Steppe: Famine, Violence, and the Making of Soviet Kazakhstan.* Ithaca, NY, 2018.

Canguilhem, Georges. *The Normal and the Pathological.* New York, 1991.

Caquel, Marie. "L'Impact du protectorat français sur l'industrie du poisson au Maroc." *French Cultural Studies* 26, no. 2 (2015): 197–208.

Carpenter, Kenneth J. *Beriberi, White Rice, and Vitamin B: A Disease, a Cause, a Cure.* Berkeley, CA, 2000.

Carroll, Christina. "Imperial Ideologies in the Second Empire: The Mexican Expedition and the *Royaume Arabe.*" *French Historical Studies* 42, no. 1 (February 2019): 67–100.

Chafer, Tony, and Amanda Sackur, eds. *French Colonial Empire and the Popular Front: Hope and Disillusion.* New York, 1999.

Chapman, Herrick, and Lara L. Frader, eds. *Race in France: Interdisciplinary Perspectives on the Politics of Difference.* New York, 2004.

Chatterjee, Partha. "Empires, Nations, Peoples: The Imperial Prerogative and Colonial Exceptions." *Thesis Eleven* 139, no. 1 (2017): 84–96.

Cherry, Haydon. *Down and Out in Saigon: Stories of the Poor in a Colonial City.* New Haven, CT, 2019.

Church, Christopher. *Paradise Destroyed: Catastrophe and Citizenship in the French Caribbean*. Lincoln, NE, 2017.

Clark, Anna. "Humanitarianism, Human Rights, and Biopolitics in the British Empire, 1890–1902." *Britain and the World 9*, no. 1 (2016): 96–115.

Clark, Hannah-Louise. "Of Jinn Theories and Germ Theories: Translating Microbes, Bacteriological Medicine, and Islamic Law in Algeria." *Osiris 36* (2021): 64–85.

Cole, Joshua. *The Power of Large Numbers: Population, Politics, and Gender in Nineteenth-Century France*. Ithaca, NY, 2000.

Conklin, Alice. "Faire Naître v. Faire du Noire: Race Regeneration in France and French West Africa, 1895–1940." In *Promoting the Colonial Idea: Propaganda and Visions of Empire in France,* edited by Tony Chafer and Amanda Sackur, New York, 2002.

——. *A Mission to Civilize: The Republican Idea of Empire in France and West Africa, 1895–1930*. Stanford, CA, 1997.

——. *In the Museum of Man: Race, Empire, and Anthropology in France, 1850–1950*. Ithaca, NY, 2013.

Connelly, Matthew. *A Diplomatic Revolution: Algeria's Fight for Independence and the Origins of the Post-Cold War Era*. Oxford, 2002.

Cooper, Barbara M. *Countless Blessings: A History of Childbirth and Reproduction in the Sahel*. Bloomington, IN, 2019.

——. "The Gender of Nutrition in French West Africa: Military Medicine, Intra-Colonial Marginality and Ethnos Theory in the Making of Malnutrition in Niger." In *Health and Difference: Rendering Human Variation in Colonial Engagements,* edited by Alexandra Widmer and Veronika Lipphardt. New York, 2016.

Cooper, Frederick. "Conflict and Connection: Rethinking Colonial African History." *American Historical Review 99,* no. 5 (1994): 1516–45.

——. *Colonialism in Question: Theory, Knowledge, History.* Berkeley, CA, 2005.

——. *Africa Since 1940: The Past of the Present*. Cambridge, 2005.

——. *Citizenship Between Empire and Nation: Remaking France and French Africa, 1945–1960*. Princeton, NJ, 2014.

Cooper, Nicola. "Colonial Humanism in the 1930s: The Case of Andrée Viollis." *French Cultural Studies 17,* no. 2 (2006): 189–205.

Coquery-Vidrovitch, Catherine, ed. "L'Afrique et la crise de 1930 (1924–1938)." Special issue of *Revue Française d'Histoire d'Outre-mer 63,* nos. 232–233 (1976): 375–84.

——. *Le Congo au temps des grandes compagnies concessionnaires, 1898–1930*. Paris, 1972.

——. "The Popular Front and the Colonial Question: French West Africa, An Example of Reformist Colonialism." In *French Colonial Empire and the Popular Front: Hope and Disillusion,* edited by Tony Chafer and Amanda Sackur. New York, 1999.

Cornet, Anne. *Histoire d'une famine: Rwanda 1927–1930*. Louvain-la-Neuve, Belgium, 1996.

Davis, Diana K. *Resurrecting the Granary of Rome: Environmental History and French Colonial Expansion in North Africa*. Athens, OH, 2007.

Davis, Mike. *Late Victorian Holocausts: El Niño Famines and the Making of the Third World*. London, 2001.

Daughton, J. P. *An Empire Divided: Religion, Republicanism, and the Making of French Colonialism, 1880–1914.* Oxford, 2006.

——. "Behind the Imperial Curtain: International Humanitarian Efforts and the Critique of French Colonialism in the Interwar Years." *French Historical Studies* 34, no. 3 (2011): 503–28.

——. *In the Forest of No Joy: The Congo-Océan Railroad and the Tragedy of French Colonialism.* New York, 2021.

——. "The 'Pacha Affair' Reconsidered: Violence and Colonial Rule in Interwar French Equatorial Africa." *Journal of Modern History* 91 (September 2019): 493–524.

de Waal, Alex. *Famine Crimes: Politics and the Disaster Relief Industry in Africa.* Bloomington, IN, 1997.

——. *Mass Starvation: The History and Future of Famine.* Medford, MA, 2018.

Debos, Marielle. *Living by the Gun in Chad: Combatants, Impunity, and State Formation.* London, 2013.

Deltombe, Thomas, Manuel Domergue, and Jacob Tatsitsa. *Kamerun! Une guerre cachée aux origines de la Françafrique (1948–1971).* Paris, 2011.

Derrienic, Hervé. *Famines et domination en Afrique noire: paysans et éleveurs du Sahel sous le joug.* Paris, 1977.

Devereux, Stephen. "Sen's Entitlement Approach: Critiques and Counter-Critiques." *Oxford Development Studies* 29, no.1 (2001): 245–63.

Drèze, Jean, and Amartya Sen. *Hunger and Public Action.* Oxford, 1989.

Duiker, William J. *Ho Chi Minh: A Life.* New York, 2000.

——. "The Red Soviets of Nghe-Tinh: An Early Communist Rebellion in Vietnam." *Journal of Southeast Asian Studies* 4, no. 2 (September 1973): 186–98.

Dutton, Paul. *Origins of the French Welfare State: The Struggle for Social Reform in France, 1914–1947.* Cambridge, 2002.

Echenberg, Myron. *Colonial Conscripts: The Tirailleurs Sénégalais in West Africa, 1857–1960.* Portsmouth, UK, 1991.

Edgerton-Tarpley, Kathryn. *Tears From Iron: Cultural Responses to Famine in Nineteenth-Century China.* Berkeley, CA, 2008.

Edington, Claire. *Beyond the Asylum: Mental Illness in French Colonial Vietnam.* Ithaca, NY, 2019.

Egg, J., F. Lerin, and M. Venin. "Analyse descriptive de la famine des années 1931 au Niger et implications méthodologiques." Paris, 1975.

Ellman, Michael. "The 1947 Soviet Famine and the Entitlement Approach to Famines." *Cambridge Journal of Economics* 24, no. 5 (September 2000): 603–30.

Ewald, François. *The Birth of Solidarity: The History of the French Welfare State.* Durham, NC, 2020.

Fall, Babacar. *Le travail forcé en Afrique-occidentale française, 1900–1946.* Paris, 1993.

Farmer, Paul. "An Anthropology of Structural Violence." *Current Anthropology* 45 (2004): 205–25.

Fassin, Didier. *Humanitarian Reason: A Moral History of the Present.* Berkeley, CA, 2011.

Fassin, Didier, and Eric Fassin, eds. *De la question sociale à la question raciale? Représenter la société française.* Paris, 2006.

Fawaz, Leila Tarazi. *A Land of Aching Hearts: The Middle East in the Great War.* Cambridge, MA, 2014.

Filipovitch, Jean. "Destined to Fail: Forced Settlement at the Office du Niger." *Journal of African History* 42 (2001): 239–60.

Fogarty, Richard, and Michael A. Osborne. "Constructions and Functions of Race in French Military Medicine, 1830–1920." In *The Color of Liberty: Histories of Race in France*, edited by Sue Peabody and Tyler Stovall. Durham, NC, 2003.

Forclaz, Amalia Ribi. *Humanitarian Imperialism: The Politics of Anti-Slavery Activism, 1880–1940.* Oxford, 2015.

Ford, Caroline. "The Inheritance of Empire and the Ruins of Rome in French Colonial Algeria." *Past and Present* (2015), supplement 10.

Forth, Aidan. *Barbed-Wire Imperialism: Britain's Empire of Camps, 1876–1903.* Berkeley, CA, 2017.

Foucault, Michel. *Security, Territory, Population: Lectures at the Collège de France, 1977–1978.* New York, 2004.

Fuglestad, Finn. "La Grande Famine de 1931 dans l'Ouest nigérien: Réflexions autour d'une catastrophe naturelle." *Revue française d'histoire d'outre-mer* 222 (1974): 18–33.

———. "Les révoltes des Touareg du Niger, 1916–17." *Cahiers d'études africaines* 13, no. 49 (1973): 82–120.

———. "Unis and BNA: The Role of 'Traditionalist' Parties in Niger, 1948–1960." *Journal of African History* 16, no. 1 (1975).

Gado, Boureima Alpha. *Une histoire des famines au Sahel: Etude des grandes crises alimentaires XIXe-XXe siècles.* Paris, 1993.

———. *Crises alimentaires en Afrique sahélienne: les réponses paysannes.* Cotonou, Benin, 2010.

Garcia, Luc. "Les mouvements de résistance au Dahomey, 1914–1917." *Cahiers d'études africaines* 10, no. 37 (1970): 144–78.

Gervais, Raymond R. "Etat colonial et savoir démographique en AOF, 1904–1960." *Cahiers québécois de démographie* 25, no. 1 (printemps 1996): 101–31.

Getachew, Adom. *Worldmaking after Empire: The Rise and Fall of Self-determination.* Princeton, NJ, 2019.

Glenzer, Kent. "La Sécheresse: The Social and Institutional Construction of a Development Problem in the Malian (Soudanese) Sahel." *Canadian Journal of African Studies* 36, no. 1 (2002).

Goscha, Christopher. *Vietnam: A New History.* New York, 2016.

Gourou, Pierre. *Les paysans du delta tonkinois: étude de géographie humaine.* Paris, 1936.

Gray, Peter. "'Potatoes and Providence': British Government Responses to the Great Famine." *Bullàn: An Irish Studies Journal* 1, no. 1 (Spring 1994): 75–90.

Greenough, Paul R. *Prosperity and Misery in Modern Bengal: The Famine of 1943–1944.* New York, 1982.

Guyer, Jane, and Gregory Mann. "Imposing a Guide on the *Indigène*: The Fifty Year Experience of the *Sociétés de Prévoyance* in French West and Equatorial Africa." In *Credit, Currencies, and Culture: African Financial Institutions in Historical Perspective*, edited by Endre Stiansen and Jane I. Guyer. Stockholm, 1999.

Harbers, Frank, and Marcel Broersma. "Impartial Reporter or *écrivain engagé?* Andrée Viollis and the Transformation of French Journalism, 1918–1940." *French History* 30, no. 2 (June 2016): 218–40.

Headrick, Daniel R. *The Tools of Empire: Technology and European Imperialism in the Nineteenth Century.* Oxford, 1981.

Headrick, Rita. *Colonialism, Health and Illness in French Equatorial Africa, 1885–1935.* Atlanta, 1994.

Healey, Kimberley J. "Andrée Viollis in Indochina: The Objective and Picturesque Truth About French Colonialism." *Asian Journal of Social Science* 31, no. 1 (2003): 19–35.

Hélénon, Véronique. *French Caribbeans in Africa: Diasporic Connections and Colonial Administration, 1880–1939.* New York, 2011.

Henry, Yves. *Economie Agricole de l'Indochine.* Hanoi, 1932.

Henry, Yves Marius. *Irrigations et cultures irriguées en Afrique tropicale.* Paris, 1918.

Herbst, Jeffrey. *States and Power in Africa: Comparative Lessons in Authority and Control.* Princeton, NJ, 2000.

Heyberger, Laurent. *Les corps en colonie: Faim, maladies, guerre et crises démographiques en Algérie au XIXe siècle, Approche anthropométrique.* Toulouse, France, 2019.

Hilton, Boyd. *The Age of Atonement: The Influence of Evangelicalism on Social and Economic Thought.* Oxford, 1988.

Howe, Paul. "Famine systems: A new model for understanding the development of famines." *World Development* 105 (2018): 144–55.

Howe, Paul and Stephen Devereux. "Famine intensity and magnitude scales: A proposal for an instrumental definition of famine." *Disasters* 28, no. 4 (December 2004): 353–372.

Hue-Tam Ho Tai. *Radicalism and the Origins of the Vietnamese Revolution.* Cambridge, MA, 1992.

Huff, Gregg. "Causes and Consequences of the Great Vietnam Famine, 1944–1945." *Economic History Review* 72, no. 1 (2019): 286–316.

Hunt, Lynn. *Inventing Human Rights: A History.* New York, 2007.

Hy Van Luong. "Agrarian Unrest from an Anthropological Perspective: The Case of Vietnam." *Comparative Politics* 17, no. 2 (January 1985): 153–74.

Jackson, Julian. *The Popular Front in France: Defending Democracy, 1934–1938.* Cambridge, 1988.

Jackson, Simon. "Transformative Relief: Imperial Humanitarianism and Mandatory Development in Syria-Lebanon, 1915–1925." *Humanity: An International Journal of Human Rights, Humanitarianism, and Development* 8, no. 2 (2017): 247–68.

Jeandel, Alice-Anne. *Andrée Viollis, une femme grand reporter: Une écriture de l'évènement, 1927–1939.* Paris, 2006.

Jennings, Eric T. *Vichy in the Tropics: Pétain's National Revolution in Madagascar, Guadeloupe, and Indochina, 1940–1944.* Stanford, CA, 2001.

———. *Curing the Colonizers: Hydrotherapy, Climatology, and French Colonial Spas.* Durham, NC, 2006.

Johnson, Jennifer. *The Battle for Algeria: Sovereignty, Health Care, and Humanitarianism.* Philadelphia, 2016.

Jones, Colin. *The Charitable Imperative: Hospitals and Nursing in Ancien Regime and Revolutionary France.* London and New York, 1989.

Kanya-Forstner, A. S. *The Conquest of the Western Sudan: A Study in French Military Imperialism.* Cambridge, 1969.

Kaplan, Steven L. *The Bakers of Paris and the Bread Question, 1700–1775.* Durham, NC, 1996.

———. *Bread, Politics, and Political Economy in the Reign of Louis XV: Second Edition.* London, 2015.

Keith, Charles. *Catholic Vietnam: A Church from Empire to Nation.* Berkeley, CA, 2012.

Keller, Richard. *Colonial Madness: Psychiatry in French North Africa.* Chicago, 2007.

Klein, Martin. *Slavery and Colonial Rule in French West Africa.* Cambridge, 1998.

Klein, Martin A., and Richard Roberts. "The Resurgence of Pawning in French West Africa During the Depression of the 1930s." In *Pawnship, Slavery, and Colonialism in Africa*, edited by Paul E. Lovejoy and Toyin Falola. Trenton, NJ, 2003.

Krasner, Stephen D. *Sovereignty: Organized Hypocrisy.* Princeton, NJ, 1999.

Kratoska, Paul H., ed. *Food Supplies and the Japanese Occupation of Southeast Asia.* New York, 1998.

Kuisel, Richard F. *Capitalism and the State in Modern France: Renovation and Economic Management in the Twentieth Century.* Cambridge, 1981.

Laqua, Daniel. "The Tensions of Internationalism: Transnational Anti-Slavery in the 1880s and 1890s." *International History Review* 33, no. 4 (December 2011): 705–26.

Laqueur, Thomas W. "Bodies, Details, and the Humanitarian Narrative." In *The New Cultural History*, edited by Lynn Hunt. Berkeley, CA, 1989.

Larcher, Silyane. *L'Autre citoyen: l'idéal républicain et les Antilles après l'esclavage.* Paris, 2014.

Laya, Diouldé. "Interviews with Farmers and Livestock Owners in the Sahel." *African Environment* 1, no. 2 (1975): 49–93.

Leach, Melissa, and Robin Mearns. *The Lie of the Land: Challenging Received Wisdom on the African Environment.* London, 1996.

Liu, Xiaoyuan. "China and the Issue of Postwar Indochina in the Second World War." *Modern Asian Studies* 33, no. 2 (May 1999): 445–82.

Lockhart, Bruce M. "The Nghe Tinh Movement in Communist Party Historiography." *South East Asia Research* 19, no. 4, Special Issue: *Revisiting and Reconstructing the Nghe Tinh Soviets, 1930–2011* (December 2011): 711–35.

Loison, Laurent. "French Roots of French Neo-Lamarckisms, 1879–1985." *Journal of the History of Biology* 44 (2011): 713–44.

Lorcin, Patricia M. E. *Imperial Identities: Stereotyping, Prejudice, and Race in Colonial Algeria.* London, 1999.

———. "Rome and France in Africa: Recovering Colonial Algeria's Latin Past." *French Historical Studies* 25, no. 2 (Spring 2002): 295–329.

Lorcin, Patricia, and Todd Shepard, eds. *French Mediterraneans: Transnational and Imperial Histories.* Lincoln, NE, 2016.

Lunn, Joe. *Memoirs of the Maelstrom: A Senegalese Oral History of the First World War.* Portsmouth, UK, 1999.

Maclean, Ken. "History Reformatted: Vietnam's Great Famine (1944–45) in Archival Form." *Southeast Asian Studies* 5, no. 2 (August 2016): 187–218.

Mamdani, Mahmood. *Citizen and Subject: Contemporary Africa and the Legacy of Late Colonialism.* Princeton, NJ, 1996.

Mann, Gregory. *From Empires to NGOs in the West African Sahel: The Road to Nongovernmentality.* Cambridge, 2015.

———. *Native Sons: West African Veterans and France in the Twentieth Century.* Durham, NC, 2006.

Marr, David G. *Vietnam 1945: The Quest for Power.* Berkeley, CA, 1995.

———. *Vietnamese Anticolonialism, 1885–1925.* Berkeley, CA, 1971.

———. *Vietnamese Tradition on Trial, 1920–1945.* Berkeley, CA, 1981.

Mbembe, Achille. *On the Postcolony.* Berkeley, CA, 2001.

McDougall, James. *A History of Algeria.* Cambridge, 2017.

Memmi, Albert. *The Colonizer and the Colonized.* Boston, 1965.

Miller, Judith A. *Mastering the Market: The State and the Grain Trade in Northern France, 1700–1860.* Cambridge, 1999.

Morton, P. A. *Hybrid Modernities: Architecture and Representation at the 1931 Colonial Exposition, Paris.* Cambridge, MA, 2003.

Moyn, Samuel. *Not Enough: Human Rights in an Unequal World.* Cambridge, MA, 2018.

Mràzek, Rudolf. *Engineers of Happy Land: Technology and Nationalism in a Colony.* Princeton, NJ, 2002.

Mukherjee, Janam. *Hungry Bengal: War, Famine, and the End of Empire.* Oxford, 2015.

Murray-Miller, Gavin. "Bonapartism in Algeria: Empire and Sovereignty before the Third Republic." *French History* 32, no. 2 (2018): 249–70.

Nally, David. "That Coming Storm: The Irish Poor Law, Colonial Biopolitics, and the Great Famine." *Annals of the Association of American Geographers* 98, no. 3 (2008): 714–41.

Ndao, Mor. "Colonisation et politique de santé maternelle et infantile au Sénégal (1905–1960)." *French Colonial History* 9 (2008): 191–211.

Ndiaye, Pap. *La condition noire: Essai sur une minorité française.* Paris, 2008.

Neill, Deborah J. "Finding the 'Ideal Diet': Nutrition, Culture, and Dietary Practices in France and French Equatorial Africa, c. 1890s to 1920s." *Food and Foodways* 17 (2009): 1–28.

———. *Networks in Tropical Medicine: Internationalism, Colonialism, and the Rise of a Medical Specialty, 1890–1930.* Stanford, CA, 2012.

Ngô Vĩnh Long. *Before the Revolution: The Vietnamese Peasants under the French.* New York, 1973.

———. "The Indochinese Communist Party and Peasant Rebellion in Central Vietnam, 1930–1931. *Bulletin of Concerned Asian Scholars* 10, no. 4 (1978): 15–35.

Nguyên Thê Anh. "Japanese Food Policies and the 1945 Great Famine in Indochina." In *Food Supplies and the Japanese Occupation in Southeast Asia,* edited by Paul H. Kratoska. New York, 1998.

Nguyen-Marshall, Van. *In Search of Moral Authority: The Discourse on Poverty, Poor Relief, and Charity in French Colonial Vietnam.* New York, 2008.

Niang, Mame-Fatou, and Julien Suaudeau. *Universalisme.* Paris, 2022.

Nord, Philip. *France's New Deal: From the Thirties to the Postwar Era.* Princeton, NJ, 2010.

———. *The Republican Moment: Struggles for Democracy in Nineteenth Century France.* Cambridge, MA, 1995.

Nørlund, Irene. "Rice and the Colonial Lobby: The Economic Crisis in French Indo-China in the 1920s and 1930s." In *Weathering the Storm: The Economies of Southeast Asia in the 1930s Depression,* edited by Peter Boomgaard and Ian Brown. Singapore, 2001.

Nouschi, André. *Enquête sur le niveau de vie des populations rurales constantinoises de la conquête jusqu'en 1919.* Paris, 1961.

Ò Gràda, Cormac. *Black '47 and Beyond: The Great Irish Famine in History, Economy, and Memory.* Princeton, NJ, 1999.

———. *Eating People Is Wrong and Other Essays on Famine, Its Past, and Its Future.* Princeton, NJ, 2015.

Ochonu, Moses E. *Colonial Meltdown: Northern Nigeria in the Great Depression.* Athens, OH, 2009.

Olivier de Sardan, Jean-Pierre. *Les sociétés songhay-zarma.* Paris, 1984.

Osborne, Michael. *The Emergence of Tropical Medicine in France.* Chicago, 2014.

Painter, Thomas M. "From Warriors to Migrants: Critical Perspectives on Early Migrations among the Zarma of Niger." *Africa: Journal of the International African Institute* 58, no. 1 (1988): 87–100.

Paxton, Robert O. *Vichy France: Old Guard and New Order, 1940–1944.* New York, 1972.

Peabody, Sue, and Tyler Stovall, eds. *The Color of Liberty: Histories of Race in France.* Durham, NC, 2003.

Pearson, Jessica Lynne. *The Colonial Politics of Global Health: France and the United Nations in Postwar Africa.* Cambridge, MA, 2018.

Pedersen, Susan. "Back to the League of Nations. *American Historical Review* 112 (2007): 1091–1117.

———. *Family, Dependence, and the Origins of the Welfare State: Britain and France, 1914–1945.* Cambridge, 1993.

———. *The Guardians: The League of Nations and the Crisis of Empire.* Oxford, 2015.

Peiretti-Courtis, Delphine. *Corps noirs et médecins blancs: La fabrique du préjugé racial, XIX-XXe siècles.* Paris, 2021.

Peters, Erica J. "Taste, Taxes, and Technologies: Industrializing Rice Alcohol in Northern Vietnam, 1902–1913." *French Historical Studies* 27, no. 3 (2004): 569–600.

Pham Cao Duong. *Vietnamese Peasants under French Domination, 1861–1945.* New York, 1985.

Pick, Daniel. *Faces of Degeneration: A European Disorder, c. 1848–1918.* Cambridge, 1989.

Pitts, Jennifer. *A Turn to Empire: The Rise of Imperial Liberalism in Britain and France.* Princeton, NJ, 2005.

Pomfret, David. "'Child Slavery' in British and French Far-Eastern Colonies, 1880–1945." *Past and Present* 201 (November 2008): 175–213.

Press, Steven. *Rogue Empires: Contracts and Conmen in Europe's Scramble for Africa.* Cambridge, MA, 2017.

Price, Roger. *The French Second Empire: An Anatomy of Political Power.* Cambridge, 2001.

Rabinbach, Anson. *The Human Motor: Energy, Fatigue, and the Origins of Modernity.* Berkeley, CA, 1990.

Rabinow, Paul. *French Modern: Norms and Forms of the Social Environment.* Chicago, 1989.

Raj, Kapil. *Relocating Modern Science: Circulation and the Construction of Knowledge in South Asia and Europe, 1650–1900.* London, 2007.

Reinisch, Jessica. "Internationalism and Relief: The Birth (and Death) of UNRRA." *Past and Present* (2011), supplement 6.

Renoult, Anne. *Andrée Viollis: Une femme journaliste.* Anger, France, 2004.

——. "André Malraux et Andrée Viollis dans la campagne de protestation contre la répression en Indochine après 1930." *Présence d'André Malraux* 13, André Malraux et le colonialisme (2016): 75–95.

Rich, Jeremy. *A Workman Is Worthy of His Meat: Food and Colonialism in the Gabon Estuary.* Lincoln, NE, 2007.

Roberts, Richard. *Conflicts of Colonialism: The Rule of Law, French Soudan, and the Faama Mademba Sèye.* Cambridge, 2022.

——. *Two Worlds of Cotton: Colonialism and the Regional Economy in the French Soudan, 1800–1946.* Stanford, CA, 1996.

Rogers, Rebecca. *A Frenchwoman's Imperial Story: Madame Luce in Nineteenth-Century Algeria.* Stanford, CA, 2013.

Rorty, Richard. "Human Rights, Rationality, and Sentimentality." In *Truth and Progress: Philosophical Papers.* Cambridge, 1998.

Rosanvallon, Pierre. *The Demands of Liberty: Civil Society in France Since the Revolution.* Cambridge, MA, 2007.

Rosenberg, Clifford. "Albert Sarraut and Republican Racial Thought." *French Politics, Culture, and Society* 20, no. 3 (Fall 2002): 97–114.

——. "The International Politics of Vaccine Testing in Interwar Algiers." *American Historical Review* 117 (2012): 671–97.

Rossi, Benedetta. *From Slavery to Aid: Politics, Labour, and Ecology in the Nigerien Sahel, 1800–2000.* New York, 2015.

Rubin, Olivier. "The Precarious State of Famine Research." *Journal of Development Studies* 55, no. 8 (2019): 1633–53.

Rudé, George E. "La taxation populaire de mai 1775 à Paris et dans la region Parisienne." *Annales historiques de la Révolution française* 28, no. 143 (1956): 139–79.

Ruedy, John. *Modern Algeria: The Origins and Development of a Nation.* Bloomington, IN, 1992.

Saada, Emmanuelle. *Empire's Children: Race, Filiation, and Citizenship in the French Colonies.* Chicago, 2012.

Salifou, André. "Quand l'histoire se répète: La famine de 1931 au Niger." *Environnement Africain, études et recherches* 1, no. 2 (1975): 25–52.

——. *Le Niger.* Paris, 2002.

Sari, Djilali. *Le désastre démographique.* Alger, 1982.

Sasges, Gerard. "Beast of (a) Burden: State, Enterprise, and the Alcohol Monopoly in Colonial Vietnam." *Journal of Southeast Asian Studies* 43, no. 1 (2012): 133–57.

Sasson, Tehila. "From Empire to Humanity: The Russian Famine and the Imperial Origins of International Humanitarianism." *Journal of British Studies* 55, no. 3 (2016): 519–37.

Sasson, Tehila, and James Vernon. "Practising the British Way of Famine: Technologies of Relief, 1770–1985." *European Review of History* 22, no. 6 (2015): 860–72.

Satia, Priya. *Spies in Arabia: The Great War and the Cultural Foundations of Britain's Covert Empire in the Middle East.* Oxford, 2009.

Sbrega, John J. "The Anticolonial Policies of Franklin D. Roosevelt: A Reappraisal." *Political Science Quarterly* 101, no. 1 (1986): 65–84.

Schaller, François. *De La Charité Privée aux Droits Economiques et Sociaux du Citoyen.* Neuchâtel et Paris, 1950.

Schneider, William H. *Quality and Quantity: The Quest for Biological Regeneration in Twentieth-Century France.* Cambridge, 1990.

Scott, James. *The Moral Economy of the Peasant: Rebellion and Subsistence in Southeast Asia.* New Haven, CT, 1976.

———. *Seeing Like a State: How Certain Schemes to Improve the Human Condition Have Failed.* New Haven, CT, 1998.

Scott-Smith, Tom. *On an Empty Stomach: Two Hundred Years of Hunger Relief.* Ithaca, NY, 2020.

Sen, Amartya. *Development as Freedom.* New York, 1999.

———. *Poverty and Famines: An Essay on Entitlement and Deprivation.* Oxford, 1983.

Sessions, Jennifer. *By Sword and Plow: France and the Conquest of Algeria.* Ithaca, NY, 2011.

Sharma, Sanjay. *Famine, Philanthropy, and the Colonial State: North India in the Early Nineteenth Century.* London, 2001.

Sibeud, Emmanuelle. *Une Science Impériale Pour l'Afrique? La construction des savoirs africanistes en France, 1878–1930.* Paris, 2002.

———. "A Useless Colonial Science? Practicing Anthropology in the French Colonial Empire, circa 1880–1960." *Current Anthropology* 53, no. 5 (April 2012): S83–S94.

Siegel, Benjamin Robert. *Hungry Nation: Food, Famine, and the Making of Modern India.* Cambridge, 2018.

Simmons, Dana. *Vital Minimum: Need, Science, and Politics in Modern France.* Chicago, 2015.

Singaravélou, Pierre. *Professer l'Empire: Les "sciences coloniales" en France sous la IIIe République.* Paris, 2011.

Skinner, Rob, and Alan Lester. "Humanitarianism and Empire: New Research Agendas." *Journal of Imperial and Commonwealth History* 40, no. 5 (2012): 729–47.

Slobodkin, Yan. "Famine and the Science of Food in the French Empire: 1900–1939." *French Politics, Culture, and Society* 36, no. 1 (Spring 2018): 52–75.

———. "State of Violence: Administration and Reform in French West Africa." *French Historical Studies* 41, no. 1 (2018): 33–61.

Smith, Justin E. H. *Nature, Human Nature, and Human Difference: Race in Early Modern Philosophy.* Princeton, NJ, 2015.

Smith, Leonard V. *Sovereignty at the Paris Peace Conference of 1919.* Oxford, 2018.

Spary, E. C. *Feeding France: New Sciences of Food, 1760–1815.* Cambridge, 2014.

Staum, Martin S. *Nature and Nurture in French Social Sciences, 1859–1914 and Beyond.* Montreal, 2011.

Stoler, Anne Laura. *Race and the Education of Desire: Foucault's History of Sexuality and the Colonial Order of Things*. Durham, NC, 1995.
Stovall, Tyler. *Paris Noir: African Americans in the City of Light*. Boston, 1996.
Surkis, Judith. *Sex, Law, and Sovereignty in French Algeria, 1830–1930*. Ithaca, NY, 2019.
Swift, Jeremy. "Desertification: Narratives, Winners, and Losers." In *The Lie of the Land: Challenging Received Wisdom on the African Environment*, edited by Melissa Leach and Robin Mearns. London, 1996.
Taithe, Bertrand. "Algerian Orphans and Colonial Christianity in Algeria, 1866–1939." *French History* 20, no. 3 (2006): 240–59.
——. "Humanitarianism and Colonialism: Religious Responses to the Algerian Drought and Famine of 1866–1870." In *Natural Disasters, Cultural Responses: Case Studies Toward a Global Environmental History*, edited by Christof Mauch and Christian Pfister. Lanham, MD, 2009.
Tanielian, Melanie S. *The Charity of War: Famine, Humanitarian Aid, and World War I in the Middle East*. Stanford, CA, 2018.
Terretta, Meredith. *Nation of Outlaws, State of Violence: Nationalism, Grassfields Tradition, and State Building in Cameroon*. Athens, OH, 2014.
Thomas, Martin. "Albert Sarraut, French Colonial Development, and the Communist Threat, 1919–1930." *Journal of Modern History* 77, no. 4 (December 2005): 917–55.
——. "Free France, the British Government and the Future of French Indo-China, 1940–45." *Journal of Southeast Asian Studies* 28, no. 1 (March 1997): 137–60.
——. *The French Empire Between the Wars: Imperialism, Politics and Society*. Manchester, UK, 2005.
Tignor, Robert L. "Senegal's Cooperative Experience, 1907–1960." In *The Political Economy of Risk and Choice in Senegal*, edited by John Waterbury and Mark Gersovitz. London, 1987.
Tilley, Helen. *Africa as a Living Laboratory: Empire, Development, and the Problem of Scientific Knowledge, 1870–1950*. Chicago, 2011.
Tilly, Louise A. "La révolte frumentaire, forme de conflit politique en France." *Annales. Histoire, Sciences Sociales* 72, no. 3 (1972): 731–57.
Todd, David. *A Velvet Empire: French Informal Imperialism in the Nineteenth Century*. Princeton, NJ, 2021.
Tran Huy Lieu. *Les soviets du Nghe-Tinh*. Hanoi, 1960.
Trentmann, Frank, and Flemming Just. *Food and Conflict in Europe in the Age of the Two World Wars*. New York, 2006.
Tusan, Michelle. "'Crimes Against Humanity': Human Rights, the British Empire, and the Origins of the Response to the Armenian Genocide (Report)." *American Historical Review* 119, no. 1 (2014).
Tworek, Heidi J. S. "Communicable Disease: Information, Health, and Globalization in the Interwar Period." *American Historical Review* 124, no. 3 (June 2019): 813–42.
Vaughan, Megan. *The Story of an African Famine: Gender and Famine in Twentieth Century Malawi*. Cambridge, 1987.
——. *Curing Their Ills: Colonial Power and African Illness*. Stanford, CA, 1991.
Velmet, Aro. *Pasteur's Empire: Bacteriology and Politics in France, its Colonies, and the World*. New York, 2020.

Vernon, James. *Hunger: A Modern History.* Cambridge, MA, 2007.

Viner, Jacob. *The Role of Providence in the Social Order.* Princeton, NJ, 1972.

Wacquant, Loïc. "Resolving the Trouble with 'Race.'" *New Left Review* 133/134 (January/April 2022).

Watenpaugh, Keith David. *Bread from Stones: The Middle East and the Making of Modern Humanitarianism.* Oakland, CA, 2015.

Watts, Michael J. *Silent Violence: Food, Famine, and Peasantry in Northern Nigeria.* Athens, GA, 2013.

Weinreb, Alice. *Modern Hungers: Food and Power in Twentieth-Century Germany.* Oxford, 2017.

White, Owen. *Children of the French Empire: Miscegenation and Colonial Society in French West Africa, 1895–1960.* Oxford, 1999.

Wilder, Gary. *Freedom Time: Negritude, Decolonization, and the Future of the World.* Durham, NC, 2015.

——. *The French Imperial Nation-State: Negritude and Colonial Humanism between the Two World Wars.* Chicago, 2005.

Will, Pierre-Etienne and R. Bin Wong. *Nourish the People: The State Civilian Granary System in China: 1650–1850.* Ann Arbor, MI, 1991.

Woodside, Alexander Barton. *Vietnam and the Chinese Model: A Comparative Study of Vietnamese and Chinese Government in the First Half of the Nineteenth Century.* Cambridge, MA, 1971.

Worboys, Michael. "The Discovery of Colonial Malnutrition Between the Wars." In *Imperial Medicine and Indigenous Societies,* edited by David Arnold. Manchester, UK, 1988.

Zinoman, Peter. *The Colonial Bastille: A History of Imprisonment in Vietnam, 1862–1940.* Berkeley, CA, 2001.

INDEX

Illustrations are indicated by page numbers in *italics*.